D1426732

MARKETING MANAGEMENT SUPPORT SYSTEMS:
Principles, Tools, and Implementation

**INTERNATIONAL SERIES
IN QUANTITATIVE MARKETING**

Series Editor:

Jehoshua Eliashberg
The Wharton School
University of Pennsylvania
Philadelphia, Pennsylvania USA

Other books in the series:

Leeflang, P., Wittink, D., Wedel, M. and Naert, P.:
  Building Models for Marketing Decisions

Wedel, M. and Kamakura, W.G.:
  Market Segmentation, 2nd Ed

Wedel, M. and Kamakura, W.G.:
  Market Segmentation

Nguyen, D.:
  Marketing Decisions Under Uncertainty

Laurent, G., Lilien, G.L., Pras, B.:
  Research Traditions in Marketing

Erickson, G.:
  Dynamic Models of Advertising Competition

McCann, J. and Gallagher, J.:
  Expert Systems for Scanner Data Environments

Hanssens, D., Parsons, L., and Schultz, R.:
  Market Response Models: Econometric
  and Time Series Analysis

Cooper, L. and Nakanishi, M.:
  Market Share Analysis

MARKETING MANAGEMENT SUPPORT SYSTEMS

Principles, Tools, and Implementation

Berend Wierenga
Erasmus University
The Netherlands

Gerrit van Bruggen
Erasmus University
The Netherlands

KLUWER ACADEMIC PUBLISHERS
Boston / Dordrecht / London

Distributors for North, Central and South America:
Kluwer Academic Publishers
101 Philip Drive
Assinippi Park
Norwell, Massachusetts 02061 USA
Telephone (781) 871-6600
Fax (781) 681-9045
E-Mail <kluwer@wkap.com>

Distributors for all other countries:
Kluwer Academic Publishers Group
Distribution Centre
Post Office Box 322
3300 AH Dordrecht, THE NETHERLANDS
Telephone 31 78 6392 392
Fax 31 78 6546 474
E-Mail <services@wkap.nl>

 Electronic Services <http://www.wkap.nl>

Library of Congress Cataloging-in-Publication Data

Wierenga, B.
   Marketing management support systems : principles, tools, and implementation/
   Berend Wierenga, Gerrit van Bruggen.
     p.cm.
   ISBN 0-7923-8615-9 (alk.paper)
     1. Marketing--Management. I. Bruggen, Gerrit Harm van, 1966-II. Title.

HF5415.13.W533 2000
658.8--dc21

                                                    00-026770

Printed on acid-free paper.

Printed in the United States of America

Contents

Preface   xi

PART I

The Demand Side of Marketing Management Support Systems

1. Introduction   3
   1.1   Marketing Decision Making   3
   1.2   The Growing Importance of Information Technology for
       Marketing   5
   1.3   What are Marketing Management Support Systems?   7
   1.4   Philosophy Behind this Book   10
   1.5   Organization of the Book   12

**2. Marketing Decision Making: A Classification of Marketing
Problem-Solving Modes**   15
   2.1   Introduction   15
   2.2   Marketing Decision-Making Experts   16
   2.3   The ORAC Model of Marketing Problem-Solving Modes   21
       2.3.1   Optimizing   22
       2.3.2   Reasoning   24
       2.3.3   Analogizing   26
       2.3.4   Creating   28
       2.3.5   Relationships between the Four Marketing
             Problem-Solving Modes   32
   2.4   Antecedents of Marketing Problem-Solving Modes   33
       2.4.1   Problem Characteristics   34
       2.4.2   Decision Environment Characteristics   35
       2.4.3   Decision Maker Characteristics   36

2.4.4   Summary of the Effects of the Antecedents of the
         Marketing Problem-Solving Modes   39

PART II

The Supply Side of Marketing Management Support Systems

3.   The Components of Marketing Management Support Systems   43

3.1   Introduction   44
3.2   Information Technology   45
       3.2.1   Computers   46
       3.2.2   Communication Networks   55
3.3   Analytical Capabilities   57
       3.3.1   What Questions   58
       3.3.2   Why Questions   59
       3.3.3   What-If Questions   60
       3.3.4   What-Should Questions   62
3.4   Marketing Data   63
       3.4.1   Internal and External Data   64
       3.4.2   Internet as a Source of Marketing Data   66
       3.4.3   Data Warehouses   67
3.5   Marketing Knowledge   68
       3.5.1   Increased Managerial Attention of Knowledge   68
       3.5.2   Different Types of Knowledge   70
       3.5.3   Sources of (Marketing) Knowledge   72
       3.5.4   Generalized Marketing Knowledge   75
3.6   The Evolving Role of the Four Components   77

4.   Data-Driven Marketing Management Support Systems   81

4.1   Introduction   81
4.2   Marketing Models   82
       4.2.1   Types of Marketing Models   82
       4.2.2   Steps in the Construction and Use of a Marketing
                Model   83
4.3   Marketing Information Systems   91
       4.3.1   Developments in Marketing Information Systems   91
       4.3.2   Architecture of Marketing Information Systems   95
       4.3.3   Examples of Marketing Information Systems   97
4.4   Marketing Decision Support Systems   103
       4.4.1   Developments in Marketing Decision Support
                Systems   104

| | 4.4.2 | Example of a Marketing Decision Support System: ASSESSOR | 105 |

4.5 The Impact of Marketing Models and Marketing Decision Support Systems 113

5. Knowledge-Driven Marketing Management Support Systems I: Artificial Intelligence, Knowledge Representation, and Expert Systems 119

5.1 Introduction 120

5.2 Artificial Intelligence 121
   5.2.1 Developments in Artificial Intelligence 122
   5.2.2 Artificial Intelligence in Management and Marketing 124

5.3 Knowledge Representation 125
   5.3.1 Rule-Based Knowledge Representation 127
   5.3.2 Networked Knowledge Representation 129

5.4 Knowledge Processing with Rule-Based Reasoning Systems 133
   5.4.1 Production Systems 134
   5.4.2 Expert Systems 137
   5.4.3 Expert Systems in Marketing 143

5.5 Marketing Knowledge-Based Systems 162

6. Knowledge-Driven Marketing Management Support Systems II: Case-Based Reasoning, Neural Networks, and Creativity Support Systems 165

6.1 Case-Based Reasoning Systems 166
   6.1.1 Reasoning by Analogy 166
   6.1.2 Principles of Case-Based Reasoning Systems 169
   6.1.3 Applications and Tools 178
   6.1.4 Case-Based Reasoning Systems in Marketing 179

6.2 Neural Networks 184
   6.2.1 Introduction 184
   6.2.2 Principles of Neural Networks 185
   6.2.3 The Application of Neural Networks to Marketing Problems 194

6.3 Creativity Support Systems 200
   6.3.1 Introduction 200
   6.3.2 Research on Creativity Support Systems 201
   6.3.3 Creativity Support Systems in Marketing 203

6.4 Marketing Management Support Technologies in Perspective 204

PART III

Matching the Demand and Supply Sides of Marketing
Management Support Systems

7.   **Integrating Frameworks**   211

     7.1   Introduction   211
     7.2   Mapping Marketing Problem-Solving Modes and Marketing
           Management Support Systems   212
           7.2.1   Object of Support   212
           7.2.2   Mode of Support   213
     7.3   From Decision Situation to Marketing Management Support
           System: An Integrating Framework   217
           7.3.1   The Complete Mapping   218
           7.3.2   Marketing Management Support Recommender   219
           7.3.3   Issues in Choosing the Type of Marketing
                   Management Support System   224
     7.4   Understanding the Evolution of Marketing Management
           Support Systems   227

8.   **BRANDFRAME: A Marketing Management Support System**
     for the Brand Manager   231

     8.1   Introduction   231
     8.2   The Tasks of the Brand Manager and the Implications
           for Decision Support   232
     8.3   The BRANDFRAME System   237
           8.3.1   Overview   237
           8.3.2   A BRANDFRAME Consultation   239
     8.4   The Knowledge in BRANDFRAME   252
           8.4.1   General Marketing Knowledge   253
           8.4.2   Knowledge About the Brand Manager's World   254
           8.4.3   Continuous Data About the Position of the Focal
                   Brand and Its Competitors   256
           8.4.4   Specific Inputs Asked of the Product Manger During
                   a BRANDFRAME Consultation   256
     8.5   Functionality of BRANDFRAME as a Marketing Management
           Support System   256
     8.6   Evaluation and Perspective   259

PART IV

Perspectives on Marketing Management Support Systems

9.   Factors That Determine the Success of Marketing Management Support Systems   265

   9.1   Introduction   265
   9.2   Empirical Research on the Effectiveness of Marketing Management Support Systems   266
   9.3   A Framework for Explaining the Success of Marketing Management Support Systems   269
          9.3.1   The Demand Side of Decision Support   270
          9.3.2   The Supply Side of Decision Support   271
          9.3.3   The Match Between Demand and Supply   272
          9.3.4   Design Characteristics of Marketing Management Support Systems   273
          9.3.5   Characteristics of the Implementation Process   275
          9.3.6   Success Measures for Marketing Management Support Systems   277

10. The Future of Marketing Management Support Systems   281

   10.1   Introduction   281
   10.2   Developments on the Demand Side   282
          10.2.1   Ever Increasing Amounts of Marketing Data   282
          10.2.2   Changes in the Marketing Decision Environment   284
   10.3   Developments on the Supply Side   288
          10.3.1   Information Technology   288
          10.3.2   Analytical Capabilities   290
          10.3.3   Marketing Data   290
          10.3.4   Marketing Knowledge   291
   10.4   Implications for Marketing Management Support Systems   291
   10.5   Research Issues for Marketing Management Support Systems   294
          10.5.1   Need for Studies in Real-World Company Environments   294
          10.5.2   Need for More Insight into Managerial Decision Processes   294
          10.5.3   The Role of Time Pressure   295
          10.5.4   From Relatively Structured to More Complex Problems   296
          10.5.5   From Date-Driven to Knowledge-Based Marketing Management Support Systems   297

10.5.6 The Optimal Combination of Managerial Judgment
and Marketing Management Support Systems 297
10.5.7 From Technical Validation to Organizational
Validation 299
10.5.8 Dynamics 299
10.6 Marketing Management Support Systems and Marketing
Science 300

References 303

Subject index 325

Author index 335

Preface

Today there is a rich collection of tools that can help marketing managers improve the quality of their decisions. Decision aids like marketing information systems, marketing models, marketing expert systems, marketing neural networks, and so on, have been developed and implemented in companies. The term *marketing management support systems* (MMSS) refers to this collection of tools; it is also the title and subject of this book.

Marketing management support systems are important because the gathering and transforming of information into actionable marketing knowledge is of utmost strategic value. Marketing management support systems are of interest to researchers who want to know how to design and develop successful ones and identify the factors that determine their effectiveness. In a sense, MMSS can be considered a link between practice and research, because they act as channels through which the results of marketing research (e.g., knowledge about marketing processes) can be brought to bear on marketing decision making in practice. Although the primary audiences for this book are academics and students, we want to emphasize the relevance of MMSS for marketing practice.

This book is the first comprehensive, systematic textbook treatment of marketing management support systems. In this monograph we deal with the principles of MMSS, with the different decision support tools currently available, and with their successful implementation in companies. In doing so we build on a wealth of earlier work on specific aspects and components of marketing management support systems. For example, there is a large literature on analytical methods, including marketing models, which are used in data-driven MMSS. Much has also been written on topics such as the "marketing information revolution." In addition, the literature on cognitive science and artificial intelligence describes the basis for knowledge-driven marketing management support systems. There are also numerous publications about special-purpose MMSS that have been developed over the last thirty years. In this book we approach marketing management support systems from the decision-making perspective and use insights from behavioral decision theory and information systems wherever these are relevant to our discussion. We also take an integrative perspective by bringing together different approaches and insights regarding marketing management support systems.

We start by discussing the *principles* of marketing management support systems. Here we follow a demand-oriented approach, taking the marketing manager and his or her decision-making processes as the object of decision support. Our underlying belief is that decision aids for marketing managers should fit with the thinking and reasoning processes of the marketing decision makers who use them. We also develop a contingency framework in which the different types of marketing problem-solving modes are linked with the most appropriate MMSS.

Next, we describe in detail the different *tools* that are currently available as marketing management support systems, including their underlying technologies. We describe not only the more conventional data-driven systems, but also knowledge-driven systems, such as marketing expert systems, marketing case-based reasoning systems, marketing neural networks, and marketing creativity support systems. These systems are relatively new (some of them very new) to the field of marketing and therefore deserve extended attention.

Finally, we address the *implementation* of marketing management support systems. We present a framework for matching demand and supply, which can guide the design and development of MMSS in specific situations. We also discuss the factors that determine the success of marketing management support systems. From the work that has been done, both in marketing and in information systems, systematic insights into the critical factors for the success of MMSS are emerging. These insights allow us to formulate research priorities for marketing management support systems.

This book should be of interest to a variety of audiences. First, it can serve as a textbook for courses on marketing management support systems. Marketing academics with a general interest in MMSS can also use it to familiarize themselves with the current state of the art of such systems. In addition to marketing students and scholars in general, a second, more specialized audience consists of researchers and doctoral students who are active themselves (or want to become active) in research on marketing management support systems. This can be in the field of MMSS as such or in fields that supply "components" to these systems, for example, marketing models, marketing data analysis methods, knowledge-based technologies for marketing, and so on. We hope that this book will stimulate creativity in developing new, effective marketing management support systems and in determining the factors that lead to their success. A third group of potentially interested readers are researchers working in information systems or knowledge-based systems in other domains. For them, the book contains interesting information on how MMSS can be used to improve the quality of decision making in a data-intensive environment that also includes relatively ill-structured problems. We think that many of the concepts and approaches developed in this book are applicable to other areas of management besides marketing.

Finally, the book should also be of interest to readers outside academia. Here we think of managers in companies who have to make decisions about investing in marketing management support systems and of the information systems and marketing people who have to implement and use such systems. We realize that the book does not provide directly implementable, hands-on solutions. However, before embarking on the installation of far-reaching and expensive MMSS in a company, these persons may find it useful to think about the desired functionality of such a system and about the match between it and the decision processes it is supposed to support. This book offers useful concepts and frameworks for reflecting on such issues. For the same reasons the book should also be useful for marketing consultants and the providers of (syndicated) marketing data services, for example, companies that operate retail, household, and Web panels.

We want to thank several people who provided inspiration for the book and/or offered direct support in actually completing the work. Our colleagues Gary Lilien and Arvind Rangaswamy, both from Penn State University, share with us a vivid interest in marketing management support systems. They provided us with stimulating comments on our work and were a continuing source of inspiration during the several projects that we have done together. Jehoshua Eliashberg (The Wharton School) was a wise and patient editor of Kluwer International Series in Qualitative Marketing (ISQM) and also gave helpful comments on material that can now be found in several chapters of the book. We also want to thank other colleagues who provided constructive comments on papers and other material that ultimately ended up in this book: John Little (MIT), John Rossiter (University of Woollongong), and Ale Smidts (Erasmus University). The ISQM reviewers gave most helpful and constructive comments on an earlier version of the book. We also want to thank our other colleagues at the Center of Information Technology in Marketing (C/IT/M) at the Rotterdam School of Management. To our deep regret our doctoral student Arco Dalebout did not live to see the publication of this book. Arco developed a real expertise with respect to marketing management support systems and was a most promising scholar. His many comments and suggestions on the book were well thought-out and immensely valuable. He is also one of the coauthors of Chapter 8, along with Soumitra Dutta from INSEAD (Fontainebleau, France). We also want to thank Zhimin Chen, another doctoral student at Erasmus University, for reading parts of the book and giving very useful comments.

A number of people played an important role in the actual production process of the book. Brian Jones, a freelance copyeditor in San Francisco, did an excellent job of editing the manuscript. We thank Wil Geurtsen of the Text Processing Department of the Rotterdam School of Management for her painstaking efforts during the copyediting process and also our secretaries, Jolanda Lenstra and Karin Birken, for their help and support during the (extended) production process of this book.

Finally, from the part of Kluwer Academic Publishers, Zachary Rolnik stimulated us to start the book and Elizabeth Murry was very supportive while we were finishing it.

We hope you will derive much pleasure, satisfaction, and valuable information and insight from reading and working with this book—and also that it will stimulate ongoing and new research in the important field of marketing management support systems. We welcome your comments and suggestions.

Berend Wierenga (bwierenga@fac.fbk.eur.nl)
Gerrit H. Van Bruggen (gbruggen@fac.fbk.eur.nl)

Erasmus University Rotterdam
Rotterdam, Netherlands

PART I

The Demand Side of Marketing Management
Support Systems

Chapter 1

Introduction

Learning Objectives

- *To understand the role of the marketing decision maker in an increasingly data-rich environment.*

- *To become aware of the growing importance of information technology for marketing management.*

- *To become acquainted with the nature and different types of marketing management support systems.*

- *To become acquainted with the approach to marketing management support systems taken in this book.*

1.1   Marketing Decision Making

Marketing decision makers are responsible for the design and execution of marketing programs for products or brands. They operate under different names, such as product manager, brand manager, marketing manager, marketing director, or commercial director. Regardless of the specific job title used in a particular company, in this book we are interested in the decision-making and problem-solving processes of persons in organizations who carry out marketing management tasks. They choose the target markets and segments for their products and services, and develop and implement marketing mixes. Because of the proliferation of products and brands, the fragmentation of markets in an ever growing number of different segments, the fierceness of competition, and the overall acceleration of change, marketing decisions are becoming increasingly complex. Furthermore, decisions have to be made under increasing time pressure. Product life cycles are getting shorter, and competition occurs not only within countries but increasingly at an international and even global level. New markets are opening up in Asia and central Europe, existing markets are being deregulated, and new distribution channels like the Internet are developing. The questions we wish to address in this book are (1) how do marketing decision makers deal with the complexities and dynamics of the environments they are operating in, and (2) how can they be supported to become more effective?

Marketing managers[1] are exposed to a constant stream of information about the markets they are operating in and the performance of their products. This information consists of data from formal information systems and market research studies as well as informal cues about customers, distributors, competitors, and so forth. Especially with consumer goods, the amounts of data collected using customer cards and point-of-sales scanning technology have multiplied. Even in business-to-business markets, however, handheld computers now make it possible for sales reps to systematically collect large amounts of data about their customers. The development of the Internet, furthermore, also offers great opportunities to collect information about existing and potential customers.

Although the exponential growth of available information offers great opportunities for marketers, it also has its downside. Usually, marketing decision makers bring a substantial amount of knowledge—experience and expertise—to bear on solving their problems. Skillful marketers make the best of the interplay between (hard) data and (soft) knowledge. However, they simultaneously cope with cognitive limitations that may inhibit them from optimally processing all the information and knowledge that is available. Simon (1957) referred to this phenomenon as "bounded rationality." Cognitive limitations may lead to the use of heuristics (Kahneman and Tversky 1974). Although sometimes an efficient and economical way of processing information, heuristics can also lead to serious decision biases when applied inappropriately (Hogarth and Makridakis 1981).

The availability of systems that help marketing decision makers to analyze data and discover the relevant issues is an indispensable condition for survival. In a project called "Dying for Information," Reuters Business

---

[1] We will use the terms *marketing manager, marketing decision maker,* and *marketer* interchangeably throughout the text. All three terms refer to a marketing decision maker in the generic sense.

Information (1996) carried out a survey among 1300 managers in the U.K., U.S.A., Australia, Singapore, and Hong Kong. They found that managers experienced increasing quantities of information as very stressful. Almost half (49%) of the managers interviewed said that they were often unable to handle the volumes of information received. Also, half of the respondents took work home or worked late as a result of having too much information. Other negative consequences mentioned were ill health and difficulties in personal relationships. An "information fatigue syndrome" sometimes occurred, with symptoms such as paralysis of analytical capacity, increased anxiety and self-doubt, and a tendency to blame others. Having too much information, especially without the proper systems for sifting through it and finding the gems among the silt, can be just as dangerous as having too little information.

The good news is that marketing decision makers can benefit from a quickly increasing supply of tools that support them in using data, information, and knowledge for decision making. Research in marketing science and information technology has resulted in systems like marketing models, marketing information systems, marketing decision support systems, marketing expert systems, and so on. We use the term *marketing management support systems* (MMSS) to refer to the whole set of tools that marketers can use to support their decision-making activities. Marketing management support systems are meant to make a marketing decision maker more effective by increasing the quality of marketing decision making. These systems are able to compensate for the weaknesses or shortcomings of human marketers; they are also the subject of this book.

1.2 The Growing Importance of Information Technology for Marketing

One of the main forces behind the development of marketing management support systems is the increasing role of information technology (IT). In companies, marketing has traditionally not been the functional domain with the highest investments in information technology. However, this is quickly changing. In areas such as finance, accounting, production management, and logistics, the important advantages of automation have been realized. Now companies are increasingly seeing marketing as an important domain where the application of IT can be beneficial. In a study done in the Netherlands, the accounting firm Moret, Ernst & Young (1995) found that, among 327 companies surveyed in 1995, 72% of the finance/accounting activities were already "automated." For logistics/supply activities, the figure was 64%, whereas for marketing it was only 49%. The same companies expected that the corresponding figures five years later would be 81% for finance/accounting, 79% for logistics/supply, and 78% for marketing. This means that a lot of "marketing automation" is expected in the next couple of years until marketing catches up with the other areas.

The same trend was found in a study done in the U.K., which showed that IT expenditures to support sales and marketing accounted for about 15% of the surveyed organizations' total IT expenditures, and that this percentage was likely to grow (Shaw 1994). In another recent study in the U.K., carried out among 111 organizations, 85% of the respondents reported that IT had already had a major impact on the marketing function and that further developments were planned. These companies most often used (or intended to use) IT in marketing for customer databases, sales analyses, sales forecasting, direct marketing, customer segmentation, external on-line data gathering, calculating optimal price levels, and measuring the effectiveness of promotions (Leverick, Littler, Bruce, and Wilson 1997).

Often, the application of IT in marketing has occurred in an ad hoc way. However, increasingly companies take a more systematic approach and install so-called marketing decision support systems (Little 1979). A study done in the Netherlands in the early nineties found that 37% of all Dutch companies with an employed marketing manager had installed some form of a marketing management support system (Van Campen, Huizingh, Oude Ophuis, and Wierenga 1991). A corresponding figure for the U.S. was 32% (Higby and Farah 1991). We assume that these figures have risen since then.

Investment costs for marketing management support systems can be substantial. The median investment in the development and implementation of an MMSS in the Netherlands amounted to U.S.\$120,000 (Van Campen et al. 1991). These figures are likely to have increased since then and will continue doing so. This means that companies are making serious financial commitments to IT in marketing and for the development and implementation of marketing management support systems. An important reason for this is that they recognize the strategic and competitive value of systematic information and knowledge about customers, markets, and competitors. The half-life of information is continuously shrinking, and competitors in principle have access to the same information (Barabba and Zaltman 1991). As the financial commitments for IT in marketing grow, these factors raise the question of how this money should be spent on MMSS that are maximally effective in creating a competitive edge. We hope that the ideas developed in this book will help companies to make the right choices with respect to their MMSS.

Marketing management support systems, although primarily developed for supporting individual marketing decision makers, can have an impact on the organization as a whole. Recently, concepts such as learning in organizations and the role of knowledge as a competitive factor (Senge 1990; Drucker 1993; Nonaka and Takeuchi 1995) have received much attention. In volatile economic times, adaptability and responsiveness become important determinants of success. Marketing managers must constantly challenge their mental models about customers, markets, and competitors—then adapt them, if necessary, on the basis of new evidence (De Geus 1988; Day and Glazer 1994). Information about markets plays an important role in this process. "Interpreting market information is key to organizational learning" (Sinkula 1994). In this respect Day and Glazer (1994) introduced the term "market-driven learning organization." Marketing management support systems can play an important role in transforming a company into a market-driven learning organization. We recognize this broader role of MMSS in the organization, but in this book we will concentrate on their decision-supporting function for the individual marketing manager.

1.3   What are Marketing Management Support Systems?

So far, we have been talking about marketing management support systems without providing a clear definition or description. We will do so now. We define a marketing management support system (MMSS) as follows:

> *Any device combining (1) information technology, (2) analytical capabilities, (3) marketing data, and (4) marketing knowledge, made available to one or more marketing decision maker(s) to improve the quality of marketing management.*

In Chapter 3 we present an in-depth discussion of each of these four components. The term *marketing management support systems* is a collective noun for a variety of systems that have been developed since the early sixties. *Marketing models* mark the start of the use of computers to aid marketing decision making; they consist of mathematical representations of marketing problems that aim at finding optimal values for marketing instruments. The philosophy underlying these systems is that it is possible to find an objective best solution. From the mid-1960s onward, marketers could make use of *marketing information systems* for the storage, retrieval, and (statistical) analysis of data. By means of manipulating quantitative information, marketing information systems assist marketers in analyzing what has happened in the market and determining possible causes of events. Whereas marketing information systems are relatively passive systems that provide marketers only with the information they are looking for, *marketing decision support systems* are more active. They provide marketers with the opportunity to answer "what-if" questions by means of making simulations. Marketing decision support systems focus not on replacing but on supporting the marketer. Using judgment, marketers will generate ideas for possible courses of action; the marketing decision support system can then help predict the outcomes of these actions. However, the marketer's judgment will still be the decisive factor in selecting the final and most appropriate course of action.

In the mid-1980s, a new generation of marketing management support systems was developed. These systems emphasized the marketing knowledge rather than quantitative data. *Marketing expert systems* were the first of these knowledge-based systems. The basic philosophy underlying these systems is to capture the knowledge from an expert in a specific domain and make that knowledge available in a computer program for solving problems in that domain. The goal of an expert system is to replicate the performance levels of (a) human expert(s) in a computer model (Rangaswamy 1993). These systems take a normative approach in searching for the best solution to a given problem. *Marketing knowledge-based systems*, introduced in the early 1990s, describe a broader class of systems than marketing expert systems. They obtain their knowledge from any source, not just from human experts but also from textbooks, cases, and so on. Furthermore, knowledge can be represented in multiple forms, that is, not only by means of rules, as in expert systems, but also, for example, by means of semantic networks and frame-based hierarchies. Unlike marketing expert systems, marketing knowledge-based systems do not focus on finding a best solution but emphasize the reasoning processes of decision makers. The third type of knowledge-based system, *marketing case-based reasoning systems,* first appeared in the mid-1990s. These systems focus on the support of reasoning by analogies. Analogous thinking is a way of solving problems in which solutions to similar past problems are taken as a starting point for solving a current problem. Marketing case-based reasoning systems make cases available in a case library and provide tools for accessing them.

Marketing neural networks are systems that model the way human beings attach meaning to a set of incoming stimuli, that is, how people recognize patterns from signals. They were inspired by the actual physical process that takes place in the human brain, where incoming signals are transmitted through a massive network of connections formed by links among neurons in the brain. Through this process, a human being is able to recognize patterns in sets of incoming stimuli, that is, a specific output is connected to input. The first examples of marketing neural networks have appeared only recently. Finally, *marketing creativity support systems* are computer programs that stimulate and endorse the creativity of marketing decision makers. Although the number of creativity-enhancement programs developed so far is limited, we expect these systems to become more popular in the coming years, given the increasing importance of creativity in marketing—for example, in the development of new products.

Type of MMSS	*Characterizing Keywords*
Marketing Models (MM)	• Mathematical representation • Optimal values for marketing instruments • Objective • Best solution
Marketing Information Systems (MKIS)	• Storage and retrieval of data • Quantitative information • Registration of "what happens in the market" • Passive systems
Marketing Decision Support Systems (MDSS)	• Flexible systems • Recognition of managerial judgment • Able to answer "why" questions (analysis) and "what-if" questions (simulation)
Marketing Expert Systems (MES)	• Centers on marketing knowledge • Human experts • Rule-based knowledge representation • Normative approach: best solution
Marketing Knowledge-Based Systems (MKBS)	• Diversity of methods, incuding hybrid approaches • Structured knowledge representation, including frame-based hierarchies • Model-Based Reasoning
Marketing Case-Based Reasoning Systems (MCBR)	• Similarity with earlier cases • Storage of cases in memory • Retrieval and adaptation • No generalization
Marketing Neural Networks (MNN)	• Training of associations • Pattern recognition • No a priori theory • Learning
Marketing Creativity Support Systems (MCSS)	• Association through connections • Idea generation • Endorse creativity in problem solving

Figure 1.1   Characteristics of Marketing Management Support Systems

In Figure 1.1 we provide a summary of the characteristics of the different types of marketing management support systems currently available. These different types of MMSS will be discussed more extensively later in the book.

1.4   Philosophy Behind this Book

So far, we have argued that both individual decision makers and organizations can benefit from investments in information technology to support marketing management. Furthermore, organizations intend to make investments to develop marketing management support systems. The question that now arises is, In which type of technologies or systems should a company invest? Our purpose in this book is to address this question. We contend that in deciding about investments in information technology for marketing, the characteristics of the marketing decision-making situation should be the starting point.

This book has several distinguishing features compared to earlier work on marketing management support systems.

First, in writing this book, we have adopted what we call a *demand-side perspective*. Developments in MMSS thus far have been driven mainly by developments in the constituting components, that is, information technology, analytical capabilities, marketing data, and marketing knowledge. These developments have resulted in a large stream of models, methodologies, and systems. Some of these systems have been very successful, whereas others have failed. So far the supply-side perspective has been dominant. However, we believe it is important to recognize that marketing management support systems are intended to support the problem-solving processes of marketing managers. Therefore, it is our premise that to be successful, an MMSS should match the thinking and reasoning processes of these managers. For this reason, this book starts with an examination of the way marketing decision makers perform their problem-solving activities. We will introduce the concept of *marketing problem-solving modes* (MPSM), which characterize the problem-solving processes of marketers. We will present a classification of four different marketing problem-solving modes, which are the four different cognitive models of how marketers solve problems. We have called this classification *the ORAC model*. The marketing problem-solving mode employed by a decision maker is an important determinant of the type of MMSS that should be implemented. At present, a mismatch often seems to exist between what the marketer needs and what the systems offer. For example, Leverick et al. (1997) indicated that 79% of the firms they investigated had major barriers to the use of IT for marketing, due to limitations in software and hardware and a misunderstanding of the needs of marketers.

Second, in writing this book, we have included both *data-driven* and *knowledge-driven* marketing management support systems. Almost all marketing decisions involve a combination of, on the one hand, data or information gathered inside or outside the company and, on the other hand, the judgment/intuition of the decision maker. Practitioners have always been convinced of the value of judgment, intuition, and experience. The value of exercising qualitative judgment and intuition in addition to using quantitative models has also been scientifically demonstrated (Blattberg and Hoch 1990; Hoch 1994; Hoch and Schkade 1996). Given the power of the combination of data and knowledge, an effective MMSS should be able to turn data into information, acting as an "information value chain" by adding value to the data (Blattberg, Glazer, and Little 1994). For this purpose, data-driven methodologies such as marketing models based on econometric and operations research techniques are available. Conversely, a marketing management support system should also be able to capture knowledge and judgment from marketing managers and represent that knowledge and judgment in computer systems so that they can be used in decision making. For this purpose, knowledge-driven methodologies such as knowledge representation and reasoning technologies from artificial intelligence and cognitive science are used. The most powerful MMSS will integrate data-driven and knowledge-driven methodologies.

A third distinguishing feature of this book is that it deals not only with the design of marketing management support systems, but also with their *effective implementation* in organizations. The acceptance and use of MMSS does not automatically follow from their availability. As early as 1970, Little observed that managers "practically never use models." Even almost 25 years later, according to Eliashberg and Lilien (1993), "the impact of operational marketing models remains far below its potential." Therefore, this book will pay attention to the factors that affect the adoption, use, and effectiveness of marketing management support systems in companies. We develop a normative framework that can be helpful in determining the type of MMSS that is most suitable for a specific organization or decision-making situation, given the nature of the marketing problem(s) being dealt with and the characteristics of the decision environment and decision maker(s). We also examine (empirical) knowledge with respect to the factors that influence the success of marketing management support systems in companies.

Finally, an important goal of ours in writing this book was to put the subject of marketing management support systems on the research agenda of the academic marketing community. This is the first book devoted solely to the phenomenon of MMSS. Over the years, many excellent books and articles on marketing models have been published. More recently, there have been books and articles in academic journals on knowledge-based systems in marketing. All this work deals with important *components* of MMSS. What seems to be missing is an integrating framework that can link these components together and also serve as a platform for further research. We hope this work will inspire others to further this line of study. Marketing management support systems are important for companies because they make marketing managers more effective. MMSS can also be seen as channels through which the achievements of research in marketing, marketing research, and marketing science become available for marketing practitioners. For this reason alone, academic researchers in marketing should be (scientifically) concerned about MMSS.

1.5   Organization of the Book

This book is divided into four parts. In *Part I: The Demand Side of Marketing Management Support Systems,* we characterize the way marketing decision makers solve problems. In Chapter 2 we introduce the ORAC model, which distinguishes four characteristic cognitive models of marketing decision making. We also present a model describing the conditions that are conducive to applying the four different marketing problem-solving modes.

In *Part II: The Supply Side of Marketing Management Support Systems,* we further describe marketing management support systems. In Chapter 3 we define the various types of MMSS and describe the constituent components. We then present an overview of both data-driven MMSS (Chapter 4) and knowledge-driven MMSS (Chapters 5 and 6).

In *Part III: Matching the Demand and Supply Sides of Marketing Management Support Systems,* we begin (in Chapter 7) by presenting an integrating framework that links the demand side (marketing problem-solving modes) to the supply side (marketing management support systems) and helps to determine the type of decision support that is appropriate in specific situations. In Chapter 8 we present an example of how the demand and supply sides can be matched: the BRANDFRAME system. BRANDFRAME, which was designed to support brand managers of fast-moving consumer goods, uses several recently developed knowledge-processing technologies in an integrated way.

Finally, in *Part IV: Perspectives on Marketing Management Support Systems,* we first (in Chapter 9) discuss the factors that drive the success of marketing management support systems and develop a framework for success in which the match between the demand and supply sides plays a prominent role. To do this, we use results from empirical research, both in marketing and in information systems. In Chapter 10, we discuss developments and issues that are relevant for the future of marketing management support systems and summarize the most important research questions surrounding them.

Key Points

- *More data does not automatically result in better information and knowledge that can be used for decision making. Managers can even be frustrated by too much data ("information fatigue syndrome"). Marketing management support systems turn marketing data into actionable knowledge that can give a company a competitive edge in the marketplace.*

- *Investments for IT in marketing are quickly increasing, which raises the question of how to spend this money for MMSS that are maximally effective.*

- *Marketing management support systems combine four major components: information technology, analytical capabilities, marketing data, and marketing knowledge. Different types of MMSS contain these components in different proportions and offer different functionalities. Two broad classes of marketing management support systems can be distinguished: data-driven MMSS and knowledge-driven MMSS.*

- *The design of marketing management support systems should be demand-driven and start with the problem-solving challenges facing the marketing manager. The match between the demand side and the functionalities of the system (i.e., the supply side) is the key factor for success.*

- *There is much marketing literature on marketing management support systems, especially on the specific components of these systems. There is, however, a need for an integrated approach that deals with the different marketing problem-solving modes and the different tools and technologies that are suitable for supporting them. In addition, more insight is needed into how MMSS should be implemented and into the factors that determine their effectiveness. These topics will be treated in the remainder of the book.*

Chapter 2

Marketing Decision Making: A Classification of Marketing Problem-Solving Modes

Learning Objectives

- *To develop a better understanding of the demand side of marketing management support systems: the marketing decision situation.*

- *To understand how marketing decision makers go about solving marketing problems and the specific role of expertise and experience in this effort.*

- *To become familiar with a classification of marketing problem-solving modes (i.e., the different ways in which marketing problems are solved) that can be used to find the right MMSS in a particular decision situation.*

- *To gain insight into the antecedents of these marketing problem-solving modes, that is, the characteristics of the decision situation that are commonly associated with each mode.*

2.1　Introduction

In this chapter we focus on the decision-making processes of individual marketing managers. These decision-making processes can take different forms; and it is our premise that in designing and implementing marketing management support systems (MMSS), one should start with the decision-making process that such systems are intended to support. In this chapter we first discuss how marketing experts go about making decisions. Then we introduce the concept of *marketing problem-solving modes* (MPSM). A marketing problem-solving mode is a cognitive model of the decision-making process or behavior of a marketer. In this chapter we present a classification of four different marketing problem-solving modes. For reasons we will explain shortly, we refer to this classification as *the ORAC model*.

After describing the four marketing problem-solving modes that a decision maker can apply, in the latter part of this chapter we describe the conditions that lead to the use of each of these four modes, that is, the *antecedents* of each MPSM. Our premise is that marketing management support systems should correlate with marketing problem-solving modes. Therefore, insight into the factors leading to the use of the different MPSM is necessary to derive conclusions about the demand for the different types of MMSS and the directions into which this demand is most likely to develop. Later in this book, after discussing the supply side of marketing management support systems, we will explicitly deal with the link between the characteristics of the decision situation and the most suitable MMSS (Chapter 7).

2.2   Marketing Decision-Making Experts

Marketers, being experts in marketing decision making, possess characteristics that are likely to lead to high-quality decision making. Experts have highly developed perceptual and attentional abilities, the sense to distinguish relevance from irrelevance, the ability to simplify complex problems, and extensive and up-to-date knowledge (Shanteau 1992). Gaining experience in making decisions will further develop and enhance these characteristics. According to Shanteau, experts perform especially well in stable environments, where they are able to develop, shape, test, and revise mental models. However, other researchers have reached the opposite conclusion. For example, Spence and Brucks (1997) state that well-structured domains do not give experts the opportunity to display their unique skills. They hypothesize that expertise will be most advantageous at moderate levels of problem structure. Empirical data from their research confirms that the benefits of expertise are most apparent in ill-structured but structurable tasks (e.g., real estate appraisal). Both Shanteau (1992) and Spence and Brucks (1997) thus acknowledge the value of experience and expertise. However, they differ with respect to the conditions under which experience and expertise will be most beneficial.

Other researchers have been more skeptical about the value of expertise. The performance of experts can, for example, be compared with the performance of novices. Camerer and Johnson (1991) found that in most clinical and medical domains, the judgment of experts was no more accurate than that of lightly trained novices. Brehmer (1980) made an even stronger statement, saying, "our faith in experience is, if not totally without foundation, so at least far from well-grounded." This is because decision biases prevent decision makers from using information that experience provides. These biases might, for example, lead to selective information processing. Dearborn and Simon (1959) found that functional experience affects information processing. This means, for example, that decision makers with a background in finance will interpret a business problem as being especially or primarily a financial problem—and will then try to solve it by implementing a financial solution. A marketing decision maker might perceive the same problem as being primarily a marketing problem and, consequently, try to solve it by means of a marketing solution. Van Bruggen, Smidts, and Wierenga (1999) report a similar finding *within* the marketing domain. Marketers with experience in advertising will more often try to solve a marketing problem with an advertising solution, whereas marketers with experience in sales will tend to try to solve the same problem by making changes in the sales force.

Given these research results, one can question whether possessing expert abilities will lead to decision-making processes that can be characterized as optimal or even rational. According to Bazerman (1998), a rational decision-making process consists of the following six steps:

1. Defining the problem.

2. Identifying the criteria.

3. Weighting these criteria.

4. Generating alternatives.

5. Rating each alternative on each criterion.

6. Computing the optimal decision.

This rational model of decision making describes what an optimal decision-making process *should* look like rather than what it often *does* look like. Often, it is impossible for decision makers to reach any high degree of rationality (Simon 1997; Hogarth and Makridakis 1981). The number of alternatives they must explore is so great, and the information they would need to evaluate these alternatives so vast, that even an approximation of objective rationality is unlikely. Actual behavior falls short of objective rationality in at least three ways (Simon 1997): First, rationality requires complete knowledge and anticipation of the consequences that will follow each choice. In reality, knowledge of consequences is often fragmentary.

Second, since consequences lie in the future, imagination must supply the lack of experienced feelings in attaching value to them. But values can be only imperfectly anticipated. Third, rationality requires a choice among all possible alternative behaviors. Yet in actual practice, only a very few of all the possible alternatives come to mind.

Simon (1957) wrote that because of bounded rationality, decision makers often will not maximize (be rational) but instead *satisfice* their decisions. This means that they look for a course of action that is satisfactory enough. Decisions are made with relatively simple rules of thumb that do not make impossible demands on the decision makers' capacity for thought. In fact, most significant decisions are made by judgment rather than by a defined prescriptive approach (Bazerman 1998). Managers make hundreds of decisions daily. Mintzberg (1973) found that an average manager engages in a different activity every nine minutes, which makes a systematic and analytical approach difficult. Mintzberg found that in making decisions, managers tend to avoid hard, systematic, analytical data and rely more on intuitive judgment. Kahneman and Tversky (1974) suggest that people rely on a number of simplifying strategies, or rules of thumb, in making decisions. These strategies are called *heuristics,* and they help in coping with the complexity that managers face. However, heuristics can also lead to serious errors. For example, Hoch and Schkade (1996) have shown that although the intuitively appealing anchoring and adjustment heuristic may perform well in highly predictable environments, it performs poorly in less predictable environments. Simplification and relying on intuition may lead to error, but there is no realistic alternative in the face of the limits on human knowledge and reasoning (Simon 1997).

Bazerman (1998) describes three general heuristics. The first one is the *availability heuristic.* Managers assess the frequency, probability, or likely causes of an event by the degree to which instances or occurrences of that event are readily "available" in memory. This heuristic can be useful since instances of events of greater frequency are generally recalled more easily than events of less frequency. Consequently, this heuristic will often lead to accurate judgment. The heuristic is fallible, however, because the availability of information is also affected by other factors that are not related to the objective frequency of the judged event. Glazer, Steckel, and Winer (1992) show, in the context of marketing decision making, that the use of this heuristic may lead to what they call "locally rational decision making." In an experimental study, they found that decision makers especially use the information that is available or easily accessible. This leads to putting a lot of effort into making decisions on variables for which (much) information is available. Decisions on these variables will probably benefit from the use of the available information. However, it may well be that these specific variables are not the most important determinants of performance and that for superior performance it would be better to focus on other decision variables, even if information on them is not as accessible.

The second heuristic is the *representativeness heuristic.* Managers assess the likelihood of an event's occurrence by the similarity of that occurrence to their stereotypes of similar occurrences. For example, managers predict the success of a new product based on the similarity of that product to past successful and unsuccessful products. A problem with this heuristic is that individuals tend to rely on such strategies even when this information is insufficient and better information exists.

A third general heuristic is the *anchoring and adjustment heuristic.* Managers make assessments by starting from an initial value and adjusting it to arrive at a final decision. The initial "anchor" may be suggested from historical precedent or from random information. So a marketer might tend to set this year's advertising budget at a level close to last year's budget even though the market may demand something completely different this year. Adjustments from the initial value often tend to be insufficient and nonoptimal since they are biased toward their initial values (Slovic and Lichtenstein 1971), which may be insufficient for present market conditions (Mowen and Gaeth 1992). Moreover, different initial values can yield different decisions for the same problem.

The problem with heuristic decision processes is that they can become so habitual or automatic that they will be applied even in situations where it would be preferable to use more formal or rational procedures and where the use of heuristics could lead to serious biases (Weber and Coskunoglu 1990). Still, Payne, Bettman, and Johnson (1993) characterize the use of simplifying, heuristic strategies that are selective in the use of information as *intelligent* responses, given that people have multiple goals for decisions. An individual's use of one of multiple decision strategies in different situations is an adaptive response of a limited-capacity information processor to the demands of complex decision tasks. People make a trade-off between the desire to be accurate (make a decision as good or rational as possible) and the desire to conserve limited cognitive resources (save mental efforts). The actual trade-off that will be made is contingent on three things: (1) the characteristics of the decision situation or problem, (2) the characteristics of the social context or environment in which the decision maker is operating, and (3) the characteristics of the decision maker.

Managerial expertise thus does not automatically imply rational decision-making processes. In fact, sometimes expertise might even be a cause of biased decision processes. However, experts possess the ability to respond intuitively and often very rapidly. They have stored knowledge because of their training and experience, which stimulates problem solving by recognition. Intuition, judgment, and creativity are basically expressions of capabilities for recognition and response based on experience and knowledge (Simon 1997). According to Simon, *analytical* (which can be interpreted as *rational*) and *intuitive* are not opposites. Among experts, relative differences may be observed in their reliance on analysis versus intuition, but large components of both, closely intermingled, can be expected to be present in virtually all expert behavior. Therefore, it is doubtful that there are two types of managers, one of whom relies almost exclusively on recognition (intuition), the other on analytical techniques. More likely, there is a continuum of decision-making styles involving a combination of the two kinds of skill. Simon concludes that it is a fallacy to contrast analytic and intuitive styles of management. Intuition and judgment—at least, good judgment—are simply analyses frozen into habit and into the capacity for rapid response through recognition of familiar kinds of situations. A manager thus should not choose between the two styles but should have command of the whole range of management skills, being able to apply them all whenever they are appropriate.

Marketing management support systems are meant to support the type of marketing experts just described. What does this characterization imply for the nature of MMSS? First, the systems should support both the analytical and the intuitive styles or components of decision making. Second, in developing marketing management support systems, one should be aware of the heuristics and biases in the decision-making processes of marketing managers. Indeed, in some situations the specific role of an MMSS may be to prevent the use of harmful heuristics. For example, Van Bruggen et al. (1998) found that a marketing decision support system may help a marketer to make better decisions by overcoming the anchoring and adjustment heuristic—in this case, overcoming the tendency to choose values of marketing instruments that are too close to their previous values. In other situations an MMSS may enhance the strength of useful heuristics. For example, as we will see later, case-based reasoning systems are meant to support the (powerful) ability of humans to recognize situations and reuse/adapt solutions that have proven effective in the past. In a way, case-based reasoning helps to overcome the bias inherent in the availability heuristic by enlarging the set of relevant experiences that are brought to bear in solving a particular problem.

We believe that MMSS can only be successful if they take as their point of departure how marketing experts actually make decisions. Therefore, in the next section we introduce a detailed taxonomy of the different modes that marketing decision makers use to solve problems.

2.3 The ORAC Model of Marketing Problem-Solving Modes[1]

In his book on cognitive science, Johnson-Laird (1988) observes that "human cogitation occurs in dazzling variety" (p. 217). At one extreme there is "mental arithmetic," where people deliberate and calculate in a consciously controlled way and where calculations have a goal and are deterministic. He calls this "the clocks of mind." At the other extreme there is the free flow of thoughts (dreams), mental processes without a goal, and varieties of creation, which he calls "the clouds of mind." Assuming that the thought and reasoning processes of marketing managers are not different from those of ordinary humans, we present a typology of marketing problem-solving modes, which represent the different positions between these clocks and clouds of the mind. Specifically, we distinguish four different modes, summarized in the acronym *ORAC:* optimizing, reasoning, analogizing, and creating (see Figure 2.1).

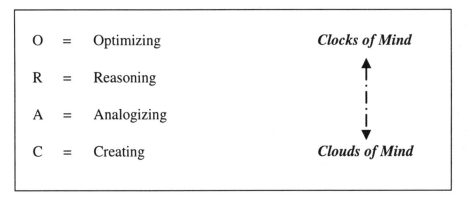

Figure 2.1   The ORAC Model of Marketing Problem-Solving Modes

Stated in a different way, the four MPSM are ordered from hard optimization by means of exact calculations to soft associations and creativity. We will now describe each of these four modes in detail.

---

[1] This section and the following are based on Wierenga and Van Bruggen (1997a).

2.3.1   Optimizing

*Marketing operations are one of the last phases of business
management to come under scientific scrutiny.*
(Kotler 1971)

The cognitive model of a marketing manager using the optimizing mode is
that of a scientist or engineer who has a clear understanding of how
marketing processes work. This is represented by a mathematical model,
which describes the relationships between the relevant variables in a
quantitative way. The decision maker searches for those values of the
decision variables that maximize the goal variable(s) for the particular
problem. These optimal values for the decision variables are determined in
the "model world." Next, they are translated into the "real world." In other
words, a marketing management problem is converted into a "marketing
programming problem" (Kotler 1971).

To solve a marketing programming problem, two basic requirements
exist: (1) a model describing the mechanism underlying the marketing
problem or phenomenon, and (2) an optimization algorithm that searches for
the optimal values for the decision variables given the objective (e.g., profit
maximization or 50% brand awareness). In the early days of optimization in
marketing, the emphasis was on the optimization *procedure*. If an
optimization procedure was available (e.g., linear programming), one was
even willing to "adapt" the marketing problem somewhat, so that it would fit
the properties of the algorithm. A case in point is the application of linear
programming to media planning, where the relationship between the effect
of an advertisement and the number of insertions was taken to be linear, not
because of theoretical reasons but because it fitted the model so nicely.
Later, however, it became clear that it is much more important to have a
correct model of the marketing phenomenon under study (since increasing
computer capacity has made it almost always possible to carry out the
optimization by some form of simulation). This gave rise to a model-
building tradition, which became a prominent school in marketing (science).
The impressive achievements of the model-building tradition in marketing
have been put on record in a series of books that appeared in intervals of
about a decade: Kotler (1971), Lilien and Kotler (1983), and Lilien, Kotler,
and Moorthy (1992). In addition, the recent book edited by Eliashberg and
Lilien (1993) pays tribute to the extensive work in marketing models.

For an overall marketing optimization—that is, where all marketing
instruments are optimized simultaneously—we would need a "comprehensive marketing system" specifying all the relevant variables and their
mutual relationships (Kotler 1971, p. 667). Although efforts have been made
to specify relationships between and within all the subsystems of a

comprehensive marketing system (e.g., BRANDAID, Little 1975), a much more easily achieved goal is to determine the optimum for *one* marketing instrument or at most *a part* of the marketing program. One of the earliest examples of a partially optimizing model is the MEDIAC model for media planning, developed by Little and Lodish (1969). The positive part of the MEDIAC model describes the relationship between the value of exposure to an advertising campaign and the planned insertions in the various media (i.e., a specific media plan). This model can then be used to find the optimal media plan, given the advertising budget on the one hand and the audience and cost of the available media on the other. The planning of sales-force operations (e.g., CALLPLAN, Lodish 1971) and supermarket shelf-space allocation (SH.A.R.P., Bultez and Naert 1988) are other domains where the optimizing mode has been successfully applied.

The example in Box 2.1 illustrates marketing problem solving using the optimizing mode.

At Syntex Laboratories, a pharmaceutical company in the U.S., management was uneasy about the size of the sales force and its allocation over products and market segments. The sales force had increased every year in an ad hoc way. The senior vice president for sales and marketing thought that there must be a better way to determine the size of the sales force needed to optimally support the sales of the company's products. Two management scientists were asked to implement such an optimization approach. Models were developed that described the relationship between sales effort and sales for the various categories of drugs in the different market segments. These models were then used in a stepwise optimization procedure, where each additional amount of sales capacity was allocated to the most profitable product/segment. Based on this approach, the corporation significantly increased the size of its sales force and altered its deployment. These changes resulted in a documented continuing increase in annual sales of $25 million (8 percent), with a return on the increased expenditures on the sales force of at least 100 percent.

Box 2.1   Marketing Problem Solving in the Optimizing Mode (*Source:* Lodish, Curtis, Ness, and Simpson 1988)

2.3.2   Reasoning

Human beings translate external events into internal models and reason by manipulating these symbolic representations. (Craik 1943)

It has long been recognized that individuals form and use mental representations of phenomena in the outside world. Such representations are called *mental models.* A mental model is a symbolic structure, a representation of a body of knowledge in the human mind (Johnson-Laird 1988, 1989). A person can use such a mental model for reasoning about a phenomenon. In cognitive science this type of approach to a problem is called *model-based reasoning* (Hayes 1985; Forbus 1988; Johnson-Laird 1989). Mental models have generated considerable interest, and the concept has been used in different domains: sometimes at the fundamental level of human perception—for example, the mental representation of a word or geometric figure, or language comprehension (Anderson 1983; Johnson-Laird 1988)—but also sometimes to describe how humans deal mentally with complex phenomena. Examples are mental models for physical systems such as the working of a calculator (Gentner and Stevens 1983), mental models that underlie public policy decisions (Axelrod 1976), managerial mental models (Courtney, Paradice, and Mohammed 1987; Day and Nedungadi 1994), and mental models as the basis for strategic planning and subjective forecasting (Klayman and Schoemaker 1993).

In the optimizing mode it is assumed that there is an objective model that provides a valid description of the marketing phenomenon under study. However, only a small part of all marketing phenomena has been brought under scientific scrutiny, so our systematic, scientifically based knowledge of marketing phenomena is limited. If a systematic world underlying marketing phenomena exists at all, it has been explored and mapped out only incompletely. In the absence of an objective model, a marketer often adopts a marketing problem-solving mode called *reasoning*. In the reasoning mode, decision makers construct a representation of the marketing phenomenon in their minds. These mental models are then the basis for the manager's reasoning about the problem. A mental model consists of variables deemed relevant and the supposed cause-and-effect relationships between these variables. Such a model helps a decision maker to diagnose and solve a specific problem.

Different marketing managers may have different mental models with respect to the same phenomenon. For example, in the case of advertising, different marketing managers may use different models to explain why a particular advertising campaign was successful. A marketer's mental model of a specific phenomenon is shaped by experience in practice, sometimes after a theoretical education. In the optimizing mode, marketers also have a mental model of the situation (hopefully consistent with the mathematical model in the optimization procedure). Compared to this model, the mental model in the reasoning mode is more qualitative, subjective, and incomplete.

Mental models can be at variance with reality. In the history of physics there are many examples of mental models that were proved wrong after thorough scientific examination. For example, for centuries heat and temperature were believed to be the same concept; this idea was only replaced by the correct model around 1750 (Wiser and Carey 1983). Although mental models may not always be correct, they are useful because they offer the marketer a framework for interpreting and reasoning about marketing problems and their solutions. As long as the truly objective and accurate scientific model is lacking, mental models must be used.

It's November 1995, and Dirk Jansen, product manager of a traditional margarine brand in the Dutch edible-fats market called Landlord has just received the new four-weekly Nielsen figures, which refer to period 10, ending the beginning of October. These figures show that Landlord's market share in period 10 is 8.4%, down from 10.7% in the previous period. This drop is quite alarming, and Dirk starts to think about possible causes. His first idea, that the fall in market share is just an occasional occurrence, is dismissed immediately, as there has been a continuous decline since period 5 (May), when Landlord's market share was 12.4%. According to Dirk's view (mental model), the Dutch edible-fats market can be divided into "standard brands" and "diet brands." He suspects that the market share of Landlord, which belongs to the standard-brands category, is going down in part because of a decline in the share of standard brands in the total market. (This share decreased from 73% in 1992 to 67% in 1994.) However, a look at the Nielsen figures shows that from period 9 to period 10 the share of standard brands did not decrease further; it even increased slightly. Indeed, within the standard-brands category, Landlord's drop in market share is even greater than its overall drop: from 16.2% to 12.5%. A check of distribution trends shows that weighted distribution is (only) 81%, and that distribution of Landlord is down in four of the five major retail chains. In the one chain where the distribution of Landlord increased, its market share also went up. Following this cue, Dirk next looks at price levels and quickly discovers that, whereas the average price of the brands in the market decreased 2% from period 9 to period 10, Landlord's price increased 3%. Duchess, a competing brand, lowered its price and saw its market share increase 18%. Following this lead, Dirk next looks at display share.

Box 2.2   Marketing Problem Solving in the Reasoning Mode (*Source:* Inspired by a real-life market situation and actual figures, though the product category and brand names have been disguised)

The example in Box 2.2 illustrates marketing problem solving using the reasoning mode. The product manager in the example in Box 2.2 is guided by a mental model of marketing phenomena that contains elements such as random versus systematic changes, the possibility of different demands in different market segments, and elements of the marketing mix such as distribution and price.

2.3.3   Analogizing

An individual's knowledge is the collection of experiences that
he has had or that he has heard about.
(Riesbeck and Schank 1989)

When confronted with a problem, a person has a natural inclination to bring to bear the experience gained from solving similar problems in the past. A doctor, faced with a patient who has an unusual combination of symptoms, may remember another patient with similar symptoms and propose the same diagnosis as in the previous case (Kolodner 1993). Analogizing is considered a fundamental mechanism in human understanding and problem solving. "Analogy-making lies at the heart of intelligence" (Hofstadter 1995, p. 63). Children automatically apply analogical thinking, and some elements of analogical thinking can even be found in apes and chimpanzees (Holyak and Thagard 1995).

For a long time the "general problem-solving" school was dominant in cognitive science. According to this school, human thought depends on a set of reasoning principles that are independent of any given domain—meaning that we (humans) reason the same way no matter what we are reasoning on or about. Simon (1979, p. xii) formulated this (standard) way of operating by "Thinking Man" as follows: "Thinking is a process of serial selective search through large spaces of alternatives guided by individual mechanisms that operate through dynamically adapting aspiration levels." The proponents of analogical reasoning have a very different view (Riesbeck and Schank 1989, p. 3): "Certain aspects of human thought may be a simpler affair than many scientists have imagined." In other words, human problem-solving behavior can often be explained by much simpler mechanisms than the general problem solver.

Analogical (or case-based) reasoning implies that the *original concrete instances* are used for reasoning, rather than abstractions based on those instances. One might deduce general principles from the experienced cases, but according to Riesbeck and Schank, such "general principles are impoverished compared to the original experience." After many repetitions of the same situation, some cases may "coalesce" into rules. However, these rules are encoded in memory separate from any particular instance of their use or the history of their creation.

Wide support exists for analogical reasoning as a model for human decision making. Studies in human problem solving reveal the pervasiveness of analogy usage (Sternberg 1977). People find analogical reasoning a natural way to reason. Car mechanics, physicians, architects, and caterers use it. In particular, case-based reasoning excels as an approach to "weak-theory domains," domains where phenomena are not understood well enough to determine causality unambiguously (Kolodner 1993).

Indeed, much of marketing problem solving probably follows the analogizing path. A marketing manager usually has a set of experiences (cases) available from memory, referring to all kinds of marketing events: new-product introductions, price changes, sales promotions, advertising campaigns, reactions of competitors, and so on. In a new situation, even without active effort on the part of the manager, one or more earlier situations come to mind that resemble the current one. Sometimes the manager will be inclined to choose the same kind of solution as in the previous case. For example, a manager may decide to execute the same sales promotion for a product in country B as the one that was so successful in country A earlier. However, in many cases the manager will not literally repeat the previous solution but will adapt it somewhat. In a sales promotion, for example, the specific premium and packaging used in country B may differ from those used in country A. Hoch and Schkade (1996) found that to arrive at a forecast, decision makers often search their experience for a situation similar to the one at hand, and then make small adjustments to it.

Basically, in these situations a process of *analogizing* or *analogical reasoning* takes place. For most problems, marketing theory is insufficient ("weak-theory domain"). Marketing managers often have no generalized rules, drawn from experience, that could serve as elements of a mental model. However, managers do have a lot of experience with more or less similar cases. Moreover, in many instances there simply isn't enough time to solve a problem by reasoning from "first principles," that is, to build a (mental) model that explains a phenomenon in terms of elementary events. In such instances, analogical reasoning is a fast and appropriate approach to problem solving.

The example in Box 2.3 illustrates marketing problem solving using the analogizing mode. A two-way transition exists between the analogizing mode and the reasoning mode. When people using the reasoning mode cannot find an adequate model, they tend to resort to analogizing. "When a causal model fails to explain some phenomenon, a person is likely to search for a useful analogy, for example, the model of a thermostat as a valve" (Johnson-Laird 1989, p. 487). On the other hand, experience with many cases in a certain domain may result in the abstraction of rules that can become the building blocks of a mental model. The cases from which these rules were derived are no longer known. Riesbeck and Schank use the term "ossified cases" to describe this situation. An example of an ossified case in marketing is the general rule that the first brand in a product category has a pioneer premium and will most likely become the market leader: "It is better to be first, than it is to be better" (Ries and Trout 1993).

Rob de Zwart, marketing director of Croky Chips, a subsidiary of United Biscuits in the Netherlands, was confronted with a drop in market share from 32% in March 1995 to 18.5% in the fall of the same year. The major cause of this dramatic decrease was the very successful Flippo campaign, launched by competitor Smith Chips in the spring. Flippos are small, round plastic disks, with Warner Bros. cartoons on them, that are put into the bags with the chips. There are all kinds of different Flippos—for example, Regular, Game, Flying, Chester, and Techno Flippos (335 different types in all)—and collecting and exchanging Flippos became a craze among teenagers and young adults as well as children. At the start of the Flippo campaign, Croky did not pay much attention to it. Flippos were thought to be too childish, and Croky instead launched an infotainment campaign (trendy texts on chips bags) combined with discounts on music CDs. When Croky realized that, against their expectations, the Flippos had really touched a chord with teenagers, they developed an analogous campaign. This Croky campaign, called Topshots, also puts plastic disks into bags of chips. However, in the case of Topshots, the disks are not round but octagonal (the disks can be used to build all kinds of constructions), and they carry not Warner Bros. cartoons but pictures of all (198) players in the highest league of the Dutch Soccer competition. This seems a clever adaptation: Soccer is by far the most popular sport in Holland, and the European Championships were not far off. First indications are that Topshots may reach the same level of popularity as Flippos.

Box 2.3   Marketing Problem Solving in the Analogizing Mode (*Source: NieuwsTribune,* no. 50, 1995)

2.3.4   Creating

Few observers would disagree that there is a considerable amount of judgment and creativity, if not art, involved in being a successful marketing manager.
(Hulbert 1981)

The last marketing problem-solving mode that we distinguish is *creating*. Using the creating mode, a marketing decision maker searches for novel concepts, solutions, or ideas in responding to a situation that has not occurred before. However, what precisely is a creative idea, and how do marketers hit upon those ideas that really make a difference in the marketplace? What was the creative process that led to successes like Post-it, the famous yellow pieces of paper from 3M, or the catchy brand name Q8, of Kuwait Petroleum?

The literal (dictionary) meaning of *create* is "to bring into being or form out of nothing." Ackoff and Vergara (1981) define creativity (in a management context) as "the ability to break through constraints imposed by habit and tradition so as to find new solutions to problems." This formulation makes clear that creating means stepping away from the conventional path. Creativity implies "divergent thinking"—that is, thinking with an open mind, expanding the set of decision possibilities, and enlarging the solution space—which is the opposite of "convergent thinking"—that is, the evaluation and screening of existing possibilities (Chung 1987). Divergent thinking has also been referred to as "restructuring the whole situation" (Wertheimer 1959), "reframing" (Russo and Schoemaker 1990), and "transformation of conceptual spaces" (Boden 1991). However, divergent thinking is not a sufficient condition to explain creativity. The element of problem finding, problem discovery, or "sensing gaps" is also important (Kabanoff and Rossiter 1994). Creativity often means coming up with solutions for problems that one was not aware of. In the management literature there are several references to this concept of problem finding (Pounds 1969; Courtney, Paradice, and Mohammed 1987; Smith 1989).

Elam and Mead (1990) emphasize the new-combinations character of creative ideas: "Creativity involves combining known but previously unrelated facts and ideas in such a way that new ones emerge." Boden (1994) defines and explains creativity "in terms of the mapping, exploration, and transformation of structured conceptual spaces." In the more applied literature, elements of value and usefulness are often part of the definition of creative output. MacCrimmon and Wagner (1994) mention the dimensions of novelty, nonobviousness, workability, relevance, and thoroughness. Bruner (1962) defines creativity as an act that produces "effective surprise." One aspect that is found in many theoretical contributions, as well as in the thinking processes of very creative persons, is that of "making connections" (MacCrimmon and Wagner 1994). This refers to the creation of new ideas through the association of existing ones (related to the new-combinations concept mentioned earlier).

It is widely accepted that marketing requires a good deal of creativity. Marketing problems are often not well defined in terms of goals, means, mechanisms, and constraints, and often do not lend themselves to the procedural or logical reasoning used in conventional computer programs or knowledge-based systems. The cognitive model of a marketer following the creating mode is one of a decision maker who—consciously or unconsciously, by means of mapping, exploring, and transforming conceptual space, expanding the number of possible solutions through divergent thinking, and making connections and associations—is searching for novel and effective ideas and solutions to strengthen the market position of the product, brand, or company. Creating can refer to all aspects of the marketing management domain, including generating ideas for new products or services, innovative advertising or sales-promotion campaigns, new forms of distribution, and ingenious pricing. Creativity is an important asset. Many companies owe their existence to a creative new product or process, and creativity is often the means for survival as well as growth.

The example in Box 2.4 illustrates marketing problem solving using the creating mode.

In the 1970s, when John Sculley was Vice President of Marketing at Pepsi-Cola, this company was struggling way behind the number one in the industry, Coca-Cola. At Pepsi-Cola there was general agreement that the most important competitive advantage of Coca-Cola was its characteristic hourglass-shaped bottle. This design had almost become the product itself. It was pleasant to hold in the hand, was easy to deal with in vending machines, and had become as American as apple pie. People at Pepsi had spent millions of dollars and many years of research to come up with a bottle for Pepsi-Cola that could play the same role as the hourglass-shaped bottle did for Coca-Cola—however, to no avail.

Then Sculley realized that Pepsi was taking the wrong approach to the problem. As long as they stayed within the solution space defined by Coca-Cola (i.e., find a competitive advantage through the shape of the bottle), it would be difficult for Pepsi to beat Coca-Cola. So Sculley ordered his people to take a fresh look at what people really do with cola. The company studied the consumption behavior of families that were allowed to order weekly (discounted) quantities as large as they wanted. It was discovered that these people always used up all their cola, regardless of the quantities bought. So the objective of a cola bottler should be to have consumers take larger quantities of cola to their homes. Once they have it, they will consume it. This conclusion triggered the development of large-size packages by Pepsi-Cola, which had a direct positive effect on their market share. Coca-Cola could not transform its hourglass-shaped bottle to larger packages and consequently lost much of its advantage in the competitive battle under the new (large packages) rules. So by "restructuring the whole situation," Sculley created the basis for Pepsi-Cola to be a strong competitor of Coca-Cola in the American market.

Box 2.4   Marketing Problem Solving in the Creating Code (*Source:* Russo and Schoemaker, 1990)

Optimizing

The marketing decision maker acts as a scientist or engineer with a precise insight in the mechanisms behind the marketing phenomea. In a strictly analytical way he has a mathematical model that explains and predicts the dependent variable(s) under study. This model is then parameterized and used for optimization.

Reasoning

The marketing decision maker constructs his own internal represesentation of the marketing phenomena. This 'mental model' is the basis for reasoning about a problem. It contains the variables deemed relevant and the supposed cause-effect relationships. Mental models are often incomplete but may contain deep knowledge.

Analogizing

The marketing decision maker, confronted with a problem, activates in his memory a similar problem which he solved before, or has witnessed being solved. The previous solution is taken as the starting point for the present case, and may subsequently be adapted, taking into consideration the differences between the present and the earlier problem. The solution is not constructed from first principles but from past cases.

Creating

The marketing decision maker is searching for novel and effective ideas and solutions by means of mapping, exploring and the transformation of the problem's conceptual space, expanding the number of possible solutions through divergent thinking.

Figure 2.2   Artistic impression of the four marketing problem-solving modes (pictures by Arco Dalebout)

There can be some overlap between the creating and the analogizing modes. Analogies can be a source of creativity: a metaphor can be a springboard for creative solutions (Tardif and Sternberg 1988) and can generate mental leaps (Holyak and Thagard 1995). However, the two modes differ in that in the analogizing mode, the search is for situations, as similar as possible, that the decision maker has already experienced or knows, whereas in the creating mode, the analogies that trigger the best ideas tend to be based on remote or dissimilar situations.

Figure 2.2 provides an artistic impression of the four modes just discussed, together with a summary of their characteristics.

2.3.5   Relationships between the Four Marketing Problem-Solving Modes

We wish to make three comments about the relationships between these four marketing problem-solving modes. The first is that the four MPSM are not mutually exclusive in the sense that a marketing decision maker can use only one mode to solve a particular problem. Some decision situations will require the use of two or more modes, sometimes in different phases of the solution process. We use the marketing problem-solving modes to refer to the *dominant mode,* that is, for a particular marketing decision situation, the MPSM that describes that situation best or comes closest to what the manager actually does. For example, consider a marketer determining the size of an advertising budget. If the elements of primary consideration are the effect of advertising on awareness, the most likely advertising efforts of competitors, and the way market share will be affected by advertising, together with some (unquantified) notion that one should not overadvertise (i.e., beyond the point where marginal returns equal marginal costs), then the dominant marketing problem-solving mode is reasoning. However, there are also elements of optimizing in this approach and maybe also some comparison with past cases (analogizing). However, reasoning is the MPSM that best or most accurately describes what the marketer actually does in this situation.

The second remark is a corollary of the first: The four marketing problem-solving modes are not completely distinct from each other, in that a decision maker can switch from using one mode to using another. For example, when using the reasoning mode, a marketer's (mental) model of a particular marketing situation becomes more refined and complete through observation and introspection. At some point this model may become sufficiently detailed and complete for the marketer to make a precise mathematical specification. When this mathematical model is then used for finding the best values for the marketing decision variables, the decision maker has segued into the optimizing mode. As already mentioned, transitions can also occur between analogizing and reasoning. A person who has observed many cases in a specific domain may generalize from these cases and develop rules to reason with (Kolodner 1993).

Third, there is an order inherent in the ORAC classification: The optimizing mode is appropriate for solving highly structured problems, the reasoning mode for moderately or only somewhat structured problems, and so on down to the creating mode, which is appropriate for highly *un*structured problems. Generally speaking, a problem that can be solved using a particular marketing problem-solving mode can also be solved using modes that assume *less* structure. In general, however, the converse is not true: a problem that is highly unstructured, which would typically require a creative problem-solving approach, cannot be solved using a mode that assumes more structure.

2.4   Antecedents of Marketing Problem-Solving Modes

Let us assume that the four marketing problem-solving modes just described constitute a useful way of classifying different modes of marketing decision making. The question now arises, What are the factors that determine which MPSM will be dominant in a particular decision situation? In this section we discuss the factors that seem most important in determining which MPSM to adopt (though we do not pretend our analysis to be complete or exhaustive). Specifically, we distinguish three sets of antecedents: problem characteristics, decision environment characteristics, and decision maker characteristics (see Figure 2.3).

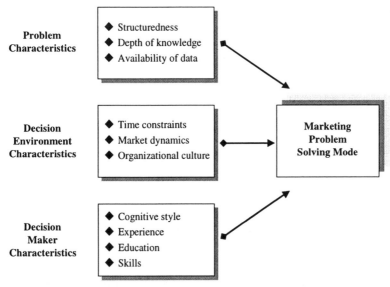

Figure 2.3   Antecedents of the Four Marketing Problem-Solving Modes

2.4.1   Problem Characteristics

We discuss three characteristics of the problem that are important for determining the dominant marketing problem-solving mode in a particular decision situation: the structuredness of the problem, the depth of knowledge about it, and the availability of data on it.

Structuredness

The term *structuredness* describes the extent to which relevant elements of a problem and the relationships between those elements are known. The notion of structuredness of a management problem has received a lot of attention in the literature (Keen and Scott Morton 1978; Sprague 1989). The concept goes back to Simon's (1960) notion of "programmability." For the optimizing mode, a high level of structuredness is required. Examples of relatively programmable and structured marketing problems are sales management and sales-force decisions and media planning for advertising. An example of a less structured problem is choosing a brand name for a new product. Such a problem requires (sometimes) analogizing and (certainly) creating. There is a relationship between structuredness and the newness of a problem. Structured or programmed problems tend to refer to decisions that are repetitive and routine, for which a procedure has already been worked out (Simon 1960). For new problems, such structured procedures are not yet available.

Depth of knowledge

Depth of knowledge refers to generalized knowledge, that is, the product of scientific research. The term *completeness of knowledge* has also been used to describe the same concept (Rangaswamy, Eliashberg, Burke, and Wind 1989). The optimizing mode requires deep knowledge. However, the required depth of knowledge (in the sense of objective, scientifically verified knowledge) decreases in the direction of reasoning, analogizing, and creating.

Availability of data

Much data is needed to develop mathematical (optimizing) models. Data also plays an important role in the formation of a marketer's mental model, used in the reasoning mode: it helps the marketer to form an impression of the mechanisms at work in a market. For analogizing and creating, however, the cognitive processes are more qualitative and subjective.

Although there may be tendencies (e.g., advertising decisions are often made by analogizing and creating, whereas distribution decisions are often made by optimizing and reasoning), there appears to be no unequivocal link between the marketing-mix instrument and the marketing problem-solving mode applied. We propose that the relationship runs through the factors structuredness, depth of knowledge, and availability of data, which can have different values for the same marketing-mix instrument. So, for example, when an advertising problem is very structured and both deep knowledge and much data are available, optimizing will be the dominant MPSM. However, when the advertising problem is unstructured and both knowledge and data are scarce, the decision maker probably has to come up with a creative solution. A similar argument applies to the applicability of different MPSM in different industries.

The three problem characteristics distinguished here are not independent. The structuredness of a problem will increase as the level of knowledge of a domain increases. Furthermore, the availability of data in a particular domain may stimulate scientific research, which in turn will increase the knowledge about the phenomena in that domain. New data sources have a major impact on developments in modeling markets (Lilien 1994). For example, scanning data have significantly increased our knowledge about the effects of sales promotions.

2.4.2   Decision Environment Characteristics

We discuss three characteristics of the decision environment that are important for determining the dominant marketing problem-solving mode in a particular decision situation: time constraints, market dynamics, and the organizational culture.

Time constraints

Time constraints often preclude the complete sequence of specifying a model, estimating parameters, and using the model in the optimizing mode. Numerous factors could cause a manager to often experience time constraints when making decisions. Some factors are internal in origin, arising from the way a company is organized—for example, fixed reporting schedules, deadlines for proposals, and the fact that a marketer usually has to divide attention between several products and brands. A marketing manager's way of operating is aptly described by Mintzberg's (1973) classical adjectives: brief, fragmented, and varying. Other factors leading to time constraints are external in origin, the most important of which is competition. Being first, making the preemptive move in the marketplace, is often more important than devising the perfect plan but implementing it too late. When time is short, the quickest way to solve a problem is to consult one's memory and to search for similar cases experienced before. Thus, time pressure clearly stimulates the analogizing mode. Some amount of reasoning can occur, but this will be confined to consulting the existing mental model. Finally, time pressure is not conducive to creativity. Creativity takes time (Tardif and Sternberg 1988), and deadlines are detrimental to creativity (Hennesey and Amabile 1988).

Market dynamics

There is a big difference between operating in a stable market and operating in a turbulent one (e.g., compare the current coffee market [Simon 1994] with the market for IT products). In stable markets, the optimizing mode will be used more often. Here mathematical models are effective tools. Under turbulent market conditions, however, marketers will be hard-pressed to understand and interpret what is going on and will therefore constantly revise their mental models of the market. If mathematical models would be feasible at all, they would have to be respecified and reestimated all the time. So in dynamic market conditions we expect that the reasoning mode will be used more often. Turbulence is also conducive to the creating mode (e.g., see the current supply of innovative IT products).

Organizational culture

A company or department will have certain prevailing attitudes and a certain standard approach to doing things (Pettigrew 1979). If in a company in general there is a positive attitude toward the use of models and quantitative analyses, this general attitude will extend to the way marketing managers go about solving problems in their domain—favoring the optimizing and reasoning modes. Similarly, more heuristic/holistic cultural attitudes favor the analogizing and creating modes. Organizations also make assumptions about the analyzability of their environment. If an organization believes that its environment is analyzable, it will try to grasp the underlying patterns through analysis and will use techniques such as correlation and forecasting. If an organization believes that its environment is not analyzable, it will rely more on soft, qualitative data, judgment, and intuition (Daft and Weick 1984).

2.4.3   Decision Maker Characteristics

We discuss four characteristics of the decision maker that are important for determining the dominant marketing problem-solving mode in a particular decision situation: the decision maker's cognitive style, experience, education, and skills.

Cognitive style

The cognitive style of decision makers refers to the process through which they perceive and process information. Most common is the classification of decision makers into two categories, *analytical* and *nonanalytical*. Sometimes the adjectives *systematic* and *heuristic* are used to label these two classes (Bariff and Lusk 1977; Zmud 1979). Analytical decision makers reduce a problem to a core set of underlying relationships. All effort is directed toward detecting these relationships and manipulating the decision variables in such a manner that some optimal equilibrium is reached with respect to the objectives. Nonanalytical decision makers look for workable solutions to the total problem situation. They search for analogies with familiar, solved problems. Common sense, intuition, and unquantified "feelings" play an important role (Huysmans 1970). All other things being equal, analytical decision makers tend toward the optimizing and reasoning modes, whereas nonanalytical decision makers are inclined to use the analogizing and/or creating modes.

Experience

A high degree of marketing decision-making experience means that a person has dealt with a large number of practical marketing problems and their solutions. This provides the marketer with the opportunity to develop a rich mental model, which favors the reasoning mode. On the other hand, all these experiences also constitute many cases, which can serve as a basis for analogizing. Which of the two modes (reasoning or analogizing) the experienced decision maker will tend to use might well depend on the individual's cognitive style, with analytical types tending toward reasoning and nonanalytical types toward analogizing.

Education

An academic education stimulates an analytical approach, favoring the optimizing and reasoning modes. Little (1979) expected that the influx of model-trained graduates in companies would lead to increased use of marketing decision support systems. Other educational institutions (e.g., professional and trade schools) emphasize examples and case histories. Consequently, their graduates are more conditioned toward analogizing and creating.

	MARKETING PROBLEM-SOLVING MODES			
Antecedents	**Optimizing**	**Reasoning**	**Analogizing**	**Creating**
Problem characteristics	• High structuredness • Precise knowledge of relationships • Quantitative data	• Moderate structuredness • Knowledge of most important variables • Quantitative or qualitative data	• Low structuredness • Weak theory • Experiences and/or cases	• No precise problem formulation • No theory • Remote associations
Decision environment characteristics	• Ample time frame • Stable market • Quantitative/analytical attitude in company	• Limited time frame • Dynamic market • Analytical attitude in company	• Little time available • Stable market • Heuristic/holistic attitude in company	• No time pressure • Dynamic market • Heuristic/holistic attitude in company
Decision maker characteristics	• Analytical cognitive style • Varies • Academic education • Quantitative skills	• Analytical cognitive style • Experienced decision maker • Academic education • Quantitative skills	• Heuristic cognitive style • Experienced decision maker • MBA or professional education • No quantitative skills	• Heuristic cognitive style • Varies • No specific education • Creative skills and intrinsic motivation

Figure 2.4   Marketing problem-solving modes and their antecedents

Skills

Skills will facilitate the use of a certain mode. For example, quantitative skills and computer literacy/proficiency are skills that stimulate the optimizing mode. However, people can be trained to develop specific skills, for example, to become more creative.

2.4.4 Summary of the Effects of the Antecedents of the Marketing Problem-Solving Modes

Figure 2.4 depicts the "pattern" of relationships between various antecedents and the four different marketing problem-solving modes. The optimizing mode, for example, is associated with conditions such as the following: high stuctucturedness, deep knowledge, and the availability of quantitative information (problem characteristics); an ample time frame, a stable market, and an analytical attitude in the company (decision environment characteristics); and an analytical cognitive style, an academic education, and quantitative skills (decision maker characteristics). In a similar way the conditions (antecedents) most likely to lead to the other marketing problem-solving modes can be gleaned from Figure 2.4.

Figure 2.4 should be interpreted as a heuristic: it shows tendencies rather than hard relationships. Nevertheless, it helps to relate the marketing problem-solving modes to actual marketing decision situations.

In this chapter, we have developed a perspective on the demand side of marketing management support systems. In the following chapters we will address the supply side of both data-driven and knowledge-driven MMSS.

Key Points

- *Decision processes are seldom completely rational. Decision makers, marketing managers included, operate under conditions of bounded rationality, which often makes them satisficers rather than optimizers.*

- *Experienced decision makers use several types of heuristics to render decision making easier, for example, the availability heuristic, the representativeness heuristic, and the anchoring and adjustment heuristic. However, such heuristics may be the cause of biased decision processes, and marketing management support systems should prevent the use of harmful heuristics.*

- *Four marketing problem-solving modes can be distinguished: optimizing, reasoning, analogizing, and creating (the ORAC classification).*

- *In the optimizing mode the marketing problem is represented by a mathematical model, which is used to find the values of the decision variables that maximize the value(s) of the goal variable(s). In the reasoning mode decision makers use a representation of the relevant marketing phenomena in their mind (a mental model) as a basis for interpretations and decisions.*

- *In the analogizing mode the decision maker uses concrete experiences in similar, prior situations as a basis for solving a current problem.In the creating mode a decision maker applies divergent thinking and, by enlarging the solution space, tries to come up with novel and effective ideas to strengthen the position of the product, brand, or company.*

- *The most important factors that determine which marketing problem-solving mode is used (i.e. the antecedents of marketing problem-solving modes) are the characteristics of the problem, the characteristics of the decision environment, and the characteristics of the decision maker. For example, the marketing problem-solving mode of optimizing is likely to occur under conditions such as a highly structured problem (problem characteristic), an ample time frame (decision environment characteristic), and an analytical cognitive style (decision maker characteristic). However, under conditions of a weakly structured problem, time pressure, and a heuristic cognitive style, the analogizing mode is more likely to be used.*

PART II

The Supply Side of Marketing Management Support Systems

Chapter 3

The Components of Marketing Management Support Systems

Learning Objectives

- *To understand the four components of marketing management support systems: information technology, analytical capabilities, marketing data, and marketing knowledge.*

- *To develop insight into how hardware and software developments have enhanced the development of powerful marketing management support systems.*

- *To become acquainted with the types and sources of data that can be part of a marketing management support system.*

- *To become familiar with the analytical capabilities currently available for analyzing marketing data.*

- *To become aware of the role of knowledge in marketing management support systems and the different types and sources of this knowledge.*

- *To understand how developments in the four components are interrelated and how they drive the development of more sophisticated marketing management support systems.*

3.1   Introduction

Part II of this book is devoted to the technologies and tools that can assist decision makers in their problem-solving activities. This is the supply side of marketing management support systems. In Chapters 4, 5, and 6 we discuss the actual *tools* of MMSS; but first, in the present chapter we discuss the *components* of MMSS that underlie these different tools. In Chapter 1 a marketing management support system was defined in terms of its components as follows:

> *Any device, combining (1) information technology, (2) analytical capabilities, (3) marketing data, and (4) marketing knowledge, made available to one or more marketing decision maker(s) to improve the quality of marketing management.*

Marketing management support systems thus comprise four components:
1. Some form of *information technology,* which is both hardware (e.g., computers, PCs, workstations, optical-scanning technology, networks, and so on) and software (e.g., database management programs, programming languages, software development environments, spreadsheets, graphics, communication software, and so on).

2. *Analytical capabilities,* which can take many different forms: statistical packages for analyzing marketing data, parameter-estimation procedures, marketing models, and simulation and optimization procedures.

3. *Marketing data:* quantitative information about variables such as sales, market shares, prices, one's own and one's competitors' marketing-mix expenditures, distribution figures, and so on.

4. *Marketing knowledge:* qualitative knowledge about such things as the structure of markets or market segments, the suitability of specific sales-promotion campaigns, typical reactions to advertisements, heuristics for the acceptance of clients, and so on.

The first two components are *general-purpose* components, whereas the latter two are *domain-specific* components. Information technology and analytical capabilities are building blocks of financial or logistical support systems as much as they are part of marketing management support systems. Marketing data and marketing knowledge are specific marketing components. The four components of an MMSS are graphically presented in Figure 3.1. These components determine the capabilities and functionality of such systems.

We will now describe the four components in more detail. An exhaustive description of each of them is beyond the scope of this book; however, we will describe the state of the art of each component and discuss the most important developments for each.

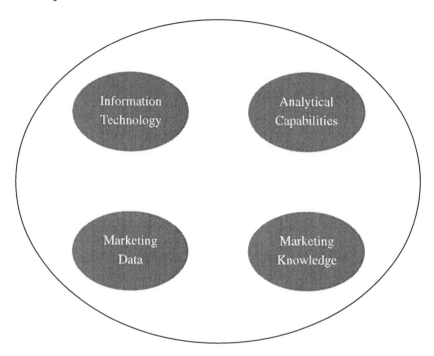

Figure 3.1   The Four Components of a Marketing Management Support System

3.2   Information Technology

In principle, marketing management support systems can be both manual and computer-based systems. However, in this book we focus on computer-based systems. Information technology (IT) is the most important factor behind the development of MMSS. Even though information technology can be conceived of as "only" the vehicle necessary to make an MMSS run, its developments have greatly stimulated the development of tools that form the building blocks of MMSS. Information technology makes it possible for marketers to collect and store enormous amounts of data and knowledge and access them in almost any way and at any time. The development of scanning technology is a case in point. This technology has revolutionized market research, especially in the packaged-goods industry (Malhotra 1999). Scanner data is collected by passing merchandise over a laser scanner at the store checkout. The scanner optically reads the bar code and links it to information about the bar code that is stored in a central computer system. Information about the sold products will also be stored in the computer system. Later, this data can be analyzed and used for decision support. In addition, modern computer systems make it possible to perform computation-intensive analyses of this data. For example, in the area of direct marketing, computer programs make it possible to perform sophisticated procedures to select from a database those names and addresses that should be targeted with a mailing.

The term *information technology* refers to the technical side of information systems. It refers to a wide variety of items and abilities used in the creation, storage, and dispersal of information (Senn 1995). Senn divides information technology into three primary components: computers, communication networks, and know-how. Since know-how will (partially) overlap the marketing knowledge component of marketing management support systems (which we will discuss in a later section), in this section we limit our description of information technology to computers and communication networks.

3.2.1   Computers

Computers are programmable devices that can be instructed to accept, process, store, and present data and information. A computer is also a device that can execute previously stored instructions (Alter 1996). The processing is done according to a set of temporarily or permanently stored instructions. The instructions for performing tasks are called software. A series of instructions is called a program.

The first generation of computers were introduced in companies in the early 1950s. The UNIVAC I, introduced in 1951, used vacuum tubes and had a memory made of liquid mercury and magnetic drums. The first computers were used in companies for structured, labor-intensive, repetitive tasks such as payroll administration. Second-generation systems, introduced in the late 1950s, replaced tubes with transistors and used magnetic cores for memories (e.g., IBM 1401, Honeywell 800). The size of computers was drastically reduced in this second generation, while their reliability significantly improved. Third-generation computers (the mid-1960s) used the first integrated circuits (e.g., IBM 360, CDC 6400) and had operating systems and database management systems. On-line systems were developed already, but most processing was still batch-oriented, using punch cards and magnetic tapes. Starting in the mid-1970s, the fourth generation of computers were introduced. The memories of these computers were made entirely of chips. Microprocessors were introduced, which started the movement of office automation. Word processors, spreadsheets, and database management programs put large numbers of people into contact with computers. However, the number of people using computers really took off with the introduction of PCs in the 1980s. Since the mid-1990s, we have seen the fifth generation of computers, with more widespread use not only of multimedia technologies but also of such technologies as voice recognition, natural and foreign language translation, optical disks, and fiber-optic networks.

Computers exist in different sizes. Senn (1995) distinguishes four categories: microcomputers, minicomputers, mainframes, and supercomputers. Microcomputers are the most frequently used. They are often called personal computers (PCs). Although the term PC is sometimes used to refer to any kind of personal computer (Macintosh, Amiga, etc.), in general PC refers to computers that conform to the PC standard originally developed by IBM. The original PC launched by IBM in 1981 used a 16-bit 8088 chip. This XT machine, as it was called, became the world's hardware standard. It was followed by the 286 (AT) in 1984, the 386 in 1986, the 486 in 1989 (a 32-bit machine instead of its 16-bit predecessors), and the Pentium in 1993. The Pentium was followed by subsequent extensions: Pentium Pro in 1995, Pentium MMX, and Pentium II. These machines have ever increasing possibilities for video, audio, three-dimensional graphics, animation, and imaging operations. Personal computers are available in many different forms—desktops, laptops, palmtops, and personal digital assistants (PDAs).

Since the first generation of computers, their storage capacity and processing speed have increased dramatically. In 1946, the world's first programmable computer, the Electronic Numerical Integrator and Computer (ENIAC), stood 10 feet tall, stretched 150 feet wide, cost millions of dollars, and could execute up to 5000 operations per second. Twenty-five years later (in 1971), Intel packed 12 times ENIAC's processing power into a 12 mm^2 chip that cost only $200. Today's personal computers have Pentium processors that perform more than 400 million instructions per second (MIPS). At the current pace of development, it is expected that by 2012 PCs will handle 100,000 MIPS (Margherio et al. 1998). The size of transistors is decreasing, which means that more of them can be placed on a chip, thereby increasing the performance of that chip. The graph line in Figure 3.2 shows how the number of transistors that can be placed on chips has grown over the years. Notice that the vertical axis of the graph is a logarithmic scale.

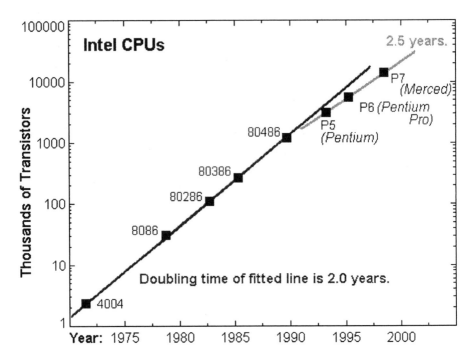

Figure 3.2   Number of Transistors that can be Placed on a Chip (*Source:* webopedia. internet.com)

The growth of processor performance follows "Moore's law." Gordon Moore, one of the founders of Intel, observed in 1965 that chips double in performance every 18 months. This exponential growth continues to this day, and semiconductor experts reckon that Moore's law for chips will face the limitations of atomic size only around 2020, after which silicon technology will probably be replaced by optical techniques such as holography (*The Economist* 1997).

While computing power has thus been doubling every 18 months for the past 30-odd years, the average price of a transistor has fallen dramatically. In six years' time (1991–1997), the cost of microprocessor computing power has decreased from $230 to $3.42 per MIPS (Margherio et al. 1998). According to the market research company Dataquest, at the end of 1996 there were 229 million PCs installed worldwide, of which 86 million were in the United States. The number of people who possess or have access to a PC is growing rapidly and will continue to do so in the coming years.

In the context of marketing management support systems, PCs are important because they are the basic tools on the desks of individual marketing decision makers. Minicomputers and mainframes are used to interconnect people and large sets of information. Minicomputers are multiuser computers that are capable of supporting from ten to hundreds of users simultaneously. Mainframes and supercomputers have significantly more capacity and are very important for the functioning of large (worldwide) networks.

A computer system consists of computers and computer-controlled devices that process data by executing programs. The physical devices in a computer system (including the equipment associated with it, such as monitors, printers, and other peripheral devices) are its *hardware*. The programs are called *software*.

Hardware

In the late 1940s, von Neumann and his colleagues published a description of the internal architecture of an idealized electronic computer. To this day most computer designs are based on this architecture (Senn 1995). The basic computer architecture consists of four components: (1) an arithmetic/logic unit to perform calculations, (2) a central processing unit (CPU) to control the sequence of operations, (3) a memory unit to hold both data and programs so that programs can be executed efficiently, and (4) input and output units.

The center of action in a computer is the central processing unit (CPU). The arithmetic/logic unit performs the four basic arithmetic operations (addition, subtraction, multiplication, and division) as well as the logical operations of comparison between two data points. All computer applications (e.g., computations, word processing, or developing graphs) are performed through these five operations. The operations of the arithmetic/logic unit are based on instructions from the CPU, which are provided by the computer program.

The primary storage, or main memory, stores data and programs for the CPU. Microcomputers contain two types of memory, random-access memory (RAM) and read-only memory (ROM). RAM is the memory in which the CPU stores the instructions and data it is processing. The larger the RAM, the larger the programs that can be stored and executed. Currently, the default amount of memory with which personal computers are shipped from the factory is 16 megabytes (MB) of RAM. Advanced operating systems and multimedia applications (i.e., the combination of sound, graphics, animation, and video) pose increasingly higher demands on RAM capacity. Therefore, the amount of RAM is often extended to 32 or 64 MB. Compared to earlier generations of PCs, the amount of RAM built in computers nowadays has grown dramatically. It was only in the early eighties that Bill Gates said that 640 kilobytes (0.64 MB) should be enough for everyone.

The clock of the computer is the component that takes care of the exact timing of all processor operations. The beat frequency of the clock determines how many times per second the processor performs operations and thus how fast the computer is. This speed is measured in megahertz (MHz) or millions of cycles per second. Currently most personal computers are shipped with processing speeds ranging from 233 to 450 MHz. Compared to the clock rate of the first 8086 processors, which was only 5 MHz, the speed of computers has thus increased dramatically.

Besides their primary storage devices, computers also use secondary storage devices to store data, information, or programs outside of the CPU. Secondary storage, which is connected to the CPU and the primary storage unit, provides computers with an enormous additional storage capacity. Secondary storage can take different forms. In the early days of computing, secondary storage devices such as paper cards and punched paper tabs were used. Now storage media are magnetic or optical. Examples of magnetic storage devices are magnetic tapes, magnetic disks (hard disks), and magnetic diskettes or floppy disks. Compared to magnetic devices, optical storage devices make it possible to store even more data because of their high storage density. CD-ROM (compact disk, read-only memory) and rewritable optical disks are examples of optical storage devices. CD-ROMs can store text, graphics, and sound. CD-ROMs have the capacity to hold 650 MB of data, the equivalent of about 250,000 pages of text. The latest generation of CD-ROMs, DVDs (digital videodisk, or digital versatile disk) can store 14 times as much information as the CD-ROM.

To be able to instruct the computer, a user needs so-called input devices to communicate with the system. Several types of input devices can be distinguished, including keyboards, point-of-sale (POS) terminals, mouse, touch screens, image scanners, bar code scanners, light pens, microphones, cameras, and magnetic ink character readers. After the computer has performed its data manipulations, it returns the results to the user(s). Output is the result of the inputting and processing of data and information; by definition, it has to be communicated to the user again. Monitors, printers, plotters, and speakers are the most important devices built into or attached to the computer through which output can be displayed, printed, plotted, or played.

The spectacular developments on the hardware side of information technology have created opportunities for developing advanced and very powerful marketing management support systems. The enormous increases in storage and computational capacity have made it possible to collect, store, manipulate, and analyze large amounts of data and knowledge within reasonable amounts of time. The technology also makes it possible to help the marketing decision maker to generate and select decision options. Technical capabilities hardly pose serious constraints to the development of MMSS these days. The challenge is to have the imagination and creativity to use these capabilities for designing systems that are attractive for marketing decision makers and effective in helping them to improve their decision quality.

Software

We tell computers what to do by using software. Software is the general term for a set of instructions that control a computer or communication network. Four types of software can be distinguished: system software, application software, end-user software, and system development software (Alter 1996).

System software refers to the combination of operating system programs that coordinate all the actions of the computer, including its peripheral devices and memory, and that execute application software or end-user software. MS-DOS, Microsoft Windows, and UNIX are examples of operating systems. Windows is currently the dominant operating system, based on market share. International Data Corp (IDC) estimated that the various Windows operating systems held a combined 86% of the operating system market in 1995, up from 76% in 1994.

Application software tells the computer how to perform tasks for specific settings. For example, application software in a sales department might include programs for forecasting sales, maintaining a customer database, and sending bills to customers. This type of software is developed for a specific purpose.

End-user software tells the computer how to perform tasks that support general business processes that apply in many settings. Users will operate the computers themselves when using this kind of software. Examples of these programs are word-processing packages (e.g., Microsoft Word, WordPerfect) and spreadsheet programs (e.g., Microsoft Excel, Lotus 1-2-3).

Finally, programmers in the process of building and enhancing information systems use *system development software.*

An application has to be written in a specific programming *language.* Since the advent of digital computers, several types of programming languages have been developed. It has become customary to classify them into *generations* of software (Turban, McLean, and Wetherbe 1996).

Software of the first generation is called *machine language.* Machine language operates directly at the machine level. Instructions have to be given about the precise representation of data and operations in the machine. For example, the computation of the combined sales of two geographical areas might involve an instruction like "add the content of storage address 14 456 to the content of storage address 34 897 and store the result in storage address 12 987." Programs in machine language are difficult to understand and are machine-dependent. However, they are very efficient in execution, which was especially important when computers had limited memories.

The second generation of computer languages are called *assembly languages.* These languages are one step further removed from the computer. The programmer does not have to keep an administration of the content of the individual storage addresses and can work with variable names such as SALESDISTR1, SALESDISTR2 and TOTSALES. As is true for all higher-generation languages, a program written in an assembly language has to be translated into machine language before it can be executed. The program, written by the programmer in the specific programming language, is called the *source code.* After it has been translated into machine language, the program is called *object code.* The translation from source code into object code is called *compilation.* A dedicated software program called a *compiler* carries out the compilation. In the case of an assembly language, the compiler is called an *assembler.*

Third-generation computer languages are much closer to natural language than first- and second-generation languages and are, therefore, easier to write, read, and change. Whereas in machine and assembly language each statement corresponds with one elementary action of the computer, in third-generation languages and higher, one statement in the language may correspond to a number of machine-language instructions. This makes programming more productive. Third-generation languages are also called *procedural languages,* because the programmer has to specify, step by step, how the computer must accomplish a task. Examples of third-generation languages are FORTRAN, COBOL, and ALGOL for mainframes and BASIC, C, and PASCAL for microcomputers.

Fourth-generation languages, also called *4GLs,* are another step closer to the user and farther away from the computer. Using 4GLs, programmers just specify the results they want, without having to detail the exact sequence of instructions the computer must follow to achieve those results. For example, to obtain a printout of sales by retail channel or sales by brand, a product manager might simply use the statements

Print sales by retail channel

or

Print sales by brand.

Since these instructions do not specify the procedures through which the results have to be obtained, fourth-generation languages are also called *nonprocedural languages.* They are well suited to developing specific applications such as marketing management support systems. Examples of 4GLs are EXPRESS, METAPHOR (both of which have been used extensively for the processing of marketing data), and KAPPA, which has a strong knowledge-processing functionality (we present an illustration of the use of KAPPA in Chapter 9). Because of how close 4GLs are to the user, nontechnical people and end users are able to develop applications in a 4GL without extensive training.

As can be derived from the foregoing description, the development of computer programming languages has moved to where more and more of the burden of programming is placed on the computer. The end user does not have to worry about how the computer should carry out the operations and can, therefore, remain closer to his or her own language and problem definition. Up to the third generation of computer languages, specialized programmers were needed. With a 4GL, however, end users can, in theory, write their own programs. Indeed, marketing managers can use EXPRESS and METAPHOR after only a short period of training. The development of easy-to-use fourth-generation languages has been possible only because of the dramatic increases in computer storage capabilities and speed. Powerful computer systems are necessary for the translation of 4GL instructions into machine language. End-user computing has especially been boosted by the advent of general-purpose software, such as spreadsheets, database management systems, word-processing systems, and desktop-publishing systems. Users do not have to write programs themselves but create their own applications within the given software. Most marketing decision makers now practice end-user computing and have access to databases and computing capabilities right on their desk.

The ultimate advance in programming is when a user can give instructions to a computer in *natural* languages such as English, Spanish, or Dutch. Systems that are able to respond to natural languages are referred to as fifth-generation computer languages. Sometime in the future these will become a reality. However, the translation of plain, natural language into a structured, computer-executable form is enormously complex, and the development of working systems will take time and even more powerful computers than the ones available today.

Object-oriented approaches

The traditional approach to software development is top-down programming, also called *structured programming,* with the program organization specifying a structured, unidirectional flow. The software system is partitioned into different processes with a well-defined hierarchy between them. Modules are built in a pyramidlike fashion, each layer taking a higher-level view of the system. Bits of data flow between these processes in a predetermined fashion. Notwithstanding their logical basic framework, many such systems, because of their large number of modules, have become complex behemoths, where the cross-links between the modules have been called *spaghetti code.* Such systems are very difficult to understand and also difficult to maintain (Turban et al. 1996; Van Hillegersberg 1997). Recently, however, a new paradigm that should be able to deal with these kind of problems has become popular in the fields of software development and computer programming. This paradigm is called *object orientation* (OO). In an object-oriented approach a system is modeled as a set of cooperating objects. An object is an entity that may represent a person, a place, or some other concept, either at an abstract or at a concrete level. An important characteristic of the object-oriented approach in systems design is that the description of a phenomenon in the system resembles the way humans think. A marketer, for example, will tend to think of concepts like brands, customers, retailers, and competitors. In an object-oriented representation such concepts are modeled as objects.

An object in the object-oriented paradigm has several characteristics. First, for each object *slots* or *attributes* that contain information about the object are specified. For example, for the object "brand," the name of the brand, sales volume, market share, product category, and type of brand (e.g., private label or manufacturer's brand) would be relevant attributes. Second, there are the notions of *class* and *inheritance*. A class is a group of objects that share the same attributes and behavior. Every object is an instance of some class (possibly only containing itself). For example, Heineken would be an instance of the class "brands." Often objects are organized in hierarchies with super- and subclasses. An example of such a hierarchy is presented in Figure 3.3.

Figure 3.3   A Hierarchy of Objects

An object "inherits" the attributes of the class to which it belongs (and of its superclass, if applicable). So if, in a hierarchical class system, the programmer creates a new instance of a beer brand, this brand will inherit the attributes of the class "brands_of_beer." A class can be seen as a template. However, a programmer can overrule inheritance for specific attributes if the inherited attributes are inappropriate.

The behavior of objects is modeled by so-called *methods*. Methods are attached to the objects to manipulate or access the object's attributes. For example, a method attached to a brand might be an algorithm "COMPUTE

ANNUAL SALES." This algorithm computes the total sales over a whole year from the numbers of the respective 13 four-week periods. Methods are invoked by *message passing* between objects. This is a mechanism through which communication between objects takes place. For example, an object-oriented system might contain an object "REPORT" that produces a review of the results for the brands over the last year. This object REPORT might then send a message to the object brand to activate COMPUTE ANNUAL SALES and receive the resulting value.

Object orientation is quickly gaining ground in the world of software development and computer programming. The most important advantages of OO are (1) easier systems development and systems building, since objects correspond to entities in the real world, (2) objects (with the imbedded software) can be used multiple times (the idea of the template), and (3) easier maintenance and repair of the system, because individual objects can be programmed individually (Van Hillegersberg 1997). Examples of object-oriented programming languages are Smalltalk and C++, Visual C++, and Visual Basic. Object-oriented concepts show promising opportunities for the development of marketing management support systems. With object-oriented concepts, it should be easier to build systems that reflect how managers think about their products, brands, and markets. Also, the reusability of modules will make it easier to exchange software parts among developers, which may foster the dissemination of special-purpose software. For example, once a module has been written—say, for analyzing the positioning of a brand—this module might be put on a Web site from which others can download it and use it in their own applications.

A high-level object-oriented programming language that has recently become popular is Java. Java, which is similar to C++ (a kind of industry standard) but simplified, was developed by Sun Microsystems and was originally called OAK. It was designed for handheld computing devices and set-top boxes. This programming language was not successful until Sun renamed it Java in 1995 and modified it so that it could take advantage of the increasing popularity of the World Wide Web. Java is a general-purpose programming language. Compiled Java code can run on most computers because Java interpreters and runtime environments exist for most operating systems, including UNIX, Macintosh OS, and Windows (http://webopedia.internet.com).

3.2.2 Communication Networks

An integral part of information technology is the ability to communicate, that is, to send and receive data and information over a communication network. A (tele)communications network is the interconnection of stations at different locations through a medium that enables people and computers to send and receive data and information. Two types of networks can be distinguished: networks at one location, known as local area networks (LAN), and networks that are dispersed across many locations, known as wide area networks (WAN). Communication networks make it possible for checkout scanner data collected in various retailing outlets to be sent to a central office, where they are received and analyzed. Communication networks also make it possible for manufacturers and distributors to exchange information, for example, by means of electronic data interchange (EDI), to improve the performance of their joint operations. There are several interesting examples of cooperation between organizations that led to improved performance for both. One of the best-known examples is the cooperation between Wal-Mart and Procter and Gamble (Buzzell and Ortmeyer 1994). With the help of EDI, the two organizations were able to improve the efficiency of their product flow. P&G's on-time deliveries to Wal-Mart improved significantly, while inventory turnover increased dramatically.

Information technology facilitates various other ways of communicating, like videoconferencing and e-mail. Recently, developments of worldwide communication networks, most notably the *Internet,* have gained much attention. The Internet (also known as the Net) is a large computer network that links several smaller computer networks. The Internet was originally developed for U.S. defense purposes; academic and commercial research institutions were also among the earliest users. Recently, however, the Internet has become very popular among many other organizations, persons, and households. The development of the World Wide Web (WWW) and browser programs like Netscape Navigator and Microsoft Explorer has made the Internet accessible to large groups of people. The number of computer systems attached to the Net is growing rapidly, as is the number of companies having access to it. The Internet makes it possible for companies to collect and distribute information. This information may pertain to the company itself or to the kinds of products it offers and the way those products can be used and obtained.

While the Internet is a publicly open medium that links different businesses and individuals, there are also networks that can only be accessed by employees of one organization. These networks are called *intranets.* They can be linked to the outside world, but they are primarily meant for internal use within a company or between a company and its trading partners (O'Connor and Galvin 1997).

Marketers can use networks like the Internet or an intranet to share information with colleagues who are located in different (physical or geographical) areas and to share information with customers or third parties like consultants or market research agencies. Furthermore, the Internet offers great opportunities for direct marketing. Manufacturers can directly communicate with their final customers without the intervention of an intermediary. By the end of 1997, more than 100 million people were using the Internet.

A particular type of architecture that is important for the wider adoption and use of marketing management support systems is the client-server architecture. Client-server computing (Senn 1995) is a type of computing in which all data and information retrieval pass over a network. This architecture facilitates the integration of geographically dispersed users. Data and applications can reside on a server and be shared by its different users. Viewing tools will reside on the client (e.g., the desktop computer of a marketer). Much of the processing is performed on the server, with the results transmitted to the client. This architecture allows all model maintenance to be done at a single location, thereby greatly enhancing the potential adoption of decision support tools at all levels of an organization. When users do not have to install or maintain systems themselves, they may be more inclined to use them.

Summarizing, we see that developments in information technology have led to a dramatic increase in computer capacities, in terms of both storage and speed. There is a rich supply of end-user software, and there are productive development environments for specific applications. Furthermore, communication networks both within and between organizations allow for the transportation of data and information. For marketers this has resulted in the opportunity to collect, transmit, and store large amounts of data and to analyze this data to develop information and knowledge. Furthermore, knowledge-processing tools (which we will discuss in more detail later) now also make it possible to collect, store, and analyze information that is of a qualitative nature rather than the more quantitative marketing data. The developments in IT have led to great opportunities to effectively support marketers. Ongoing developments will further increase these opportunities. It has now truly become possible for a company to create a strategic competitive advantage by means of an advanced marketing management support system. Such systems help companies to discover trends and opportunities in the market before their competitors do, and also offer efficient support in finding those marketing policies that are most effective in reaching desired goals.

3.3   Analytical Capabilities

To process and transform data into information that is meaningful for marketers, marketing management support systems should contain analytical capabilities. In this section we describe the nature of these analytical capabilities. Our description here is restricted to analytical capabilities for manipulating quantitative data. In section 3.5 we pay attention to techniques for manipulating qualitative knowledge.

To categorize the various analytical capabilities that can be part of a marketing management support system, we use a classification scale related to four levels of questions (Wierenga, Oude Ophuis, Huizingh, and Van Campen 1994):

1. *What* happened?
2. *Why* did it happen?
3. *What* will happen *if?*
4. *What should* happen?

The first level refers to a situation in which systems are able to perform "status reporting" (Little 1979) tasks. Analytical capabilities that facilitate status reporting can help answer so-called *what happened* questions. The second level of analytical capabilities is able to answer *why did it happen* questions or "response-reporting" (Little 1979). The third level of analytical capabilities aims at finding answers to *what happens if* questions. Finally, the fourth, and most advanced, level of analytical capabilities focuses on providing the marketer with ready-to-use solutions. It answers the *what should happen* question. These four categories of analytical capabilities have been developed mainly within the fields of statistics, econometrics, and operations research/management science.

3.3.1   What Questions

Once there is raw data in the database of a marketing management support system, marketers first want to know what has happened ("status reporting"). This calls for descriptive analyses. The simplest analyses would be to make straightforward counts and show frequencies. Next, summary statistics such as the mean, median, mode, and standard deviation can be computed. These statistics give marketers a general idea of the performance of their product and/or brands in the market. Once certain statistics have been generated, marketers will be interested in questions such as the following: Does the level of sales differ between different regions? To what extent have sales changed compared to last year? One can simply compare means across different time periods and different sales areas. However, it will often also make sense to test to what extent observed differences are statistically significant. To analyze differences (e.g., between regions or segments), marketers can make use of a rich collection of both parametric and nonparametric statistical techniques. Examples are analysis of variance (ANOVA) and t-tests with their nonparametric counterparts, such as the Kruskal-Wallis and Friedman test (see, for example, the books of Bagozzi 1996, 1997; Siegel and Castellan 1988; Churchill 1999; Winer 1971).

To answer the what question, basic analysis procedures can mostly be used; and either most database systems will already contain these procedures or they will be very easily programmable and implementable.

3.3.2   Why Questions

Determining what happened is the first step when analyzing data. However, to be able to develop a marketing policy, marketers need to know more. They need insights into the causes and consequences of what happens in the market. Why did sales decline in the last quarter, or why did distribution coverage increase, and what will be the effects of increasing advertising expenditures? To answer these kinds of questions, marketers need to investigate relationships between variables. Correlation and regression analyses are the best-known techniques to investigate relationships. *Correlation analysis* determines the relationship between two variables by calculating their joint variation. Results of this analysis show the extent to which variables move up and down together or move in opposite directions. For example, what is the statistical relationship between sales and price? *Multiple regression analysis* can be used when the relationships between one dependent variable (e.g., sales) and several independent variables (e.g., price, advertising expenditures, and distribution) are of interest. Correlation and regression analyses are well-known techniques, and most database packages (e.g., SPSS, SAS) contain standardized procedures to conduct these analyses. Regression-based econometric techniques play a major role in the analysis of marketing data (Naert and Leeflang 1978; Leeflang et al. 2000; Hanssens, Parsons, and Schultz 1990). Other advanced techniques to study associations between variables are multivariate techniques such as discriminant analysis, factor analysis, cluster analysis, and structural equation modeling.

Discriminant analysis shares similarities with regression analysis in that its primary purpose is to determine the relative importance of predictor variables. However, discriminant analysis is different in that the dependent (criterion) variable is a dichotomy or multichotomy, whereas in regression analysis this variable is interval or ratio scaled. With the help of discriminant analysis one could, for example, classify customers as loyal versus nonloyal and then try to analyze if the difference is caused by their background characteristics (e.g., education, age) and the marketing-mix efforts that were targeted at them.

Factor analysis can be used to investigate the extent to which different variables share common variation that may be the result of a common underlying factor. A marketer can use factor analysis to analyze, for example, whether different buying behavior phenomena are all caused by the same underlying factor, such as risk sensitivity.

Cluster analysis can be used to classify objects (e.g., customers) in homogeneous subgroups. This classification can be performed on the basis of various variables such as, for example, buying behavior demographic variables, income, and psychological variables. The results of the cluster analysis can provide marketers with insights into why their products do better with some buyers than with others and thus form the basis for market segmentation.

In addition to the techniques described above, other more advanced techniques are available to study the associations between (sets) of variables. *Structural equation modeling* is a technique that combines factor analysis and regression analysis to study the relationships between variables that cannot be measured directly (i.e., latent constructs) but for which indicators are available. For example, it might be hard to measure a person's risk sensitivity directly. However, one's risk sensitivity might possibly be derived from a series of responses to particular stimuli (items). By means of confirmatory factor analyses, the indicators (the items) will be linked to their underlying constructs (risk sensitivity, in this example); and by means of regression analyses, the relationship with other constructs (e.g., attitudes or purchasing intentions) can be investigated. Using structural equation modeling, these analyses will be performed simultaneously. LISREL, PLS, and AMOS are the names of well-known software packages that can be used to perform structural equation modeling.

The data analysis techniques discussed in this section constitute a powerful set of tools for answering the why question. Most of these techniques are relatively mature, and excellent discussions of them can be found in textbooks such as Churchill (1999) and Malhotra (1999). Other techniques that can be helpful to answer why questions are logit analyses, chi-square automatic interaction detection (CHAID), and latent class modeling. Bagozzi (1996, 1997) provides a description of these analytical capabilities.

3.3.3   What-If Questions

After having determined what has happened in the market and how this could be explained, marketers next want to know what actions they have to take to reach their goals. For this purpose they need to have systems that can answer what-if and what-should questions. Analytical capabilities are needed that are predictive and/or normative in nature. These systems will take the form of *models* as far as the manipulation of quantitative data is concerned. (With qualitative knowledge, such systems are called *expert systems;* see Chapter 5.) Marketing models are extensively dealt with in Naert and Leeflang (1978); Lilien, Kotler, and Moorthy (1992); and Eliashberg and Lilien (1993).

Decision support models support decision making. With these models conditional predictions can be made; for example, what happens to sales if we increase our price by 5 percent? Besides this, decision models can contain optimization modules that help to find optimal solutions and in a sense provide users with a ready-to-implement solution. So with decision models we are in the realm of what-if and what-should questions.

Marketing models relate the variables the marketer can make decisions about (and that are under his or her control) to variables (objectives) he or she wants to influence. Controllable variables are marketing decision variables like price, advertising budgets, selling efforts, and so on. If possible, the influence of noncontrollable variables such as the weather and competitors' actions should also be taken into account. Objectives the marketing decision maker wants to influence are variables such as sales, market share, profit, and brand awareness. A brand manager might, for example, use a model that relates advertising expenditures to brand awareness levels. Such a model can help to predict, for example, the effect of a 10% increase in advertising expenditures on brand awareness. In a similar way a sales manager may want to have a model that relates sales efforts to sales, so as to predict the effect on sales of an increase in the number of salespeople. Such response models (Lilien and Rangaswamy 1998) can differ with respect to the numbers of variables included, the nature of the relationship (linear or nonlinear, dynamic or static, individual or aggregate), and the level of demand (market share or sales) that is analyzed.

Statistical techniques such as regression analysis can be used to determine the value of parameters that link marketing decision variables to output variables in predictive marketing models. Predictive models can also be developed by using managerial judgment with respect to the relationship between input and output. In Chapter 4 we will elaborate on the ways (predictive) marketing models can be calibrated.

A technique that is especially useful for simulation purposes is conjoint analysis (Green and Rao 1971; Green and Wind 1973). Conjoint analysis can be used to determine how customers make trade-off judgments between attribute levels of a product. If this information is known, it can be used to estimate customers' preferences for different product alternatives (i.e., different combinations of alternatives). Making these estimates is an attempt to answer what-if questions. For example, what happens to the customers' preferences for a car if we increase its maximum speed or decrease its price, and so on.

Predictive marketing models are an important type of analytical capability for marketing management support systems. Marketers can use these models to generate all kinds of decision alternatives and predict their outcomes. This activity is called *simulation*. It is important to recognize, though, that the decision maker still has to choose which decision would be best. The model functions only as a sparring partner for the human decision maker, providing that person with feedback on his or her ideas. It will not, however, tell the marketer what to do.

3.3.4   What-Should Questions

To answer what-should questions, decision makers need normative or prescriptive decision models. In 1954 Dorfman and Steiner proposed a theorem with conditions that should be satisfied in order to find optimal values for marketing decision variables. Using this theorem, marketers can determine a theoretical optimal resource allocation or marketing program. With the entry of operations research/management science approaches in marketing in the 1960s, normative models started to be developed that actually determine optimal marketing decisions in terms of numerical values for marketing instruments (Eliashberg and Lilien 1993). Most of these models solved the decision problem of one specific marketing-mix variable (Gatignon 1993). Examples are MEDIAC (Little and Lodish 1969), which supports media allocation decisions, and CALLPLAN (Lodish 1971), which supports sales-force time allocation decisions. In Chapter 4 we describe examples of both descriptive and normative models in more detail.

The purpose of descriptive models was to predict the outcome of alternative values for marketing decision variables. Normative models go a step further in that their output consists of a guideline of what the value of the marketing decision variable should be. Typically, normative models will consist of an objective function that is subject to one or more constraints. Normative models will contain an optimization part next to the descriptive part. These optimization parts are methods developed in the field of operations research, such as linear programming, integer programming, nonlinear programming, and dynamic programming (Eppen, Gould, and Schmidt 1993; Nemhauser and Wolsey 1988; Bellman 1957). For example, the CALLPLAN model (Lodish 1971), which is discussed in more detail in Chapter 4, uses a linear programming approach to determine the optimal sales-force time allocation. And the MEDIAC model (Little and Lodish 1969) uses a dynamic programming approach to develop an optimal media allocation schedule.

When it is difficult or impossible to find an optimum using an analytical method, simulation methods are available to determine optimal solutions in a numerical way.

Developments in the fields of statistics, econometrics, operations research (OR), and management science have provided marketers with a rich collection of tools to help them answer the various types of questions they are confronted with. The analytical capabilities of an MMSS can be related to the four marketing problem-solving modes of the ORAC model, which we discussed in Chapter 2. Analytical capabilities are especially helpful for the support of decision makers if they solve problems using either the optimizing or the reasoning mode. If a decision maker solves a problem by means of optimizing, the use of normative marketing models that provide answers to what-should questions is appropriate. Solving a problem by means of reasoning can be supported with tools that answer what, why, and what-if questions.

Looking at historical developments in the use of analytical capabilities, we observe that marketing scientists have not followed a logical order in trying to develop tools that support decision makers in their problem-solving approach. They did not start by attempting to answer the least complicated questions (what and why). On the contrary, researchers have started by trying to develop tools that help answer the most difficult question, the what-should question. Already in the late 1950s and 1960s, there were attempts to automate marketing problem solving. This was the time that operations research/management science entered the marketing domain after having been successful in other management domains such as production and logistics. However, it turned out that most marketing problems were too complex for straightforward optimization with standard OR methods. (In Chapter 7 we will return to the circumstances under which particular types of marketing support, for example, optimization, are appropriate.) Later, in the 1970s and 1980s, marketing researchers concentrated on developing marketing models that relate marketing inputs to marketing outputs. These so-called "market response reporting systems" (Little 1991) did not try to automate marketing decision making but focused on decision support (Little 1979) and answering what-if questions. Nowadays, it seems that researchers in marketing science are focused on developing sophisticated methodologies for measurement and estimation, and in a sense have made a step back in order to better answer the basic what and why questions. The recent data explosion is an important impetus behind this trend. Various sophisticated procedures to analyze scanner panel data are regularly published in journals like *Journal of Marketing Research* and *Marketing Science*. Much effort has also been put into developing and refining advanced data-analysis procedures such as structural equation modeling and latent class modeling (DeSarbo, Manrai, and Manrai 1997; Wedel and DeSarbo 1997; Wedel and Kamakura 1998). This backtracking move toward basic issues in measurement and modeling may well lay the groundwork for MMSS with more advanced what-if and what-should features in the future.

3.4 Marketing Data

Marketing emphasizes the use of numerical measurement and has always been in the forefront of collecting current and accurate data (Frank and Ganly 1983). Information processing is an important part of marketing. Hence, marketing data constitutes an important component of marketing management support systems. For all four of the question levels described in the last section—what, why, what-if and what-should—data about the market is very relevant. The development of analytical capabilities as described above has greatly benefited from the increasing availability of marketing data. Scanner data has made the development of a new generation of marketing models possible (Little 1991).

In a sense the abundance of data can sometimes become almost as problematic as a lack of data. The amount of POS data that can be collected by means of retail checkout scanners, for example, is enormous. A single store may generate around 50,000 transactions per day. Transactions may involve 25,000 to 30,000 different SKUs for a (U.S.) supermarket and up to 1.5 million different SKUs for a department store. In both segments, the size of a retail marketing database with weekly movements, SKU per store, will be on the order of 12 to 16 gigabytes (Ing and Mitchell 1994). It requires great skills, advanced analytical capabilities, and sophisticated information technology to transform this data into actionable marketing knowledge.

3.4.1   Internal and External Data

Marketing data can be classified according to its source. Roughly speaking, companies can generate or collect data themselves (*internal data*) or get or buy data from outside sources (*external data*). Internal data concerns a company's own actions, performances, and situations. Examples would be data about the various products and brands offered by a company with respect to sales (ex-factory), prices, reseller margins, advertising expenditures, promotional activities, distribution figures, personal selling efforts, and so on. Mostly these kinds of data can be extracted from the departments of marketing, sales, accounting, and operations. Enterprise resource planning (ERP) systems facilitate data exchange between different departments.

The data generated within a company will, in general, only be a part of the marketer's database. Data about competitors, customers, and general market conditions will be difficult to generate from within the company itself. However, it is this type of information that is strategic and of great value to marketers. To obtain this information, marketers can turn to specialized outside sources. These can be market research agencies but also sources like trade organizations, governmental organizations, and academic institutions.

Market research companies can collect various types of information. Basically, we distinguish two types of external data: data that is collected on a continuous basis, for example, by means of panels (these can be panels consisting of consumers or retailers), and data that is collected on an ad hoc basis. In general this second type of data will be collected for a specific purpose, for example, to determine the brand awareness of a product or to test whether consumers like the taste of a new food product.

Consumer panels supply data about purchasing behavior of consumers on a continuous basis. For example, the market research agency A.C. Nielsen operates consumer panels in 15 countries around the world, capturing actual purchase behavior for over 100,000 households. More than half of these countries makes use of home scanning technology. Panel members record their purchases of each shopping trip. They record price, promotions, and quantity purchased. Furthermore, characteristics like the age and gender of the shopper are already registered. Purchases are collected from all outlet types where the consumers go to buy their products. This provides marketers with information about who the buyers of products are, where they buy from, how often they buy, how loyal they are to brands, and how they respond to promotional activities.

Retail store audits supply information on sales, market share, availability (distribution), and inventories of different brands, as recorded at the checkout registers of the shops. Information Resources Inc. (IRI) and also A.C. Nielsen are providers of this kind of information. Nielsen's SCANTRACK services provide customers with scanner-based marketing and sales information, gathered on a weekly basis. The information is collected at the checkouts of retailers. This provides marketers with the ability to monitor performance trends and evaluate price and promotion effectiveness. Furthermore, it provides marketers with information about the performance of competing products and brands.

Besides consumer purchase panels and retail store audits, a third source of continuous external marketing data is specialized agencies that collect very specific types of information, for example, on the advertising expenditures for different brands. IRI records, for example, all the newspaper advertising and special in-store displays (Little 1991). These three sources collect data on a continuous basis and will regularly report to their clients.

In addition to the market research agencies operating in this way, there are also a lot of market research companies that collect data on an ad hoc basis. Marketers can consult these agencies when they need information with respect to, for example, the awareness of their brands or the way (potential) customers perceive their products. Also, tests concerning new products can be performed by these kinds of agencies.

Market research agencies will, in general, supply data that directly concerns the company, the products it markets, and its competitors. Data about more general economic indicators like overall growth and productivity, inflation and employment rates, or trends in an industry can be obtained from government or trade organizations. Such organizations publish statistics that are publicly available, which means a company's competitors can see them as well.

Traditionally, consumer-goods environments have been more data-intensive than business-to-business environments. Consumer-goods marketers hardly ever interact directly with their final customers. Therefore, to become familiar with the opinions and behavior of their customers, they need market research studies. Business marketers, on the other hand, often interact directly with their customers, of which the number is also much smaller than it is for consumer-goods marketers. Therefore, information about the opinions and behavior of their customers will often be stored in the head of the business-to-business marketer and will typically be more qualitative and anecdotal than data in consumer-goods environments as well. Recently, however, marketers have recognized that the systematic collection of information is important in business-to-business environments as well. Given the high costs of sales calls and the often prevalent desire to cut costs, collecting data from business customers about their needs and buying behavior and systematically analyzing that data is becoming more common. Salespeople equipped with laptop computers can immediately enter data about sales visits. This data can be systematically analyzed and used in developing marketing programs. Furthermore, several market research agencies specialize in collecting information in business-to-business markets. Dunn & Bradstreet is an example of a company that provides business marketers with marketing and financial data about (potential) customers.

3.4.2   The Internet as a Source of Marketing Data

A relatively new source of marketing data is the Internet. Organizations can develop Web sites through which they can provide their customers with all kinds of information concerning the company and the products or services it sells. Internet sites also make it possible for companies to collect data from their customers. Site owners can develop questionnaires and ask customers to fill them out. In this way, customers can express their opinions, perceptions, and experiences about the products or services the company offers. By tracing customers' movements or purchases on the site, organizations can also collect valuable data. Subsequently, this data can be used in determining offerings to individual customers based on their past behavior and background characteristics. Virtual retail sites like Amazon (http://www.amazon.com) and CDNow (http://www.cdnow.com) already offer customers a recommendation service. By using the data they have about an individual customer and performing mathematical analyses on that data, these companies can suggest products that may match an individual customer's preferences (see, for example, Figure 3.4).

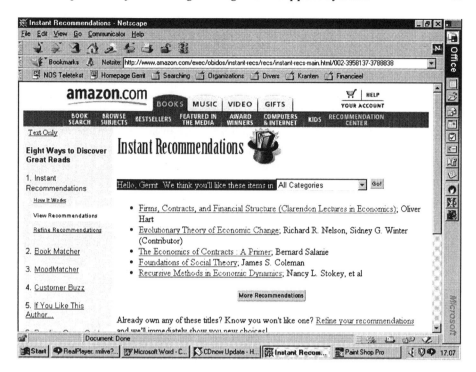

Figure 3.4   Using Internet-Based Data to Develop Personalized Marketing Programs

3.4.3   Data Warehouses

Many organizations, such as (virtual) retailers, banks, and insurance companies, are developing enormous databases from their interactions with clients. This data needs to be organized in such a way that it is easy to transform it into information and knowledge. For the storage of data from all kinds of different sources, the development of *data warehouses* is becoming popular. Data warehouses are databases that hold high-level operational, historic, and customer data for the entire organization and make it available for decision-making purposes (O'Connor and Galvin 1997). The recognition that there are two fundamentally different types of information systems in organizations (i.e., *operational systems* and *informational systems*) is an important driver of the data warehouse movement (Orr 1997). Data warehouses combine and store data that is extracted from various operational systems. Data warehouses contain decision support data that is kept outside the operational and transactional systems. Operational systems help run an organization's day-to-day operations. Information systems have to do with analyzing data and making decisions, often major decisions, about how the organization will operate, both now and in the future.

Data warehouse tools help to build and extract data from the data warehouse. These tools can be grouped into three categories based on their activities (Sakaguchi and Frolick 1998): (1) *Acquisition tools* extract data from various sources and transform that data (via conditioning, cleaning, and so on) to make it usable in the warehouse. These tools also generate information about where data is stored. (2) *Storage tools* manage the databases. Finally, (3) *access tools* support users in accessing and analyzing the data in the warehouse in various ways. Examples of access tools are data-mining tools such as multivariate statistical analyses, neural networks, and knowledge discovery tools (see also Chapter 6). These tools sift through millions of data points to find patterns (Sakaguchi and Frolick 1998). On-line analytical processing (OLAP) is a category of software technology that enables decision makers to gain insight into data through fast, interactive access to a wide variety of possible views of information that has been transformed from raw data. Data warehouses will become of increasing importance in providing an important input for MMSS, that is, marketing data.

Data or quantitative information is only part of what marketing decision makers use in problem solving. Knowledge, either generalized marketing knowledge or marketing knowledge pertaining to particular situations and/or specific decision makers in the form of expertise, experience, and judgment, also plays an important role in decision making. Increasingly, knowledge is also recognized as a separate element of marketing management support systems. We discuss the marketing knowledge component of MMSS in the next section.

3.5   Marketing Knowledge

An important component of marketing management support system is marketing knowledge. There are different types of (marketing) knowledge and also different sources for this knowledge.

3.5.1   Increased Managerial Attention on Knowledge

Whereas marketing data consists of concrete figures that can be looked at (and almost touched), either individually or in summary form in tables and graphs, marketing knowledge is less visible and tangible. Of course this statement applies not only to marketing knowledge but to knowledge in general. For more than 2500 years, philosophers and other scholars have been pondering the nature of knowledge and how it can be obtained. Plato (427–347 B.C.), for example, is widely known for his inquiries into the sources of knowledge. Later philosophers, such as Descartes, Locke, Hume, and Kant, have devoted themselves to thinking about knowledge. Knowledge is a multidimensional concept and, as we shall see, there are many different types of knowledge. Over the years, especially since the Enlightenment, the amount of human knowledge has increased steadily, mainly as a result of systematic, scientific research. Because of the unprecedented level of research efforts and the amplifying effects of research in different disciplines, over the last 50 years the store of human knowledge has grown at an exponential rate.

In this section we are interested in the role of knowledge in the context of marketing management support systems. For this purpose we first look at the role of knowledge in management and, of course, especially in *marketing* management. Two major developments can be observed. First, the attention on knowledge in management has increased drastically. Knowledge used to be applied to tools, processes, products, and work, but it is now also applied to knowledge itself. Knowledge has become a resource and utility that has to be maintained, developed, updated, and extended. Peter Drucker (1993) observed that knowledge has become "the *one* factor of production, sidelining both capital and labor." Companies are very concerned about the knowledge that their employees have and how that knowledge can be used optimally; they also wonder how they can convert themselves into a *knowledge-creating organization* (Nonaka 1994). Knowledge definitely has become a primary source of the competitive strength of companies.

The second development in the role of knowledge in management, which is related to the first one, is a heavy emphasis on learning. Where the environment in which companies operate is changing rapidly and the pace of knowledge development (and obsolescence) is also rapid, not just knowledge itself but also the ability to acquire new knowledge (i.e., to learn) has become an important competitive weapon. The ability to learn has been called "the fifth discipline" (Senge 1990). As we argued in the last chapter, decision makers, including marketing managers, use mental models to guide their interpretations of the world and to help them develop strategies and actions. Because of the dynamics of the situations in which managers operate, these mental models should not be static. They have to be updated constantly based on new evidence and knowledge.

Thus, in the current era, inquiries into knowledge appeal not only to philosophers but to everyone. Knowledge is a concrete, day-to-day concern for marketing managers; it is also something that can be put into computers. In this section we pay attention to the role of knowledge as a component of marketing management support systems. We discuss here the different types of knowledge, sources of marketing knowledge, and the state of generalized marketing knowledge. Later, in Chapters 4, 5, and 6, we deal with knowledge acquisition, knowledge representation, knowledge processing, and learning.

3.5.2   Different Types of Knowledge

Knowledge can be classified according to several dimensions (see Figure 3.5).

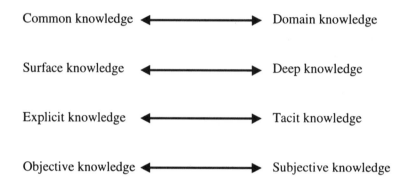

Figure 3.5   Dimensions of Knowledge

First, we can make a distinction between *common knowledge* and *domain knowledge. Common knowledge* refers to what is often called "common sense," the knowledge that everyone has (or should have). Examples of this kind of knowledge are as follows: bread is a food; when it rains you get wet; a telephone can be used for direct communication with a person not in your neighborhood. *Domain knowledge,* on the other hand, is specialized knowledge, referring to a specific problem area or a specific task. Marketing knowledge is an example of domain knowledge, but usually domains are defined at an even narrower level of specialization, for example, knowledge about the domain of sales promotions. It is relatively easy to develop systems with specialized domain knowledge, for example, building a marketing management support system to support sales-promotion decisions. Because of the enormous amount of relevant common knowledge, it is much more difficult to equip a system with a sufficient amount of common sense to allow it to operate in a wider environment. Even a very sophisticated sales-promotion support system will behave outside its domain less adroitly than a five-year-old child. At the University of Austin (Texas), researchers are trying to build a knowledge base of common human knowledge that is meant as a commonsense infrastructure on which future knowledge bases could be built. This megaproject by Douglas Lenat involves several millions of rules and commonsense facts, and it may take more than ten years before it is completed (Lenat and Guha 1990).

Another distinction that can be made is the one between *surface knowledge* and *deep knowledge. Surface knowledge* consists of simple heuristics about specific solutions that are known (from experience) to work in specific conditions, without knowing the precise mechanism between the solution as input and its outcome. An example of surface knowledge is the knowledge of most drivers that turning the ignition key makes the engine of a car start running. However, often (usually) they have no idea *why* this happens. In the same way, a marketer may know that advertising leads to sales without having a clear idea about the underlying process that makes advertising increase sales. *Deep knowledge,* on the other hand, means that one also knows the mechanism behind a phenomenon, for example, what exactly causes that engine to start or how advertising leads to increased purchases. Deep knowledge is required for so-called "reasoning from first principles." An example of reasoning from first principles is the reasoning process of a marketing manager who predicts the sales of a new product. He or she starts with a model (the mental model) of the decision process of an individual consumer and the factors that determine whether or not that consumer will buy the new product. Next, the marketing manager makes assumptions about the differences between the decision processes of consumers in different market segments. He or she then combines this knowledge with estimates of the relative sizes of the different market segments and in this way arrives at a sales estimate. This is called reasoning from first principles because the chain of causes and effects is explained in terms of elementary events (choices of individual consumers). As we shall see later, expert systems can work with surface knowledge. Marketing models, however, are an example of reasoning from first principles. In Chapter 2 we indicated that depth of knowledge is an important antecedent (or determinant) of which marketing problem-solving mode is used. Having deep knowledge facilitates applying the reasoning and optimizing modes.

Next, we can divide knowledge into *explicit knowledge* and *tacit knowledge. Explicit* or *codified knowledge* refers to knowledge that is transmittable in formal, systematic languages. Probably this type of knowledge is only the tip of the iceberg of the entire body of knowledge that a person has. In other words, "We know much more than we can tell" (Polanyi 1966). The part of knowledge that we cannot transmit to others via words and language is called *tacit knowledge. Tacit knowledge* refers to know-how, crafts, and skills; it is personal, context-specific, and therefore hard to formalize and communicate. A major challenge in building knowledge-based systems is to acquire and capture this tacit knowledge from human experts. The articulation of tacit elements is a key factor in the creation of new knowledge. It has been claimed that U.S. managers focus on explicit knowledge, whereas Japanese managers focus on tacit knowledge. According to Nonaka and Takeuchi (1995), the key to the economic success of Japan in the 1980s was that Japanese managers knew how to convert tacit knowledge into explicit knowledge.

Finally, we can distinguish *objective knowledge* from *subjective knowledge. Objective knowledge* is knowledge in the interpretation of classical epistemology, whereas *subjective knowledge* is seen as "justified true beliefs." *Objective knowledge* is obtained by systematic scientific research and can be found in scientific journals and textbooks. It represents the body of knowledge about a specific field, the total of facts and relationships (sometimes called laws) that experts in that field agree on. Although the possibility of falsification remains (i.e., some aspect of objective knowledge could be proved wrong at some future date), as long as this has not occurred, objective knowledge is considered to be true. *Subjective knowledge,* on the other hand, refers to the perceptions and beliefs of individuals, for example, marketing managers. The mental models of managers tend to be combinations of objective knowledge (e.g., from textbooks and what they learned in school) and subjective knowledge, mainly based on their own specific experiences. Since we do not have many generalized relationships (i.e., true knowledge) in marketing, the mental models of marketers tend to have a substantial subjective component. Ultimately, a manager will always act on his or her mental model of a situation. For a company, therefore, the quality of the mental models of its managers and the maintenance of this quality are important strategic considerations. The recent interest in empirical generalizations in marketing can be an important factor in favor of giving greater weight to objective knowledge in marketing decisions (Bass and Wind 1995).

A variety of different types of knowledge thus exist. Apart from common knowledge, all the different types of knowledge discussed here—domain knowledge, surface knowledge, deep knowledge, explicit knowledge, tacit knowledge, objective knowledge, and subjective knowledge—can be elements of marketing management support systems.

3.5.3   Sources of (Marketing) Knowledge

After having discussed the different types of knowledge, we now turn to the sources of the knowledge that can be used in marketing management support systems.

General knowledge

Inquiries into the sources of knowledge in general go back to the roots of ancient philosophy. Plato stressed the importance of absolute, pure reason. He developed the theory of "ideas," which are seen exclusively through the mental eye and which form the ultimate ideals that the human spirit aspires to know. To obtain real truth and wisdom, in Plato's view, humans should focus on their own thinking and be disturbed as little as possible by what is caught by the eyes, ears, and other senses. Plato's student Aristotle (384–322 B.C.) had a different view. He emphasized the importance of the senses as a source of knowledge, as well as the experiences that people obtain from operating in an environment. Once practitioners have gone through a lot of experiences in a particular domain, they are able to apply the knowledge they have acquired to new cases in that domain. Aristotle's recommendation, therefore, was that if you have a problem, do not ask a philosopher; ask an old, wise man. Aristotle also started to collect empirical data on plants and animals and carried out astronomical observations. These different views about the role of observation versus reasoning resulted, many centuries later, in two schools of thought, *rationalism* and *empiricism.* Descartes (1596–1650) is the most prominent representative of the rationalist school. To him, human reason and the human mind were most important: he held that beliefs (knowledge) were acquired by means of logical reasoning. Descartes assumed that human beings have mental objects or constructs by which they apply their reasoning (we would now call them mental representations or models). Descartes was suspicious of all perceptual experiences, claiming that perception is inherently uncertain. The only thing he was completely sure of was his own thinking: *Cogito, ergo sum* ("I think, therefore I am").

Perhaps the most outspoken proponent of the empiricist school is David Hume (1711–1776). In opposition to Descartes, Hume believed that our ideas are based on experiences in the external world and our reflections on these experiences. Yet reason also plays a role in Hume's philosophy: reason combines simple ideas into complex ideas or relations. Hume did not content himself with observations from the external world as such, but he was heavily interested in the causal laws between observed phenomena. For example, does lightning "cause" thunder?

It is interesting to observe that there are geographical differences with respect to people's preferences for the rationalist and empiricist schools. At least in the social sciences, the European continent has traditionally shown a relative preference for the rationalist way of thinking, whereas the Anglo-Saxon world (including the United States) has traditionally favored the empiricist approach, with its heavy emphasis on data collection and measurement. The German philosophy tends to favor Plato, whereas the Anglo-Saxons have a greater liking for Aristotle (Störig 1990).

The German philosopher Immanuel Kant (1724–1804) proposed a synthesis between rationalism and empiricism. His view was that both the mind and experience are sources of knowledge. The mind has a capacity to structure and order incoming experiences, for example, in space and time. So the mind provides the structure for knowledge, whereas experience from the external world provides the facts to fill the mental structures (Haberland 1994). The following statement by Kant has become famous: "Gedanken ohne Inhalt sind leer. Anschauungen ohne Begriffe sind blind" ("Mind without observations is empty, observations without mind concepts to interpret them, is blind") (Kant 1787). The way we think a marketing decision maker operates comes close to Kant's view: A marketing manager has an a priori mental model of how the market works (formed by education and experience), which he or she then uses to interpret incoming facts and solve marketing problems.

Marketing knowledge

We define *marketing knowledge* as insights about marketing phenomena and processes that can be used for explanation and prediction. Marketing knowledge can be objective or subjective, surface or deep, and explicit or implicit. In this book we are interested in the role that marketing knowledge plays in the context of marketing management support systems. Two different roles can be distinguished here: (1) *existing* marketing knowledge can be put into an MMSS and in this way provide guidance for marketing decision makers, and (2) an MMSS can be used to produce *new* marketing knowledge that is of practical value to decision makers in the company where the MMSS is used. With respect to existing marketing knowledge, there are two different sources:

1a. Marketing science: generalized insights about marketing phenomena that have been acquired in scientific research. Examples of such knowledge include knowledge of consumer choice processes, knowledge of new product diffusion processes, knowledge of distribution channels, knowledge of advertising response functions, and knowledge of the effects of sales promotions.

1b. Mental models that marketing experts use to reason about marketing decision situations and arrive at solutions. These models usually consist of "if-then" rules. For example, *if* you are introducing a new brand, *then* you have to spend substantial amounts on advertising to create brand awareness. Such expert rules have a general reach and are not confined to the situation of a specific product or company.

Marketing science has a strong empirical tradition, and marketing knowledge source 1a is clearly empiricist. Source 1b, however, with its imbedded if-then rules and logical way of reasoning, is more akin to the rationalist tradition. Of course, the first source of marketing knowledge is the most objective, whereas the second source is dependent on the subjective views of the experts from whom the knowledge is acquired.

With respect to new knowledge that is generated by MMSS, there are also two different sources:

2a. Statistical relationships observed between relevant marketing variables in the environment of the company that uses the MMSS. An example would be the estimated relationship between advertising expenditures and sales, using data from the data warehouse of that company. This is also relatively hard (objective) knowledge, albeit only applicable in that specific situation. Knowledge of such "locally hard relationships" is very useful for the solution of the company's practical marketing problems.

2b. The events that occur in day-to-day marketing life. The daily experiences to which a marketing decision maker is exposed create a kind of informal knowledge called *expertise* or *intuition,* which cannot easily be described or transmitted to others but can be very valuable as judgmental knowledge in making decisions. An MMSS can merely help this process of tacit knowledge formation by reporting facts, events, and data, but an MMSS can also actively support this process by providing pattern recognition–based systems such as case-based reasoning or neural networks. It is very important that (marketing) employees learn maximally from the events in their environment.

We will elaborate on knowledge from the first source, the generalized body of knowledge of marketing (1a), in the next section. For the acquisition of locally hard knowledge from marketing data (2a), data-driven marketing management support systems are needed. These are described in Chapter 4. For dealing with knowledge from the other two sources, expert knowledge (1b) and soft knowledge from day-to-day events (2b), knowledge-driven marketing management support systems are needed. These are described in Chapter 5 (expert systems) and Chapter 6 (case-based reasoning systems and neural networks).

3.5.4   Generalized Marketing Knowledge

The first source of knowledge that marketing decision makers can use is generalized marketing knowledge. This knowledge is the product of scientific research in marketing; it can be thought of as the body of knowledge of the marketing discipline. According to Bass (1993), one of the most influential contributors to marketing science, serious research on marketing topics (i.e., applying advanced research methods) started in the early 1960s. In the three and a half decades since then, the field has made important progress, the results of which are documented in an enormous number of papers, articles, books, conference proceedings, and so on. However, it takes many studies in a specific area before truly empirical generalizations can be formulated, that is, regularities and relationships between variables that hold under a large variety of circumstances.

From time to time inventories are made of generalizable findings in a specific area of marketing, for example, advertising, pricing, or new product introductions. One possibility to accumulate knowledge across studies is to perform a *meta-analysis*. A *meta-analysis* is an "analysis of analyses," the statistical analysis of a large collection of analysis results from individual studies with the purpose of integrating their findings. An example is the meta-analysis by Tellis (1988) of the effect of price on sales. Based on his analysis of 337 studies, he concluded that the *grand mean* for price elasticity for branded goods is –1.76. Such a figure can be used in a marketing management support system as a default value. If there is no additional information, the best value for price elasticity in a particular case is –1.76. For a particular variable, not only is a grand mean estimated over all the studies included in the analysis, but the effects of specific conditions on the parameter under study are also examined. For example, in the Tellis study it was found that price elasticity is 0.63 lower (in an absolute sense) for a food product compared to a nonfood product and 0.50 higher for a European market compared to a U.S. market. Similar meta-analyses have been carried out for other areas of marketing. For example, it was found that the grand mean of short-term advertising elasticity is 0.27, and that the grand mean of the carryover effect is 0.39 (Assmus, Farley, and Lehman 1984). A comprehensive review of empirical generalizations in marketing can be found in a special issue of *Marketing Science* (Bass and Wind 1995). The empirical generalizations presented in this issue concern many domains of marketing, including diffusion, consumer choice behavior, market response to marketing instruments (price, advertising, and sales promotions), brand awareness, distribution, consumer satisfaction, order of entry, R&D spending, and bargaining. Generalizations are not limited to first-order effects but can also refer to interactions, for example, the interaction of price and advertising (Kaul and Wittink 1995).

The development of marketing knowledge is also reflected in the contents of textbooks. The evolution of marketing knowledge over the last 30 years can be traced by examining the subsequent editions (since 1967) of Philip Kotler's *Marketing Management* (Kotler 1997). Some of the findings and recommendations mentioned there can be implemented directly, for example, as rules in MMSS. Similarly, the evolution of consumer behavior can be traced by looking at the series of editions of Engel, Blackwell, and Miniard (1995), which was first published in 1968. Some textbooks make an explicit effort to formulate the results from research in such a way that they are directly translated into managerial recommendations. An example is the Rossiter and Percy (1987, 1997) book on advertising and promotion. An illustration of a recommendation from their book is the following: "If the motivation of the consumer is informational and the product category is low involvement, then it is not necessary for people to like the ad." Such recommendations are in a form that can be directly implemented in marketing knowledge-based systems, one of the different types of MMSS (for an actual implementation of this type of knowledge, see Chapter 8).

The prospects for the further growth of generalized marketing knowledge are excellent. The last several decades of research in marketing have not only produced gains in fundamental knowledge, but also—and what may be more important—the development of a system for further developing the science of marketing (Bass 1993). Nevertheless, marketing is still a young science, and at this moment there are in this field insufficient empirically generalized relationships for a marketing manager to derive management guidelines exclusively from this source of knowledge. Both for the time being and for the foreseeable future, the other three sources of marketing knowledge mentioned in section 3.5.3 will remain very important for marketing decision makers. How to deal with them in marketing management support systems is the topic of Chapters 4, 5, and 6.

3.6   The Evolving Role of the Four Components

The four components described in this chapter have contributed to the development of the different marketing management support systems. Of these four components, information technology has been the most constant and strongest driving force behind the development of MMSS. Since the first computers began being used in companies in the 1950s, marketers have actively been exploring opportunities to use them for marketing management. As we have seen, computers have dramatically increased the ability to collect and store data and have stimulated the development of computation-intensive data analysis procedures. The other three components of marketing management support system have played varying roles over time. The analytical capabilities component (i.e., operations research, mathematical modeling, and econometric methods) produced the first wave of MMSS, starting in the 1960s. This component has produced an impressive number of marketing models and marketing decision support systems.

In the late 1970s and 1980s, the marketing data component was the major driver behind the development of MMSS. Scanning data collected at checkouts in supermarkets was especially important during this time. It has been estimated that scanning data increased the quantity of data that an average brand manager was confronted with by a factor of 1400 in a period of less than five years (Eskin 1993).

Not only has progress in information technology produced better options for how to deal with data, but the developments in knowledge-based systems and artificial intelligence have also produced many tools for the representation and manipulation of knowledge. This is important for the fourth component of marketing management support systems, marketing knowledge. Technologies became available to deal with qualitative knowledge and to incorporate this knowledge into systems that support decision makers. Examples are expert systems, knowledge-based systems, case-based reasoning systems, and neural networks. In the 1990s these knowledge-oriented technologies became an important driving force behind developments in MMSS.

At the end of the 1990s, it is evident that information technology has become such an important driving force in the development of marketing management support systems that it should be considered an independent component. The same is true for marketing knowledge. The importance of (qualitative) knowledge has been recognized, and knowledge technology has made it possible to capture this knowledge in computer programs and make it available to support marketing decision making. Figure 3.1 (see the beginning of this chapter) may remind some readers of a four-component framework for marketing decision support systems that was presented 30 years ago by Montgomery and Urban (1969) and later modified by Little (1979). The four components in their models were *models, statistics, optimization,* and *data.* Our framework encompasses the Montgomery and Urban framework. Their elements *models, statistics,* and *optimization* are included in our analytical capabilities component, and, like Montgomery and Urban, we also have a (marketing) data component. Our extension of their model consists of adding the information technology and marketing knowledge components, which shows the progress that has taken place.

The different types of marketing management support systems differ with respect to the prominence of each of the constituting components. For example, marketing models and marketing decision support systems make extensive use of analytical capabilities, whereas marketing information systems and marketing neural networks lean heavily on marketing data, and marketing expert systems and marketing knowledge-based systems rely most on marketing knowledge. The information technology component is an enabling capability for all types of MMSS. The relationships between the four components and the different kinds of MMSS are graphically shown (heuristically) in Figure 3.6.

Having discussed in this chapter the four components underlying the different types of marketing management support systems, in the following three chapters we deal with these systems themselves. In Chapter 4 we discuss data-driven MMSS, whereas in Chapters 5 and 6 we describe knowledge-based MMSS.

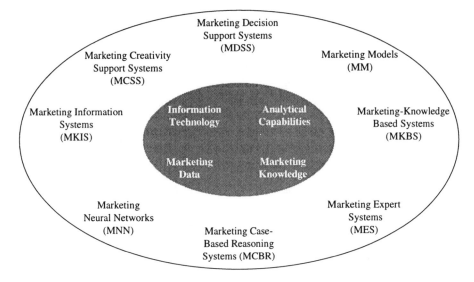

Figure 3.6   The Four Constituting Components and the Various Types of Marketing
Management Support Systems

Key Points

- *Marketing management support systems are a combination of information technology, analytical capabilities, marketing data, and marketing knowledge.*

- *The developments in the information technology component (both hardware and software) have greatly stimulated the development of tools that form the building blocks of MMSS. The development of communication networks has strongly enhanced communication opportunities.*

- *Ongoing developments in information technology will further stimulate the development of powerful MMSS. Particularly promising, for example, are the developments in object-oriented programming.*

- *The fields of statistics, econometrics, and operations research/management science have produced a large set of powerful analytical capabilities that can help marketers a great deal in obtaining relevant insights into their markets.*

- *Marketing management support systems can be provided with marketing data from various sources. Both the quantity and the quality of available data are still increasing. Furthermore, the Internet is an important source of new marketing data; and data warehouses are becoming increasingly popular for storing the data from different sources.*

- *There are different sources of knowledge for the marketing knowledge component of MMSS: generalized marketing knowledge from marketing science, marketing experts, results from analysis of the data from the company's own database, and day-to-day marketing events in the company environment. Marketing knowledge used in MMSS can be objective or subjective, surface or deep, and explicit or implicit.*

- *Although major progress has been made over the last several decades, the generalized body of knowledge of marketing science is still far from sufficient to answer all practical marketing questions. Therefore, marketing management support systems will require marketing knowledge from different sources for a long period to come.*

- *The developments in the four components have influenced each other and have led to more powerful MMSS. Information technology, for example, has stimulated the collection of more and better data. The availability of this data has then triggered the development of sophisticated analytical capabilities. And applying these tools has led to the creation of marketing knowledge.*

Chapter 4

Data-Driven Marketing Management Support Systems

Learning Objectives

- *To develop an overview of the different types of data-driven marketing management support systems.*

- *To understand what a marketing model is, how it is constructed, and how it can be used to support marketing decision making.*

- *To become familiar with marketing information systems, including their architecture and what real-world examples look like.*

- *To obtain insight into the ways a marketing decision support system can support marketing decision making.*

- *To begin to understand the effects of applying marketing models and marketing decision support systems in actual practice.*

4.1 Introduction

The attempts to use the various components of marketing management support systems to support marketing decision making have resulted in several types of systems that marketers can use to support their decision-making activities. These systems have appeared from the early 1960s onward. Continuous developments in the various components have stimulated the ongoing development of newer and more advanced types of systems. Roughly speaking, we can say that the first three decades of MMSS have been dominated by what we call *data-driven marketing management support systems.* These are systems that heavily emphasize the marketing data and analytical capabilities components. In this chapter we describe three types of data-driven marketing management support systems: marketing models, marketing information systems, and marketing decision support systems.

4.2   Marketing Models

This overview introduces the basic concepts and developments in the field of marketing models (MM). For a more detailed and in-depth treatment we refer readers to the excellent textbooks of, for example, Naert and Leeflang (1978), Lilien, Kotler, and Moorthy (1992), Eliashberg and Lilien (1993), and Lilien and Rangaswamy (1998).

4.2.1   Types of Marketing Models

Marketing models signify the start of the use of computers for marketing decision making (Bass et al. 1961; Frank, Kuehn, and Massy 1962; Buzzell 1964). This work in the early 1960s was the beginning of a model-building tradition in marketing that continues through today (Lilien, Kotler, and Moorthy 1992). Developments in the fields of operations research/ management science and econometrics led to the start of marketing modeling. The field of operations research/management science (OR/MS) emerged during World War II and focused first on problems in production, operations, and logistics. Because of the successes achieved in these areas, the practitioners in this field attempted to tackle problems in other areas. The OR/MS approach entered marketing in the early 1960s (Eliashberg and Lilien 1993). Several types of models have been developed since then. Lilien, Kotler, and Moorthy (1992) distinguish three types: measurement models, decision support models, and stylized theoretical models. Our interest in this section is in *decision support models.* Work in the area of stylized theoretical models (Eliashberg and Lilien 1993) is important for the development of marketing knowledge. However, these models do not directly aim at supporting actual marketing decision processes. Measurement models are descriptive and intended to describe decision or other processes. Such models may be developed in the process of constructing a decision support model, of which they can be a module.

Within the category of decision support models, we distinguish two subcategories, predictive and prescriptive models. *Predictive models* aim at predicting future events. In the context of decision models, this generally means predicting the effects of alternative marketing actions, the so-called what-if simulations. For example, a decision maker may want to predict the market share for a product at alternative price levels, advertising spending levels, distribution efforts, and/or package sizes. The other category of decision support models, *prescriptive* (or *normative*) *models,* have, as one of their outputs, a recommended course of action. This implies that an objective has been defined against which alternatives can be evaluated and compared. When we talk about marketing models in this book, we specifically mean prescriptive models, those that aim at finding an optimal solution. In terms of the ORAC model, marketing models follow an optimizing mode.

4.2.2 Steps in the Construction and Use of a Marketing Model

In the marketing-modeling approach to problem solving, a mathematical representation of the relevant marketing phenomena is first developed. This mathematical representation is the descriptive part of the marketing model. In developing it, a marketer must take three steps (Naert and Leeflang 1978; Lilien, Kotler, and Moorthy 1992): model specification, model para-meterization, and model validation.

Model Specification

The model development process starts with specification. This means that the marketer must develop a structure or representation of the most important elements of a real-world system in mathematical terms. This involves two steps:

1. Specifying the variables to be included in the model and making a distinction between those to be explained (the dependent variable) and those explaining (the explanatory or independent variables). The dependent variable can be a variable like the demand or preference for a product (in terms of, for example, sales or market share), the brand awareness or distribution coverage for brands, and so on. The independent variables will usually be variables that can be controlled by the marketer, such as marketing-mix variables. However, variables such as industry characteristics, competitor tactics, and seasonal effects can also be incorporated as independent variables.

2. Specifying a relationship between the dependent and the independent variables, that is, specifying a *response function* (Lilien and Kotler 1983). Saunders (1987) presents an overview of the various forms a relationship between dependent variables (effects) and independent variables (efforts) can take. These include linear relationships (which can cross the origin), relationships with decreasing returns to scale of effort, relationships where a certain level of effect (the saturation level) cannot be exceeded, relationships with increasing returns to scale of

effort, relationships with both increasing and decreasing returns to scale of effort (S-shaped), relationships where first some level of effort (the threshold level) must be exceeded before there is any effect, and relationships in which beyond a certain effort level the effect even declines. This last effect is called supersaturation.

The marketer thus has a rich supply of mathematical forms available from which to choose the specification that fits best with the characteristics of the market. Relationships can differ between market segments, between brands, and between time periods. Furthermore, interaction effects can be specified in which the effect of one independent variable will depend on the levels of other variables. The effects of promotional efforts, for example, will often depend on the distribution efforts. Dynamics can also be incorporated in the model. The effect of advertising efforts, for example, will often have both a short-term and a long-term component. In the model specification these kinds of dynamics should be taken into account.

Each form has its advantages but also its drawbacks. Lilien, Kotler, and Moorthy (1992) mention criteria that can be used to evaluate the various relationship forms and to determine which form is most appropriate in a given case. They introduce three types of soundness as criteria that can be used to determine whether a model form is appropriate: theoretical soundness, descriptive soundness, and normative soundness. A model form is theoretically sound if there is theoretical reason to believe that the relationships between independent variables and dependent variables take the form that is present in the mathematical representation. Descriptive soundness refers to the way the model form fits the data and whether it does so better than alternative models. A model is descriptively sound if it conforms to historical or judgmental data. The third criterion, normative soundness, is concerned with the kind of suggestions the model produces. A model is normatively sound if the guidelines it produces are believable.

Model parameterization

When the model has been specified, the value of its parameters, linking the independent variables to the dependent variables, has to be determined. This step is called *parameterization* or *estimation*. In order to estimate parameters, the users of the model need data. According to the kind of data available, a distinction will be made between data-based or objective parameterization (which is parameterization from historical data) and judgment-based or subjective parameterization.

When quantitative, historical data is available, several types of econometric (regression) methods can be used to determine the values of the regression coefficients (i.e., the parameters of the model) mathematically.

Depending on the characteristics of the data, techniques such as ordinary least squares (OLS) and generalized least squares (GLS) can be used to estimate parameter values. Generalized least squares will be applied when the marketing data does not satisfy the standard assumption of the OLS approach. This will happen in case of heteroscedasticity (i.e., the error terms do not have the same variance) and/or autocorrelation (i.e., the error terms are not independent). In the case of nonlinear models, one can try to see whether it is possible to transform the model to a linear form. If not, numerical procedures exist that can be used to come up with parameter values.

Econometric, data-based techniques for determining parameter values are valid within the range and time period of the collected data. Extensions beyond the data, whether in time or in space, may be difficult to justify (Lilien, Kotler, and Moorthy 1992). When no quantitative data is available, or when one assumes that the model will be used in circumstances very different from those in which the data was collected, models can also be parameterized subjectively. This means that parameter values will be determined based on the subjective judgments of experts (e.g., the manager who normally makes the decisions the model has to support) in the area for which the model was built (Lilien, Kotler, and Moorthy 1992). Little (1970) introduced the decision calculus concept in marketing; it provides a procedure for determining model parameters in a subjective way.

Little demonstrated the approach of incorporating managerial judgment by developing a model of sales response to advertising (the ADBUDG model). In building the model, Little made the following assumptions with respect to the response function:

1. If advertising is cut to zero, brand share will decrease, but there is a floor, *min,* to which share will fall by the end of one time period.

2. If advertising is increased to a saturation level, brand share will increase, but there is a ceiling, *max.*

3. There is an advertising rate that will maintain the initial share.

4. An estimate can be made of the effect of a 50% increase in advertising over the maintenance rate on brand share by the end of the period.

Based on these assumptions, the following function can be specified:

$$\text{share} = min + (max - min)(\text{adv})^{\gamma} / [\delta + (\text{adv})^{\gamma}]$$

The constants *min, max,* δ, and γ can be determined by asking a product manager to make judgments about the assumptions listed above. The questions would be the following:

- To what level would your brand share drop if you spent no money on advertising?

- What would be the ceiling above which your brand share would not rise even with very high advertising expenditures?

- At what level of advertising will your brand share stay at the current level?

- What would be your brand share if advertising expenditures were increased by 50%?

Since the introduction of the decision calculus concept, several models have been developed using this technique to determine the parameter values. The best known among these are the CALLPLAN model (Lodish 1971) and the BRANDAID model (Little 1975a). In addition, we used the decision calculus approach in developing the advertising module of the BRAND-FRAME system (see Chapter 9).

Besides the purely data-based (objective) and purely subjective methods of estimating parameter values, methods that use *both* data and judgment are also available. These are called *Bayesian analyses* (Lilien, Kotler, and Moorthy 1992). In such an approach a distinction is made between a prior distribution and a posterior distribution with respect to the probability distribution of parameters. A *prior distribution* is a probability distribution of the parameters before any data is observed. It is a judgmental assessment about the value of the parameters. A *posterior distribution* is an update of the prior distribution after data has been observed. The posterior distribution combines subjective assessments and objective data.

Model validation

After the functional relationship has been specified and parameter values have been determined, the quality of the model has to be assessed. Validation of a model and its parameters implies assessing the quality or success of the model. Naert and Leeflang (1978) mention a number of criteria of success, including the following:

1. The degree to which the results are in accordance with theoretical expectations or well-known empirical facts.

2. The degree to which the results pass a number of statistical criteria or tests.

3. The degree to which the results of a modeling effort correspond to the original purpose:

a. Is the model useful for clarifying and describing market phenomena?

b. Is the model accurate in predicting the level of certain variables?

c. Can the model be used as a basis for determining optimal marketing policies?

In our conceptualization of marketing models, their distinguishing characteristic is that they aim to find the best solution. Therefore, after the descriptive part of the model has been developed and optimal values for the independent marketing-mix variables controlled by the marketer, the decision variables have to be derived. To do this, differential calculus and OR techniques such as linear programming, integer programming, and simulation (Lilien, Kotler, and Moorthy 1992, p. 8) are available.

The growth of operations research strongly stimulated the development of marketing models. In terms of the four components of MMSS, marketing models heavily emphasize analytical capabilities. For the purpose of parameter estimation, marketing data and (sometimes) managerial judgment are also important. When the values of the parameters are determined objectively, econometric techniques are required as another form of analytical capabilities. The heavy emphasis on analytical capabilities was also stimulated by the characteristics of the persons that developed the first marketing management support systems. These first MMSS were developed in the 1960s by engineers, scientists, and applied mathematicians applying the OR/MS approach in the area of marketing rather than by people with a background in marketing, who became more dominant only recently (Eliashberg and Lilien 1993).

Over the years, especially in the seventies and eighties, a large collection of marketing models have been developed. These models support decisions on a variety of marketing variables. Among the most prominent were models like MEDIAC (Little and Lodish 1969), SPRINTER (Urban 1970), GEOLINE (Hess and Samuels 1971), CALLPLAN (Lodish 1971), DETAILER (Montgomery, Silk, and Zaragoza 1971), ADMOD (Aaker 1975), STRATPORT (Larréché and Srinivasan 1981), and SH.A.R.P. (Bultez and Naert 1988). In section 4.5 we present a more exhaustive list of marketing models.

Example of a marketing model: CALLPLAN

To illustrate the marketing-modeling approach, we will now describe a well-known marketing model, the CALLPLAN model developed by Lodish (1971). CALLPLAN is an interactive computer system designed to aid sales management in allocating sales-call time more efficiently. The objective of the model is to determine call frequency norms for each client and prospect that maximize adjusted anticipated sales minus travel costs.

First the descriptive part of the model is developed. I is the total number of clients and prospects that are considered. Call frequencies are the number of calls per *effort* period, which is the time period on which the allocation is based. Expected sales to clients and prospects over a *response* period are assumed to be a function of the average number of calls made per effort period. The solution to the mathematical program is the optimal number of calls to be made on each client and prospect.

A descriptive response function that relates expected sales to account i to the number of calls x_i made on this account is determined. The salesperson, usually with the help of his or her manager, carries out the determination of the response function: $r_i(x_i) =$ the expected sales to account i during the response period if x_i calls are made during an average effort period. Parameters in the response functions can be determined using either the subjective judgmental approach (in which the sales manager gives the parameter estimates directly) or a quasi-objective method in which a relationship is fitted based on data provided by the salesperson. In this latter, decision calculus approach, the salesperson has to provide information for each client with respect to five variables:

1. The expected sales during the response period with zero calls during an average effort period (ZER).

2. The expected sales if only one-half of the present number of calls are made.

3. The expected sales if the present call level is continued.

4. The expected sales if the present call level is increased by 50%.

5. The maximum sales level with saturation sales-call effort (SAT).

Using the data points, the computer fits a smooth curve through these five numbers. The four-parameter curve takes the following form:

(4.1) $r_i(x_i) = \text{ZER} + (\text{SAT} - \text{ZER})\, x_i^{\sigma} / (\gamma + x_i^{\sigma})$

The response function can assume both an S-shaped and a concave form. The fitted values of $r_i(x_i)$ for all feasible values of x_i are shown to the user for all clients and prospects. If a user does not agree with function values, these can be changed. Both the model specification and its validation are thus done in close cooperation with the user of the system.

The expected sales to a client or prospect are multiplied by an account-specific adjustment factor, a_i, to obtain a number that more accurately represents the contribution of the product mix of the specific account or management priorities on account types. In some other cases this adjustment factor has been used to reflect differences in average commission rates to accounts.

The salesperson's territory can be divided into J mutually exclusive geographic areas. Each account is identified by the geographical area in which it is located. Thus, g_i is the geographic area in which account i is located. If we assume that the salesperson is already in the geographical area of account i, each call takes an average of t_i time units (e.g., hours, minutes), including the average time it takes to travel to account i from within its area. The number of trips made to a geographical area during an effort period is assumed to be the maximum number of times any one account in the area is called on during the effort period. Each trip to a geographical area j is assumed to take an average time of u_j time units and to cost c_j in out-of-pocket expenses. NT_j is the number of trips made to area j during an average effort period. If there are e effort periods in each response period, then the number of trips to be made to area j during a response period is $e \times NT_j$.

To find an optimal solution, we state the problem in terms of mathematical programming. The objective is to find x_i for $i = 1, \ldots, I$ that maximizes z, the total adjusted expected sales from all accounts and prospects minus travel costs over the response period, where

(4.2) $$z = \sum_{i=1}^{I} a_i\, r_i(x_i) - e \sum_{j=1}^{J} N\, T_j c_j$$

The amount of time spent on selling and traveling must be less than T, the amount of time available during an average effort period:

(4.3) $$\sum_{i=1}^{I} t_i\, x_i + \sum_{j=1}^{J} NT_j u_j \le T$$

The number of trips to an area is a function of the number of calls made to each account in the area:

(4.4) $$NT_j = Max\{x_i\ such that\ g_i = j\}\ for\ j = 1, \ldots, J.$$

The call frequencies are constrained to be within minima (Min_i) and maxima (Max_i) input by the salesperson. This means that

(4.5) $$Min_i \le x_i \le Max_i\ for\ i = 1, \ldots, I.$$

The problem now is to find x_i for $i = 1, ..., I$ to maximize z subject to constraints (3), (4), and (5). This can be done by means of mathematical programming.

The CALLPLAN model as described here is thus a typical example of a normative or prescriptive marketing model, which consists of both a descriptive part (the response function) and an optimization part. After its user has provided the system with (judgmental) inputs with respect to the response function and the characteristics of the sales domain, the model will compute an optimal allocation of sales-force time.

The type of problems on which the CALLPLAN model focused (i.e., the allocation of sales-force time) can be characterized as relatively structured. In Chapter 2 we argued that this is a problem characteristic that favors the optimizing mode. Therefore, we could expect that applications of the CALLPLAN model would be successful. Fudge and Lodish (1977) studied its effectiveness in a field experiment at United Airlines. At the time of their study, United Airlines had a sales force that called on travel agents and corporations to promote passenger travel on its airlines. A smaller United Cargo sales force called on a multitude of firms to promote its air freight operations. Both of these sales forces were concerned with allocating their time, as a scarce resource, to maximize the effects of their efforts on United's sales and profits. In the experiment eight passenger and two cargo sales representatives used the model. The ten CALLPLAN participants were chosen randomly from ten pairs of salespeople who were individually matched by local management using personal characteristics and compatibility of territory size, revenue, and account mix. The remaining ten salespeople in the control group were told that they were participating in an experiment, and each of them manually estimated anticipated sales to compare their estimates against those of the CALLPLAN group. Fudge and Lodish (1977) report that the users were initially skeptical of the system. However, after they used the model, they realized that they were in control of it and viewed the experience as productive. After six months the average CALLPLAN salesperson had 8.1% higher sales than his matched non-CALLPLAN counterpart. Combining both judgmental and objective data in a mathematical program resulted in behavioral changes that significantly improved sales performance. This field experiment thus demonstrated how the implementation of a marketing model for the support of relatively structured and operational marketing decisions could improve the effectiveness of such decisions. The findings were confirmed in a study at Syntex laboratories (see Box 2.1) (Lodish, Curtis, Ness, and Simpson 1988). Here model use helped the corporation to decide to significantly increase the size of its sales force and change its deployment. This resulted in an 8% annual sales increase valued at $25 million. The CALLPLAN model itself has been implemented successfully in several companies. Furthermore, several other systems have since been developed that also use the approach originally developed for CALLPLAN.

Using the CALLPLAN model does not completely eliminate the role of marketers. As we described, marketers were important in providing input for the specification and calibration of the response models. However, this type of marketing model does aim to provide its user with a best solution, given the characteristics of the problem at hand. The role of the marketer is therefore diminished substantially on account of the new role of the model in determining the optimal solution.

4.3   Marketing Information Systems

Marketing information systems (MKIS) emerged in the second half of the 1960s when the concepts and approach of *management* information systems (MIS) were applied to the field of marketing.

4.3.1   Developments in Marketing Information Systems

Management information systems were (usually) computer-based systems intended to retrieve, extract, and integrate data from various sources in order to provide timely information necessary for managerial decision making (Turban and Aronson 1998). These systems had been most successful in providing information for routine, structured, and anticipated types of decisions. They were successful in storing large quantities of detailed data concerning transaction processing. MIS were developed for applications such as production control, where they produce reports regularly. Most management information systems were built with a focus on the internal organization. *Marketing* information systems differ in that they especially contain market data from outside the organization.

At the time that the concept of marketing information systems was introduced, businesses were caught in an "ironic dilemma" (Brien and Stafford 1968). Enormous amounts of data were generated (already then), the sheer volume of which appeared to increase exponentially. Despite this abundance of information, managers complained that they had insufficient, inappropriate, or untimely information to support their decision making. The process of developing timely, pertinent decision data for marketing management was characterized as the function of an MKIS rather than simply marketing research.

The importance of marketing information increased as companies grew larger and became more complex and marketers got further removed from firsthand contact with the "scenes of marketing action" (Kotler 1966). Marketers increasingly had to rely on secondhand information to get a picture of what was happening in the market. According to Kotler (1966) this information suffered from a number of problems. Too much information of the wrong kind was available, while not enough of the right kind was. With respect to management information systems in general, Ackoff (1967) also observed that managers did not so much lack relevant information as they suffered from an overabundance of irrelevant information. In designing information systems, therefore, one should try to resolve this problem. According to Ackoff the two most important functions of an MIS were filtration and condensation. Furthermore, information was often highly dispersed through the company, which meant that great effort was needed to locate simple facts and that important information often arrived too late to be useful. This, in the view of Kotler, led key executives to be often ignorant of important marketing developments. They did not optimally use the existing information and tended to distort information in passing it on.

Kotler called for a systematic solution in order to let executives make effective marketing decisions in an age characterized by intensifying competition, frequent product changes, and shifting consumer wants.[1] At the time of the introduction of the concept of marketing information systems, marketing research tended to be rather unsystematic, emphasizing data collection per se rather than the development of useful information for the support of marketing decision making. Furthermore, the focus was on isolated problems, which led to the ad hoc collection of data (Brien and Stafford 1968). Marketing research followed an eclectic path (Berenson 1969) in which, for example, one time the prices of one product line were examined, while another time competitors' packaging innovations were examined. Usually marketing research departments provided only part of the data needed to make decisions that had great and far-reaching impact on the company.

Marketing information systems were an attempt to more systematically provide marketing management with the kind of information they really needed. Brien and Stafford (1968) pointed at the need for a sustained flow of decision information and defined a marketing information system as "a structured, interacting complex of persons, machines and procedures designed to generate an orderly flow of pertinent information collected from both intra- and extra-firm sources, for use as the bases for decision-making in specified responsibility areas for marketing management." Berenson (1969) emphasized that MKIS provide a continuous study of the marketing factors that are important to an organization. MKIS use many more data sources than marketing research does. MKIS did not so much emphasize the generation of larger quantities of data as they focused on providing really useful decision support in a more structured manner.

---

[1] Surprisingly, the terminology of 1966 shows striking similarities to that of today.

With respect to the type of data in a marketing information system, Berenson (1969) listed several types of data that can be represented. These are invoice data (prices, purchased quantities, order dates, customer names, and so on), annual reports (of customers, suppliers, and competitors), market research inputs (audit and panel data, special projects, customer demand schedules, questionnaire responses), sales data (by product, by customer class, by region, and so on), financial data (credit, discount analysis, promotional allowances), and data about profitability (by product, product line, customer class, and so on). In a study of over 400 Belgian companies, Langerak, Commandeur, and Duhamel (1998) found that the MKIS of these organizations especially contained data about customers, sales prices, sales quantities, and distribution (see Table 4.1).

Table 4.1   Types of Data in Marketing Information Systems (*Source:* Langerak, Commandeur, and Duhamel 1998)

Type of Data	Percentage of MKIS Containing These Data
Customer data	94%
Own sales price data	86%
Own sales data	74%
Own distribution data	75%
Own market share data	75%
Own advertising data	55%
Literature references	38%
Competitors' market share data	39%
Competitors' price data	25%
Competitors' advertising data	10%
Competitors' distribution data	7%

According to Montgomery and Urban (1970) the key purpose of the database is to maintain data in its most elementary, disaggregated form. Maintaining disaggregated data enhances the flexibility of future use. Amstutz (1969) also mentions that a disaggregated data form lies at the heart of every successful information system.

The first marketing information systems did not put too much emphasis on the role of computers. Berenson (1969), for example, warned that systems should not be based solely on the computer. Although he perceived the computer to be a vital tool, he maintained that "old-fashioned" forms and procedures might also be quite good. Furthermore, since computers had such an enormous capacity, their use might make information too detailed and wide ranging. In his view, the goal of MKIS should especially be the structured provision of the *right* information. Although this is of course true, we should realize that with the amounts of data that are generated today, filtering, condensing, and evaluating masses of information into useful managerial input is crucial, making information technology an indispensable component of any MKIS.

The first marketing information systems were mainly a combination of marketing data and information technology, that is, systems with an emphasis on data storage and retrieval. Later, statistical procedures (analytical capabilities) were added (see Figure 4.1).

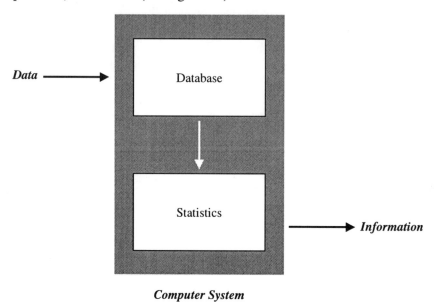

Computer System

Figure 4.1   The Basic Design of a Marketing Information System

Kotler (1966) distinguished information flows that are relevant for marketing information systems. The first flow is the marketing intelligence flow (*external information*). This flow consists of facts about institutions and the environment of an organization that affect its opportunities and performance. Major sources of marketing intelligence are its suppliers, complementary producers, markets, channels, competitors, and, in the broader environment, culture, law, technology, and the economy. A company should regularly monitor these sources for marketing intelligence. Marketing intelligence covers raw data, summary statistics, qualitative inferences, expert opinions, and even rumors. Kotler uses the analogy of the marketer as a military decision maker. The high-level military decision maker is usually far removed from the battlefield and therefore totally dependent on secondhand information in directing the battle. He (or she) requires a continuous stream of data on the current situation, the plans of the enemy, and so on. The marketing executive is in the same position. He or she fights for markets, with channels as allies against an enemy (its competitors) for a prize (sales). The second information flow as distinguished by Kotler concerns internal information that may be useful for marketers. Data from these two flows will typically be present in the database of a marketing information system.

4.3.2   Architecture of Marketing Information Systems

Kotler (1966) developed one of the first blueprints of "an organizational unit that promises to improve the accuracy, timeliness, and comprehensiveness of executive marketing services." He labeled this the *marketing information and analysis center,* or MIAC (see Figure 4.2). A MIAC would function as the marketing nerve center for an organization. It would perform three kinds of functions: information gathering, information processing, and information utilization. *Information gathering* is involved with the effort to develop or locate information that is needed by marketers. It is made up of three services: search, scanning, and retrieval. *Search* concerns specific requests for information—the more ad hoc type of information needed when a marketer suddenly raises a question. *Scanning* concerns the more regular assembly of general marketing intelligence. Kotler (1966) mentions newspapers, magazines, trade journals, special reports, and individuals as sources to judge the state of affairs. *Retrieval* concerns the efficient location of needed information.

The second function of a MIAC is *information processing.* Information should be evaluated with respect to its reliability and credibility. Next, information should be abstracted. Summary statistics are needed because marketers lack the time and mental capacity to process huge amounts of raw data. Information should be indexed so that it can be stored and retrieved efficiently. Information should also be organized in such a way that each potential user can be provided with the information he or she needs.

The third function of a MIAC is *information utilization.* Information should be provided in such a way that it can be used easily. Computer programs should enhance opportunities to use the information in the system and increase the user's power to make decisions and control operations. Complex marketing decisions can be supported and evaluated both before and after the fact through a thorough analysis of the available data.

The services offered by the MIAC largely coincide with three components that a marketing management support system normally contains. Information gathering is concerned with the various data sources. Information processing can be done by means of analytical capabilities. Finally, information technology will stimulate the possibility of active interaction between the decision maker and the information system.

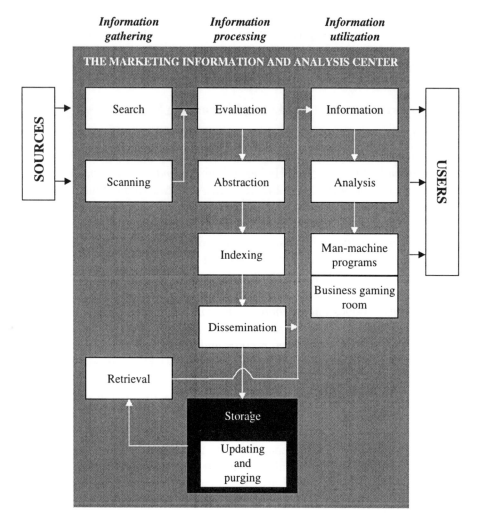

Figure 4.2   Architecture of Kotler's Marketing Information and Analysis Center (*Source:* Kotler 1966)

It was especially in the late 1960s and early 1970s that the marketing literature paid a lot of attention to marketing information systems, and many of the concepts and ideas developed at that time are still valid today. In the early 1990s Barabba and Zaltman (1991) came back to this topic with their introduction of the inquiry center. This center is in many ways similar to the concept of MKIS. It weaves together, in a meaningful pattern, all information from a variety of sources, leading to wise decisions. An inquiry center makes possible a more effective use of knowledge in general and market knowledge in particular in organizational decision-making processes. The concept of the inquiry center refers to a set of attitudes that can improve organizational thinking and action.

Some of the proposed marketing information systems of the early days were systems that tried to contain all marketing management support system components and in a way tried to automate the marketing process. However, if one looks at how these systems have evolved, it appears that the data component has become the heart of these systems and that the marketer is still in command.

Nowadays, many marketing management support systems in companies are de facto marketing information systems. The main function of an MKIS is to provide information (predominantly quantitative) about what is going on in the market, that is, to answer the question "What happened?" MKIS are basically passive systems. They provide information. However, it is up to the marketing decision maker to attach conclusions to this information and to decide whether or not to act on those conclusions. In Chapter 9 we discuss an MMSS that actively involves the decision maker when analyzing the data, including calling for action if necessary.

Although only limited attention has been paid to marketing information systems in the academic literature, in companies they are much more prominent than marketing models. In terms of the components of marketing management support systems, MKIS strongly emphasize the marketing data and information technology components. Furthermore, some analytical capabilities, in the form of statistical analyses, tend to be available in these systems.

4.3.3 Examples of Marketing Information Systems

To illustrate what actual marketing information systems look like, we describe two examples. These are A.C. Nielsen's INF*ACT system and Baan Company's FrontOffice system.

*INF*ACT*

An example of a marketing information system used by many companies is the well-known INF*ACT system, developed by A.C. Nielsen. The INF*ACT system is a computer-based tool that facilitates the storage, retrieval, integration, analysis, and presentation of information. The program provides marketers with the opportunity to control massive amounts of raw data. Nielsen's INF*ACT Workstation enables decision makers to access, analyze, and integrate marketing information and other key data from throughout their own enterprise. However, in the first instance the data will be those collected in Nielsen's own scanner-based retail audit and consumer panel. In a typical marketing information system, data from other sources can also be stored. Next, using statistical tools, users can consistently track and measure performance and monitor the markets they are operating in. By using INF*ACT, a decision maker can address such business issues as the following: What are the distribution changes when launching a line extension? In how many shops are the two varieties present? And is it worthwhile to increase my distribution, given the additional costs?

In Figure 4.3 we present three illustrative screens a marketing decision maker will typically face when consulting the INF*ACT system. In the first screen a user of the system can select from the products list those products about which he or she wants information. In the second screen the user can then select the time period for which information is wanted. The graph in the third screen shows the sales volume and distribution figures for the selected product in the selected time period. This particular INF*ACT database (on the Dutch pet food market) has four dimensions (i.e., markets, products, facts, and periods), with several items per dimension. The INF*ACT database consists of 3136 products, 24 markets, 24 facts, and 120 periods, resulting in 216,760,320 data points. By selecting items from the four dimensions, a marketer can retrieve and display marketing data and perform ad hoc analyses on it. Furthermore, by using the macro option, the marketer can produce standard reports. The production of standard reports on a regular basis is an important function of a marketing information system.

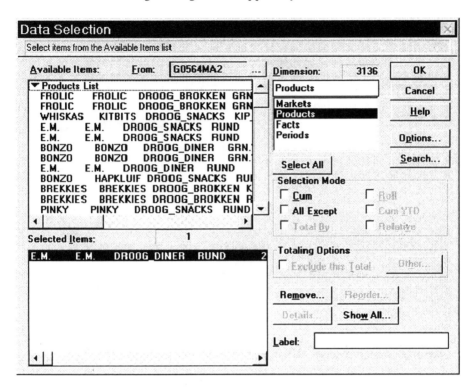

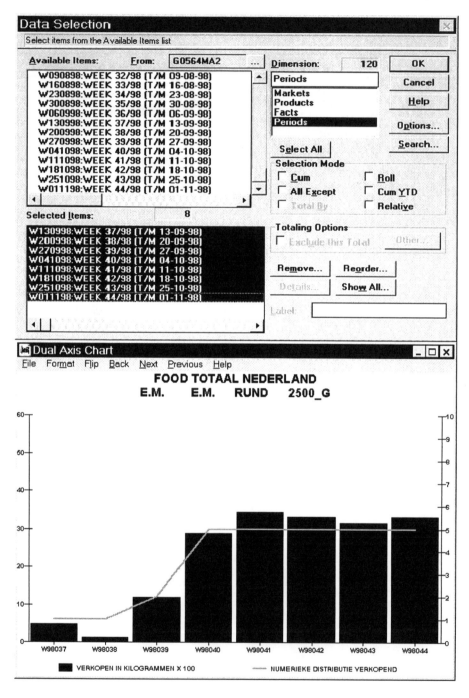

Figure 4.3   Illustrative Screens of A.C. Nielsen's INF*ACT Marketing Information System

Using the INF*ACT program, a marketer is able to monitor the market and track changes in all kinds of marketing variables. INF*ACT combines the components of information technology, marketing data, and analytical capabilities. These analytical capabilities mainly concern statistical analyses that make it possible to answer especially the "what happened" question.

BaanFrontOffice

As we have argued above, marketing information systems are especially useful in environments where a lot of data/information is available and where this information needs to be organized in a structured and usable form. Consumer-goods markets, especially those in which scanner data is collected, are often characterized by these traits. Therefore, MKIS will be very useful in these environments. However, in business-to-business markets, information systems have also become more popular. These systems can, in terms of their functionalities, also be characterized as MKIS. Compared to consumer-market systems, the data intensity of these systems is usually lower. Furthermore, the data will normally be represented at a lower aggregation level. Often the data will concern individual clients, whereas data in consumer MKIS will more often be measured at the level of market segments. However, the goal of business-to-business MKIS is the same as that of consumer MKIS. Both aim at the structured collection and storage of marketing and sales information, which makes it possible to track developments in the market and support decisions for products and brands in these markets. In general, for MKIS that are used in business-to-business settings there will be more emphasis on the support of sales activities.

An example of a business-to-business application of an MKIS is Baan Company's FrontOffice. BaanFrontOffice is a suite of products consisting of BaanSales, BaanConfiguration, and BaanCallCenter. FrontOffice provides a set of integrated components that give the marketing decision maker comprehensive customer information across the enterprise. The system aims at making marketers more knowledgeable in dealing with customers. It offers such tools as customer interaction and tracking, forecasting, sales funnel and opportunity management, and telemarketing and telesales campaign management. An important resource for exchanging information is the back-office/ERP applications.

BaanSales, one of the components of FrontOffice, aims at enhancing the effectiveness and efficiency of sales activities. It insures that the (mobile) sales force has the most current information available about leads, customer data, and product and pricing information. At the same time, salespeople in the field can upload (or transmit) new customer information and orders back to the corporate office. Figure 4.4 shows a screen with the sales funnel. This funnel summarizes the status of potential customers (*status* here meaning the number of activities that have been performed to transform potential customers into actual ones).

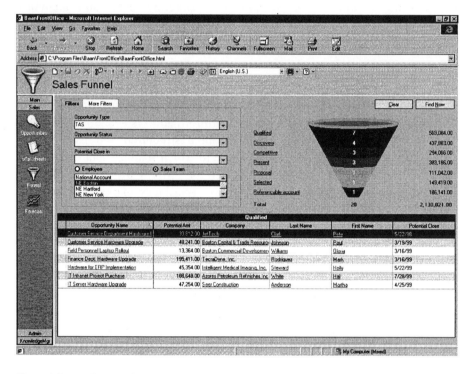

Figure 4.4   A Screen of the BaanSales Application

BaanConfiguration, the second element of the suite, allows sales representatives to quickly assess customer needs and tailor complex product and service configurations to meet those needs. This tool supports the operational sales activities, which will lead to more deals closed at the point of sale and shorter sales cycles. Furthermore, it enables users to configure complex product and service offerings, generate proposals, browse electronic catalogs, and build products to order.

Finally, BaanCallCenter applications (see Figure 4.5) facilitate interactions with customers. This application features components for telemarketing and telesales, customer service, and support. It provides management and tracking of marketing activities throughout the lead qualification process. Furthermore, it automates the planning and implementation of marketing campaigns, customer inquiry tracking, lead qualification and follow-up activities, and call scripts.

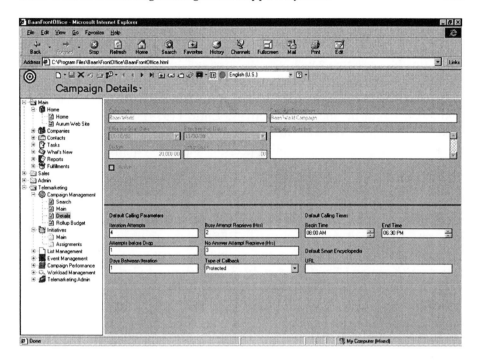

Figure 4.5   A Screen of the BaanCallCenter Application

Besides its three main components, the BaanFrontOffice system also contains tools for obtaining information from the Internet and intranets and for OLAP (on-line analytical processing).

BaanFrontOffice is especially focused on the support of operational marketing and sales activities. Although this kind of system is not as sophisticated as most of the other types of marketing management support systems, it is probably the type of system that has the highest adoption rate in companies. Like INF*ACT, this type of marketing information system is very much data and information oriented. As we have seen, the availability of data strongly stimulates the development of sophisticated systems like marketing models. Therefore, the adoption and use of this type of MKIS probably forms a good basis for the future adoption of more sophisticated systems.

4.4   Marketing Decision Support Systems

Marketing modeling primarily took a normative approach, with a concentration on developing solution techniques. A reason for this was that operations research was a young discipline, with little or no contact with management reality (Naert and Leeflang 1978). However, as the discipline became more mature and better two-way communication developed between management scientists and managers, models became more predictive and descriptive rather than normative (Naert and Leeflang 1978). This led to more flexible systems, which were focused not so much on coming up with one optimal solution as on helping decision makers develop solutions to less structured problem situations. At approximately the same time that Naert and Leeflang made their observations, Little (1979) wrote his paper on "Decision Support Systems for Marketing Managers." These developments led to the introduction of marketing decision support systems.

4.4.1   Developments in Marketing Decision Support Systems

Marketing decision support systems (MDSS) represent the more general concept of decision support systems (DSS) in the field of marketing. This concept emerged in the 1970s and caught on quickly in the management literature (Keen and Scott-Morton 1978; Sprague and Carlson 1982). Scott-Morton (1971) defined *management* decision support systems as interactive computer-based systems that help decision makers use data and models to solve unstructured problems. Note that this description of the first type of DSS defined them as a kind of combination of models and information systems. Compared to classical operations research, which was the main source of inspiration for marketing models, a DSS takes a more practical and flexible approach to problem solving. Its focus is on semistructured, rather than structured, tasks. Its purpose is to support rather than replace managerial judgment, and to improve the effectiveness of decision making rather than its efficiency. Moreover, DSS aimed at supporting top management rather than managers at lower organizational levels.

Little (1979) defines a *marketing* decision support system as "a coordinated collection of data, models, analytical tools and computing power by which an organization gathers information from the environment and turns it into a basis for action." An MDSS makes it possible for marketing managers to model marketing phenomena according to their own ideas (mental models). In that sense a marketing decision support system can be conceived of as a "relaxed" version of the more rigorous marketing models. On the other hand, an MDSS can also be seen as an extension of a marketing information system. Like an MKIS, an MDSS consists of a combination of information technology, marketing data, and analytical capabilities, but with much more emphasis on the last component. An MDSS contains an explicit model base. Whereas an MKIS is particularly geared toward answering "what" questions (What is happening in the market?) and "why" questions (Why did it happen?), an MDSS is especially equipped to answer "what-if" questions (What will happen if?). Taking advantage of its model base, the user of an MDSS can carry out simulations in order to answer such questions. The type of models in MDSS will be of a predictive rather than a normative nature.

Examples of marketing decision support systems described in the marketing literature are the ADBUDG system (Little 1970), which predicts market shares for given advertising budgets (an MDSS "avant-la-lettre"), and ASSESSOR (Silk and Urban 1978), which predicts the market share of a new product given its attributes and the introduction campaign. Other well-known MDSS are systems like BRANDAID (Little 1975a), TRACKER (Blattberg and Golanty 1978), and SCAN*PRO (Wittink et al. 1988). SCAN*PRO, which estimates promotional effects based on Nielsen's SCANTRACK data, aims at providing brand managers with an understanding of the impact of promotional activities. Alternative sales-promotion programs can be compared in terms of their impact on sales. The system has been very successful and has been used by A.C. Nielsen in more than a thousand applications.

4.4.2 Example of a Marketing Decision Support System: ASSESSOR

To illustrate the concept of marketing decision support systems, we will now describe a specific example of such a system in more detail. ASSESSOR (Silk and Urban 1978) is a measurement and modeling system designed to estimate the sales potential of new packaged goods before they are test-marketed. The goal of this system is to reduce the incidence of new product failures in test markets, thereby cutting the costs of new product development. The system aids marketers in evaluating new packaged goods before test-marketing when a positioning strategy has been developed and executed to the point where the product, packaging, and advertising copy are available and an introductory marketing plan (price, promotion, and advertising) has been formulated. The system then aims to do the following:

1. Predict the new brand/product's long-run market share.

2. Estimate the sources of the new brand's share (i.e., cannibalization of the firm's existing brand[s] and/or drawing from competitors' brands).

3. Produce actionable diagnostic information for product improvement and the development of advertising copy and other creative materials.

4. Permit screening of elements of alternative marketing plans (e.g., advertising copy, price, and package design).

This last function especially is a typical task of marketing decision support systems. By performing what-if analyses, the system will give the marketer feedback on various alternative marketing programs.

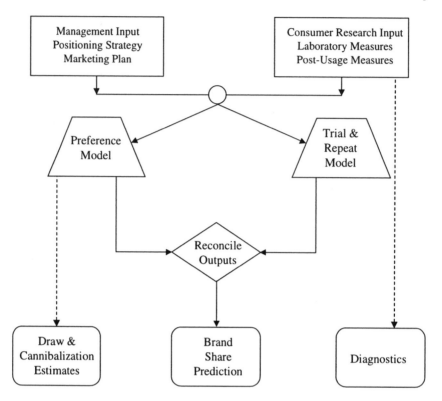

Figure 4.6   Structure of the ASSESSOR System (*Source:* Silk and Urban 1978)

The ASSESSOR system (see Figure 4.6) consists of two models that together should predict the new brand's market share. The first model is a *preference model* that relates preference to purchase probability. The other one models a *trial-and-repeat process*. The input for the two models is obtained through laboratory and usage tests. The data collection follows a design structure parallel to the model structure shown in Figure 4.6. Figure 4.7 summarizes the design of the data collection procedure.

Design	Procedure	Measurement
O_1	Respondent screening and recruitment (personal interview)	Criteria for target group identification (e.g., product class usage)
O_2	Premeasurement for established brands (self-administered questionnaire)	Composition of "relevant set" of established brands, attribute weights and ratings, and preferences
X_1	Exposure to advertising for established brands *and* new brand	
$[O_3]$	Measurement of reactions to the advertising materials (self-administered questionnaire)	Optional, e.g., likability and believability ratings of advertising materials
X_2	Simulated shopping trip and exposure to display of new and established brands	
O_4	Purchase opportunity (choice recorded by research personnel)	Brand(s) purchased
X_3	Home use/consumption of new brand	
O_5	Post-usage measurement (telephone interview)	New brand usage rate, satisfaction ratings, and repeat-purchase propensity; attribute ratings and preferences for "relevant set" of established brands plus the new brand

O = Measurement
X = Advertising or product exposure

Figure 4.7   The ASSESSOR Data Collection Procedure

Data is collected by means of a laboratory-based experimental procedure. A sample of consumers are confronted with advertising for the new product and a small set of the principal competing products already established in the market. Next, the consumers enter a simulated shopping facility where they have the opportunity to purchase quantities of the new and/or established products. The ability of the product to attract repeat purchases is assessed by follow-up interviews with the same respondents conducted after enough time has passed for them to have used or consumed a significant quantity of the new product at home.

Preference model

In the model the probability that consumer i chooses brand j ($P_i(j)$) is related to the consumer's preference for that brand. The relationship between preference and probability is described as

$$(4.6) \qquad P_i(j) = \frac{[V_i(j)]^\beta}{\displaystyle\sum_{k=1}^{m_i} [V_i(k)]^\beta}$$

where

$V_i(j) =$ consumer i's preference for brand j
$m_i \quad =$ number of brands in consumer i's relevant set of alternatives (the consideration set)
$\beta \quad =$ parameter to be estimated

Parameter β is an index that reflects the rate at which preferences will convert into purchase probabilities. It is estimated using the preference scale values for the established brands derived from data obtained in the premeasurement questionnaire (O_2) in Figure 4.7 and from information about the last brand the respondents reported that they purchased. One can now assume that parameter β is a stable parameter whose value will remain unchanged after the introduction of a new brand. Given measures of consumers' preferences for the new brand plus the established brands, which are obtained after a period of trial usage of the new brand, an individual's probability of purchasing a new product can be computed as follows:

$$(4.7) \qquad L_i(t) = \frac{[A_i(t)]^\beta}{[A_i(t)]^\beta + \displaystyle\sum_{k=1}^{m_i} [A_i(k)]^\beta}$$

where

$L_i(t) =$ probability that consumer i chooses brand t after having tried the new brand
$t \quad =$ index for the new brand
$k \quad =$ index for established brands

$A_i(t) =$ estimated preference of consumer i for the new brand t after having tried the new brand

$A_i(k) =$ estimated preference of consumer i for the established brand k after having tried the new brand

The predicted probabilities are conditional on the brand being an element of each consumer's relevant set. In calculating an expected market share for the new brand, ASSESSOR takes into account that the new brand will not necessarily become an element of the relevant set of brands for *all* consumers. Therefore, the expected market share is computed as follows:

$$(4.8) \qquad M(t) = E(t) \frac{\sum_{i=1}^{N} L_i(t)}{N}$$

where

$M(t) =$ expected market share for the new brand t

$E(t) =$ proportion of consumers who include brand t in their relevant set of alternatives

$L_i(t) =$ predicted probability of purchase brand t by consumer i, $i = 1, ..., N$

To assess how the new brand affects the market shares of existing brands, we must compute the market share equilibrium. One must recognize that under the new steady-state conditions the market will consist of two subpopulations, those who have the new brand in their relevant (or consideration) set and those who do not. The proportions of the total market of these two groups are $E(t)$ and $1 - E(t)$. The addition of a new brand is expected to be manifested in the preferences for the established brands as expressed in the post-usage survey *after* exposure to the new brand, that is, in the quantities $A_i(k)$. Furthermore, it is supposed that consumers whose relevant set does not include the new brand will continue to purchase established brands after the introduction of the new brand, in the same way as they did before its entry.

One can now derive expected market shares for the established brands. If the new brand is present in a consumer's set, the purchase probability for any established brand j can be computed as follows:

(4.9) $$L_i(j) = \frac{[A_i(j)]^\beta}{[A_i(t)]^\beta + \sum_{k=1}^{m_i}[A_i(k)]^\beta}$$

$$k = 1,...,j,...,m_i$$

The new brand's market share in the submarket of consumers whose relevant set includes the new brand is computed as follows:

(4.10) $$M'(j) = \frac{\sum_{r(j)} L_i(j)}{N}$$

where the summation $\sum_{r(j)} L_i(j)$ is over the $r(j)$ individuals who include the established brand j in their relevant sets.

For consumers who do not include the new brand in their relevant sets, the probability of purchasing any established brand j can be obtained from equation (6), and within the subpopulation of all such consumers the market share of any established brand j will be

(4.11) $$M''(j) = \frac{\sum_{r(j)} P_i(j)}{N}$$

In order to obtain the established brand's expected market share in a total market, one weights the "unadjusted" shares (equations 10 and 11) by the relative sizes of the two subpopulations:

(4.12) $$M(j) = E(t)M'(j) + (1 - E(t))M''(j)$$

where

$M(j)$ = expected market share for the established brand j after the introduction of new brand t

One can now determine the extent to which a new brand draws from existing brands by comparing the prior market share with the market share after the introduction of the new brand.

Trial-and-repeat model

The trial-and-repeat model in the ASSESSOR system computes the market share that a new brand will obtain by combining new brand trial-and-repeat measures obtained from the laboratory experiment. The market share for new brand t is computed as follows:

$$(4.13) \qquad M(t) = TS$$

where

$T =$ ultimate cumulative trial rate for the new brand t (proportion of all buyers in the target group who ever try the new brand)

$S =$ ultimate repeat purchase rate for the new brand t (new brand's share of subsequent purchases in the product category made by users who have ever made a trial purchase of the new brand)

Trial is assumed to come about in one of two ways: by the receipt and use of free samples or by initial purchases. The incidence of first purchase of the new brand is assumed to depend on the awareness level induced by advertising or other forms of promotion and by the extent of its retail availability. The probability of becoming aware of the new brand and the probability of its availability are presumed to be independent. It is also assumed that the probability of a consumer making a first purchase is independent of the probability of that consumer receiving and using a sample. Using these assumptions, trial is modeled as follows:

$$(4.14) \qquad T = FKD + CU - (FKD)(CU)$$

where

$F =$ long-run probability of a consumer making a first purchase of the new brand assuming awareness and availability (i.e., proportion of consumers making a trial purchase in the long run given that all consumers were aware of it and distribution was complete)

$D =$ long-run probability that the new brand is available to a consumer (i.e., proportion of retail outlets that will ultimately carry the new brand weighted by their sales volume in the product category)

$K =$ long-run probability that a consumer will become aware of the new brand

$C =$ probability that a consumer will receive a sample of the new brand

$U =$ probability that a consumer who receives a sample of the new brand will use it

The probabilities are averages for the particular target group under consideration. To estimate F, we can use the proportion of respondents who purchased the new brand in the laboratory on their simulated shopping trip (O_4 in Figure 4.7). The parameters K, D, and C depend on the type and magnitude of marketing efforts. The translation of the marketing plans into the values of these parameters is done by obtaining managerial judgment and using experiences with similar products, or by analyzing historical data. The value of C is determined in a straightforward manner by looking at the scale of the sampling program. The value of U is determined by looking at the results of similar products or by performing small experiments.

The ultimate repeat-purchase rate (S) is modeled as the equilibrium share of a first-order, two-state Markov process:

$$(4.15) \qquad S \frac{R(k,t)}{1 + R(k,t) - R(t,t)}$$

where

$R(k,t)$ = probability that a consumer who last purchased any of the established brands k will switch to the new brand t on the next buying occasion

$R(t,t)$ = probability that a consumer who last purchased the new brand will repurchase it on the next buying occasion

The estimates of $R(k,t)$ and $R(t,t)$ are derived from measurements obtained in the post-usage survey (O_5 in Figure 4.7).

The two models described above predict the market share for a new product. Convergence increases our confidence in the estimates, whereas divergence may lead to a critical evaluation of the assumptions made. Marketers can use the ASSESSOR model for marketing decision support. Management can evaluate the outcomes of alternative marketing mixes of a new brand (advertising efforts, sales efforts, and so on) before test-marketing the product. Performing this kind of what-if analysis supports the reasoning processes of the marketer. He or she can fine-tune the setup of the marketing mix in such a way that results in the test market will be maximized.

The ASSESSOR system has been very successful in practice. Several hundreds of companies have used it, and its impact on marketing decisions has been substantial. In a large study among firms in which ASSESSOR was applied, Urban and Katz (1983) found that 66% of the products that passed ASSESSOR were successful in the test market. This figure can be compared with the 35.5% success rate that A.C. Nielsen arrived at after systematically studying the success of products in test markets over two decades. In their study Urban and Katz also found that six products were test-marketed despite a negative pretest evaluation; all of them subsequently failed in the test market. This clearly demonstrates the value of a system like ASSESSOR.

4.5   The Impact of Marketing Models and Marketing Decision Support Systems

In this chapter we have presented some specific examples of data-driven marketing management support systems that have been successful in supporting marketing decision making. However, many more such systems have been developed and implemented. More information about the effectiveness of these systems can be obtained from a survey that we carried out among their developers. This survey was restricted to systems that have appeared in the academic literature. For our data collection we identified 44 MMSS by scanning the marketing literature (marketing journals and well-known books on marketing models, such as Lilien, Kotler, and Moorthy 1992 and Eliashberg and Lilien 1993). For each of these MMSS, we sent a questionnaire to the first author of the paper describing the system. The questionnaire contained questions with respect to characteristics of the systems, the problems they were developed for, and the impact they had. Ultimately, 38 questionnaires were returned, a response rate of 86%. Table 4.2 lists the names of the specific MMSS in our database by type, along with the developers of these systems.

The classification of the actual systems into the different categories of marketing management support systems was done by applying two criteria: First, whether a quantitative model (marketing model, marketing information system, marketing decision support system) or qualitative knowledge (marketing expert system, marketing knowledge-based system, marketing case-based reasoning system) was used. Second, whether the system

a. Focused on finding the best solution (marketing model, marketing expert system).

b. Helped the user in developing, adapting, and/or using mental models (marketing information system, marketing decision support system, marketing knowledge-based system).

c. Made descriptions of similar problem situations in the past available to its user (marketing case-based reasoning system).

d. Was able to recognize patterns and to learn (marketing neural networks).

Table 4.2   Marketing Management Support Systems in our Survey

Type of MMSS	Systems in the Sample
Marketing Models (MM)	MEDIAC (Little and Lodish 1969)
	SPRINTER (Urban 1970)
	GEOLINE (Hess and Samuels 1971)
	CALLPLAN (Lodish 1971)
	DETAILER (Montgomery, Silk, and Zaragoza 1971)
	ADMOD (Aaker 1975)
	MODEL FOR ALLOCATING RETAIL OUTLET BUILDING RESOURCES (Lilien and Rao 1976)
	STRATPORT (Larréché and Srinivasan 1981)
	PRICESTRAT (Simon 1982)
	DEFENDER (Hauser and Shugan 1983)
	SALES TERRITORY ALIGNMENT MODEL (Zoltners and Sinha 1983)
	SH.A.R.P. (Bultez and Naert 1988)
	SIMOPT (Green and Krieger 1989)
Marketing Expert Systems (MES)	INNOVATOR (Ram and Ram 1988)
	NEGOTEX (Rangaswamy et al. 1989)
	ADCAD (Burke et al. 1990)
	DEALMAKER (McCann and Gallagher 1990)
	PROMOTION DETECTIVE (McCann and Gallagher 1990)
	TEXTBOOK PROMOTION ADVISOR (McCann and Gallagher 1990)
	ESWA (Neibecker 1990)
	SHANEX (Alpar 1991)
Marketing Decision Support Systems (MDSS)	ADBUDG (Little 1970)
	THE SYSTEM OF PROMOTIONAL MODELS (Rao and Lilien 1972)
	NEWPROD (Assmuss 1975)
	BRANDAID (Little 1975a)
	THE A/S RESPONSE MODEL (Rao and Miller 1975)
	PERCEPTOR (Urban 1975)
	MAPLAMOD (Bloom and Stewart 1977)
	TRACKER (Blattberg and Golanty 1978)
	ADVISOR2 (Lilien 1979)
	ASSESSOR (Silk and Urban 1978)
	NEWS (Pringle, Wilson, and Brody 1982)
	SCANPRO (Wittink et al. 1988)

Type of MMSS	Systems in the Sample
Marketing Knowledge-Based Systems (MKBS)	PROMOTOR (Abraham and Lodish 1987) CAAS (Kroeber-Riel 1993) DATASERVER PARTNERS/COVERSTORY (Schmitz et al. 1990)
Marketing Case-Based Reasoning Systems (MCBR)	ADDUCE (Burke 1991) CASE-BASED REASONING SYSTEM FOR FORECASTING PROMOTIONAL SALES (McIntyre et al. 1993)

The distinction between marketing models and marketing decision support systems was based on whether the system just contained models (marketing decision support system) or also contained optimization procedures (marketing model). In the first case the user can carry out what-if analyses and in that way develop a mental model of the market. In the case of marketing models the system can be used to answer the what-should question, that is, to find the best solution. Based on these criteria, ADBUDG, for example, is classified as a marketing decision support system and CALLPLAN as a marketing model, despite the fact that both systems use the same decision calculus approach for determining the response function. However, CALLPLAN aims at finding one optimal account call schedule, whereas ADBUDG will provide the decision maker with various outcomes for alternative advertising decisions. The difference between marketing models and marketing decision support systems is related to the distinction between normative (MM) and predictive (MDSS) marketing models (Naert and Leeflang 1978).

As we mentioned already, marketing information systems are predominantly developed in practice, but most of them are not documented in the literature; therefore, they are not included in the survey. Apart from the data-driven marketing management support systems, such as marketing models and marketing decision support systems, we did include knowledge-driven systems such as marketing expert systems and marketing case-based reasoning systems in the survey. (These systems are described in the next two chapters.) However, since the use of knowledge-based systems in marketing has only started recently, the majority of the systems in the survey are either marketing models or marketing decision support systems.

The results in Table 4.3 show that both marketing models and marketing decision support systems have been successful in supporting marketers. Even though several of the systems were not developed with the primary aim of being implemented in real-life decision situations, on average per system a relatively high number of companies have adopted them. Furthermore, especially in the case of marketing models, the endurance of their use was also high. A substantial number of companies are still using the data-driven MMSS that they once adopted. If a company did adopt a system, usually these systems were very successful in terms of their impact on the decisions that were actually made. Users were also highly satisfied. Finally, the figures in the table show that there is a large variance in the success of the systems.

Table 4.3   The Success of Marketing Models and Marketing Decision Support Systems
              (standard deviations are in parentheses)

Indicators of Success	Marketing Models		Marketing Decision Support Systems	
Number of companies that have adopted the system	41.77	(66.44)	72.67	(108.57)
Percentage of companies that adopted a system and still use it	46.67	(45.00)	22.78	(33.74)
Impact on actual decisions (very small = 1, very large = 7)	5.64	(1.12)	5.25	(1.55)
Successfulness of implementations (not successful = 1, very successful = 7)	6.09	(0.83)	5.25	(1.49)
Satisfaction of users (not satisfied = 1, very satisfied = 7)	5.73	(0.79)	5.25	(0.75)

Most of the data-driven marketing management support systems were described in the marketing literature in the late 1960s and 1970s. In the 1980s the number being described in the literature dropped. During this decade a new category of MMSS—knowledge-driven marketing management support systems—started to be described in the literature (see Figure 4.8). In Chapters 5 and 6 we discuss this category of systems.

Number of Systems

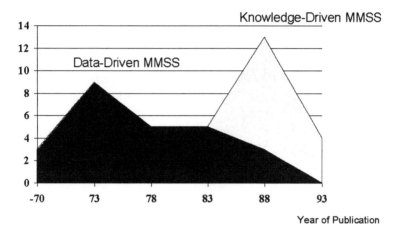

Figure 4.8   Appearance in the Literature of Data-Driven and Knowledge-Driven Marketing Management Support Systems (the numbers refer to the midpoints of five-year periods)

Key Points

- *From the early 1960s onward, marketing management support systems have been developed. The first three decades of their existence have been dominated by so-called data-driven systems. These systems emphasize marketing data and analytical capabilities.*

- *Marketing models, marketing information systems, and marketing decision support systems are the most prominent types of data-driven MMSS.*

- *Marketing models represent the start of the use of computers to support marketing decision making. They take a normative approach and aim at providing a decision maker with an optimal solution.*

- *To build a marketing model, a marketer must take three steps: (1) specify a functional form, (2) determine parameter values, and (3) validate the model.*

- *Marketing information systems intend to manage data from various sources in order to provide marketers with the information necessary for marketing decision making.*

- *Most MMSS that are actually used in companies can be classified as marketing information systems.*

- *Marketing decision support systems are flexible systems that recognize the importance of two-way communication between the marketer and the system. They do not replace the marketer but stimulate and support him or her in solving problems that are not very well structured.*

- *The marketing models and marketing decision support systems that have been developed by marketing academics and implemented in real-world situations have had significant impact on the quality of marketing decision making.*

Chapter 5

Knowledge-Driven Marketing Management Support Systems I: Artificial Intelligence, Knowledge Representation, and Expert Systems

Learning Objectives

- *To acquire insight into developments in artificial intelligence and cognitive science and how these developments have given rise to knowledge-based decision support systems.*

- *To become familiar with the most important methods for knowledge representation.*

- *To learn about knowledge-processing methods, in particular, rule-based reasoning methods.*

- *To become familiar with the principles of expert systems.*

- *To understand the application of expert systems in marketing so far.*

- *To understand the characteristics of marketing problems that make them suitable for applying expert systems.*

5.1   Introduction

A marketing manager is exposed to a continuous stream of data and information, which he or she combines with the knowledge and experience in his or her mind in order to detect problems and react to opportunities in the market. A marketer is constantly trying to figure out what is going on and why (monitoring and diagnosis) and constantly devising marketing actions and programs that should lead to developments in the desired direction (planning and design). The purpose of marketing management support systems is to help the marketing decision maker in carrying out these tasks.

Typically, marketing problems involve large numbers of variables with complex relationships between them. Often marketing problems can be expressed at least partly in numbers; therefore, at least some of the activities of marketing managers are *quantitative* in nature. The marketer usually has data about important market variables, such as sales, market shares, prices, and marketing efforts (e.g., advertising and personal selling expenditures). The marketing management support systems that were discussed in the last chapter (marketing models, marketing information systems, and marketing decision support systems) deal with these quantitative data. Therefore, we called these systems *data-driven* marketing management support systems. Such MMSS can be used to analyze trends, find the causes of phenomena in the marketplace (e.g., the causes of a major decrease in market share), and determine optimal values for the marketing instruments. However, often a marketing problem can be quantified only partially, and especially as marketing problems are more complex and ill structured, their qualitative aspects play an important role. Consequently, the monitoring/diagnosis and planning/design activities of the marketer will practically always involve qualitative aspects. Even though, for example, a marketing manager may have a mathematical model available for quantitatively predicting the effect of sales promotions on sales and market share, he or she still has to consider the effect of a promotion on the long-run reputation of the brand or the possibility of a retaliate response by a competitor. Both are more qualitative aspects. Certain marketing decisions are intrinsically qualitative. An example of such a decision is the design of an advertisement. Finally, and most important, human reasoning itself is more qualitative than quantitative in nature. This general observation also applies to the particular ways marketing managers reason about marketing phenomena. When a marketing decision maker is reasoning, his or her view of the world (mental model) plays an important role. Furthermore, experience with earlier cases and pertinent information (facts) about marketing phenomena (e.g., actions of competitors) are also important for the way a marketing decision maker solves problems. In this context we speak of the *knowledge* of a marketing decision maker and how this knowledge is used in solving problems. Marketing decision making, to a great extent, is the processing of this knowledge.

In this chapter and the next we address the question of how marketing management support systems can deal with knowledge, and we describe *knowledge-driven* marketing management support systems. In order to reason with qualitative knowledge, a marketer needs methods of knowledge representation and knowledge processing. Specific examples of MMSS that use these methods and in which the marketing knowledge component is the primary element include marketing expert systems, marketing knowledge-based systems, marketing case-based reasoning systems, marketing neural networks, and marketing creativity support systems. The principles of knowledge-driven marketing management support systems come from cognitive science, especially the field of artificial intelligence (AI).

We deal with knowledge-driven marketing management support systems in two chapters, this one and the next. Following this introduction, we begin the present chapter with a brief discourse on the field of artificial intelligence. The subsequent section presents the most important *knowledge representation* schemes as they are used in MMSS. Then we discuss knowledge manipulation, or *reasoning with knowledge,* which involves generating new knowledge from existing knowledge. One important technique for reasoning with knowledge is a (rule-based) *expert system,* which we describe in the last section of this chapter. Chapter 6 starts with another reasoning technology, *case-based reasoning.* After that we elaborate on one of the more recent developments in AI, *neural networks,* and describe how they can be used in marketing. Chapter 6 concludes with a discussion of *creativity support systems.* For each of these topics in the two chapters on knowledge-based MMSS, we start with the (general) principles and then describe implementations in marketing.

5.2 Artificial Intelligence

Since World War II numerous researchers have been interested in exploring the workings of the human mind. These researchers have a variety of different backgrounds, including cognitive psychology, neurophysiology, linguistics, anthropology, philosophy, and artificial intelligence. This emerging, interdisciplinary field, which studies how humans acquire and use knowledge, is mostly referred to as *cognitive science.* Many different aspects of the workings of the human mind have been objects of research. Examples are vision (how do people see?), language and speech, movement (e.g., walking), perception, memory, thought, reasoning, and problem solving. The driving factor behind the explosion of research on the human mind was the invention of the programmable digital computer and the accompanying development of the theory of computation. An important question that has been asked is, To what extent can human thinking be represented in algorithms that can be run on digital computers? Far before the advent of computers David Hume (1711–1776) already held the view that "cognition is computation," implying that the different operations of the mind can be described as algorithmic computations. In the nineteenth century there were already efforts to build programmable machines that could carry out human reasoning tasks such as simple calculations (e.g., Charles Babbage in 1835). In the middle of the twentieth century the modern computer arrived, and around the same time Alan Turing (1950) made important contributions to the theory of computation. His conclusion was that a digital computer has great potential for acting as a thinking device, that is, to mimic and simulate human thought. As the first computers were emerging, Turing foresaw that "machines will eventually compete with men in all purely intellectual fields." A large stream of approaches and programs in which machines actually simulated human thought and reasoning has followed these reflections on the theoretical possibility of representing human thought in computer programs.

Within cognitive science *artificial intelligence* (AI) is the field that emphasizes the building of computer programs that mimic human perception, information processing, thinking, and reasoning. The basic, scientific purpose of artificial intelligence is to understand human intelligence by building computer programs that reproduce it. In pursuing this goal, AI has produced a lot of concepts, tools, and methods for developing computer programs that contain intelligence and knowledge and can be used for solving a broad variety of practical problems. Over the years these tools have been applied successfully in a multitude of different fields. In this book we will approach AI from the perspective of how we can use its concepts and methods in systems that support marketing managers in making decisions, that is, marketing management support systems.

5.2.1   Developments in Artificial Intelligence

The term *artificial intelligence* was coined at a historic conference that took place at Dartmouth University in 1956. The expectations and orientations of AI have changed substantially over its lifetime. First, there was the optimistic idea that a relatively simple, general mechanism underlies all human reasoning and that the representation of that mechanism in a computer would constitute a powerful device for simulating human reasoning in every domain. This was when Simon and Newell developed their "logic theorist" and their general problem solver (GPS), which were meant as general-purpose reasoning devices. These first programs were able to solve puzzles and to prove theorems of symbolic logic. However, they appeared to be weak in solving practical, real-life problems. General-purpose algorithms were unable to deal with the peculiarities of practical problems in specific domains.

A new phase in the development of AI started in the late sixties with the recognition of the importance of *domain knowledge*. This perspective emerged after positive experiences with programs such as DENDRAL and MYCIN. DENDRAL (Buchanan and Feigenbaum 1978) is able to analyze a spectrum produced by a mass spectrometer and infer the underlying molecular structure. MYCIN (Shortliffe 1976) finds the causes of infectious diseases in blood based on the outcomes of tests and measurements. In both cases the programs are fed large amounts of knowledge about the specific domain, obtained from human experts. It was found that the power of an AI program in solving problems depends heavily on the amount and quality of the domain knowledge these programs contain. The emphasis of AI thus shifted from finding general-purpose algorithms to finding methods for encoding and using domain-specific knowledge. This resulted in a distinction between, on the one hand, the reasoning mechanism, and, on the other hand, the domain knowledge to which this mechanism is applied. Thus the concept of an *inference engine* emerged.

An inference engine is a device that contains generic knowledge about how to reason. Such a device reasons with the domain knowledge from a specific field. The combination of these two components is the principle of operation of an expert system. Expert systems have grown into a very important area of AI; thousands of them have been developed and deployed in all kinds of industries. Later in this chapter we will return to the subject of expert systems and their use in marketing.

A more recent development in AI is the emergence of (artificial) neural networks. These are inductive devices for pattern recognition and classification that are based on the architecture of the human brain. Like expert systems, neural networks have also caused a big boom in AI and have led to many practical applications. As we will see later, neural networks are also useful for marketing. Apart from the developments of expert systems and neural networks, which have drawn widespread public attention, there has been a lot of other useful research in AI on topics such as knowledge acquisition, knowledge representation, reasoning with knowledge, planning, and learning. Of particular importance for marketing are the different modes of knowledge representation and the different ways of reasoning that have been developed. Examples are rule-based reasoning and case-based reasoning. In this book we will limit the discussion to those areas of AI that are directly relevant for the development of marketing management support systems, such as problem solving, reasoning, and learning.

AI has developed a number of other subfields such as, for example, natural language processing, speech recognition, speech synthesis, computer vision, and robotics. AI became a commercial industry, with many start-up companies trying to sell their knowledge technologies to interested clients in business and government. In the year 1986 the total revenue of the AI industry exceeded $1 billion for the first time (Newquist 1994).

From its conception, the field of AI has been in the public limelight. The very term *artificial intelligence* appeals to the human imagination, and over time the field has drawn a lot of attention through publications in the general press, science fiction books, games, and movies (e.g., *2001: A Space Odyssey,* made in 1968). Mysterious overtones got connected to the term AI ("machines that outsmart men"), partly caused by exaggerated claims that were made early on. The development of AI has been strongly influenced by public (governmental) funding, first in the United States (especially through DARPA, the Defense Advanced Research Project Agency), later also in the United Kingdom, France, other European countries, and Japan (The Fifth Generation Project). Compared to its original claims, the achievements of AI have progressed more slowly than expected. However, significant progress has definitely been made. In the late fifties Simon and Newell (1958) predicted that within ten years a computer would be world chess champion. It was not until 10 February 1996 that the computer program Deep Blue won a chess game from the governing world chess champion, Gary Kasparov. On 11 May 1997 Deep Blue even won a match from Kasparov. Although this achievement happened almost 30 years later than Simon and Newell had predicted, for many it still came as a shock.

In these few pages we have sketched only a broad outline of developments in the fields of cognitive science and artificial intelligence. For more information we refer the reader to books such as Johnson-Laird (1988), Luger and Stubblefield (1993), Haberlandt (1994), Luger (1995), and Nilsson (1998). A more applied introduction is Dutta (1993). We also did not deal with the controversies that AI has raised. These controversies have been discussed in books with such illustrative titles as *Mind over Machine* (Dreyfus and Dreyfus 1988), *The Emperor's New Mind* (Penrose 1989), and *The Brain Makers* (Newquist 1994).

5.2.2   Artificial Intelligence in Management and Marketing

In the area of *management* support systems, quantitative approaches applying the methods from operations research have traditionally been the dominant perspectives. This is especially true for areas of management such as production, logistics, and physical distribution, where problems are relatively well structured. More recently the work of Herbert Simon, one of the founding fathers of AI as well as a management theorist and winner of the Nobel Prize in Economics, became more influential. Books such as *The New Science of Management Decision* (Simon 1960) and *Human Problem Solving* (Newell and Simon 1972) have had a major impact on the way researchers approached decision making in organizations. In marketing we can observe a parallel development. As we saw in Chapter 4, the field of *marketing management* support systems also started with a model-building approach (Montgomery and Urban 1969; Kotler 1971). However, because of the recognition that marketing problems seldom have a purely quantitative character and also because of the advances that have been made in the field of AI, we increasingly see knowledge-based/intelligent systems that are used for the support of marketing management. The adoption and use of concepts and tools from AI for solving marketing problems has started only in the second half of the eighties. So far, we have seen applications of expert systems, knowledge-based systems, case-based reasoning systems, and neural networks in marketing. Later in this chapter and in the following chapter we discuss several examples. However, before that we introduce the principles underlying these tools, beginning with a discussion of methods for knowledge representation.

5.3   Knowledge Representation

In order to deal with knowledge, we need a precise language in which we use words, phrases, and sentences to represent and reason about elements in the real world, their properties, and their mutual relationships. Problem solving with knowledge involves (1) knowledge representation schemes that put knowledge into a form that makes it accessible to a problem-solving procedure and (2) procedures that can carry out operations on the knowledge and derive solutions from it. The latter requirement is often referred to as *knowledge processing, knowledge manipulation,* or *reasoning with knowledge.* The present section deals with knowledge representation; the next one, with knowledge processing.

In the field of artificial intelligence there are basically two approaches to knowledge representation. The *symbolic representation* school, sometimes called the "classical" school, starts from the premise that intelligence resides in physical symbol systems. In this view knowledge manipulation is conceived of as performing operations on symbol patterns. Intelligent activity, in either humans or machines, makes use of symbol patterns to represent a problem domain. Problem solving means operating on symbol patterns, generating possible solutions, and then selecting a solution from these possibilities. The alternative view, the *connectionist* approach, does not start from patterns of symbols. In this view intelligence arises from the collective behavior of large numbers of interacting components that are not in themselves interpretable. The knowledge of a connectionist system is contained in the structure and weights of the connections between the components. These weights are determined by fitting the system to observations. No concepts or symbols are specified a priori. Since the structure of connectionist systems is derived from neural systems in the brain, these systems are often called *neural networks*.

The symbolic representation school can be subdivided into (1) rule-based representation of knowledge and (2) networked representation of knowledge. In *rule-based representation* schemes knowledge is treated as a collection of separate fragments of knowledge, expressed as propositions or rules. In *networked representation* schemes knowledge is organized in thematically related structures. Figure 5.1 gives a schematic picture of the different methods for knowledge processing and the sections where they are discussed in this book.

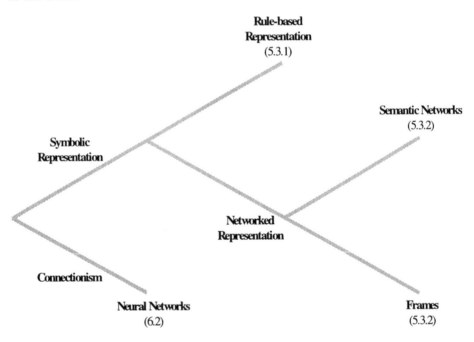

Figure 5.1   Classification of Knowledge Representation Methods with the Sections where they are Discussed in this Book

Apart from *knowledge representation* methods, we also have *knowledge processing* methods. Examples are expert systems and case-based reasoning systems. Expert systems make use of rules, whereas case-based reasoning systems most often use networked representation of knowledge. Because of their close relationship, we will discuss these knowledge-processing methods immediately after the symbolic methods of knowledge representation (starting in section 5.4). The last part of Chapter 5 will be devoted to expert systems and their applications in marketing, while the first part of Chapter 6 will discuss case-based reasoning systems. Then, in the second part of Chapter 6, we will deal with the connectionist approach and discuss the principles of neural networks and their use in marketing.

5.3.1   Rule-Based Knowledge Representation

Artificial intelligence primarily deals with the qualitative aspects of a problem. From its earliest development, logic has been used as a means to express what we know about the world; logic is also the basis of rule-based knowledge representation. In particular, predicate calculus, a branch of formal logic with well-defined formal semantics and complete inference rules, is used for this purpose. The building blocks of knowledge are "propositional symbols." A propositional symbol is a statement about the world that is either true or false. Examples of such statements are "it is raining" or "sales are up." We can create a "predicate," for example, weather, which describes the relationship between a date and the type of weather. Like propositional symbols, predicates are either true or false. For example, if the predicate **weather** (Tuesday, rain) is true, this implies that it is raining on Tuesday. Inference rules are used to derive true/false statements about propositions from true/false statements about other propositions. An important inference rule is *modus ponens,* which says that if both

P *is true*   (1)

and

$P \rightarrow Q$ (2)

then

Q *is true*   (3)

In words: If we know that P is true (1), and it is also known that P implies Q (2), then we can conclude that Q is true (3). For example, if we know that "Socrates is a man" (P), and it is also known that "all men are mortal" (P $\rightarrow$ Q), then the conclusion must be that "Socrates is mortal" (Q). This classical syllogism is an application of *modus ponens.* In this way new knowledge is inferred from existing knowledge.

The rules in rule-based knowledge representation schemes can be represented in two different ways:

a. Formal logical expressions using the syntax from predicate calculus. We might, for example, have the following predicates:

   (1) **Likes** (X, Y) which is defined to be true if person X likes brand Y

   (2) **Dutch** (X) which is defined to be true if X is Dutch

   (3) **Jenever** (Y) which is defined to be true if Y is a brand from the product category Jenever[1]

We can now write down the logical expression

$$\forall X \ \forall Y \ \textbf{Dutch} \ (X) \ \text{and} \ \textbf{Jenever} \ (Y) \ \textbf{Likes} \ (X, Y) \qquad (5.1)$$

This expressions says that for all X and Y, if **Dutch** (X) is true (i.e., X is Dutch; see predicate (2)), and **Jenever** (Y) is true (i.e., Y is a Jenever brand; see predicate (3)), then **Likes** (X, Y) is true, implying that X likes Y (by predicate (1)).

In this expression $\forall$ is the so-called universal quantifier ("for all"), which indicates that the expression is true for all of its values.

So if the following would be known:

Dutch (Jansen), implying that Jansen is Dutch (by predicate (2))

and

Jenever (Bols), implying that Bols is a brand of Jenever (by predicate (3)),

then equation (5.1) would immediately produce the conclusion that Jansen likes Bols.

b. Expressions in the form of rules. Such expressions have the following general structure:

IF *antecedent* THEN *conclusion.*

The antecedent is the condition. If the condition is fulfilled, then the conclusion is drawn. It is said that the rule then "fires." A rule can

---

[1]   Jenever is a very popular product in Holland, a kind of brandy.

have one or several antecedents. In the latter case the general structure is as follows:

IF *antecedent 1* AND *antecedent 2* AND ...
(*additional antecedents*) THEN *conclusion*   (5.2)

With this syntax the same statement as expression (5.1) would be formulated as follows:

IF "the person is Dutch" AND "the brand is of the product category jenever" THEN "that person will like the brand."

We will return to rule-based knowledge representation in our discussion of expert systems in section 5.4.

5.3.2   Networked Knowledge Representation

There are two main forms of networked knowledge representation: semantic networks and frames.

Semantic Networks

In the rule-based knowledge representation schemes, knowledge is represented as a collection of separate, small pieces. Although this representation makes knowledge easily accessible for logical operations, it is probably not the way information is stored in human memory. Humans tend to think in terms of ideas or concepts, and concepts derive their meaning from networks of similarities with other concepts. There is evidence from cognitive psychology that the storage of knowledge in the mind of a human can be conceived of as coherent networks of concepts linked by semantic relations. These networks of relations are called *semantic networks*. For example, the concept "Coca-Cola" in the mind of a marketer might be networked to other concepts as shown in Figure 5.2.

For a marketer Coca-Cola is first of all the prototype of a global brand. Therefore, Coca-Cola is linked to the concept of global brands, and in this way it has semantic relations with other global brands, such as Heineken. The word *Coca-Cola* will also immediately prompt the name of that other cola brand, its eternal rival Pepsi. Coca-Cola also has of course a direct semantic link with the concept of soft drinks and, perhaps at a somewhat larger distance, with the concept of parties. Through the concept of parties, there is another link with Heineken, which is also a drink offered at parties. Furthermore, Coca-Cola may have associations with the concept of Diet Cola, and in this way it may be connected to concepts such as Diet Pepsi and health.

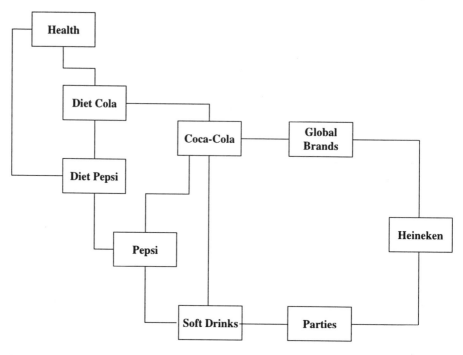

Figure 5.2   Network of Coca-Cola in the Mind of a Marketer

The notions of how humans store information as coherent structures of knowledge have inspired the networked knowledge representation schemes in AI. Whereas the logical (rule-based) representation grew out of the work of philosophers and mathematicians, networked representations can be traced back to psychologists and linguists. Networked representation schemes for knowledge take the mutual links between concepts as the starting point. In these representation schemes the nodes in the networks can be either relatively simple concepts or more complex data structures. Examples of the latter occur when the nodes represent entire structures, for example, frames, scripts, scenarios, or cases. Especially *frame-based* representation is increasingly used in marketing management support systems; we will elaborate on this topic next.

Frames

The concept of a frame has been proposed by Minsky (1981). A frame is a data structure for representing well-understood, stereotyped situations. Framelike structures seem to organize our knowledge of the world. When we think of, for example, the concept "supermarket" we use the stereotype of a large room with a series of aisles that are stocked on both sides with products on parallel shelves, with special compartments for vegetables and meat. Customers walk between the aisles filling their shopping carts and purchase their selections at one of the checkout counters, where the bar codes of their purchases are read optically. Such a stereotype can be called a *frame*. Marketing decision makers also use frames in their thinking. For example, for a product manager a brand in the category FMCG (fast-moving consumer goods) would be a stereotypical situation. The brand would be competing for sales and market share with other brands, would fight for shelf space in supermarkets, and would use advertising and sales promotions to reach its goals. We can think of frames as networks of nodes and relations. The concept "brand," for example, is related to the concept "supermarket" and also to the concept "sales promotion."

A frame has a data structure in the form of "slots" or attributes. The product manager of a particular brand of beer would, for example, think about that product in terms of such attributes as the strength of the brand name (brand added value), its stage in the product life cycle, awareness, purchase frequency, price, market share, perceptual attributes (e.g., color, taste), loyalty, and percentage of alcohol. In a frame-based representation there would be slots corresponding with all these attributes (see Figure 5.3).

Frame-based representation of knowledge in AI employs *hierarchical structures*. This approach is inspired by the way humans store information. There is experimental evidence that in the human mind knowledge is stored in a hierarchical fashion, with the more general (abstract) concepts at the higher levels, and that information is stored at the highest appropriate level of the taxonomy. We know, for example, that a canary is a bird and that a bird is an animal. From animals we know that all animals can breathe and have a skin. So the latter information is stored at the animal level. That they can fly and have feathers is specific for birds; therefore, this knowledge is stored at the bird level. Finally, a canary can sing and is yellow. Since this does not apply to all birds, the human mind seems to store this information at the canary level. In a classic experiment Collins and Quillian (1969) demonstrated that it takes longer for subjects to answer the question "Can a canary fly?" than to answer the question "Can a canary sing?" Their explanation for this is that the information about singing is directly stored with "canary," whereas to answer the question about flying, the respondent must go up to the level of "bird." The answer to the question "Does a canary have a skin?" took even longer, since in this case the respondent has to travel even farther up the memory hierarchy, to the level of "animal."

Knowledge representation based on frame-based systems follows this hierarchical structure. Classes are defined, and for each class it is known what the "parent class" is and which (sub)classes it has as "children." For example, there might be a class "brands_in_FMCG" of which the subclass "brands_of_beer" would be a child. An "instance" is a concretization with its own identity. Examples of instances of the subclass "brands_of_beer" are

Heineken, Amstel, and Grolsch. Related to the hierarchical structure is the phenomenon of inheritance. A child inherits, in principle, the slots and their values from its parent. These can be considered as default values, which can be overruled by additional information. For example, in Figure 5.3 some of the slots will have different values for different brands of beer (for example, for brand added value, awareness, or market share). For other slots, however (for example, purchase frequency and alcohol percentage), the values might be equal and determined at the level brands_of_beer.

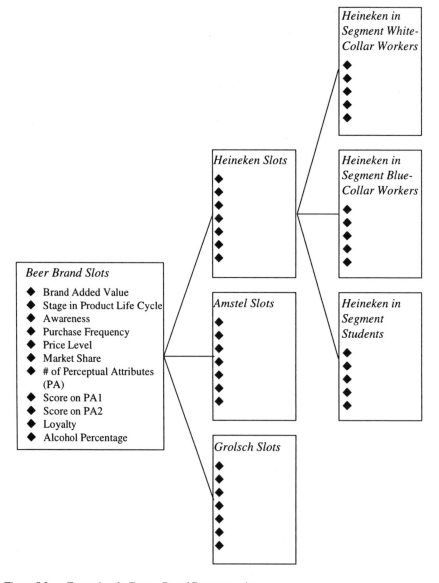

Figure 5.3   Example of a Frame-Based Representation

It is possible to define additional slots at a lower hierarchical level. The slot "alcohol percentage," for example, is not relevant for all the subclasses in the general class brands_in_FMCG and is, therefore, more properly defined at the subordinate class brands_of_beer. Each concept, represented by a frame, is called an object. The inheritance property is very useful in case of the creation of new objects. Suppose we are interested in the position of Heineken in the market segment blue-collar workers. For this purpose we create an object Heineken in the segment blue-collar workers. The same frame can be used for the brand Heineken in general with, for the most part, the same values. We only have to enter new values for those attributes about which we have specific, unique information for the segment blue-collar workers.

The reader may have observed that the terminology of frames is very similar to that of objects (the building blocks of object-oriented systems), which we discussed in Chapter 3. This observation is correct. Concepts such as stereotypes, classes, slots, and inheritance have emerged from the AI literature as well as from the field of computer science (Harmon 1995). The role of objects in object-oriented systems is directly comparable to the role of frames in cognitive science. The fact that humans tend to think in framelike structures with hierarchically organized information storage may well be an explanation for the quick acceptance of the object-oriented paradigm by managers.

We have now discussed two major knowledge representation schemes that have been developed in AI and that are used in marketing management support systems: rule-based and networked knowledge representation. Although these paradigms are conceptually very different, increasingly we see the use of hybrid systems (Luger and Stubblefield 1993) that incorporate both rule-based and frame-based knowledge representation. Such "hybrid environments" combine the advantages of the realism of networked knowledge representation with the rigor of logical reasoning. Frames are very good at representing a specific domain. Rules are very good at describing heuristic problem-solving knowledge. Advanced frame-based development environments such as KAPPA (used for the BRANDFRAME system, described in Chapter 8) offer these hybrid features.

5.4 Knowledge Processing with Rule-Based Reasoning Systems

In the last section we discussed representation methods for existing knowledge. Knowledge *processing* refers to the creation of new knowledge out of existing knowledge. People, in their minds, are manipulating knowledge all the time; this is called *reasoning*. How do humans process knowledge, and how can these processes be represented in computer programs? We will discuss two major knowledge-processing techniques or reasoning methods that have been developed in AI and that are very relevant for marketing: rule-based reasoning systems (in the remainder of this chapter) and case-based reasoning systems (in the first part of Chapter 6). It will be clear that for rule-based knowledge processing, rule-based knowledge representation is used. As we mentioned earlier, for case-based reasoning, the network paradigm is the dominant mode of knowledge representation.

5.4.1   Production Systems

After having monitored many human subjects in various problem-solving activities, Newell and Simon (1972) came to the conclusion that there is a basic mechanism through which humans solve problems. The problem-solving process starts from a set of *initial conditions* and a *goal* that has to be reached. There is a sequence of operations that leads the decision maker in a series of steps from the initial conditions to the goal. The "resources" that the individual has available to perform this sequence of steps is his or her knowledge, expressed as a set of "condition-action pairs." Operators used to transform knowledge into new knowledge or actions are called *productions*. These are of the form: IF (condition1, ..., condition *n*) THEN (action 1, ..., action *m*); see Payne, Bettman, and Johnson (1993). Expression (5.2) is an example of such a production. Hence, the name *production system* exists for this type of reasoning mechanism.

The productions constitute the problem-solving skills of a person. They are stored in the so-called *long-term memory*. Productions can be invoked by the pattern of a particular problem instance and then used to produce new knowledge. The problem-solving process starts from the initial conditions, which will usually contain knowledge that makes the antecedent conditions true of one or more production rules that a person has in his or her long-term memory. If the antecedent condition of a particular rule is satisfied, such a rule is said to be executed or "to fire," which will produce new knowledge. The *working memory* refers to the current focus of attention of the problem solver and contains the propositions that are known to be true at that particular stage of the decision process. In summary, a production system consists of the following elements (Luger and Stubblefield 1993, Chap. 5):

1. The set of production rules, the "productions." A production is a condition-action pair (as discussed above) and defines a single piece of problem-solving knowledge.

2. The working memory that contains the current state of the world in the reasoning process. At any stage of the reasoning process a number of

propositions are known to be true and others are not (yet) known to be true.

3. The recognize-act cycle, which is the structure that controls the reasoning process from the initial conditions to the true/not-true declaration of the goal.

We will illustrate these concepts with a marketing example. Suppose the category manager of salad dressings of the (imaginary) supermarket chain Super has to make a decision whether or not to introduce a private-label dressing under the name Super. Let's assume that the category manager derives his solution from the rules in his long-term memory, as described in Figure 5.4.

---

(1) If the private label has an attractive margin, and if it is possible to offer the private label with a guaranteed quality level, then we will introduce a private label in this product category.

(2) If one of the A-brand manufacturers is willing to produce the private label, it is possible to produce a private label with a guaranteed quality level.

(3) If there is no strong price competition among the existing brands, a private label can have an attractive margin.

(4) If the leading brand holds a dominant position, there is no strong price competition among the existing brands.

Figure 5.4   Rules in the Mind of Super's Salad Dressing Category Manager

---

A.   The leading brand holds a dominant position in the market.

B.   There is no strong price competition among the existing brands.

C.   A private label has an attractive margin.

D.   It is possible to produce a private label with a guaranteed quality level.

E.   One of the A-brand manufacturers is willing to produce the private label.

F.   The advice is to introduce a private label in this product category.

Figure 5.5   Elementary Propositions

In these rules we can distinguish the elementary propositions, as described in Figure 5.5.

The first rule of Figure 5.4 contains three of these elementary propositions: the private label has an attractive margin (C), it is possible to offer the private label with a guaranteed quality level (D), and introduce a private label in this product category (F). The rule says: If C is true, and if D is true, then the decision is F. This can be summarized by the expression C & D → F. In this way we can summarize the four rules of Figure 5.4 in terms of the elementary propositions, as follows:

(1) C & D → F
(2) E → D
(3) B → C
(4) A → B

The assumption underlying rule 4 might be that a dominant brand will act as a price leader, with the other brands acting as followers, in this way preventing price competition. The heuristic behind rule 3 is that in the case of limited price competition the prices of manufacturer's brands tend to be high and, hence, it will be relatively easy to introduce a private label at a lower price that still has an attractive margin for the retailer. Rule 2 expresses the category manager's confidence that a current producer of an A-brand will be able to produce the private label at Super's quality specifications. Finally, rule 1 is a managerial rule, saying that the private label will be introduced if an attractive margin can be realized and if there are no serious quality risks. Proposition F is called the *goal*.

How would the category manager solve a problem with this information? Suppose for the particular situation of the salad dressing market that the manager has the following case-specific information:

In the salad dressing market the largest brand has a 70% market share, and the number two in the market (with an 18% market share) is willing to produce salad dressing under the Super label.

According to the production system approach, the problem-solving process of the category manager can be described as follows. The information in italics constitutes the *initial conditions*. The category manager has to use this information, together with the knowledge from his long-term memory (the rules from Figure 5.4) to arrive at a conclusion about the *goal*, that is, whether or not to introduce a private label. As a start, the information in italics about the market share of the largest brand makes the antecedent condition of rule 4 true (market leader holding a dominant position). Rule 4 thus fires. We know that its conclusion (no strong price competition among existing brands) is true. From the initial conditions we also know that the antecedent condition of rule 2 (an A-brand manufacturer willing to produce the private label) is true, and, therefore, this rule will also fire. This produces the conclusion that a private label with a guaranteed quality level is possible. At this stage, both antecedent conditions of rule 1 are true. Hence, this rule fires, too, and the managerial conclusion "introduce a private brand" is drawn.

5.4.2   Expert Systems

We will now deal with several aspects of expert systems.

Principles of Expert Systems

Expert systems have been developed out of the notion of production systems. Humans are supposed to solve a problem/reach a goal by moving, in a number of if-then steps (productions), to a final conclusion or action (Newell and Simon 1972). If these rules are put into a machine, along with the mechanism that carries out the sequence of if-then steps needed to travel from the initial conditions to the final conclusion, we have a (rule-based) expert system. The name *expert system* stems from the fact that the rules are often deduced from the knowledge of experts in the domain to which the system applies. For example, the rules in Figure 5.4 are deduced from the expertise of the category manager of the supermarket chain. Expert systems are computer programs that use heuristic strategies developed by humans to solve specific classes of problems. In expert systems there is a principal separation of domain knowledge and procedural knowledge. The latter refers to the way a program, in a step-by-step fashion, tries to establish whether the goals are true or not-true. For this purposes it uses the initial conditions (the data) and the rules from the so-called *knowledge base,* a set of rules that refer to a specific domain. If the knowledge base is small (in the private-label decision example we had a knowledge base of only four rules), this reasoning is straightforward. However, in the case of large knowledge bases (there are expert systems with thousands of rules) this reasoning process has to be handled by specific computer algorithms. This capability to manipulate with data and rules is called the "inference engine" of an expert system. Such an inference engine can be applied to any problem domain, as long as the knowledge is available in the form of data and rules.

The idea of separating domain knowledge and inference capabilities was developed in the 1970s at Stanford University, where the MYCIN system was developed. This is a system for diagnosing and recommending treatment for meningitis and blood infections (Shortliffe 1976). A version of MYCIN in which the specific-domain knowledge (about meningitis and blood infections) was removed from the system has become an archetype of rule-based expert systems. This "stripped" version, called EMYCIN ("empty MYCIN") contained just the reasoning mechanism (inference engine). Such a reasoning mechanism without domain knowledge is called an *expert system shell*. Such a shell can, in principle, be applied to a knowledge base in any domain. Knowledge engineers at Stanford University, for example, used EMYCIN to build an expert system for a different domain, pulmonary problems affecting inpatients (PUFF). The use of an expert system shell greatly reduces the time required for building an expert system. Figure 5.6 presents a sketch of a generic expert system.

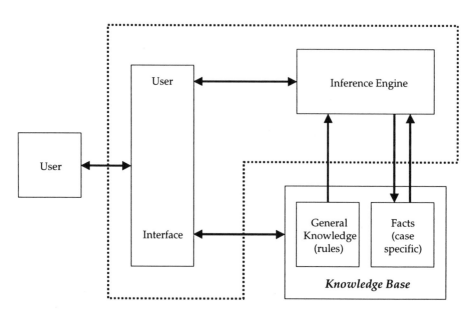

Figure 5.6   Structure of a Generic Expert System

The heart of the expert systems is the knowledge base, which consists of two parts. The first part (shown to the left in Figure 5.6) contains the rules that apply to the domain for which the expert system has been developed (e.g., sales promotions). The second part (shown to the right) contains the facts that apply to the specific case for which a solution has to be found (e.g., data about the brand for which a sales promotion has to be developed). If an expert system has to be developed for the private-label decision discussed earlier, the rules in Figure 5.6 would be included in the left-hand part of the knowledge base, whereas the facts for a specific situation would be stored in the right-hand part. The inference engine applies the rules from the knowledge base to the facts of the actual problem and in this way tries to find a solution. During this process the knowledge in the right-hand part of the knowledge base is growing. The user interface of an expert system may employ different modes of communication, for example, question-and-answer, menu-driven, or even natural language. Separating the problem-solving knowledge from the inference engine has the advantages that knowledge can be entered in a natural fashion (if-then rules) and that the expert system builder does not have to worry about lower-level control structures. The dotted line in Figure 5.6 separates the modules of the expert system shell from the knowledge base.

It has been found that the quality of the knowledge in an expert system is much more critical to the success of the system than the particular inference engine that is used. Edward Feigenbaum, a prominent contributor to the field of expert systems, formulated this finding as the *knowledge principle*. This principle states that "the power of artificial intelligence programs to perform at a high level of competence on problems of intellectual difficulty depends on the amount of knowledge and the quality of the knowledge these programs contain about their problem domain. The reasoning method, while necessary, plays a secondary role" (Feigenbaum, McCorduck, and Nii 1989, p. 7).

Forward Chaining and Backward Chaining in Expert Systems

To arrive at a conclusion with respect to the goal(s) in an expert system, there are basically two different ways of reasoning. They differ in the way the solution space is searched. With *forward chaining* the reasoning starts from the data (this type of search is also called data-driven) and proceeds from there toward the goal. In the private-label decision example of the last section, the data implies that A is true. Using rule 4, we conclude that B is true. Using rule 3, we conclude that C is true. The facts also tell us that E is true, and using rule 2, we conclude that D is true. Knowing that C and D are true and using rule 1, we conclude that F is true, so the advice is to introduce the private brand. The other way of reasoning is called *backward chaining,* which starts not from the data but from the goal(s) (another term for backward chaining is goal-driven search). The task is to find the conditions under which the goal(s) can be made true or not-true. In our example one can see that for F to be true, C has to be true *and* D has to be true. To make C true, B has to be true. And for B to be true, A has to be true, which is the case because of the facts (dominant leading brand). To make D true, E has to be true, which is also the case because of the facts (willing manufacturer); therefore, the final conclusion is that goal F is true.

Backward and forward chaining can be related to human reasoning processes. In some instances we want to reach a goal (for example, finishing writing a book by a specific date) and, by backward chaining, infer which conditions have to be fulfilled in order to reach this goal. In other circumstances our behavior can be driven by the initial conditions. For example, a person might start writing a book at a certain point in time and, from there, reason about the expected opportunities to work on the book in the future and thereby calculate when the book might be finished. Forward chaining and backward chaining ultimately search the same state space and should come to the same conclusion. However, for a problem with a large state space (i.e., having many more rules than in this example) one way of searching can be more efficient than the other. If the number of data is large relative to the number of goals, a goal-driven or backward chaining search is more efficient. However, when there are few data relative to the number of goals, a data-driven or forward chaining search is the more efficient procedure. More advanced expert systems support both forward and backward chaining. Sometimes it is efficient to employ both types of searches alternately. For example, to find the cheapest or fastest way to fly from Rotterdam to Philadelphia (if there is no direct flight between these two cities), it may be useful to reason from the destination as well as from the point of departure.

Dealing with Uncertainty in Expert Systems

So far, we have assumed that the user provides the expert system with facts that are either true or not-true. However, most expert systems can also deal with uncertainty. A user can express his or her (subjective) uncertainty about the state of nature (a proposition) or about an if-then relationship (a rule) by means of a *confidence factor* (CF). A confidence factor is a number between -1 and 1 and expresses one's confidence in a proposition or rule. A confidence factor with a value close to 1 implies a strong belief that the proposition is true. A confidence factor close to -1 implies a strong belief against the proposition, and a CF of around 0 means that there is not much evidence one way or the other, neither in favor of nor against the proposition. The way of computing with confidence factors is based on heuristic principles, not on axiom-based formal theory such as the Bayesian probability theory. These heuristics have become known as the "Stanford Certainty Factor Algebra" (Shortliffe 1976).

As example we give the heuristic of the *uncertain premise,* which can be formulated as follows: Assume we have a proposition A and a rule $A \rightarrow B$. The confidence factors for the proposition and the rule are CF1 and CF2, respectively. Now, if we know that A is true with confidence factor CF1 and that A implies B with confidence factor CF2, then the heuristic of the uncertain premise says that the confidence factor of B is CF1 times CF2 (in the same way as one would multiply conditional probabilities).

For an example we go back to the private-label decision of the last section. Suppose the category manager attaches a confidence factor of 0.80 to the proposition that the leading brand holds a dominant position in the market (A) and a confidence factor of 0.70 to the rule that in the case of a dominant leading brand there is no strong price competition among the existing brands (i.e., A is true with confidence factor 0.80 and A → B is true with confidence factor 0.70). Then the confidence factor for B (the proposition that there is no strong price competition among existing brands) is 0.80 × 0.70 = 0.56.

Confidence factors make it possible to deal explicitly with uncertainty in expert systems.

Languages and Shells

Specific AI languages have been developed to implement the representation and control structures, discussed before, in computers. The two most prominent AI languages are PROLOG and LISP (Luger and Stubblefield 1993, Chaps. 6–7). PROLOG is a logic programming language. (Its name is derived from PROgrammining in LOGic.) A logic program is a set of specifications in formal logic. The PROLOG interpreter responds to questions about this set of specifications. We could, for example, write a small program that answers the question from section 5.3.1, whether Mr. Jansen likes jenever. In PROLOG such a program would look as follows (the PROLOG statements are on the left, their meaning in normal language is given on the right):

?-**likes** (Jansen, Bols)	Does Jansen like Bols?
Dutch (Jansen)	Jansen is Dutch.
Jenever (Bols)	Bols is a brand of Jenever.
$\forall$X $\forall$Y **Dutch** (X) and	
Jenever (Y) **Likes** (X, Y)	X likes Y if X is Dutch and Y is a brand of jenever.

This program would return the answer "yes" as its response to the question posed. PROLOG was developed by Alain Colmerauer and his colleagues at the University of Marseilles around 1970. PROLOG is a rule-based system that only allows backward chaining. As the example shows, in PROLOG knowledge about a problem is entered in a completely formal system by means of predicates. What is known with respect to a specific problem is entered as data in the PROLOG syntax, and the PROLOG interpreter responds to queries about these specifications. It uses pattern-directed searches to find out whether these queries follow logically from the database.

The other important AI language is LISP. The name is an acronym of LISt Processing, which indicates that in this language operations are carried out on "lists," symbolic expressions that can contain both program and data structures. Important is the principle of *recursivity*. A list can contain other lists that, in turn, can contain other lists, and so on. A LISP program evaluates the list presented to it and returns the result of the evaluation. LISP has built-in functions, such as cond, which takes condition-action pairs as arguments. For example, the function

    (cond   (<condition 1> <action 1>)
             (<condition 2> <action 2>)
             . . .
             (<condition n> <action n>))

checks whether the conditions 1, 2, ..., n are true. As soon as a condition is found to be true, the corresponding action is executed, and the result is returned as the value of the cond expression. Such an evaluation, using a cond function, could be imbedded somewhere in a recursive procedure.

LISP has been the dominant AI language in the more than 35 years that it has existed. In the early days of AI, many artificial intelligence programs were implemented directly in LISP. Later, LISP was also used for the implementation of AI tools like, for example, expert system shells.

Users of knowledge-based systems in application areas such as marketing would not normally write their own programs in PROLOG, LISP, or another AI language. This work is left to specialized programmers during the system development stage. Expert system *shells* (which themselves may be written in LISP, PROLOG, or C) offer the opportunity to users to provide information for the knowledge base in normal English (or some other language, depending on the target group of users). Thus the antecedents and conclusions can be provided as input to the system in a form such as that given in Figure 5.4. Numerous different shells are available today. Examples of shells that have been used to develop marketing systems are VPEXPERT, PERSONAL CONSULTANT, M1, LEVEL5, and OPS5. The wide availability of shells has been the primary driver behind the boom of expert systems applied in a broad variety of industries such as the chemical industry, medicine, computers, finance, insurance, and accounting. In 1990 the total number of expert systems was estimated to be more than 5000 (SEI Center Results). Some expert systems have acquired a worldwide reputation, for example, the XCON system used by Digital Equipment Corporation to configure computer systems, which contains 17,500 rules (Barker and O'Connor 1989).

Over time, expert system shells have become more sophisticated and have become development environments. Examples of these new generation tools are CLIPS 6.04, LEVEL5 OBJECT, LPA Flex Expert System, GOLD-WORKS III, EXSYS Professional, and PROKAPPA. For up-to-date information about expert systems software, we refer the reader to the following Internet sites: http://www.faqs.org/faqs/ai-faq/expert/ (general), http://www.ghg.net/clips/CLIPS.html (for CLIPS), http://www.15r.com (for Level5) and http://www.lpa.co.uk/flx.html (for LPA Flex).

Once an expert system has been developed for solving a particular type of problem in a specific consultation, the user has to provide the facts for only that specific case. This can be done through an interactive dialogue between the user and the system, as we will see in the ADCAD example described in the next section.

5.4.3   Expert Systems in Marketing

Having completed our discussion of the *general* principles and features of expert systems, we now turn our attention to expert systems in *marketing.* When considering marketing expert systems (MES) in this book, we primarily refer to systems that use *rule-based* knowledge representation and reasoning, that is, the type of systems we discussed in the previous section. This has been the dominant approach in the first generation of expert systems in marketing, which emerged in the second half of the 1980s. We use the term *marketing knowledge-based system* (MKBS) to refer to a more general class of computer programs that represent and use knowledge to solve marketing problems and that may apply any kind of formalism and algorithms, including rules. MES also have a more normative orientation than MKBS. Given the knowledge about the situation, an MES indicates what the *best* decision is, which is definitely not the case for all MKBS. Thus marketing expert systems constitute a subset of marketing knowledge-based systems.

The first papers on marketing expert systems started to appear in the second half of the 1980s, with working papers on both sides of the Atlantic in 1986: Rangaswamy, Burke, Wind, and Eliashberg (1986) in the United States and Choffray and Charpin (1986) in Europe. Books and journal articles followed, for example, Gaul and Schader (1988), McCann and Gallagher (1990), Rangaswamy, Eliashberg, Burke, and Wind (1989), and Burke, Rangaswamy, Wind, and Eliashberg (1990). In 1991, the *International Journal of Research in Marketing* devoted a Special Issue to expert systems in marketing.

In this section we first take a closer look at the way a marketing expert system operates. For that purpose we describe ADCAD, a rule-based system designed to support advertising decisions. ADCAD, which was developed at the Wharton School by a team of researchers (Burke, Rangaswamy, Wind, and Eliashberg 1990), is a well-developed, high-quality exponent of the class of expert systems that apply rule-based knowledge representation to problems in the marketing domain. After that, we take a broader look at the experiences with expert systems in marketing and examine what has been learned so far.

An Example: The ADCAD System

The ADCAD system was designed to assist advertisers of consumer products with the formulation of advertising objectives, copy strategy, and the selection of communication approaches. The ADCAD system ("ADCAD" stands for ADvertising Communication Approach Design) uses the expert system methodology to codify and synthesize prior research, theory, and personal expertise. A user who wants to obtain ADCAD's advice in a specific situation has to provide ADCAD with information about the brand, the product class, and the target market. This is done in a dialogue session between the user and ADCAD, where ADCAD asks a series of questions (usually about 30). The answers to these questions are stored as "facts" in the knowledge base. The inference engine of ADCAD then applies the generic part of its knowledge base (rules that represent general knowledge about the working of advertising) to the facts and tries to generate advertising recommendations for the specific situation. Figure 5.7 shows a schematic representation of ADCAD and its use in a consultation.

ADCAD's Knowledge Base

As expressed by the knowledge principle (quoted above), the most important part of an expert system is its domain knowledge. In ADCAD there are two important sources for this knowledge. The first is *published material,* that is, existing theories of how advertising works and about its effectiveness. These theories can be found in the literature in sources such as Lavidge and Steiner (1961), Rossiter and Percy (1987), and so on. In addition, more practice-oriented literature was used as input, giving heuristics with respect to advertising "do's and don'ts" (e.g., Ogilvy [1983]). From these published sources, rules were derived that describe the relationships between advertising copy factors, market characteristics, consumer behavior, and the psychological processes driving that behavior. The second source of knowledge was *practitioners' knowledge,* which was provided by the creative staff of a major advertising agency (Young and Rubicam, New York). These "experts" were asked to discuss the background information and reasoning underlying their choice of copy strategies in past advertising work. This information was then converted into rules that were added to the ADCAD knowledge base.

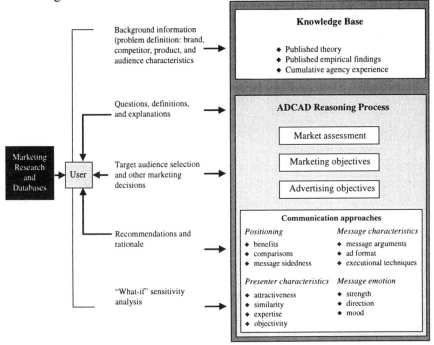

Figure 5.7   A schematic representation of ADCAD and its use in a consultation

As Figure 5.7 shows, there is a top-down structure in ADCAD's knowledge base, going from the level of "market assessment," to "marketing objectives," to "advertising objectives," to "communication approaches." The knowledge base of ADCAD contains separate sets of rules that correspond to the respective links between these levels. The first set of rules translate market assessment facts into marketing objectives. The second set of rules transfer knowledge about marketing objectives into advertising objectives, and so on. ADCAD concentrates on four areas of attention within communication approaches: *positioning, message characteristics, presenter characteristics,* and *message emotion.* Each of these areas has its own set of rules. ADCAD's reasoning starts with the market assessment, based on information that is provided by the user in the dialogue session. ADCAD then uses its rules to develop, successively, marketing objectives, advertising objectives, and communication approaches. Figure 5.8 presents examples of rules in three of the categories referred to above (two example rules per category).

These rules are in the format we discussed in section 5.3.1. Rules to determine marketing objectives (the first category of Figure 5.8) use market assessment information as input. For example, as one of the first questions in any consultation, ADCAD asks its user in which stage of the product life cycle the product category is. This stage of the product life cycle is also the first antecedent of the first marketing objectives rule in Figure 5.8. Figure 5.8 also illustrates how the output of a specific stage acts as input to the next stage. For example, the first rule for marketing objectives determines whether or not stimulate_primary_demand is true. The first rule for advertising objectives (the next block of Figure 5.8) uses this knowledge to decide whether or not to convey product category information. The six rules given in Figure 5.8 are only a subset of the total of 188 procedural rules that ADCAD contains for dealing with substantive advertising knowledge. Apart from that, the program contains many declarative rules imposed by the semantics of the concepts, rules to regulate the interaction between ADCAD and the user, and technical rules required by the syntax of the shell. Altogether the database consists of hundreds of declarative statements and rules. A printout of all the ADCAD rules takes up over 50 pages. The particular shell used for ADCAD is M1 (a product from the Teknowledge Company), a goal-driven (i.e., backward-chaining) inference engine. The reasoning starts from the alternative communication approaches and copy strategies and searches back through the rules to conditions in the knowledge base (the facts) and to input from the user(s) to determine whether or not the antecedents for the various communication alternatives are fulfilled.

Marketing Objectives (11 rules)
* IF product life cycle stage = introduction AND innovation type = discontinuous THEN marketing
  objective = stimulate primary demand
* IF brand usage = none THEN marketing objective = stimulate brand trial

---

Advertising Objectives (18 rules)
* IF marketing objective = stimulate primary demand AND product purchase motivation
  direction = negative THEN ad objective = convey product category information
* IF marketing objective = stimulate brand trial AND brand purchase motivation direction
  = positive THEN ad objective = convey brand image

Positioning (24 rules)
* IF ad objective = convey brand image or reinforce brand image AND brand purchase motivation
  = social approval AND brand usage visibility = high THEN possible benefit = "status"
  (cf. Holbrook and Lehmann 1980)
* IF ad objective = convey brand information or change beliefs AND perceived differences between
  brands = small or medium AND perceived relative performance = inferior or parity AND relative
  performance = superior AND current brand loyalty = competitor loyal THEN message comparison
  = direct comparison against competition

Figure 5.8   Examples of Rules in ADCAD

Illustrative Application for the Yalac Brand

We will illustrate the way ADCAD works by using the system to develop an advertising approach for a new brand in the product category health drinks in the Dutch market. This category consists of dairy-based drinks with a health association that is based on the use of a particular lactic acid bacterium. It is claimed, among other things, that this bacterium has a favorable effect on the cholesterol content of the blood. The health drinks category has been formed over the last two years with the successful introduction of three brands. Our (imaginary) new brand, Yalac, will be the fourth brand in this category. Yalac is positioned at the high end of the market: it is relatively high priced, claims a unique type of lactic acid bacterium, and comes in a container that is easier to use than those of the existing brands. The main target group for the advertisement is the elderly. Figure 5.9 shows a printout of the first part of the dialogue about Yalac between the user and ADCAD.

In the dialogue, ADCAD first asks for several pieces of information about the brand, the product category, and the consumption behavior of the target group. During the consultation ADCAD actively reasons with the information it has collected so far and tries to translate it into marketing and advertising strategies. When there is insufficient information, the user is consulted. For example, after having learned that the target group (the elderly) has a low usage rate of health drinks and no past usage of Yalac (it's a new brand), ADCAD suggests to the user that "reinforce primary demand" might be considered as a marketing objective. It is true that the first rule of Figure 5.8 contains conditions for stimulating primary demand, but these are not fulfilled at this point. ADCAD knows that the product class is in the growth stage of the PLC (which is thus not the introduction stage as mentioned in the rule). Furthermore, there is not enough information about the type of innovation (discontinuous?) to fulfill the second antecedent of the first rule. Therefore, ADCAD consults the user to determine if stimulating primary demand is a good idea. During this consultation, ADCAD comes up with similar suggestions a number of times.

What is the name of the brand for which you want to develop an ad?
>> yalac

In which product category does yalac belong?
Before responding, carefully consider the major brands and products with which yalac competes.
>> health drinks

Give a name to the segment to which the ad will be targeted.
Use a maximum of ten letters.
>> elderly

At what stage of the life cycle is the product category health drinks?
1. introduction
2. growth
3. maturity
4. decline
>> 2

How would you characterize the level of usage of health drinks in segment elderly?
1. none
2. low
3. high
>> 2

Is the purchase interval for health drinks long, medium, or short?
>> medium

What is the rate at which consumers in segment elderly use or consume health drinks?
1. never
2. infrequently
3. frequently
>> 2

How would you characterize loyalty to yalac in segment elderly?
1. loyal to brand
2. loyal to competitor
3. favorable brand switcher
4. unfavorable brand switcher
5. split loyalty
6. nonuser
>> 6

Figure 5.9   Partial dialogue about Yalac between the user and ADCAD

The printout of the dialogue also shows that it is possible to specify uncertainty. For example, although the advertising manager tends to think that there is no physical risk involved in making a wrong brand decision, he is not completely sure for this health-sensitive product category. Therefore, he gives a confidence factor of 60 to this belief. In the M1 shell the confidence factor runs from 1 (no confidence at all) to 100 (completely confident). The full set of input values provided to ADCAD in the case of Yalac is given in Figure 5.10.

1.	life cycle stage of health drinks	growth
2.	health drinks usage elderly	low
3.	product purchase interval	medium
4.	product usage frequency	infrequently
5.	brand loyalty	nonuser
6.	yalac past usage elderly	none
7.	product motive	problem avoidance
8.	brand motive	problem avoidance
9.	time of brand decision	prior to purchase
10.	advertising level	low
11.	publicity level	low
12.	promotion level	low
13.	package usability	low
14.	physical risk	low (cf 60)
15.	brand type	new
16.	age	elderly
17.	product complexity	high (cf 80)
18.	perceived performance difference	medium
19.	price of yalac	high
20.	decision-making unit	individual
21.	yalac attitude	neutral
22.	actual relative performance	superior
23.	relative price	high
24.	actual performance differences	medium
25.	product performance evaluation	subjective
26.	benefit delivery	high
27.	benefit uniqueness	high (cf 50)
28.	benefit importance	high
29.	perceived relative performance	superior
30.	level of competition	high
31.	education	high school
32.	benefit visibility instead	low
33.	share trend	gaining
34.	product anxiety	high

Figure 5.10   Complete input for the Yalac situation

The communication strategy recommendations that ADCAD produces for this set of input variables are presented in Figure 5.11. Basically, ADCAD recommends to strongly emphasize the quality of Yalac, in a rational rather than emotional approach, and to have an expert with a high degree of objectivity (e.g., a medical doctor) presenting the advantages of Yalac. Furthermore, there are several recommendations with respect to the presentation technique, for example, brand name repetition (consumers should learn the name of the new brand) and strong arguments.

Components of the communication approach

1.	benefit	quality
2.	benefit presentation	strongly positive
3.	benefit presentation	can mention many benefits
4.	information strategy	two-sided messages
5.	information strategy	focus ad on the brand
6.	format	customer interview
7.	format	testimonial by product user
8.	emotion in ad	authenticity of emotions can be low
9.	emotion in ad	portray positive emotions
10.	emotion in ad	emotion can be weak
11.	emotion in ad	relaxation
12.	presenter attribute	high likability
13.	presenter attribute	need not be familiar
14.	presenter attribute	high expertise
15.	presenter attribute	male
16.	presenter attribute	high objectivity
17.	presentation technique	jingle/rhyme/slogan
18.	presentation technique	animation/cartoon/rotoscope
19.	presentation technique	brand name repetition
20.	presentation technique	short headline
21.	presentation technique	nouns in headline
22.	presentation technique	personal reference
23.	presentation technique	visual/verbal integration
24.	presentation technique	strong arguments
25.	presentation technique	supporting information
26.	presentation technique	implicit conclusion
27.	presentation technique	surrogate indicators of performance

---

Figure 5.11. ADCAD's recommended communication strategy

ADCAD allows the user to ask for explanations of the different recommendations. For example, if we ask why the message should be two-sided (recommendation 4), ADCAD gives the answer as reproduced in the upper part of Figure 5.12. This explanation shows how theory and results from the literature have been used to develop the ADCAD knowledge base.

"Two-sided message" ... because:

"Consumers are well educated, very knowledgeable about the products, are highly involved in the decision. However, they have a negative attitude toward our brand or have been exposed to a lot of contradictory information from competitors. We should acknowledge any negative characteristics of our brand in our advertising and then counter this with a number of strong positive arguments. This will inoculate the consumer against competition claims."

"One-sided message" ... because:

"The consumers in this segment have poor knowledge of the products and are not highly involved in the decisions. Further, their education level is low, making it more difficult for complex messages to succeed. We should present strong positive arguments in favor of buying our brand using a one-sided brand message."

Figure 5.12   An Example of ADCAD's Explanation of Its Recommendations

Apparently, the education level of the target group, which in this case is specified as high school, inspires the choice for a two-sided message. It is possible to carry out what-if analyses with ADCAD. We might wonder what the effect on ADCAD's recommendations would be if, for example, we specify the education level of the target group as "grade school" instead of "high school." The answer is that the recommended message strategy changes to "one-sided message," with the explanation given in the lower part of Figure 5.12. This what-if feature of ADCAD is attractive since it enables the user to simulate different market situations. It can also be useful in solving conflicts in opinions among decision makers. ADCAD can explain differences in preferred communication strategies among advertising experts by making the different assumptions behind these preferences explicit.

ADCAD is a fairly representative example of the type of marketing expert systems that were developed in the early 1990s. Apart from the group at Wharton, who developed ADCAD along with several other marketing expert systems, researchers at the Fuqua School of Business of Duke University also actively produced a series of marketing expert systems. Several of these (i.e., Promotion Advisor, Marketmetrics Knowledge System, Promotion Detective, and Dealmaker) have been described in McCann and Gallagher (1990). Apart from the systems produced by these groups, other researchers developed several marketing expert systems. We will discuss these systems in the following section.

The First Generation of Expert Systems in Marketing

After having discussed one marketing expert system in detail, in this section we will look at the broader picture of expert systems in marketing. Between the mid-1980s and the beginning of the 1990s several expert systems for the support of marketing decisions were developed. It is interesting to know what kind of systems have been developed, for which types of marketing questions they were designed, to what extent these systems have been validated, and what is known about their use by companies. This section is based partly on an inventory of MES made in the early nineties (Wierenga 1990, 1992). However, this information is complemented with insight from more recent sources.

The 1992 inventory was confined to the academic literature, that is, articles, book chapters, and working papers. This implies that it is not exhaustive. Marketing expert systems that have been developed in companies but have not been published are not included. Twenty-seven MES were identified and included in the inventory. Figure 5.13 provides an overview of the systems and their purposes. More specific information can be found in Wierenga (1992).

No.	Author(s), Year, Name	Purpose
1.	Abraham & Lodish (1987) PROMOTOR	To evaluate sales promotions, notably, to determine the baseline (what sales would have been without promotion) using rules of thumb
2.	Alpar (1991) SHANEX	To help the product manager analyze Nielsen data, concentrating on changes in market share, features share, or relative price
3.	Bayer & Harter (1991) SCANEXPERT	To trace significant changes in market share and find the causes: trade support, retail distribution, or competition
4.	Bayer, Lawrence & Keon (1988) PEP	To find the right type of sales promotion given the market position of the brand and management objectives
5.	Böchenholt, Both & Gaul (1988, 1989) DANEX	To find and carry out appropriate data analysis method (e.g., MDS cluster analysis) given the data structure
6.	Burke (1991) ADDUCE	To predict consumer response to advertising on the basis of theory and empirical knowledge by drawing analogies with earlier cases
7.	Burke, Rangaswamy, Wind & Eliashberg (1990) ADCAD	To make recommendations for advertisement development on different aspects, given the marketing goals and characteristics of the situation
8.	Collopy & Armstrong (1991)	To make forecasts on the basis of time series data
9.	Gaul & Schaer (1988), Gaul & Both (1990) MEXICO	To predict sales and market share and make go/no recommendations given the product and the marketing plan for a new product
10.	Girod, Orgeas & Landry (1989) TIMES	Media planning: design of a television advertising campaign based on client's data (accounts, commercials, marketing targets) and TV databases (audience, prices, etc.)
11.	Kroeber-Riel, Lorson & Neibecker (1992), Esch & Muffler (1989) CAAS	To offer computer-aided advertising support in the creative search as well as the evaluation (diagnosis) stage of advertising
12.	Schmitz, Armstrong & Little (1990) COVERSTORY	To find the news in a huge amount of data; to select the major events and identify their causes
13.	McCann & Gallagher (1990) DEALMAKER	To predict the impact of a deal offer in two layers: (1) participation/nonparticipation of chain and (2) prediction given participation
14.	McCann & Gallagher (1990)	To guide the analysis of large amounts of (scanner) data; automatic modeling
15.	McCann & Gallagher (1990) MARKETMETRICS	To give advice about the type of promotion given the strategy and situation characteristics

No.	Author(s), Year, Name	Purpose
16.	McCann & Gallagher (1990) PROMOTION DETECTIVE	To spot a promotion by looking at weekly scanning data; subsequently, to report the effects of a promotion
17.	McGann & Gallagher (1990) PROMOTION ADVISOR	To give advice about the type of promotion
18.	McGann, Tadlaoui & Gallagher (1990) RAD (Retail Ad Designer)	To design a weekly retail newspaper advertisement for promoted products based on scanner data
19.	McCann, Lahti & Hill (1991) BMA (Brand Manager's Assistant)	To assist the brand manager in writing reports based on insights obtained using an MIS
20.	Mitchell (1988)	To provide support in designing a media plan; decision support and knowledge added
21.	Mockler (1989)	To determine the local introduction strategy of a globally marketed new health care product
22.	Mockler (1989)	Media planning
23.	Neibecker (1990) ESWA	To select among alternative copy proposals in the pretest stage of advertisement
24.	Ram & Ram (1988) INNOVATOR	To screen new product ideas in the financial services industry based on attributes of products, the brand, and companies
25.	Rangaswamy, Eliashberg, Burke & Wind (1989) NEGOTEX	To offer support for a negotiating strategy in terms of preparation, team composition, communication approach, and behavioral response based on the characteristics of the situation
26.	Rangaswamy, Harlem & Lodish (1991) INFER	To automate the interpretation of scanner data; knowledge based on interpretive results of statistical analysis
27.	Schumann, Gongla, Lee & Sakamoto (1987) ADVISOR BUS.STRAT.	To make strategic recommen-dations based on the position of a business in the BCG matrix and in a technology portfolio matrix

Figure 5.13   An Overview of the Marketing Expert Systems in the Survey

Characteristics of the Systems

In this subsection we discuss the most important characteristics of the marketing expert systems included in the inventory. Figure 5.14 shows the distribution of these systems over the subfields of marketing for which they were developed.

Type of Marketing Decision	# of Systems	% of Systems
Sales promotion	7	26%
Monitoring markets & writing reports	5	19%
Advertising	4	15%
Media planning	3	11%
New products	3	11%
Automated data analysis	2	7%
Negotiations	1	4%
Strategy	1	4%
Prediction	1	4%

Figure 5.14   Subfields of marketing for which the marketing expert systems in the survey were developed

Sales promotion is the marketing domain for which the largest number of marketing expert systems have been developed. MES support such sales-promotion tasks as the following:

- Evaluating the effect of sales promotions (1, 4, 13, 16, 17).[2]

- Finding the right type of sales promotion, given the position of the brand and the management objectives (4, 15).

- Spotting competing promotions (16).

- Designing weekly newspaper advertisements for promoted products (18).

Marketing expert systems that support monitoring markets also occur with a relatively high frequency. Especially because of the "scanning revolution," marketing decision makers are swamped with data and need support for finding the "news" in these large quantities of tables and numbers. CoverStory (12) and its successor, SalesPartner (Schmitz 1994), do exactly that. There are several other systems (e.g., systems 2 and 26) that also aim at automating the interpretation of scanner data. Advertising and media planning are also the object of support for MES relatively often. We described ADCAD (7) already. There are several other systems that support, for example, the search for a creative advertising design (11), the selection of ad copy from several proposed alternatives (23), and media planning (10, 20, and 22). Furthermore, MES have been developed that support the introduction of new products and for a few other purposes. The majority of the systems (63%) were developed for products in the FMCG category.

---

[2]   Numbers refer to the numbers of the marketing expert systems listed in Figure 5.13.

Figure 5.15 provides information about the sources of the knowledge that was used in developing the 27 marketing expert systems.

Source of Knowledge Base	# of Systems	% of Systems
• General scientific knowledge (textbooks, published literature)	9	33%
• Informal interview(s) with professionals/experts	9	33%
• Expertise of the authors	7	26%
• Analysis of earlier cases	3	11%
• Survey among experts	2	7%
• Expertise of system designer	2	7%
• Formal assessment from expert	1	4%

Figure 5.15   Sources of knowledge used in the marketing expert systems in the survey

Formal knowledge acquisition methods are used only seldomly for marketing expert systems. In the 1992 inventory, in only one case out of 27 were formal interviews held to capture knowledge from experts. This is different from how expert systems are developed in other fields. In one-third of the systems included in the inventory, the knowledge came from general scientific sources. For another third, informal interviews with experts were conducted, while in two cases a survey was held among experts. Mostly the authors/developers of the systems also acted as providers of the knowledge.

With regard to the methods for knowledge representation and knowledge manipulation, the inventory found that in the majority of systems (63%) rule-based knowledge representation was applied. The tool for reasoning with this rule-based knowledge representation was implemented in an expert system shell (82%) or in PROLOG (18%). For the other systems (37%), knowledge representation was done by means of frames, a combination of rules and frames, or other methods, or the type of knowledge representation could not be deduced from the description of the system.

Validation of Expert Systems

The application of ADCAD to Yalac showed how a marketing expert system can make policy recommendations in a more or less realistic setting. An important issue with respect to an expert system is its *validity*. How can we be sure that the system makes recommendations that are really good, given the objectives of the user? In the case of Yalac, the recommendations do have *face validity*, but how can we know that there are no alternative strategies that would be (much) better? Validity is hard to establish for an expert system. One option is to look at the *substantive content* of the knowledge base (i.e., the rules). Although the truth claims of individual rules in the knowledge base can be judged (the ADCAD rules are largely based on empirical research), it is not easy to think through what the expert system will recommend when these rules are applied in different combinations and orders. Usually, the number of possible combinations is huge. Another option is *validation against expert judgment.* For a variety of problems, the system's recommendation should be compared with the recommendations a human expert would make when confronted with the same problem. In computer science this way of validating has become known as the *Turing test* (Turing 1950). An MES passes the Turing test if the marketing manager who requested the advice is not able to tell whether the advice he or she receives was produced by an expert system or a human adviser (see Figure 5.16).

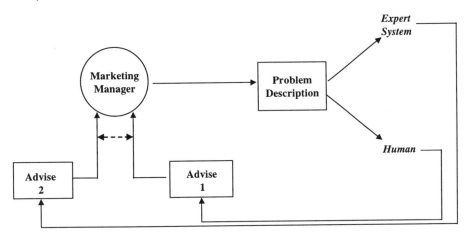

Figure 5.16   Validating an Expert System (Turing Test)

Recently, methods have become available to test the logic of a knowledge base, that is, whether the rules are mutually consistent and do not contain contradictions (Ayel and Laurent 1991; Meseguer and Preece 1995; Preece and Shingal 1995). These *verification methods* can be used to examine the formal validity of (large) marketing knowledge bases.

However, the ultimate validation of an expert system is *validation in use,* which consists of determining whether use of the system results in better performance compared to not using it, for example, in terms of sales, market share, and/or profits. To carry out such a validation, an appropriate test design would be to create two comparable groups of decision makers of which one would be provided with the system while the other would not. Over an extended time period the performance of the two groups could then be compared. Fudge and Lodish (1978) carried out this type of experiment for the CALLPLAN system (see Chapter 9).

In the description of the systems in our 1992 inventory, little attention was given to validation. In 60% of the cases validation was not mentioned at all. For a few systems soft tests had been carried out (e.g., soliciting comments from users), whereas for three systems the output from the system was compared with actual outcomes or results from other procedures. For three of the MES in our sample, validation studies were reported later. Neibecker (1996) validated his ESWA model, an advertising evaluation system, based on theories about communication and the working of advertising (number 23 in Figure 5.13). He compared predictions of ESWA with results from pretest studies of advertisements in the consumer population. Neibecker used 103 advertisements, each of which was pretested by a sample of about 120 respondents. For each advertisement he computed the (aggregated) score on four dimensions: recall, imagery, acceptance, and emotionality. For the same advertisements ESWA produced performance predictions ("Wirkungsprognosen") on the same four dimensions. It turned out that, for the four dimensions considered, the pretest results were significantly correlated with the ESWA predictions. The correlation coefficients ranged from 0.24 to 0.38. Thus theory-based expert systems for advertising can produce valid information about the actual performance of an advertisement.

Validation studies were also carried out for the MYCIN system for medical diagnoses (discussed in section 5.4.2). Both the system and real-life experts had to recommend therapies (antibiotics) for patients with specific symptoms. Over several such studies the agreement between experts and the system ranged from 43% to 65%. This provides some perspective for the accuracy of the advertising expert system. In making the comparison we should note that there is much more unexplained variance in the working of advertising than in the relatively well-researched area of infectious diseases.

Ram and Ram (1996) provide validation results for their INNOVATOR system, which screens ideas for new products in the financial services industry (system 24 in Figure 5.13). INNOVATOR evaluates new product ideas. An example is a financial corporation that currently offers stocks and bonds and that may wish to evaluate adding mutual funds or annuities to its portfolio. INNOVATOR's knowledge base has been developed on the basis of knowledge acquisition sessions with five (top) experts in the industry. These persons were called the *donor experts*. For the validation test five other experts were recruited who had not been involved in the knowledge acquisition process (*nondonor experts*). A test was conducted wherein the recommendation that INNOVATOR made for a particular scenario was compared with the recommendations of experts for the same scenarios. Fifteen new product scenarios were presented to INNOVATOR and to the nondonor experts as well as to the donor experts. It turned out that the nondonor experts' judgments perfectly matched with INNOVATOR's recommendations on 10 of the 15 scenarios. For the other scenarios there was a partial match, with some experts agreeing with INNOVATOR and some not. For the donor experts there was a perfect match between their recommendations and those of INNOVATOR for all 15 scenarios. (However, these scenarios were new, that is, not used in the knowledge acquisition process.) The results of this validation study indicate that a reasonable degree of validity is possible with this type of expert system.

Finally, the negotiation expert system NEGOTEX (system 25 in Figure 5.13) was evaluated in an actual negotiating setting (Eliashberg, Gauvin, Lilien, and Rangaswamy 1992). In an experiment, a situation was created in which a Chinese manufacturer sold computers to an American distributor. Pairs of negotiators had to reach an agreement about a one-year contract that would specify the quantity of computers sold to the American distributor and their unit price. Each of the (66) negotiating pairs consisted of an American and a Chinese party (both students). The experimental manipulation consisted of providing different types of negotiation training to the American negotiator: (1) reading material, (2) a course on negotiation, or (3) the expert system NEGOTEX. Whereas just using reading materials contributed the least to the performance of the American negotiators, taking the course and using NEGOTEX showed a statistically equivalent impact on the actual *outcomes* of their negotiations. However, these two type of training differed in their impact on the negotiation *process*. American negotiators who took the course tended to need more preparation time than those using the expert system. It thus seems possible to assemble the knowledge (about negotiation) that one would otherwise have learned in a course in an expert system that can produce comparable outcomes more quickly.

Implementation

At the time the first inventory was made (1992) many of the systems (60%) were not operational but in a prototype or even preprototype stage. In eight cases the systems were complete and ready to use. However, in only four cases were applications mentioned. The results of the 1992 inventory can be supplemented with information from a more recent survey conducted among developers of marketing management support systems (see Chapter 4). Eleven of the marketing expert systems listed in Figure 5.13 were included in this later survey. For six of these systems implementations in companies were reported. These six systems were Innovator, ESWA, CAAS, COVER-STORY, NEGOTEX, and PROMOTOR. The average number of different companies in which a system was implemented was 39.3, with an average of

6.6 different implementations per company. According to the developers of these systems, their use had a considerable impact on actual decision making (an average score of 5.5 on a seven-point scale). The users of these systems were also reported to be quite satisfied with them (an average score of 6.2 on a seven-point scale). So MES clearly have an impact for marketing decision making in practice.

Summarizing, we learn the following from the first generation of MES:

- These systems have been geared toward fast-moving consumer goods, with sales promotions and monitoring of markets as frequent applications.

- The knowledge in these systems is predominantly from marketing textbooks and informal sources (including the authors of the systems).

- Validation of the systems was not a preoccupation of the developers, but the validity of several of these systems has been confirmed since their development.

- The (admittedly limited) information about their use seems to indicate that these systems are effective.

Evaluation of Marketing Expert Systems

What can be said about the current and possible future role of (rule-based) expert systems in marketing and about the type of marketing problems that are especially suitable for expert systems?

An expert sample, consisting of marketing faculty and marketing PhD students from five universities ($n = 41$; U.S. and Europe) concluded that expert system problems (i.e., problems suitable for expert systems) are distinct from nonexpert system problems in that they are *narrower, less deep, more structured,* and *more programmable* (Wierenga 1992). Expert system problems are also more *operational* and more often the type of task that a marketing decision maker would *delegate* to someone else. Finally, expert system problems are problems for which there is *more agreement* among experts than there is for nonexpert system problems. In the view of these "expert respondents," the suitability of expert systems is thus restricted to a particular subset of all marketing problems: those that are relatively structured and primarily diagnosing/monitoring in character. Problems with evident managerial and strategic dimensions would not easily be entrusted to an expert system. These outcomes are in agreement with what we found about the application domains of MES in the last section and also with the observation of Mitchell, Russo, and Wittink (1991) that marketing problems that are amenable to expert systems "reflect the more repetitive and mechanical aspects of the data analyst's task." For these types of tasks expert systems can be of major help.

Expert systems clearly have *limitations*. Expert systems are "brittle" (Mitchell et al. 1991), meaning that they can break down with minor changes in their task and that the addition of new variables may require an extensive redesign of the system. Also, an expert system often does not have all the knowledge that an analyst has about a problem (major managerially relevant variables may be missing). It is interesting to observe that many of the limitations attributed to expert systems also apply to models, for example, that they are suitable for structured problems, that they are designed more for diagnosis than for strategy, and that their knowledge is often incomplete (simplification of reality). As with mathematical models, it is relatively easy to say, "You left something out of your system." One should be aware of this limitation when interpreting the recommendations of an expert system. Another objection that can be raised against rule-based expert systems (again, something that also applies to models) is that the knowledge they contain is static and that no learning takes place. These characteristics restrict expert systems to relatively static environments. (In the next chapter we discuss neural networks, a type of MMSS that can learn.)

The limitations just mentioned apply to expert systems in general. There may be one particular issue that is more specific for expert systems in marketing environments, and that is the level of *agreement* among experts about a solution. As there is more agreement about the solution, it is easier to have a problem solved by an expert system. However, there is often not that much agreement among marketing experts about how to deal with a specific marketing problem. This may well pose the most important limitation on the use of expert systems in marketing, especially when compared to the engineering domains where expert systems have been so successful (Mitchell et al. 1991). Unlike expert systems in marketing, those used in engineering domains deal with relatively "hard" relationships determined in the physical sciences. This lack of agreement is probably also the reason that the knowledge built into MES is relatively infrequently captured from real-life marketing experts.

In conclusion, for most of the marketing tasks we will continue to need the expertise and judgment of the individual marketing decision maker. Expert systems will not replace marketing managers. However, for specific tasks that are relatively structured and repetitive and for which agreement exists about how they should de dealt with, expert systems can produce important efficiency gains. An example is scanning data, where huge amounts of data can be monitored and diagnosed by means of expert system technology in a very short time. For other purposes we need other technologies to support marketing decision making. These will be dealt with in the next chapter.

5.5   Marketing Knowledge-Based Systems

In this book we use the term *marketing expert system* to refer to systems that employ rule-based representation of knowledge with a generic structure, as depicted in Figure 5.6. Marketing knowledge-based systems (MKBS) refer to a broader category of systems than marketing expert systems. If we follow Rangaswamy's straightforward definition of knowledge-based systems—that is, "decision models that use AI methods" (Rangaswamy 1993, p. 750)—all developments in AI have the potential to add new and useful features to MKBS.

Marketing knowledge-based systems do not stand for just one particular approach to dealing with knowledge in marketing but encompass a diverse collection of knowledge representation methods and procedures for reasoning, learning, and problem solving that can be brought to bear to support marketing decision making. This applies in the first place to the source of knowledge. In (marketing) knowledge-based systems the knowledge originates from any source, not just from human experts but also from textbooks, cases, and so on. Second, the set of possibilities to represent knowledge is much richer and not limited to rule-based representation. Specifically, semantic networks and frame-based knowledge representation (as discussed in section 5.3.2) are important alternatives for the representation of knowledge. In the survey we discussed earlier (Wierenga 1992) several marketing systems were encountered that already used frame-based representation, and this type of system has the potential to be widely applied in marketing (Rangaswamy 1993). Burke (1991) used frames in ADDUCE, a system for reasoning about consumer response to advertising. For example, he uses a frame for an advertisement, which contains the attributes exposure, presenter, message emotion, argument, format, and technique. He also uses a frame for presenter, with attributes such as age, sex, relation to brand, expertise, and objectivity. Another example of a marketing knowledge-based system using an object-oriented design is Brand Manager's Assistant (McCann, Lahti, and Hill 1991), which supports brand managers by monitoring, analyzing, and designing tasks related to their brands. Increasingly, knowledge systems make use of "hybrid environments" (Luger and Stubblefield 1993, p. 537) in which multiple representation paradigms are combined into a single integrated programming environment. Rules and frame/object-based representations can, for example, be combined to benefit from the relative advantages of both approaches. The BRANDFRAME system, described in Chapter 8, is an example of an MKBS that combines frames and rules. However, in the next chapter we will first discuss two knowledge technologies—case-based reasoning and neural networks—that originated from AI but have become so substantial that they have each become separate fields in their own right.

Key Points

- *The field of artificial intelligence (AI) is still relatively young but has produced many useful concepts and methods for representing and processing knowledge; these concepts and methods form the basis for knowledge-based computer-aided decision support tools.*

- *There are basically two different paradigms for dealing with knowledge: the symbolic representation school and the connectionist school. Both approaches can be used in marketing management support systems.*

- *The most important symbolic knowledge representation methods for MMSS are rule-based and networked knowledge representations, the latter including hierarchical frame-based representation.*

- *Production systems, which constitute the basis for expert systems, start with initial conditions and then, by executing a sequence of if-then rules in a logical way, reach the final goal, that is, the solution of the problem. It has been claimed that this is the mechanism underlying all human problem solving.*

- *In expert systems this process of executing if-then rules is carried out by a computer. The breakthrough leading to the success of expert systems was the separation of domain knowledge and procedural knowledge. A given expert system or shell can be loaded with domain knowledge from any domain. By now there is a rich supply of expert system software (shells) available.*

- *The ADCAD system is an expert system for the support of advertising decisions. From initial conditions defining the position of the brand, ADCAD uses its knowledge base (expressed in the form of rules) to arrive at recommendations with respect to the characteristics of the advertisement. ADCAD is a representative example of a marketing expert system.*

- *Many applications of expert systems in marketing have taken place. Predominantly these pertain to fast-moving consumer goods, with sales promotions and the monitoring of markets being the dominant applications. Several of these systems are used on an ongoing basis by companies and have considerable impact.*

- *Marketing problems amenable to expert systems are relatively structured, repetitive, operational problems for which agreement exists about what the solution should be. For such types of problems—for example, the monitoring and diagnosis of scanning data—expert system technology can produce substantial efficiency gains. However, marketing problems with less structure that are more strategic in character do not easily lend themselves to being solved by an expert system.*

Chapter 6

Knowledge-Driven Marketing Management Support Systems II: Case-Based Reasoning, Neural Networks, and Creativity Support Systems

Learning Objectives

- *To understand the basic philosophy underlying case-based reasoning as a tool for processing knowledge.*

- *To become familiar with the concepts and techniques used in case-based reasoning, such as representation of cases, measures of similarity between cases, retrieval of cases, adaptation, and revision of cases.*

- *To learn about the current application of cased-based reasoning in marketing and the prospects for its extended use.*

- *To understand the principles of connectionism or neural networks as a pattern-recognition tool.*

- *To become familiar with the basics of designing, training, and testing (artificial) neural networks.*

- *To understand how neural networks can be applied to time-series data and cross-sectional data in marketing and to learn about the results of studies comparing neural networks with conventional methods.*

- *To learn about the role of creativity support systems in problem solving and their contribution to the creativity of solutions.*

- *To acquire an overall perspective on the different marketing management support technologies discussed in this and the last two chapters.*

6.1   Case-Based Reasoning Systems

In this book we discuss two major techniques for knowledge processing or reasoning with knowledge. In the previous chapter we dealt with the first one, *rule-based reasoning* (which is the basis of expert systems). In this chapter we discuss the second technique, *case-based reasoning*. The idea underlying case-based reasoning is that, when solving a new problem, a person remembers a previous, similar problem situation and reuses information and knowledge from that prior problem to solve the current one. *Case-based reasoning systems* are computer programs that follow this principle and consist of a "case base" of earlier cases and mechanisms for storing, retrieving, adapting, and learning from cases.

6.1.1   Reasoning by Analogy

Case-based reasoning systems find their origin in two basic notions. The first is that humans tend to understand a novel situation in terms of one that is already familiar. In the last two decades, the power of the *analogy* has become apparent to cognitive psychologists. Some of the greatest scientific discoveries have emerged through analogies, for example, the double helix that triggered Watson and Crick's discovery of the structure of DNA. The great astronomer Kepler was a prolific *analogizer;* in 1609 he used the analogy of light to understand gravity (Gentner and Markman 1997). Like light, gravity is not something material or tangible, yet it has demonstrable effects. (Kepler lived many centuries before the discussion about the wave/particle nature of light.) Not only have the great discoverers made use of analogies, but we all use them all the time. Professionals such as physicians and automobile mechanics do not go back to basic theories of how the human body or a car engine works. They use experiences (similar symptoms shown by earlier patients or cars) to generate hypotheses about what's the matter with a patient or car and to come up with solutions and therapies. Architects and caterers also tend to recall, merge, and adapt old design plans to create new ones (Kolodner 1993).

Analogical reasoning also occurs in marketing. For example, Goldstein (1993) examined how product managers use scanning data. He found that product managers organize what they have learned from analyzing scanner data into a set of *stories* about their products and marketing environments. Thus humans often use experiences instead of general rules to solve problems. "Human experts are not systems of rules, they are libraries of experiences" (Riesbeck and Schank 1989, p. 15). Therefore, analogical reasoning is a plausible model for human problem solving in general and marketing problem solving in particular. Although case-based reasoning and analogical reasoning are sometimes used as synonyms, it is more appropriate to consider case-based reasoning as a specific form of analogical reasoning, that is, the type of reasoning that uses *intradomain* analogies. Analogies can also serve as a source of creativity. In that situation, typically, a problem in a particular domain is solved by using an analogy with another, often very remote domain (e.g., the double helix as a model for DNA). These are called *interdomain* analogies.

The second notion lying at the origin of case-based reasoning systems is the idea that analogical reasoning, which apparently is very powerful in humans, can also be used as a model for computer reasoning. In the early 1990s this thought gave rise to a new field in AI: case-based reasoning. Since that time a substantial literature about case-based reasoning has accumulated, case-based reasoning (software) tools have been developed, and many applications have been reported. Important references on case-based reasoning (which also served as sources for our discussion in this chapter) are Schank (1982), Riesbeck and Schank (1989), Kolodner (1993), Schank, Kass, and Riesbeck (1994), and Leake (1996). Applications of case-based reasoning in business environments are described in Althoff, Auriol, Barletta, and Manago (1995) and Watson (1997).

To illustrate the idea of case-based reasoning systems, we describe the computerized case-based reasoning system that is used at George Washington University. The APACHE[1] system (Newquist 1994) helps to evaluate a patient who has been brought into the intensive-care ward. When a patient is admitted to the hospital, doctors enter 27 pieces of data about that person (vital signs, level of consciousness, lab results, and so on) into the APACHE system. The system then compares this patient's file with the file of 17,448 records of other patients in a case base. Based on the similarity of the new patient's condition with that of previous patients, APACHE makes an assessment of the new patient's chances of survival. Based on this assessment, the doctor can determine how to care for the patient and what treatment(s) to choose.

The transition from intensive care to marketing is relatively straightforward. Consider a marketing manager confronted with a brand whose market share is tumbling. The marketing manager has several other pieces of information about the brand: brand awareness, customer loyalty, (relative) price, perceived quality, distribution, actions of competitors, gains of competitors, and so on. If the manager had a file with historical cases of brands that have been in similar circumstances, including the actions taken and the outcomes of these actions, this file could help him or her determine what to do with the brand and, if there is sufficient perspective, what treatment to choose.

---

[1]   APACHE stands for Acute Physiology, Age, and Chronic Health Evaluation.

The application domains of case-based reasoning can be divided into two categories: (1) the use of case-based reasoning for *classification* tasks, including diagnosis, predicting/forecasting, and assessment, and (2) the use of case-based reasoning for *synthesis* tasks, including planning and design. The APACHE system just described belongs in the first category. Designing a sales promotion would be an example of a synthesis task. Compared to rule-based reasoning, which forms the basis of expert systems, case-based reasoning does not require specialists (experts) to describe their know-how as logical rules. In this way case-based reasoning overcomes what has historically been one of the stumbling blocks in building expert systems. A case-based reasoning system can handle domains that are not fully understood and where many exceptions to rules exist. Case-based reasoning is a very flexible methodology. Compared to rule-based systems, case-based reasoning can deal with broader areas and with more irregularities. Case-based reasoning systems are less "brittle": they still come up with a solution even if there is no perfect fit. Although a case-based reasoning solution is not always perfect for the problem at hand, in every situation you can find a closest case that can suggest a default solution. This makes case-based reasoning a robust methodology, with a rich application potential, especially in complex domains.

Apart from its direct contribution to decision making by solving problems at hand, case-based reasoning systems have additional benefits in that they help preserve the know-how of the most talented experts in an organization. Expertise can be transferred from the skilled to the novice, and a corporate memory can be built (Althoff et al. 1995). Case-based reasoning is still in the early stage of its life cycle. However, for the reasons described below, we think that case-based reasoning has great potential as a knowledge-processing method for marketing management support systems.

Marketing is not blessed with a large amount of generalizable knowledge at this point in time (see section 3.5). Case-based reasoning does not make use of generalized knowledge but instead uses the specific knowledge of previously experienced concrete problem situations. All the knowledge pertaining to a case is left intact. This can be an advertising campaign, the introduction of a new product, or a sales-promotion activity. The rich, coherent whole of all the elements describing a marketing problem is preserved. Rule-based reasoning, the knowledge-processing method discussed in the last chapter, represents knowledge as a set of fragments logically related to each other. This approach is probably more suited for reasoning in well-structured domains than it is for reasoning in the complex, semistructured, or weakly structured domains that we encounter in many areas of marketing.

The importance of cases in marketing was recognized a long time ago, long before the advent of case-based reasoning. Think, for example, of the important role of cases in marketing education. There is an ongoing production of cases in marketing all the time. All marketing events taking place for a product—be it an advertising campaign, a sales promotion, a new product introduction, or a threatening competitive move—are cases that contain relevant marketing knowledge. In FMCG companies such as Unilever or Procter and Gamble, which are active in a range of product classes in a large number of markets with many different brands, tens of thousands of such cases are produced every year. The data of such cases could easily be stored, not only for events pertaining to the company's own brands, but also for events pertaining to the brands of the competition. Apparently, the case format is an efficient way to describe marketing problems and reason about their solutions.

6.1.2   Principles of Case-Based Reasoning Systems

The heart of a case-based reasoning system is the database of earlier cases, the so-called *case base*. Cases are stored with as much relevant information as possible (referring to the problem, the solution, and the outcome, respectively). When a new problem arises, the system searches for a problem that is as similar as possible to the new one (according to some specified criteria) and presents the solution for that problem as a suggested ("ballpark") solution for the new problem. An adaptation may be necessary to derive a solution for the new situation from the "old" solution. This solution may then be implemented and, subsequently, retained in the case base as an additional case or a revision of the original case. An overall picture of the case-based reasoning cycle is depicted in Figure 6.1.

A new problem is solved by *retrieving* one or more previously experienced cases, *reusing* the case(s) (possibly adapting it or them), *revising* the solution suggested by the earlier case(s), and *retaining* the new experience by adding it to the case base. As Figure 6.1 shows, a case-based reasoning system not only contains cases (contextual pieces of knowledge), but can also include a certain amount of general knowledge. Such general knowledge concerns the way that a comparison between the new problem and the cases in the case base can be made, how similar cases can be efficiently found in the case base, and how the adaptation strategies can be applied.

How exactly would this process work in a marketing context? Suppose a manufacturer of sauces and dressings wants to carry out a sales promotion. Looking in his case base, he finds the case of a successful joint promotion of a Mexican salsa with a brand of potato chips. The two products taste really good together. This triggers the idea of a joint promotion of a salad dressing with fresh salad. Although the principle of this joint promotion is the same, several adaptations have to be made in the implementation of the promotion.

One difference is that chips are a packaged product that can easily be stored together with salsa on the shelves of a supermarket, whereas salad is sold fresh in the produce department, which implies different arrangements for the joint presentation of the two products and also a shorter duration for the sales promotion.

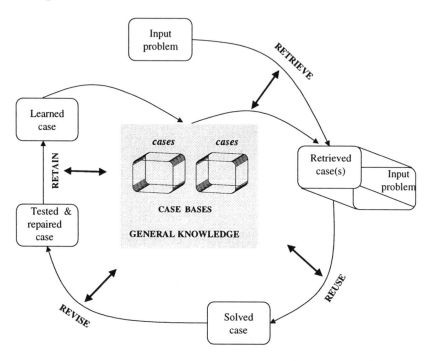

Figure 6.1   The Case-Based Reasoning Cycle (*Source:* Aamodt and Plaza 1994)

Although the principle of case-based reasoning is fairly straightforward, there are several issues in the case-based reasoning cycle that need to be elaborated on. We will now discuss a number of these issues in detail, including the representation of cases; the retrieval and indexing of cases; the adaptation of the case resulting in a solution for the new problem; and case revision, retention, and learning. During these discussions it will be helpful to refer to Figure 6.2, which provides a more detailed schematic of the process between problem input and solution in case-based reasoning.

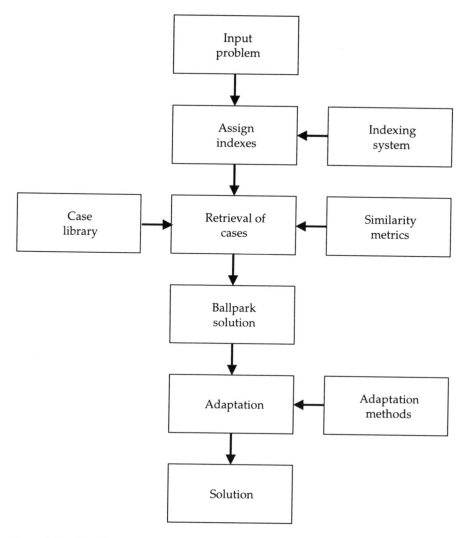

Figure 6.2   Case-Based Reasoning Systems: From Input to Solution

Representation of Cases

The *representation* problem in case-based reasoning concerns the decision of what knowledge to store about a case and how to represent that knowledge. There are three major parts to any case:

1. The problem situation.
2. The solution.
3. The outcome.

The particular attributes chosen for the representation of cases will depend on the domain. Assume, for example, that a company in FMCG has a case-based reasoning system that can help to design sales promotions for its brands based on a description of the brand and its situation in the market. In the description of a particular sales-promotion case, the *problem situation* part contains information about the type of brand, product class, current market share of the brand, consumer behavior with respect to the product, recent actions of competitors, and so on. The *solution* describes the specific sales promotion chosen, that is, the type of promotion (e.g., temporary price discount), its duration, the amount of advertising spending, and so on. The *outcome* part contains the result of the sales promotion in terms of additional sales and the effects on profit and market share. A case can be useful even without all three parts filled in. For example, cases that include only a problem and a solution can still be used in developing solutions to new problems. However, they are less useful if the purpose is to evaluate solutions.

Within the problem situation part of the case, three major components can be distinguished: goals, constraints, and features. The most important element, the *goal,* defines the aims of the actor. Possible goals of a sales promotion could be to create brand awareness or increase sales. Figure 6.3 provides an example of a case description for a sales promotion. It shows how the management of a newspaper might have used case-based reasoning to arrive at a successful sales promotion. (We do not know whether the particular analogy was actually instrumental in finding the promotion.)

Constraints are specific limitations, such as the maximum budget for sales promotions or institutional constraints (e.g., the fact that it is against the law to use advertising in combination with a sales promotion for cigarettes). *Features* of the problem situation can refer to any description of the case that is deemed useful in reaching the goal. In general, these features have to be determined by a specialist in the domain. It is important to choose the right level of abstraction for these features. Furthermore, it should always be possible to add additional features while using a case-based reasoning system.

One can use different knowledge representation methods for representing the knowledge about the cases in the case-based reasoning system. For organizing the data that make up a case, frame-based representation is very well suited. With frames a case can be represented as one coherent structure, and the cases can be organized efficiently in an inheritance hierarchy (see section 5.3.2). For the adaptation of cases, which mostly implies changes in individual attributes, rule-based approaches can be useful.

In the opinion of the marketing management of the Dutch newspaper *Algemeen Dagblad* (AD), the paper has a somewhat dusty image. It wants to change that by communicating a more attractive lifestyle, thereby improving its image and attracting new customer groups. The usual promotion instruments (e.g., temporary reductions of the subscription price for specific groups) are overused in the category and have lost most of their effectiveness. AD's promotion budget is limited, and after discussing the options, the AD management decides to do an event promotion. This promotion should radiate a modern lifestyle, should attract a new audience, and should create "rumor around the brand"; moreover, it should be possible to combine it with other sales-promotion activities.

Suppose AD has a case base that serves as a repository for storing interesting promotional events. The management looks in the case base for a source analogy: a promotion that was organized within a similar situation to AD's, where a company had used a sales promotion to achieve goals similar to AD's current goals.

The case that is retrieved is the "Camel Trophy" event, where the cigarette brand Camel started to organize an annual motor car competition that attracts a lot of attention (free publicity) and associates the Camel brand with a young, sportive lifestyle. Camel has set up all kinds of connected activities, for example, a special line of clothing. Using the Camel Trophy as the source analogy, AD decides to sponsor the annually held "North Sea Jazz Festival," a three-day, high-profile event in The Hague/Scheveningen that attracts thousands of visitors from the desired demographic and is televised extensively.

AD has now sponsored the event for two years with great success. It has combined the sponsoring with other sales-promotion activity such as a Special Issue of the newspaper devoted to the Festival, the sale of special CDs, and sampling of the newspaper at the Festival. Sponsoring the North Sea Jazz Festival is not the same as organizing an event such as the Camel Trophy: the promotion has been "adapted" to the specific circumstances of AD (for instance, the limited budget). Nevertheless, the source (organizing the Camel Trophy) and target analogy (sponsoring the North Sea Jazz Festival) are very similar at a higher level of abstraction.

Figure 6.3   An Example of a Case Description for a Sales Promotion (*Source:* This case was developed based on an idea by Arco Dalebout)

Retrieval

Retrieval involves searching the case library to identify those cases that match the new situation well. For the retrieval of cases, two elements are important: indexing and similarity. The goal of case *indexing* is to select a subset of the attributes in order to make faster retrieval possible. The capability of a case-based reasoning system to retrieve relevant cases is mainly determined by the quality of its indexing system. Indexes have to be chosen in a way that is related to their usefulness in solving new problems. For example, think of a multinational company in the FMCG sector that wants to set up a case-based reasoning system with a case base of all its sales promotions worldwide. In such a situation indexes might run from product class to country to whether or not the sales promotion was especially aimed at children. Indexes can be concrete or abstract. The weight of a package unit would be an example of a concrete index; at a certain point in a consultation it might be useful to be able to retrieve all sales promotions with small package sizes. Strategy would be an example of a more abstract index (for example, fighter brands versus cash cows). In developing an index, one should take the *vocabulary* of the prospective users of the system into account. The elements of the discourse about (the same) food products would be quite different for marketers as opposed to nutritionists, for example. Therefore, in choosing the indexes, people with expertise about the domain should be involved. The better the person choosing the index understands the domain, the better the index tends to be.

The case-based reasoning tool searches the case base for cases that closely resemble the new problem in terms of the specified attributes. *Similarity metrics* are needed to determine the *match* of a case in the case library with a new problem. Retrieval can take place on the basis of superficial or *syntactical similarities* or on the basis of features that refer to deeper *semantic similarities.* The first approach, also called "knowledge poor," makes use of only a limited amount of domain knowledge. A case-based reasoning system that uses only superficial attributes like product class, country, and size of the company for the retrieval of similar sales-promotion cases is an example of such a simple approach. Methods based on semantic similarities, also called "knowledge intensive," are able to use the contextual meaning of a problem description and the general insights of a domain. For example, for sales promotions the reputation of a brand and its associations (e.g., with quality, health, or honesty) may be more important for the suitability of a particular sales promotion than its product class. A case-based reasoning system using such types of information when retrieving cases would follow a *semantic similarities* approach.

Similarity basically is a distance concept. So (inverse) similarities can be computed as distances in the multidimensional (index) space. A straightforward approach to finding the best matching case is the *nearest-neighbor method.* However, several other similarity metrics are possible, ranging from the city-block metric to the weighted Minkowski metric (Althoff et al. 1995, p. 7).

Figure 6.4 presents an example of similarity computations according to different distance metrics. Suppose the brand manager of Mybrand plans a sales promotion for her brand. She wants to search the sales-promotion case base of her company for sales promotions that were applied for brands in market situations similar to that of Mybrand. If we assume that the relevant problem attributes for this sales-promotion decision are position of the brand in the market, brand prestige, price category, media advertising, and strength of competition, the scores of Mybrand and three cases in the case base might look like those shown in Figure 6.4.

Problem Attributes	Scores on Problem Attributes			
	CASES IN CASE BASE			
	A	B	C	*Mybrand*
Position of brand in the market (1 = largest brand; 2 = largest but one; etc.)	1	2	4	2
Brand prestige (1 = high; 5 = low)	3	1	1	3
Price category of the brand (1 = highest; 5 = lowest)	4	1	2	4
Intensity of media advertising (1 = high; 5 = low)	1	4	4	1
Strength of competition (1 = very strong; 5 = very weak)	4	3	3	1

	DISTANCE FROM *Mybrand*	
Similarity Metric	Nearest Neighbor	City block
Case A	10	4
Case B	26	10
Case C	25	11

Figure 6.4   Computing the Similarity of the Problem Situation of Mybrand with Cases A, B, and C in the Case Base: Different Similarity Metrics

The results of the computations for two different distance metrics, nearest neighbor and city block, respectively, are given in the lower half of the figure. Nearest-neighbor similarity is the Euclidean distance (generalized Pythagorean rule) between the two cases.[2] City-block distance simply adds the distances per attribute into an overall measure. As can be seen in the table, case A matches best with Mybrand, which is reflected in both metrics. So the brand manager of Mybrand is probably most interested in the kind of sales promotion that was carried out for case A. The problem situations of cases B and C are more different from Mybrand. Of these two, according to the nearest-neighbor metric, case C is slightly more similar to the situation

---

[2]   Figure 6.4 gives the squares of these distances.

of Mybrand, but according to the city-block metric, case B is slightly more similar.

It is not always wise to concentrate exclusively on the best-matching case. An alternative approach is to have the case-based reasoning system produce an initial set of relatively good–matching cases and then, in interaction with the user, determine which is the most useful given the objective of the consultation.

For the retrieval of similar cases in a case base, not only is a similarity metric needed, but a case-based reasoning system should also contain retrieval algorithms to carry out the search in an efficient way. The simplest approach is exhaustive serial search to a flat memory (list). In that case one is certain of finding the best case (i.e., closest to the new problem according to the attributes specified). However, the procedure can become very time-consuming if the case base is large. It is often possible to apply more intelligent search procedures that make use of the structure in the case base. If, for example, the case base has a hierarchical structure (e.g., a tree or graph structure), this knowledge can be used to develop so-called "deep" index structures that make it possible to search only subsets of the case library. The order in which these different parts of the knowledge base are searched may be based on rules that have (inductively) been discovered by analyzing the case base. For example, it might have been observed that successful sales promotions for soft drinks occur much more often in the second half of the year than in the first half. Using this information in the retrieval process is sometimes referred to as *inductive retrieval* (Watson 1997, p. 28).

Adaptation

The basic idea of case-based reasoning is that solutions that have been employed earlier can be reused in subsequent, similar situations. The best-matching case is taken as the *ballpark solution*. When the differences between the new problem and the past case are small or considered irrelevant, the solution can be transferred to the new problem without alteration. However, often the new and the old situation are not that similar, and the old solution has to be adapted to make it applicable to the new problem situation. Whereas case retrieval is a task at which computers are very good, the human decision maker has to play an important role in the adaptation stage.

Basically, there are two adaptation methods in the reuse of past cases: transformational reuse and derivational reuse. In the case of *transformational reuse* the old solution is *transformed* into a solution for the new problem. We encountered an example of this in Chapter 2 when Croky "reused" the sales-promotion idea of its competitor Smith Chips. Croky also put plastic disks into bags of chips but used pictures of soccer players instead of cartoons. Another transformation is "parameter adjustment," a heuristic for adjusting numerical parameters of an old solution. An example is changing the running time of a coupon action from one to two months. In the case of *derivational reuse* it is not so much the original solution that is adapted. Here the method that was used for generating that solution is "replayed" for the conditions of the new problem. For example, if season was the "method" used by a supermarket organization to hit on a highly successful wine action in the fall, the same method might suggest an action with fresh fruits in the spring.

There is no general solution to the case adaptation problem. Domain characteristics, to a large extent, determine the options for adaptation. Case adaptation is easier for classification than for synthesis tasks. In prediction tasks, for example, it may not be possible to find a case that exactly equals the problem at hand. However, one may find several cases that differ from the present problem on only a few attribute values. It may then be possible to have a computer make a forecast that carries out adjustments for these differences (*interpolative adaptation*). For planning and design tasks, where the users are often highly educated and skilled, adaptation is usually left to human experts.

Case Revision, Retention, and Learning

The case solution generated by the reuse of an existing solution might not be successful. In such a situation *case revision* (the stage after solution in Figure 6.1) has to take place. This implies that the errors in the case base are repaired. Sometimes it takes time before a solution can be evaluated (e.g., in the case of particular medical treatments); as a consequence, the possible revision in such a case has to wait. The human memory is continuously changing as the result of new experiences. Schank (1982) used the term "dynamic memory" to describe this phenomenon. Accordingly, a case-based reasoning system should also have this dynamic feature. It should have the capacity to add new cases and to help the user to learn from experiences. For this purpose, a case-based reasoning system has capabilities for *case retention* and *learning*. This is the process of incorporating what is useful to retain from the new problem-solving episode into the existing knowledge. After every cycle the case base of a case-based reasoning system is updated. If a problem was solved using a previous case, the old one may subsume the present case. If the present solution is an adaptation of an existing one, then the new solution may be stored as a separate case. A new case is also entered when the problem was solved by other methods, including asking the user. This ever growing case base constitutes a first opportunity for learning. Learning can also take place when information is stored about how successful (or unsuccessful) it was to use a specific solution in reaction to a specific feature of a problem. This will strengthen/weaken the association between a specific feature and a specific case. In this way the system learns from successes as well as from failures. A third form of learning takes place if the system not only records the solutions that were chosen but also stores the traces of how those solutions were derived. Capturing these reasoning traces for reuse ("replay") in a future problem situation also represents learning. Induction methods can be used to learn from the cases in the case base. For this purpose methods from another area of artificial intelligence, *machine learning,* can be used. In this context the expression *case-based learning* is sometimes used. Neural networks, which we will deal with later in this chapter, can be used to learn from the cases in a case base.

6.1.3   Applications and Tools

Although case-based reasoning (CBR) is a young field, many real-life CBR-based decision aids have been developed already. Examples of case-based reasoning applications for *classification* tasks include the following: the APACHE system, which supports decisions with respect to intensive-care patients; Battle Planner, which can help to develop strategies and tactics for battles; Casey, a system for diagnosing heart problems; and several help-desk support systems (Leake 1996). Other CBR systems primarily support *synthesis* and *design* tasks, for example, the configuration of an autoclave (convection oven); systems for meal planning, landscape design, or the design of electrical devices; and systems that support the design task of architects. Applications of case-based reasoning systems in companies include areas such as technology (process control, engineering), finance and insurance (credit assessment), telecommunications, manufacturing, and transportation (Althoff et al. 1995; Watson 1997).

So far applications of case-based reasoning in marketing seem to be lagging. However, it is easy to think of marketing tasks that lend themselves very well to case-based reasoning. Obvious application areas are finding out what happened in the market on the basis of market data (diagnosis), developing marketing plans (planning), constructing sales promotions and media plans, and developing new products (design). In the next section we will discuss case-based reasoning systems in marketing.

Several tools are becoming available for case-based reasoning. Ideally, a decision maker who wants to use CBR should be able to concentrate on case acquisition and case engineering without having to worry about the system itself. Software tools are now being developed for the construction of CBR systems. Complete CBR shells are also available on the market already. Some of these shells provide mechanisms to support retrieval, such as nearest-neighbor retrieval, or to automatically generate decision trees (using machine learning). The ReMind shell (Cognitive Systems 1992), for example, offers an interactive environment for the acquisition of cases, domain vocabulary, indexes, and prototypes. The user may define hierarchical relations among attributes and similarity measures. The system supports several case retrieval methods from which the user can choose. ReMind also has case adaptation capabilities. Althoff et al. (1995) provide an in-depth comparison of five case-based reasoning tools: CASE-BASED REASONING EXPRESS, ESTEEM, KATE, REMIND, and S3-CASE. In Watson (1997, Chap. 6) these CBR software tools are also discussed, together with several additional ones, including ART*Enterprise*, RECALL, CASE-1, CASEADVISOR, and CASEPOWER. Watson also provides vendor information.

In this brief introduction to case-based reasoning we have dealt only with the basic principles. The literature on case-based reasoning is extensive and growing quickly. Readers who want a more in-depth discussion of these basic principles and of many other aspects of CBR are referred to the monographs and readers on this topic mentioned earlier.

6.1.4   Case-Based Reasoning Systems in Marketing

Whereas there have been several implementations of rule-based reasoning and expert systems in marketing already, the experiences with case-based reasoning in marketing are still limited. Burke's (1991) ADDUCE system uses analogical reasoning for predicting how consumers will react to new advertisements by searching for relevant past advertising experiments and generalizing the results across similar contexts. However, this system is not a case-based reasoning system in a strict sense since it uses, in addition to the cases, a knowledge base with theory about the working of advertising. This theory, which directs the search for similarities in ADDUCE, makes it different from a standard CBR system.

We will now discuss two case-based reasoning systems developed for the support of marketing problem solving that have not yet appeared in the literature.

A Case-Based Reasoning Promotion Planning System

McCann, Hill, and McCullough (1991) developed the case-based reasoning Promotion Planning System to support sales-promotion decisions in FMCG markets. In their system a particular sales promotion is represented by three classes of features, which they call item profile, event profile, and results profile. The indexes used in their system are listed and illustrated for a particular case in Figure 6.5.

Item Profile	
Name	Magic Bean
Size	one pound
Category	coffee
Number in case	8
Price	2.50
Cost	2.25
Involvement	low
Inventory risk	low
Franchise strength	strong

Event Profile	
Value type	price cut
Action type	immediate
Popularity scope	more popular
Line scope	in line
Selection scope	selective
Market scope	regional
When to promote	in season
When to announce	early
Duration	short
Frequency	low
Discount rate	deep
Terms	loose
Market	Miami
Date to be offered	15 May 1988
Date to be started	1 June 1988
Length of promotion	4 weeks
Discount	0.20

Results Profile	
Regular price	
Deal price	
Feature	
Display	
Units	
Revenue	
Advertising	

Figure 6.5   Indexes in the Case-Based Reasoning Promotion Planning System

The three classes of features in Figure 6.5 can be related to the three generic parts of a case representation referred to above: the problem situation, the solution, and the outcome. The *item profile* describes the problem in terms of brand name, type of product, costs, consumer involvement with buying the item, the possibilities for stocking the item (inventory risks), and strength of the brand (franchise). The *event profile* describes the actual sales promotion. The features in this class, which are listed in Figure 6.5, are self-explanatory. The most important items of the *results profile* are the number of units moved and the resulting revenues.

In the Promotion Planning System the user can input planned promotions, and the system will then search for matches in the case base (see Figure 6.6).

For this search the indexes (see Figure 6.5) are used. The user can set feature weights, which makes it possible to weight different features differently in determining similarities. The system searches the case base and comes up with the best-matching case. In Figure 6.6 the user has selected the planned promotion Magic Bean in Miami (upper-left pane) as the input problem. The system searches through the case base of past promotions (partly visible in the upper-middle pane of Figure 6.6) and comes up with several close matches, ordered according to their (dis)similarity to the input problem (see the upper-right pane).

CBR: PROMOTION MATCHER			
Planned Promotions	**Past Promotions**	**Matches**	
Java Lava in Seattle	Magic Bean St. Louis 87	**Magic Bean Atlanta 86**	**0.224**
Yank M Crank in Boston	Magic Bean NY 87	Java Lava Chicago 87	0.241
Magic Bean in Miami	Magic Bean Atlanta 86	Java Lava Dallas 87	0.241
	Java Lava USA 88	Magic Bean Bangor 87	0.243
	Yank M Crank DC 88	Magic Bean St. Louis 87	0.243
	Magic Bean Bangor 87	Java Lava USA 88	0.261
	Magic Bean LA 87	Magic Bean LA 87	0.263
	Java Lava Dallas 87	Yank M Crank DC 88	0.280
	Yank M Crank XC 86	Yank M Crank XC 86	0.281
	Java Lava Chicago 87	Magic Bean NY 87	0.393
Differing Slots			
Price	1.8	2.99	
Cost	1.25	2.5	
Involvement	high	low	
Franchise strength	strong	weak	
When to promote	off season	in season	
Frequency	low	high	
Discount rate	deep	shallow	
Terms	loose	tight	
Market	Miami	Atlanta	
Discount	8.15	8.11	
Similar Slots			

Figure 6.6   User Input in the Promotion Planning System

In this application it turned out that Magic Bean Atlanta 86 is the closest match. The lower half of Figure 6.6 shows the similarities and differences of the input problem with the most similar past case. In the Promotion Planning System the user can develop a complete draft solution (in terms of specifying values for event profile features) for the input problem and then search for a match in the case base. It is also possible to specify only the problem (item profile) and then search for cases that represent a solution for that problem. Such a solution would be called a "seed" and the case-based reasoning Promotion Planning System has a so-called Promotion Critiquer that produces "cautionary comments" about implementing this seed solution for the problem situation at hand.

In the situation that a sales promotion had to be developed to support the introduction of a new product, Promotion Critiquer might give the following comment:

> *The case that you are looking at used 4 price packs. Price packs are not strong trial generators. However, it also used one sample event, which is a good way to generate trial. You may want to consider a trial size.*

Such cautionary comments may induce the user to adapt the solution for the current problem.

We described McCann et al.'s Promotion Planning System to demonstrate some of the features of a case-based reasoning system for sales promotions. It uses a limited number of attributes to represent a case, and it does not have mechanisms for supporting the adaptation of cases or learning. Now let us look at another, slightly more sophisticated system.

A Case-Based Reasoning Forecasting System for Retail Sales

McIntyre, Achabal, and Miller (1993) developed a system that uses case-based reasoning to forecast the sales generated by sales promotions in a retailing environment. Accurate sales forecasts are very important for a supermarket organization; they can reduce overbuying, increase inventory turnover, decrease clearance markdowns, and reduce stock-outs (the situation when the store is out of stock of an item) and thus lost sales. Expert buyers make sales forecasts; McIntyre et al. discovered that these expert buyers do not use well-established rules to develop forecasts, but rather reason by analogy. Expert buyers select past promotional analogies, review the differences with the planned promotion, and adjust these analogies if they are different from the planned promotion. This intuitive sales-forecasting strategy of expert buyers thus follows the structure formalized in a case-based reasoning approach. McIntyre et al. developed a CBR system that resembles the approach of the expert buyers.

In their system a sales promotion is represented by ten factors:

1. Price (ratio of regular to promotional price).
2. Trend.
3. Seasonality.
4. Number of days at the promotional price.
5. Type of display during promotion.
6. Percentage of stores participating.
7. Number of TV spots.
8. Number of radio spots.
9. Quality of print ads.
10. Number of print ads.

The purpose of the system is to make a sales projection for a given sales-promotion plan. This is done as follows: The three cases most similar to the current plan are selected from the case base. This retrieval is carried out by computing the nearest-neighbor distances on the basis of the ten factors that characterize a case (actually, the system applies an additional step and considers only the sales promotions for similar product types). For each of the three retrieved cases the system then makes an adaptation, based on so-called *adjustment tables.* In the terminology discussed earlier, this method of case adaptation can be called *transformational-through-parameter adaptation.* The adjustment coefficients are determined in interaction with the expert buyers. Next, the sales forecast for the given plan is computed as the weighted average of the adjusted sales for the three most similar cases, where the weights are the inverses of their nearest-neighbor similarity with the plan.

McIntyre et al. had a case base of only 39 cases. Using the bootstrapping technique—that is, leaving one case out as the "plan" and considering the 38 remaining cases as the case base from which the forecast was made—and repeating this procedure for all cases, the developers of this system made 39 forecasts. These were compared to the expert buyer's estimates for the same sales promotions. It turned out that the system was more accurate than the expert buyer, measured by the mean average percentage error (MAPE) and mean absolute deviation (MAD). The system also had a slightly higher percentage of wins. So the system, although operating from fewer historical analogs than the best expert buyer of the organization, successfully matched or exceeded the expert buyer's intuitive forecasting of promotional sales.

This study, being one of the first in a practical marketing situation, empirically demonstrated the usefulness of the case-based reasoning approach in a marketing context. Note that in the approach taken by McIntyre et al., case-based reasoning was used only to *evaluate given solutions*. The results are encouraging. However, the real value of case-based reasoning lies in *generating new solutions* based on the similarities of the new problem with problems solved earlier. Case-based reasoning should help a decision maker to generate better solutions. More research is needed on the contribution of CBR to the solution of marketing problems and on the conditions under which these pattern-matching techniques are most effective (Hoch and Schkade 1996).

The application of case-based reasoning to sales-promotion decisions is straightforward and offers just one example of a marketing application of CBR. However, for many other (and more complex) marketing decision areas, it is possible to set up case bases of earlier events and to use case-based reasoning systems to bring this knowledge to bear on decisions for new situations. Examples of such areas are the selection of customers, the development of advertising campaigns, the introduction of new products, entry in new markets, and reactions to competitive actions. The data in a case base constitutes "knowledge" that a company has about specific areas—notably, about what has been successful (and not) in the past. A company can learn from this knowledge. As mentioned earlier, when the case base is sufficiently large, machine-learning techniques such as neural networks, to be discussed in the next section, can be used for this learning.

6.2   Neural Networks

After rule-based and case-based reasoning, the next knowledge technology we deal with is the neural networks or connectionist approach. As we described in section 5.3, this approach is completely different from the symbolic representation school. The connectionist approach tries to rebuild (on a very small scale) the "physical machinery" of the human brain in a computer. It takes as its starting point the structure of the brain and the processes that take place when the brain processes information. By building artificial analogies of these structures and processes in computers, the connectionist approach tries to reproduce elements of human intelligence.

6.2.1   Introduction

One can question in what respect(s) people are smarter than computers. Human beings are not as good as computers at performing complex computations (number crunching) or at thoroughly and consistently searching through large databases. However, people perform much better than computers at tasks such as recognition (e.g., a face, a situation) and making associations (e.g., solving cryptograms). People are not only extremely fast at such tasks but also very robust. Frequently, objects and events do not appear complete and in full clarity. Often, they are only partly visible, distorted, blurred, and messy. Nevertheless, in many cases human beings are still able to recognize them and (re)act in an adequate manner. Experience and expertise, to an important degree, are based on pattern recognition. An experienced marketer, when exposed to a complex marketing situation, often immediately comes up with a correct diagnosis or with a plan for action. Sometimes this is called "solving by intuition," but according to Simon (1995), a better label would be "solving by recognition." Somehow, the manager *recognizes* something in the situation that triggers a reaction.

In data-rich environments (such as marketing), it is important to equip computers with such pattern-recognition capabilities. Suppose that a company has a database describing a large number of past introductions of new products. For each introduction a record is available that describes the product introduction (characteristics of the new product, the market, the competitors, data about the introduction campaign, and so on). Furthermore, the record contains information about whether the new product became a success (S) or a failure (F). An experienced marketer would learn from earlier product introductions, and this education would help him or her to predict the success of a new introduction. We can train an (artificial) neural network to do exactly the same things. Such a network would be shown, for a series of new product introductions, the data on the characteristics of the product introduction and the corresponding success/failure outcome. The product introduction characteristics would be the *input* of the network, the outcome (success or failure) would be the *output,* and the network would train the associations between input and output patterns. After this training the network would be able to classify other new product introductions (not used during the training) as successes or failures. Such a trained network could then be used to assist managers in judging new product proposals.

6.2.2   Principles of Neural Networks

Since the purpose of an artificial neural network is to replicate in computers the capacity for quick recognition and making associations, it is important to know where this capacity resides in the brain. Quick recognition is not restricted to humans; other animals also have this capacity. A hawk, for example, recognizes its prey in less than a second. Research in neurobiology and cognitive science has established that a wide range of phenomena in recognition, learning, and memory can be accounted for by the structure of the brain, which consists of a huge number of small processing units (neurons) operating in parallel. These processing units are *connected* to each other, which is why we use the expression *neural networks*. We will first examine the way this process takes place in the biological world and then look at systems that are built to replicate this capacity for recognition and association in a computer.

Biological Neural Networks

The neuron is the building block of the human nervous system. A neuron is a communication station that receives information and transmits this information to other neurons with which it is connected. The human brain contains about 10^{15} neurons (Haberlandt 1994). A neuron (see Figure 6.7) consists of a cell body (the soma), dendrites through which information is received from other neurons, and the axon, a kind of tube through which the information is sent to the terminal buttons. At these terminal buttons the information, in turn, is received by neighboring neurons through their dendrites.

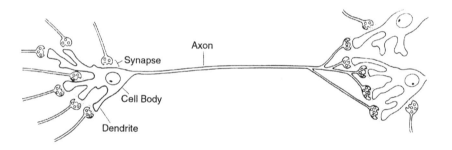

Figure 6.7   A Neuron

The transmission of signals from one neuron to the other takes place at the synapses. A synapse is the small gap between neurons. Transmission of signals at the gaps is performed by so-called neurotransmitters, molecules in which the signals are chemically coded. The action potential in the sending neuron causes neurotransmitters to be released and to travel to the receiving neuron, where they are chemically bound to receptor molecules. The transmission of a signal from one neuron to the other can have an excitatory or an inhibitory effect. *Excitation* means that the receiving neuron reacts positively to the input signal, whereas *inhibition* implies a negative reaction. When a neuron receives both excitatory and inhibitory inputs, these signals may cancel each other out. The neuron's response to stimulation is of the "all-or-nothing" type. Either the stimulus is too weak, falling below a certain threshold, and the neuron does not respond from its resting position, or the stimulus is stronger than the threshold and the neuron *fires,* that is, sends a signal to the neurons with which it has output connections. The associations between neurons are determined by the strengths of their connections. As Figure 6.7 shows, one neuron can be connected to more than one other neuron. The number of connections of one particular neuron can be as high as 6000.

Artificial Neural Networks

Already in the 1940s, researchers in psychology started to build models of (artificial) neuron systems that they used to explain memory and learning phenomena (McCulloch and Pitts 1943.) However, it was not until the 1980s that neural network technology really took off and started being applied to many problem areas. Very influential were the two volumes on "Parallel Distributed Processing": Rumelhart, McClelland and the PDP Research Group (1986) and McClelland, Rumelhart, and the PDP Research Group (1986). Although they use the terms *parallel distributed processing, connectionism,* and *(artificial) neural networks* interchangeably, we will mainly use the term *(artificial) neural network.* In the following section we discuss the structure and function of (artificial) neural networks.

A neural network consists of a set of artificial neurons, usually referred to as *units* or *nodes,* that are placed in a structure of two or more *layers.* A neural network has at least one *input layer* (where the signals come in) and one *output layer.* Since a two-layer network is severely limited in representing the relationship between input and output, a network usually possesses one or more layers of units between the input and the output layers. Such intermediary layers are called *hidden layers.* We will only deal with the principles of neural networks and discuss one particular type (feed-forward network with back propagation). For more information about neural networks, we refer the reader to McClelland and Rumelhart (1986), Lippmann (1987), Johnson-Laird (1988, Chap. 10), Dutta (1993, Chap. 9), Haberlandt (1994, Chap. 6), and Mehotra, Mohan, and Ranka (1997).

Figure 6.8 shows an example of a neural network with an input layer, one hidden layer, and an output layer. This network has four input units, three hidden units, and one output unit. The network in Figure 6.8 is a so-called *feed-forward network:* each unit feeds its signals into the units of the next layer.

Output
Layer

Hidden
Layer

Input
Layer

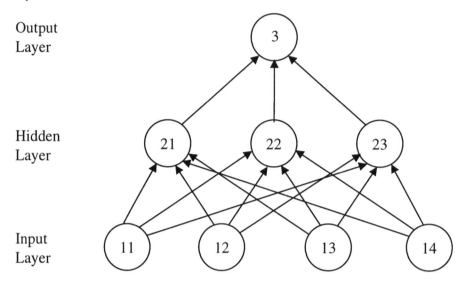

Figure 6.8.   Example of a Neural Network

The network in Figure 6.8 can represent a network that learns about new product introductions, a situation discussed above. The input units are the characteristics of a new product introduction, while the output node represents success (S) or failure (F). A network can be characterized by the strengths of the connections between its units. These strengths are expressed by the so-called connection *weights.* For example, in Figure 6.9, which shows a part of the network of Figure 6.8, $W_{11/22}$ is the connection weight between unit 11 in the input layer and unit 22 in the hidden layer.

Signals are transmitted from unit to unit, weighted by the connection weights between these units. This transmission takes place in two phases. In Figure 6.9 this process is illustrated for unit 22 of the hidden layer. Unit 22 receives signals from the input units 11 to 14. The strengths of these input signals are X_{11} to X_{14}, respectively. The *input* to unit 22 (I_{22}) is the weighted sum of the signals sent by the units from the input layer. To determine the *output* of unit 22, a *transfer function* is applied to the input.

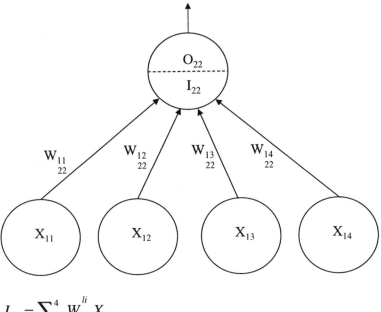

$$I_{22} = \sum_{i=1}^{4} W_{22}^{li} X_{li}$$

$$O_{22} = T(I_{22})$$

Figure 6.9   Connection Weights in Neural Networks

As Figure 6.10 shows, for the transfer function a step function is used. An S-shaped curve can be considered an approximation of a step function.

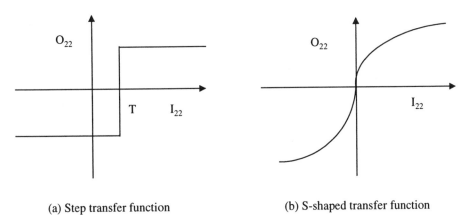

(a) Step transfer function   (b) S-shaped transfer function

Figure 6.10   Two Different Forms of Transfer Functions

The application of the step(like) transfer function has the consequence that the output signal is either very weak or very strong, which is a direct parallel of what occurs in the biological system. When the transfer function reaches its high value, the (artificial) neuron *fires*.

Training the Network

When the weights between the units are known, the network will produce an output for every set of inputs presented to it through the computational procedure just described. The connection weights reflect the associations of inputs with output patterns. In the human brain the connections between neurons are the synapses, and research shows that the synaptic junctions are formed through experience and learning. In artificial networks a *training process* determines the connection weights. Pairs of input and output items are presented to the network, and the network learns the associations between inputs and outputs. The results of this learning are expressed in the values of the connection weights. We only consider the situation of "supervised" learning here, where for each input there is a desired or actual output. The network is trained in such a way that the network, as faithfully as possible, reproduces the actual outputs. For that purpose the *error* between the output produced by the network in its current state and the desired output is propagated back into the network, and the weights are then updated. This entire feedback process is called *back propagation* (See Figure 6.11).

Training of the network is an iterative process. At the start small random values are assigned to the connection weights in the network. Next, inputs from a set of input-output pairs are fed to the network. Using its initial weight values, the network computes output values. Subsequently, the error between the desired output and the network output is calculated. Then a recursive algorithm, starting at the output nodes and working back toward the input nodes, adjusts the weight values so that the error is reduced. For the adjustment of the weights, the so-called delta rule is usually used (see Figure 6.12).

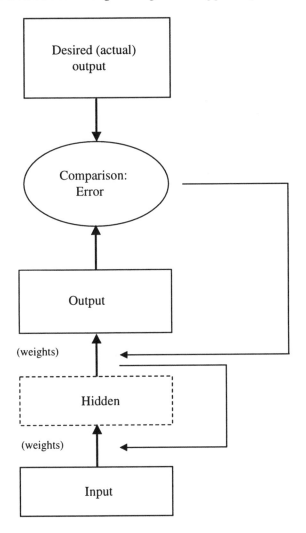

Figure 6.11. Back Propagation in a Neural Network

As can be seen in Figure 6.12, the weight of the connection from node *i* to node *j* (W$_{ij}$) is increased more, as this is more effective in reducing the error (expressed by $\delta = -dE/dW_{ij}$) and as the output from node *i* (O$_i$) is larger. The value of the weight in the previous iteration is also taken into account. By setting certain parameters (i.e., the learning rate and the momentum para-meters), the user can influence the speed of the learning process. These iterative steps are repeated until the error term is sufficiently small. During the process the algorithm repeatedly cycles through the entire training set. Each cycle through the whole training set is called an *epoch*. The main objective of training the network is to be able to generalize to new cases. Because of this generalization purpose, care should be taken that learning from the examples in the training set should not go too far, in which case overfitting can occur. This means that the network becomes very good on the training examples but that the error on new examples increases.

$$\Delta W_{ij}(t) = \eta \, \delta O_i + \alpha \, \Delta W_{ij}(t-1)$$

where: ΔW_{ij} =   change in the weight W_{ij}

δ = $-dE/dW_{ij}$, i.e., the (at-the-margin) decrease of the error per unit increase in W_{ij}

η =   learning rate (to be set by the user)

α =   momentum parameters, which may speed up the learning process (also to be set by the user)

O_i =   output from node i

Figure 6.12   The Delta Rule

Design of the Network and Neural Network Software

Designing the network involves decisions about the type of network, the number of layers, and the number of nodes or units per layer. There are no strict guidelines, although some rules of thumb have been developed (Bailey and Thomson 1990). Experimentation can also be done to establish the best parameters of a neural network in a given situation. With respect to the number of layers, we have already remarked that a network with only two layers (i.e., input and output) is very restricted in its representation possibilities. Increasing the number of layers makes it easier to fit the network to the training data. However, training time increases quickly with the size of the network. Moreover, there is the danger of overfitting, resulting in poor generalization capabilities. As a consequence, most multilayer networks developed in practice consist of three layers: an input layer, one hidden layer, and the output layer.

With respect to the number of units per layer, for the input and output layers these numbers mostly follow directly from the purpose of the network and the problem situation. If a network has to be developed for the new product situation described above, the number of input nodes is equal to the number of variables, per new product introduction, for which we have data. The number of output nodes also follows directly from the problem, that is, two nodes (for success and failure). With respect to the number of hidden units, a rule of thumb from Bailey and Thomson (1990) is that the maximum number of hidden units can be computed as follows:

(number of inputs + number of outputs) × 2

In the network of Figure 6.8 this would amount to a maximum of 10 hidden units. This number can be taken as an upper bound. By experimenting with different numbers of hidden units, the developers of a system can determine which number is best in terms of the adaptation and generalization capabilities of the network in the specific situation.

Decisions about the functional form of the transfer function also have to be made. This concerns the learning rate η and the momentum parameter α. With the current knowledge on neural networks, experimentation is the best way to make decisions on these issues. Of course, such experimentation is easier with larger databases. One can then separate out a subset of the data (the holdout sample) to carry out experiments to find out about the most suitable number of hidden units and the best values for the other parameters. Next, the remaining data can be used for actually training (and validating) the network. The software packages that are available for rapidly building neural network applications usually have default values for the parameter values, which the user can change. For example, NeuralWorks (NeuralWare, Pittsburgh, PA), one of the best-known neural network software packages, employs the default value 0.6 for the learning rate η and 0.9 for the momentum parameter α. Other software packages for neural network applications are 4Thought (Right Information Systems, London/Newbury, MA), Neuroshell (Ward Systems Group, Frederick, MD), and Neural Connection (SPSS).

Comparison with Symbolic Approaches

Neural networks differ, in a fundamental sense, from the knowledge technologies rule-based representation, networked representation, and case-based representation, which we discussed above and in Chapter 5. The latter approaches are based on the so-called *physical symbol hypothesis,* which takes its starting point in concepts ("symbols") in the mind of the decision maker. According to this hypothesis, knowledge processing implies carrying out operations on symbols or systems of symbols. The connectionist approach, while using an architecture derived from the structure of the human brain, takes its starting point in the real world, without any a priori assumptions about concepts (symbols) and relationships among concepts. The connectionist approach is a bottom-up method (starting from facts or data) and is strong in knowledge discovery, pattern recognition, classifi-cation, and dealing with fuzzy situations (Minsky 1991). Neural networks are able to derive generalizations from events in noisy environments. Another advantage of neural networks over rule-based systems is their capacity to learn. Rule-based systems are typically static, whereas neural networks continuously adapt themselves to changes in the environment. However, a drawback of neural networks is their poor explanation facilities. A network does not tell why it associates a particular input pattern with a specific output. Another drawback is that relatively large data sets are needed to apply neural networks.

6.2.3   The Application of Neural Networks to Marketing Problems

Although the field of neural networks is still young, an impressive selection of applications can already be mentioned. These range from process control and fault diagnosis (manufacturing), signal detection (defense), traffic control (airlines), diagnosis (health care), credit approval and fraud detection (finance), and recognition of human faces (police) to the targeting of customers in direct marketing. In this section we discuss the applications of neural networks to marketing in three specific areas: time-series analysis, direct marketing, and data mining.

Time-Series Analysis

We will demonstrate the use of neural networks (NN) for the analysis of time-series data by using real-life data pertaining to market shares and marketing-mix efforts for five competing brands of an FMCG product in a large western European country (Wierenga and Kluytmans 1996). Together, the five brands cover the whole market (actually, brand E is a summary brand). The data is traditional (bimonthly) Nielsen data and covers the span from period 6 of 1984 to period 2 of 1993. For those 51 periods, for each of the five brands the authors had data on the following variables:

• Market share (volume).
• Relative price.
• Advertising share.
• (Weighted) distribution.
• (Weighted) out-of-stock.
• Trend.

The authors developed a neural network with the purpose of learning the association between market share, on the one hand, and the marketing-mix variables (and a trend variable), on the other. In this case the network has five input variables and one output variable (market share). For the training of the network a subset of the data was used. This subset, called the "training set," contained the 43 data points from 1984 to 1991. The 8 data points from 1992 and 1993 were used as fresh data for validation purposes; in neural network terminology, this subset is called the "test set." The authors specified a neural network with one hidden layer consisting of six units. In a test run involving only one brand and only the data from the training set, it turned out that the results did not improve when the number of hidden units was increased above six. After the association between the marketing-mix variables and market share was trained, the resulting neural network was used to make predictions of the market shares for the five brands, given the values for the marketing-mix variables and the trend. The prediction was made for each of the 51 data points in the sample, that is, for the training set as well as for the test set. The training of the neural network was carried out for each brand separately, with no provision made that the sum of the predicted market shares should be one. The actual discrepancies at this point turned out to be small, though. Figure 6.13 provides information about the quality of the predictions by showing the (RMS)[3] errors for each of the brands A to E (the left-hand side of the table refers to the NN results).

	Neural Network (NN)		Regression	
Brand	Training Set $n = 43$	Test Set $n = 8$	Training Set $n = 43$	Test Set $n = 8$
A	0.39	0.96	0.42	1.08
B	0.49	0.68	0.62	0.75
C	0.60	1.02	0.77	2.88
D	0.84	1.05	0.86	1.74
E	0.57	2.10	0.72	2.64
Average	0.58	1.16	0.68	1.82

Figure 6.13   Quality of the Predictions of a Neural Network: RMS Errors

The errors for the test set are of course larger than those for the training set (since the former data was not used to train the net). However, as Figure 6.13 shows, for the test set the performance of the neural network is still quite good, with a discrepancy between predicted and actual market share of around 1 point for brands A through D and of around 2 points for the (aggregate) brand E.

For the same data set a linear regression was also carried out, with market share as the dependent variable and the marketing-mix variables (plus trend) as independent variables. In this analysis the data was also split

---

[3]   RMS = root mean square.

into a training set and a test set. (In econometric work the test set is usually referred to as the *validation sample*.) The prediction errors for the regression model are presented in the right-hand side of Figure 6.13. We can conclude that while the neural network does somewhat better than the regression model on the training set, it does much better than the regression model on the test set. The latter set is of course the real arbiter. The mean RMS error is more than 50% higher for the regression model than for the neural network. It turned out that in 31 of the 40 (8 times 5) prediction occasions of the test set, the prediction of the neural network was closer to the actual market share than the prediction of the regression model. This implies a significantly better performance on the part of the neural network.

To illustrate the differences between both approaches, we can consider the market leader, brand C (which has over 40% market share). This brand increased its price significantly during the 1992–93 period (the test period). The regression model predicted a sharp decline in market share as a consequence of this price increase. However, the neural network had a better sense of the latent stability of the market and correctly predicted a more moderate reaction (in terms of the market share of brand C) to the price increase of this brand.

The application of neural networks to time series is presented as an example only. We cannot yet draw any general conclusions from the good performance of these systems here. Only one data set was used, and the neural network was compared with the simplest regression model. Nevertheless, it is clear that neural networks have potential for time-series analysis in marketing. In a study where neural networks were compared with regression and where Nielsen data was also used, Hruschka (1991, 1993) obtained the same result that neural networks outperformed econometric models. The strength of neural networks for forecasting tasks in a time-series context has also been demonstrated in a study by Hill, O'Connor, and Remus (1996), who found that neural networks outperformed six traditional statistical forecasting methods (Box-Jenkins, exponential smoothing, etc.) However, more research is needed regarding the conditions under which it is better to use neural networks in a marketing time-series analysis as opposed to other methods such as regression.

Direct Marketing and Other Cross-Sectional Data

In direct marketing the supplier of a product or service makes an offer directly to individual customers or prospects. This can be done by means of mailings, telemarketing, personal sales calls, and so on. A direct marketing action can be made more profitable by selecting those prospects that have a relatively high probability of responding. Therefore, it is important to find a relationship between the characteristics of a prospect (e.g., family type, income, lifestyle, education, type of house, past purchasing behavior, reactions to earlier campaigns, and so on) and his or her response probability. Traditionally, regression was used for this purpose. Recently, neural networks have also been explored. From a data set that contains actual responses of prospects (e.g., to a pilot mailing), a neural network can learn the relationship between prospect characteristics and response probability. Subsequently, the trained neural network can be used to select the most promising addresses from the remaining database for the full-scale mailing.

Recently, under the auspices of the Dutch Direct Marketing and Sales Association (DMSA) a series of case studies were carried out. These studies compared the performance of neural networks (and several other "adaptive" techniques) and regression analysis on a number of large databases (Wagenaar, Den Uyl, and Van der Putten 1997; Den Uyl and Langendoen 1997). Databases were made available by eight companies that are active in direct marketing—banks, insurance companies, railways, and charities.

One of the case studies used a database of 60,000 clients of an insurance company. For each of the clients the database contained information on 60 (socioeconomic and demographic) variables and on whether or not the client had bought a particular insurance product that had been offered. The selection of addresses to send a mailing to, based on the 60 variables, was determined with three different techniques. The results of these three techniques were mutually compared; they were also compared against a random selection. The results of these comparisons are presented in Figure 6.14.

Figure 6.14 is a so-called *gains chart*. A gains chart presents the response rate (as a percentage) for different selections from the database. The prospects are ordered from the most promising prospect to the least promising one. The ordering of the prospects is done using a particular prediction method. In Figure 6.14 three different prediction methods are compared: (1) regression, (2) a neural network with back propagation, and (3) another variant of neural networks, one based on resonance theory (see Mehotra, Mohan, and Ranka 1997, Chap. 5). (The company that developed the software baptized the latter method "Datadetective.") The gains chart shows that all three methods performed significantly better then random selection and that the two neural network methods both outperformed regression. Figure 6.14 is based on raw data. In this situation the resonance-based neural network outperformed the back-propagation neural network (at least up to a 50% selection from the database). After the raw data was cleaned, though, the back-propagation neural network performed best, with a response rate that was 1.5 to 2 times higher than that of a random selection of prospects.

As a result of their experiments with the different databases in the project, Den Uyl and Langendoen (1997) concluded that in direct marketing, adaptive techniques such as neural networks perform better than regression. This enhanced performance is especially evident for small selections of the database, for example, for the top 10 or 20%. Apparently, neural networks are particularly good at selecting the most promising prospects. Furthermore, the advantages of neural networks are greater if the number of variables per prospect is higher, that is, several hundreds of variables per prospect rather than 50 or 60. This is usually the case with internal databases, which tend to include a lot of relevant information on the past purchase behavior of clients. However, external databases (lists purchased from database companies) usually contain limited numbers of variables per prospect, in which case the advantages of neural networks over regression analysis tend to be modest (Wagenaar et al. 1997).

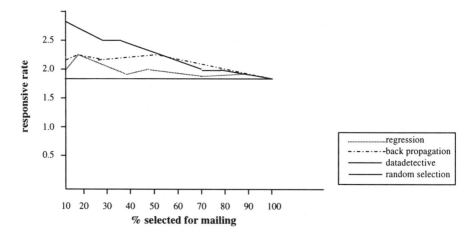

Figure 6.14   Results of Different Selection Techniques: A Gains Chart

In direct marketing neural networks are used for cross-sectional analyses. In two other studies using cross-sectional data, in-depth comparisons of neural networks with regression analysis were carried out. Kumar, Rao, and Soni (1995) compared neural networks to logistic regression using 1-0 data as the dependent variable (supermarket buyer decisions). They found that neural networks were relatively strong in classification accuracy, whereas logistic regression rated higher on interpretability. West, Brockett, and Golden (1997) predicted supermarket shopper behavior (whether or not a consumer is a frequent shopper at a particular retail chain) using scores on 19 store image characteristic scales as independent variables. They used discriminant analyses, logistic regressions, and neural networks as alternative prediction methods, and the neural networks outperformed the statistical methods in terms of explained variance and out-of-sample predictive accuracy. All these results show that neural networks are very promising for the prediction of buyer behavior.

Data Mining

Earlier in this book we referred to the "data explosion" in marketing. This explosion, which is a consequence of developments in information technology, leads to an enormous increase in the amount of marketing data. Human decision makers are simply not able to cope with these mountains of information. They lack the time to examine the data at any depth. Furthermore, it is often necessary to analyze a combination of several variables to really see the message in the data, and this kind of analysis is difficult to carry out manually.

In Chapter 3 we discussed the development of *data warehouses,* very large databases that contain historical data on customers, competitors, distributors, marketing events, and/or other entities, which may be used for decision support. For the extraction of knowledge from (large) databases the expression *knowledge discovery in databases* (KDD) has come into vogue (Fayad, Piatetsky-Shapiro, Smyth, and Uthurusamy 1996). Knowledge discovery in databases can be described as "the non-trivial extraction of implicit, previously unknown, and potentially useful knowledge from data" (Adriaans and Zantinge 1996, p. 5). An important stage in knowledge discovery in databases is *data mining,* which is the discovery stage of the KDD process. The metaphor of mining is chosen because of the parallels with the physical mining process, where the purpose is to discover the valuables (jewels, precious metals) amidst the surrounding dirt and dust. Data mining uses computer programs that aim at learning from the data in the (often very large) database and at discovering interesting associations. Neural networks constitute an important type of learning algorithms that are used to extract knowledge from databases. (Other approaches are machine learning and genetic algorithms.) Neural networks can be trained to learn the association between a specific output variable (e.g., whether a client has decided to switch to another supplier or to stay with the focal company) and the client in the data warehouse. Such a neural network can help to detect customers that have a relatively high probability of leaving the company as a client. For example, the analysis might show that clients who placed their most recent order on the last day of the workweek have a relatively high tendency to defect. This knowledge would certainly entice the supplying company to take a critical look at its order processing and delivery systems on Friday. Neural networks and other learning techniques can make an important contribution to the discovery of managerially relevant knowledge in large databases.

After analyzing the applications of neural networks in marketing so far, Pandelidaki and Burgess (1998) concluded that their performance is encouraging. In most cases they perform better than, or at least as well as, statistical methods. However, several issues, mainly concerning architecture and methodology, remain to be solved by additional research on neural networks in marketing.

6.3   Creativity Support Systems

The last type of marketing management support systems discussed in this chapter are creativity support systems.

6.3.1   Introduction

The fourth marketing problem-solving mode in the ORAC model is *creating* (see Chapter 2). Nobody will disagree that creativity is an important element of marketing management. After all, the field is driven by "marketing imagination" (Levitt 1983). There is a continuous pressure to generate creative ideas for new products and services. Creativity is also important for other marketing-mix instruments, such as advertising, package design, and sales promotions. The present chapter and the last one deal with knowledge-driven approaches to marketing management support. There exists a direct link between creativity and knowledge. On the one hand, creativity (e.g., generating new ideas and new ways to solve problems) implies the production of *new knowledge.* In the present economy and society, the ability of an organization to create (new) knowledge is of critical importance for innovation and future competitive advantage. Nonaka and Takeuchi (1995) speak of the *knowledge-creating company.* On the other hand, however, the new knowledge that is produced by means of creativity often consists of *new combinations* of existing knowledge components. Creativity *adds value to knowledge* by transforming knowledge from one form into another and in this way makes knowledge more useful (Kao 1996).

Although creating involves existing knowledge ("making new combinations of," "adding value to"), there is also an element of discontinuity. New knowledge is not always derived from existing knowledge in a linear way. Sometimes there are "jumps" of imagination. Creating is therefore probably the most elusive marketing problem-solving mode, and so far only a few *computer-aided* support systems have been developed to support it. Although marketing has applied techniques for stimulating the creativity of decision makers for a long time (brainstorming, lateral thinking, morphological analysis, etc.; see Crawford 1997), these methods operated without computers. In this section we discuss a new breed of *creativity support systems* (CSS): computer-based tools that enhance the creativity of decision makers and help them to produce new and useful ideas that keep an organization competitive in the marketplace (Abraham and Boone 1994; Massetti 1996).

The question of whether or not a computer program can be creative is much debated. Boden (1991) tends to give a positive answer to this question. Hofstadter (1995) observes that many "so-called creative systems" do not go much beyond a reshuffling of components (for example, pieces of prose or pieces of music) that were put into the program in the first place. We are not so much interested here in the creative abilities of computer programs as such (i.e., in the question of whether or not a computer program can be creative), but rather in the capabilities of information technology to make human marketing decision makers more creative. According to Kao (1996) information technology provides a powerful *amplifier* for creativity, but a computer is a tool and not a substitute for creativity. "Creativity still comes out of your brain" (p. 140). In this context it is important to distinguish between two different definitions of creativity, that is, creativity as a trait and creativity as an achievement (Eysenck 1994; Wierenga and Van Bruggen 1998). Creativity as a *trait* is a *dispositional* variable: the characteristics of a person lead him or her to produce acts, items, and instances of novelty. Creativity as an *achievement* refers to the creative *product* or the output of a creative *process,* for example, the number and quality of ideas that a person produces in a certain setting. Creative achievement will depend on the creativity of the individual as a trait, but also on other variables. Here we can think of personality variables (e.g., intelligence, motivation, and confidence), cultural factors, and environmental variables. The last variable includes *the availability of a computer-based creativity support system.* Assuming that an individual user has creativity as a trait, an effective creativity support system increases the creative output of his or her overall problem-solving process.

6.3.2 Research on Creativity Support Systems

In the literature on information/decision support systems, several experimental studies have reported the results of the use of creativity support systems. Typically, such a study contains the following elements:

- A *problem* that has to be solved by the respondents, for example, how to convince a company to make specific software changes, how to make the U.S. industry more innovative, how to deal with airline no-shows, how to deal with the homeless problem, how to improve an ailing doughnut franchise, and so on.

- A specific *creativity support system:* a software package that enhances the creative output of the problem-solving process. The several software packages use different mechanisms for enhancing creativity. For example, one package, ods/Consultant (Elam and Mead 1990), structures the decision process and has the respondents work on solutions in a stepwise fashion. The GENI system (*GEN*erating *I*deas) of MacCrimmon and Wagner (1994) has "making connections" as its leading principle: the creation of new ideas occurs through the association of entities from the problem domain with other entities, which can be as remote as the fragments of a poem. The software package IdeaFisher (Robbin 1990) provides the user with an idea bank of over 705,000 possible associations of topics, phrases, and words.

- A specific *experimental design,* which can be either *between respondents,* where some of the respondents work with the creativity support software and others solve the problem without it, or *within respondents,* where each respondent solves different problems either with the creativity support software or without it. Often a "noncreative" control system is used in the "without" condition. For example MacCrimmon and Wagner (1994) use an adapted form of a word-processing system as a control system.

- Independent *judges* who score the produced solutions and ideas on quality and creativity. In order to determine the net effect of the software, the outcomes have to be corrected for differences between respondents in creativity as a trait ("baseline creativity") using an appropriate creativity test.

From the several experiments on the effects of creativity support systems reported so far—for example, Elam and Mead (1990), Marakas and Elam (1997), MacCrimmon and Wagner (1994), and Massetti (1997)—we can draw the following conclusions:

1. In general, using a creativity support system significantly increased the creative output of the problem-solving process. However, this is not automatically the case for all systems advertised as "enhancing creativity." For example, one of the systems used by Elam and Mead (1990) seemed to actually *undermine* creativity rather than enhance it.

2. There is a strong positive correlation between the number of ideas generated and the quality of those ideas. This confirms the common belief in creativity research that "quantity breeds quality." Thus it is important to have systems that help respondents increase their *flow* of ideas. This will also enhance the quality of those ideas.

3. The treatment groups that produce the most creative solutions tend to take more time to complete their tasks (Elam and Mead 1990). This is a confirmation of the thesis that "creativity takes time" (Tardif and Sternberg 1988).

4. Creativity support systems may help the top group of respondents (those who have on average the best ideas) more than they help the worst-performing group. This was found in the study by MacCrimmon and Wagner (1994); it remains to be seen whether or not this result can be generalized to other CSS software. The baseline creativity of a person might well be a factor in determining which type of CSS software is most effective for enhancing that person's creativity.

The general conclusion here—that the use of creativity support systems can indeed enhance the creativity of decision makers—is an important one for marketing, where creativity plays such an important role.

6.3.3   Creativity Support Systems in Marketing

The work on creativity support systems has emerged in the general area of information systems/decision support systems. To our knowledge, the question of how software systems can enhance the creativity of *marketing* decision makers has not been dealt with systematically, although the more general question of what drives marketing creativity recently received some attention (Andrews and Smith 1996). We are aware of one creativity support system that was specifically designed for marketing purposes, the Computer Aided Advertising System (CAAS). CAAS was developed at the University of Saarbrucken by Kroeber-Riel and his coworkers (Kroeber-Riel 1993; Esch and Kroeber-Riel 1994; Siekmann 1994). The purpose of CAAS is to support the development and diagnosis of advertisements. It consists of several modules, of which the so-called Search System supports the creative process of generating visual ideas, persuasive motives, or pictures and ideas for effective pictorial execution (Kroeber-Riel 1993). The goal of the system is to stimulate the user's own creativity by providing a multitude of visual ideas and cues for the creative search process, using the ground rule from the creativity field that "quantity produces quality." The process starts with the system requesting the user to provide a "search concept" as input. This is a possible attribute that might be used for the positioning of the product or brand. If the concept provided by the user is among the 220 central concepts stored in its knowledge base, CAAS immediately moves on to the next stage, the development of visual ideas. If the search concept is *not* among its central 220 concepts, CAAS uses the 70,000 associations stored in its knowledge base, a semantic network that connects the central positioning concepts with other concepts. The associations are used to find the central concept that is most closely connected to the input search concept. Starting from the central positioning concept, CAAS helps the user to find suitable visual ideas to communicate that concept. The user is first invited to produce spontaneous associations and is then supported in making associations by means of several creativity stimulation methods (development of opposites, choosing pictures that are symbolic for the brand, wordplays, and so on). In a number of subsequent steps, the user can give commands to the system, such as "Find pictures with high attention value," "Play with body language," and "Can you use key excitements" (Siekmann 1994). In this way, in a heavily interactive session between the user and CAAS, the complete trajectory from concept search to visual ideas, pictures, pictorial schemes, and pictorial execution is covered. CAAS was developed to be used by advertising agencies (Kroeber-Riel 1993). We are not aware, at this moment, of reports with systematic analyses of the effectiveness of the CAAS system. The area of creativity support systems, in general, is underdeveloped territory in marketing.

6.4   Marketing Management Support Technologies in Perspective

In this and the last two chapters we have discussed several types of technologies for the support of marketing decisions. Figure 6.15 puts the different approaches into perspective. (This figure is an adaptation and extension of a figure by Mott 1993.) In Figure 6.15 the different knowledge technologies are placed on a continuum according to the amount of knowledge about the domain that is required for the technology. However, as the figure shows, there are also other systematic differences between the five technologies.

Starting from the left in Figure 6.15, we find algorithms for numerical analysis, which refer to the quantitative models of the data-driven marketing management support systems we discussed in Chapter 4. Next to that we find rule-based systems (expert systems), which we discussed in Chapter 5. Then follow the three knowledge technologies that we dealt with in the present chapter: case-based reasoning systems, neural networks, and creativity support systems.

Amount of Knowledge About the Domain

HIGH ◄————————————————————————————————————► LOW

	Numerical analysis *Algorithms*	**Rule-based systems** *Expert systems*	**Case-based reasoning** *CBR/Induction*	**Neural networks** *Pattern recognition*	**Creativity support systems** *Associations*
Target domains	Finite relationships; closed world	More complex relationships; somewhat bounded world		Raw, simple data; lots of data points	Open world; divergent thinking
Typical limitations	Precise but very limited answers	Brittle; knowledge engineering problem; hard to maintain	Need cases	Operates as a black box	Dependence on quality of generating process
Explanation/ learning	Knowledge-static explanation within model framework; no learning	Minimal explanation; learning difficult	Rich explanation; learning automatic	No explanation; learning automatic	Discontinuous; "jumps" in knowledge

Figure 6.15   Technologies for the Support of Marketing Management

Quantitative models operate in a closed world and provide very precise answers that apply in very specific conditions. The knowledge contained in these models is static. No learning is taking place. Rule-based systems fit static and well-understood domains quite well, but they can be brittle and hard to maintain. Furthermore, expert systems exhibit little capacity for explanation and learning. The (mostly qualitative) answers that they produce are precise and meant to be optimal, but they can be narrow and (too) absolute. Case-based reasoning technologies require less overall knowledge about the domain than rule-based systems, but, on a case-by-case basis, they can be rich in representation and explanation. CBR automatically implies learning. Neural networks do not need (symbolic) knowledge of the domain. They just need large numbers of observations in order to discover interesting patterns.

Finally, creativity support systems require limited knowledge of a domain and try to find new solutions in a solution space that is as wide as possible. Creative solutions are by definition discontinuous, since they represent "jumps" from existing knowledge. Reading the figure from left to right, we observe that the amount of domain knowledge is decreasing, that the solution space is becoming less bounded, but that, as a consequence, the answers and solutions are also becoming less precise. Other differences between the various knowledge technologies are the amount of explanation that they offer (high for numerical methods and case-based reasoning but low for neural networks) and whether or not a particular technology has the capacity to learn. Case-based reasoning systems and neural networks are able to learn, while numerical analysis and rule-based systems are not.

Key Points

- *Making analogies with other situations or earlier experiences is a powerful method that human beings use for interpreting new events. Marketers use analogies in their reasoning very often and organize their experiences in a series of cases or stories.*

- *Case-based reasoning (CBR) is a recently developed branch of artificial intelligence that is based on the notion of analogies. It has found applications for classification and synthesis tasks in many fields.*

- *When a new problem arises, a CBR system searches in the case base for a problem that is similar to the new one, the solution of which, after a possible adaptation, can become the solution of the new problem. A CBR system is equipped with specific techniques for the representation, retrieval, and adaptation of cases.*

- *CBR is a very promising technology for a weak-theory domain such as marketing. Applications to areas such as sales-promotion decisions are straightforward, but there is also potential for more complex marketing problems to be solved using CBR.*

- *Using the architecture of the human brain, neural networks are able to discover patterns in and to learn from large databases without a priori knowledge. Neural networks are robust and can make generalizations from events in noisy environments.*

- *In designing a neural network, the developers have to make decisions about the number of layers in the network, the numbers of units or nodes per layer, the transfer function, the learning rate, and the momentum parameter. The network can be trained on existing data by means of back propagation. A holdout data set can then be used for testing the pattern-recognition capabilities of the network after training.*

- *In marketing neural networks have been introduced in environments with time-series data as well as cross-sectional data. An important example of the latter is direct marketing environments, where neural networks are used to recognize promising prospects for a mailing. For both types of data, studies in which neural networks were compared to conventional statistical methods have produced encouraging results. Neural networks are also increasingly used for data mining: finding interesting pieces of knowledge in large databases (e.g., customer databases).*

- *Creativity support systems (CSS) are intended to increase the creativity of solutions that decision makers produce. A series of experiments in the DSS literature have established that such systems do indeed enhance the creative output of human decision makers. The experience with CSS in marketing so far is limited but deserves extension.*

- *The different technologies for marketing management support discussed in the last three chapters can be put on a continuum in the following order: numerical analysis (models/optimization techniques), rule-based systems, case-based reasoning systems, neural networks, and creativity support systems. In this order the amount of required domain knowledge for the application of the support technologies is decreasing, the solution space becomes less bounded, but the solutions provided also become less precise. Furthermore, the technologies differ with respect to aspects such as the amount of explanation that they offer and their ability to learn.*

PART III

Matching the Demand and Supply Sides of Marketing Management Support Systems

Chapter 7

Integrating Framework

Learning Objectives

- *To become familiar with a conceptual framework that relates the demand and supply sides of marketing management support systems.*

- *To understand that there can be different objects of support for marketing management support systems and also that marketing management can provide different modes of support.*

- *To know which type(s) of marketing management support systems is (are) most appropriate for each of the four marketing problem-solving modes.*

- *To learn how the conceptual framework can be used to recommend the most appropriate type of marketing management support system for specific marketing decision situations.*

- *To develop an understanding of the evolution of marketing management support systems over time.*

7.1   Introduction

To be effective, marketing management support systems should match the requirements of the marketing decision situation. In Chapter 2 we discussed the demand side of MMSS and developed a classification of *marketing problem-solving modes,* the ORAC model. In Chapters 4, 5, and 6 we dealt with the supply side of marketing management support, that is, data-driven and knowledge-driven MMSS. This chapter is concerned with the *match* between the demand side and the supply side. We take the ORAC model as our starting point for determining the most appropriate marketing management support system to use in a given decision situation.

In the following sections we develop a contingency framework that indicates the suitability of specific marketing management support systems for specific decision situations. In section 7.2 we describe the match between marketing problem-solving modes and marketing management support systems. In section 7.3 we link decision situation characteristics to the MPSM and MMSS. We illustrate the framework by using it to determine the required support for three different marketing decision situations, that of a media planner, that of a product manager in an FMCG industry, and that of a new business manager in an IT company. Finally, in the last section of this chapter we show that insight into the relationship between the demand and supply sides of marketing management support (which the framework provides) can also help us to understand the evolution of MMSS over time.

7.2   Mapping Marketing Problem-Solving Modes and Marketing Management Support Systems

For the design of management support systems, Dutta, Wierenga, and Dalebout (1997a) delineate two important dimensions: the *object* of support and the *mode* of support.

7.2.1   Object of Support

Three different objects of support can be distinguished: *the outcome, the process,* and *learning.* The *outcome*-oriented view of decision support is primarily concerned with the final decision. The emphasis is on insuring that the best or "correct" output is produced for the appropriate set of inputs. This is a matter of finding the most efficient computation algorithm. However, for many problems there does not exist a best solution in an objective sense. In these cases the decision *process* can be taken as the object of support. The process-oriented view of decision support focuses not on the final outcome but on the process by which decisions are made. In this situation a support system is conceived of as an intervention in the decision process that should increase the quality of this process. A process-oriented approach to decision support is especially relevant when there is uncertainty in the environment
and when the problem is not very well structured. Finally, when *learning* is the object of decision support, the relevant question is how to improve the decision and the decision process. The ability to question decision procedures and to adopt new, innovative ones is a critical component of a decision maker's learning capabilities.

7.2.2 Mode of Support

Three different modes of decision support can be distinguished: *automating, informating,* and *stimulating. Automation* of decision making has been the traditional strength of operations research/management science approaches. Management support systems that emphasize automation have certain decision procedures and mechanisms hardwired into the system as optimization procedures. Zuboff (1985) first used the term *informate* to denote the capability of intelligent technology to capture and provide information. Zuboff referred primarily to the *informatization capabilities* of large databases. *Informating* has a more active connotation than *informing:* the attention of the decision maker is drawn to specific events. Finally, in the *stimulating* mode of decision support, the system aids the decision maker in finding new solutions by questioning existing frames and norms, noticing special features in the decision environment, making (remote) associations, and so on.

There are "dominant matches" between the objects and modes of decision support (Dutta, Wierenga, and Dalebout 1997a). These dominant matches can be related to the three types of management support system characteristics identified by Silver (1991). These characteristics are *restrictedness, guidance,* and *customizability.* If the object is to support the *outcome* of a decision, the dominant match is with the *automating* mode. This leads to *restrictive* systems that are prescriptive and normative in nature. Many of the traditional management support systems fall into this category. If the object of support is the decision *process,* the decision support should have a *guidance* role, which is offered by the decision support mode *informating.* The *learning* view of decision support calls for greater emphasis on *stimulation.* It is important that support systems stimulate decision makers to use exploratory modes of problem solving. The support system should continuously be adapted to the changing needs of the environment. In such a situation the system should have a high degree of *customizability:* decision makers should have a lot of leeway in choosing how to apply the system.

When we apply the design dimensions *object of support* and *mode of support* to the ORAC classification, we arrive at a mapping of marketing problem-solving modes and the most appropriate type of marketing management support system(s), as given in Figure 7.1 (adapted from Wierenga and Van Bruggen 1997a)[1].

---

[1] For the different systems we use the abbreviations introduced earlier: MM = Marketing Models, MES = Marketing Expert Systems, MKIS = Marketing Information Systems, MDSS = Marketing Decision Support Systems, MNN = Marketing Neural Networks, MKBS = Marketing Knowledge-Based Systems, MCBR = Marketing Case-Based Reasoning Systems, and MCSS = Marketing Creativity Support Systems.

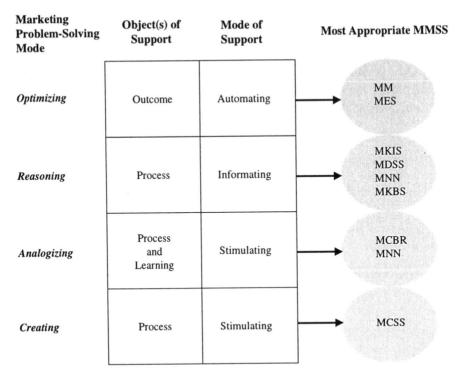

Marketing Problem-Solving Mode	Object(s) of Support	Mode of Support	Most Appropriate MMSS
Optimizing	Outcome	Automating	MM MES
Reasoning	Process	Informating	MKIS MDSS MNN MKBS
Analogizing	Process and Learning	Stimulating	MCBR MNN
Creating	Process	Stimulating	MCSS

Figure 7.1   Framework for Mapping Marketing Problem-Solving Modes and Marketing Management Support Systems

Optimizing

In the case of optimizing, a best solution exists, and the marketing management support system should insure that this solution is found. So the emphasis is on the final solution, that is, the *outcome* of the decision process. In principle, decisions can be *automated* and left to a computer. In this situation there is typically a high degree of structure and little uncertainty in the decision problem, and users can have low domain skills. Typical examples of marketing problems that can be approached in this way are media allocation, shelf-space allocation, and sales-force planning.

The first type of MMSS that became available to match the design requirements of the optimizing mode were marketing models. Marketing models provide a mathematical representation of the marketing problem and can be used, in combination with an optimization algorithm, to find the objectively best solution for the values of the marketing instruments. Given the input data (objectives, resources, and so on), the algorithm produces a solution like the best media plan, the optimal shelf-space allocation in a supermarket, or the optimal sales-call schedule. The solution of the problem can be delegated to a relatively low skilled employee who need not have a lot of marketing expertise. Whereas marketing models provide the best *quantitative* solution, marketing expert systems aim at providing the best solution if the problem is described in terms of *qualitative* relationships between the variables. Under the optimizing mode, a marketing model might be used to determine the advertising budget, and a marketing expert system might subsequently be used to find out what the copy should be and what the execution of the advertisements should look like. Again, since the expertise is in the system, within the predetermined solution space a relatively low skilled person can (in principle) find the solution.

Everyone familiar with marketing decision making will recognize that solving a marketing problem purely by optimizing is rare. Elements of managerial judgment, which cannot be put into a computer system, practically always come into play in marketing. Often, however, *parts* of a marketing problem can be defined as structured subproblems that are amenable to optimization by means of models or expert systems. This is also true for the problems mentioned above. Media allocation, shelf-space allocation, and sales-force planning are usually specific subproblems within more comprehensive marketing problems.

Reasoning

The reasoning mode takes the mental model of the decision maker as its starting point. No objective true representation of the decision situation exists. Ultimately, the final decision will be the result of a process in the decision maker's mind. Therefore, in the reasoning mode, the object of support for the decision maker should not be a particular *outcome* (a precise recommendation on what to do) but rather the marketing manager's decision-making *process*. The basic mode of support in this situation is *informating*. Under the reasoning mode, an MMSS should provide information about what is going on in the market and actively draw a manager's attention to significant events.

Marketing management support systems can support the reasoning mode in two different ways:

1. By supporting the formation and maintenance of mental models of managers.
2. By reasoning with these mental models.

In the first method, information is needed about what happens in the market, that is, actual facts and data (answering the "what" question). This is the main function of marketing information systems. Because of its model base, a marketing decision support system can also help the decision maker to understand the mechanisms in a market by providing systematic insight into the relationships between key marketing variables, such as advertising expenditures and brand awareness or advertising expenditures and sales. By means of simulation (i.e., answering "what-if" questions), a marketer can use a marketing decision support system to explore the consequences of alternative marketing strategies. Marketing neural networks can also help to explore what is going on in a market. A marketing neural network can discover patterns in the interdependencies between marketing variables. For example, it can capture the characteristics that distinguish successful new products from unsuccessful ones.

In the second method, it is necessary to represent a decision maker's mental model in a computer and reason with this model. A marketing knowledge-based system is particularly suited for this purpose. Systems can be built for monitoring and diagnosing market events and suggesting appropriate actions in the same way as the manager would do. An example of such a system is CoverStory (Schmitz, Armstrong, and Little 1990; Schmitz 1994). CoverStory produces short reports and graphs about the most important events in a market (*informating*), based on an analysis of scanning data. Such marketing knowledge-based systems can search very large amounts of data for significant marketing events and act as an efficient electronic assistant to a marketing decision maker. In the current era of the "marketing information revolution," such systems are becoming indispensable.

Analogizing

In the analogizing mode the decision maker uses solutions from earlier, similar decision situations to develop a decision for a current problem. In the analogizing mode, therefore, the primary object of support is the *process* of finding suitable cases and adapting them for the current problem situation. In the analogizing mode the MMSS should *stimulate* the decision maker by actively coming up with solutions of earlier cases and proposing transformations of these solutions to adapt them to the current problem situation. *Learning* will take place so that future decisions can benefit from current experiences. Marketing case-based reasoning systems are the type of MMSS that match the requirements of the analogizing mode. The development of case-based reasoning technology was inspired by the desire to support the analogy-seeking behavior of decision makers. As we saw in the last chapter, case-based reasoning systems consist of (large) sets of cases stored in a computer, with efficient indexing systems for finding the cases that are similar to a problem situation at hand, and with the capacity to transform or adapt earlier solutions to the current problem situation. For example, a product manager who has to develop a sales promotion for his or her brand can be inspired by a campaign (present in the case base) that has been successful for a similar product in a different market. Or the sales potential of a new outlet of a service company in a city not yet covered may be estimated on the basis of the sales figures of existing outlets in cities that are comparable in terms of size, customers, and the competition. The strength of a computerized case-based reasoning system is that it augments a decision maker's memory by providing access to a large collection of relevant cases. Human decision makers are fairly good at adapting these cases to the situation at hand (Dutta, Wierenga, and Dalebout 1997b). Ultimately, in the analogizing mode, as the number of cases in the case base grows larger, some form of generalization takes place (learning from experience). For that purpose, marketing neural networks might be used here also, in order to search for patterns in the cases of the case base.

Creating

In the creating mode the marketing decision maker searches for concepts, solutions, or ideas that are novel, often in response to a situation that has not occurred before. Here an MMSS should support the creative *process* and should fulfill a *stimulating* role, that is, generate cues and ideas that trigger the user. Creativity consists to a large extent of making connections and associations between (remote) concepts. This process can be facilitated by a marketing management support system. As we have seen in Chapter 6, there is an emerging class of creativity support systems that match up well with the demand for creativity support in the domain of marketing. However, research is needed on how to use this approach to solve marketing problems. Pursuing this path will lead to a new type of MMSS: marketing creativity support systems.

This concludes our discussion of the match between marketing problem-solving modes and marketing management support systems. In the next section we will expand the framework by including the link with decision situation characteristics.

7.3 From Decision Situation to Marketing Management Support System: An Integrating Framework

In the last section we linked marketing problem-solving modes to marketing management support systems. In Chapter 2 we discussed the antecedents of the marketing problem-solving modes. We distinguished three classes of decision situation characteristics: problem characteristics, decision environment characteristics, and decision maker characteristics. Now we expand the framework by connecting the decision situation characteristics to marketing management support systems. This is shown graphically in Figure 7.2.

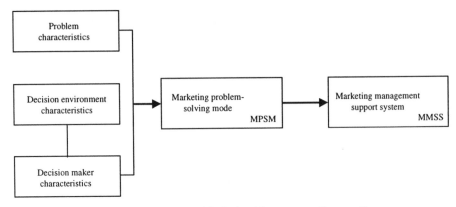

Figure 7.2   From Decision Situation to Marketing Management Support System

In Figure 7.3 we present a list of problem characteristics, decision environment characteristics, and decision maker characteristics. For a discussion of these characteristics and their links to the marketing problem-solving modes, see Chapter 2.

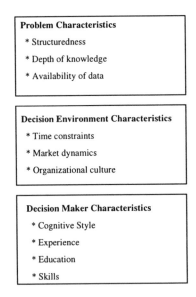

Figure 7.3   Decision Situation Characteristics

7.3.1   The Complete Mapping

Our framework aims at transforming decision situations, via marketing problem-solving modes, into requirements for decision support. By doing so, the framework can determine the MMSS that fits best with the decision situation. The complete mapping of decision situation characteristics and MMSS is shown in the integrating framework of Figure 7.4.

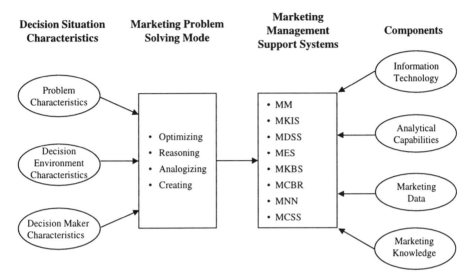

Figure 7.4   Integrating Framework of Marketing Problem-Solving Modes and Marketing Management Support Systems

This framework encompasses the complete stretch between, on the one hand, the characteristics of the decision situation (left side of the figure) and, on the other hand, the components that constitute marketing management support systems (the right side of the figure). The decision situation characteristics are translated into marketing problem-solving modes, and the constituting components, into marketing management support systems. The heart of the framework is the centerpiece of successful support: the fit between MPSM and MMSS.

7.3.2   Marketing Management Support Recommender

We can use the integrating framework to recommend the type of marketing management support system to use in specific situations. That is, we can use it as a *marketing management support recommender*. We will illustrate the procedure by making recommendations for three typical marketing decision situations: (1) that of a media planner, (2) that of a product manager in an FMCG industry, and (3) that of a new business manager in an IT company.

First, we have to typify the three decision situations in terms of decision situation characteristics. We use a simplified scheme in which each characteristic can have only two levels, high or low. The actual scores are given in Figure 7.5.

Decision situation characteristics		Marketing decision situation		
		(1) Media Planner	(2) FMCG Product Manager	(3) New business manager of IT Company
Problem characteristics				
Structuredness	High	◆	◆	
	Low			◆
Depth of knowledge	High	◆		
	Low		◆	◆
Availability of data	High	◆	◆	
	Low			◆
Decision environment characteristics				
Time constraints	Yes		◆	◆
	No	◆		
Market dynamics	High			◆
	Low	◆	◆	
Organizational culture	Analytical	◆	◆	◆
	Holistic			
Decision maker characteristics				
Cognitive style	Analytical	◆		
	Heuristic		◆	◆
Experience	High		◆	◆
	Low	◆		
Education	Science	◆		
	Other		◆	◆

Figure 7.5   Characterizing Three Different Marketing Decision Situations in Terms of Problem Characteristics, Decision Environment Characteristics, and Decision Maker Characteristics

We posit that a media planner typically deals with highly structured problems and has ample knowledge, that much data is available to him or her, and that media planning usually does not take place under significant time pressure and is often carried out in relatively stable markets (low dynamics). At the other end of the spectrum, a new business manager of an IT company is typically confronted with relatively unstructured problems (technologies and applications are constantly changing). Furthermore, low levels of knowledge (e.g., about the preferences of customers and the capabilities of competitors) exist, little data is available to that manager, severe time pressure exists (being first with a new IT product is very important), and markets are dynamic. Finally, the decision situation of a product manager in an FMCG industry is positioned somewhere between these two extremes (see Figure 7.5).

The characteristics discussed so far are more or less tied to the decision situation in a particular industry. But the characteristic of organizational culture is independent of the particular industry. The culture will be specific to the company; for our present purposes, we assume that the organizational culture is analytical in all three decision situations.

Finally we have the decision maker characteristics. In principle these are also independent of the industry. For example, one can find analytical as well as heuristic persons as product managers in FMCG companies. Let's assume that the media planner has an analytical cognitive style, little experience and an education in science. In the case of the product manager in FMCG and the new business manager in IT, we assume (also for illustrative purposes) a heuristic individual with a lot of experience and a nonscientific background.

Next, we link the decision situation characteristics to the marketing problem-solving modes of the ORAC model. In Figure 7.6 we present a scheme that contains the relationships between the various decision situation characteristics and the marketing problem-solving modes.

In Figure 7.6 we use a simple constant-sum scale in which a total of four points (equal to the number of different MPSM and represented by plus signs in the figure) per level (e.g., low or high) of a characteristic (e.g., structuredness) are distributed over the different MPSM. The number of points allocated to a specific mode will depend on the applicability of this specific mode given the level of the decision situation characteristic. For example, in the case of *high structuredness* the points are equally divided between optimizing and reasoning, because both modes are equally applicable. In the case of *low structuredness* the points are equally divided between analogizing and creating. Of course there is a certain amount of arbitrariness in this distribution of points. We think that the overall picture has validity, though.

Decision Situation Characteristics		*Marketing Problem Solving Mode*			
		O	**R**	**A**	**C**
Problem characteristics					
Structuredness	High	++	++		
	Low			++	++
Depth of knowledge	High	+++	+		
	Low		+	++	+
Availability of data	High	+	+++		
	Low		++	+	+
Decision environment characteristics					
Time constraints	Yes		++	++	
	No	+++	+		
Market dynamics	High		+	++	+
	Low	++	++		
Organizational culture	Analytical	++	++		
	Holistic			++	++
Decision maker characteristics					
Cognitive Style	Analytic	++	++		
	Heuristic			++	++
Experience	High		++	++	
	Low	++		++	
Education	Science	+++	+		
	Other			++	++

Figure 7.6. Mapping of Decision Situation Characteristics and Marketing Problem-Solving Modes

The combination of the mappings from the two last figures result in the assignment of points to the marketing problem-solving modes for each marketing decision situation, dependent on their characteristics. This is shown in Figure 7.7.

Decision Situation Characteristics	Marketing Decision Situation											
	(1) Media Planner				(2) FMCG Product manager				(3) New Business Manager IT Comp.			
	O	R	A	C	O	R	A	C	O	R	A	C
Structuredness	++	++			++	++					++	++
Depth knowledge	+++	+				+	++	+		+	++	+
Available Data	+	+++			+	+++				++	+	+
Time constraints	+++	+				++	++			++	++	
Market dynamics	++	++			++	++				+	++	+
Organiz. culture	++	++			++	++			++	++		
Cognitive style	++	++	++				++	++			++	++
Experience	++		++			++	++			++	++	
Education	+++	+					++	++			++	++
	20	14	2	0	7	14	10	5	2	10	15	9
	O	**R**	**A**	**C**	**O**	**R**	**A**	**C**	**O**	**R**	**A**	**C**

Figure 7.7   The Marketing Management Support Recommender: from Marketing Decisions Situation to Recommended MMSS

Figure 7.7 shows that, based on the decision situation characteristics, in the case of the media planner, the marketing problem-solving mode predisposition is toward optimizing and reasoning. For a product manager in FMCG, the emphasis is on reasoning and analogizing, whereas for the new business manager in IT, analogizing, reasoning and creating are the dominant modes.

In this way we have obtained a connection between marketing decision situations and marketing problem-solving modes, which, as per Figure 7.1, can be translated into recommendations for marketing management support.

The media planner would be appropriately supported with marketing models and marketing expert systems. The FMCG product manager needs marketing information systems, marketing decision support systems, and marketing neural networks in order to form and update his (or her) mental model of the market and to be able to simulate alternative marketing strategies. This product manager would also be served by a marketing knowledge-based system that represents his (or her) knowledge of the market. Such a system could assist the product manager, for example, by monitoring the position of a brand through the analysis of scanning data. The new business manager in IT needs a marketing information system in order to constantly update his (or her) mental model of the very dynamic market. This manager may also need a case-based reasoning system that can help draw useful parallels between the movements in his (or her) market and similar events in other markets. In this context marketing neural networks can help for pattern recognition. Finally, creativity support systems can help to generate new application ideas for the ever increasing technological possibilities.

These examples show how the framework can be used as a marketing management support recommender: the decision situation characteristics are given as input, and the most appropriate type(s) of MMSS are given as output. The introduction of the concept of marketing problem-solving modes results in a huge savings of effort to determine decision support requirements. By using the concept of MPSM, we can map a large number of different problem situations (in our example of Figure 7.7, 2^9 different decision situations are possible) into four marketing problem-solving modes and, subsequently, determine the most appropriate type(s) of marketing management support system.

7.3.3   Issues in Choosing the Type of Marketing Management Support System

Although the procedure just described is straightforward in finding the most suitable marketing management support systems in a given marketing situation, a number of issues deserve consideration.

(1) Should the marketing problem-solving mode actually employed be unconditionally taken as the starting point for deciding on the type of support?

The marketing problem-solving mode is, to a great extent, determined by factors that are given by the market characteristics, for example, the structuredness of the marketing problem, depth of knowledge, the availability of data, time constraints, and market dynamics (see Figure 7.7). These elements are external factors. However, other (internal) factors, such as company culture (e.g., a prevailing holistic instead of an analytical attitude) and decision maker characteristics, which also have their impact on the marketing problem-solving mode employed, are specific to an individual company. As a consequence, the marketing problem-solving mode actually employed may differ from the one that would be derived from the external characteristics of the decision situation. For example, there are financial institutions with a lot of data, which would enable them to use the optimizing mode (through sophisticated direct-marketing campaigns). However, they do not employ that marketing problem-solving mode because of an opposing organizational culture, a lack of analytical capabilities, an insufficient education level on the part of their marketing personnel, or a combination of these (internal) factors. In such a situation, it might not be in the best interests of the company to uncritically follow the existing MPSM. This would imply to provide the marketers with MMSS that fit their predisposition (e.g., give them marketing information systems only) whereas this particular company could do much more with advanced marketing models. A similar problem would arise when very analytically oriented decision makers would have to use heuristic tools, for example, creativity support systems, for generating new product ideas in an IT environment. Such decision makers would probably feel more comfortable using analytically oriented tools.

As marketers well know, it is very difficult to go against the prevailing attitudes of consumers and users. This statement is as true for marketers themselves as for any other group. Trying to force decision makers to use systems that do not match their predisposition(s) is counterproductive; realistically, such systems will not be used. In order to increase the likelihood of changing the dominant marketing problem-solving mode, a deliberate and well-planned change program is needed. Sometimes it may be possible to "drag the decision maker along." For example, a product manager with a heuristic style who operates in a data-rich FMCG environment might be enticed to use a (very user-friendly) marketing decision support system that will stimulate (quantitative) reasoning and maybe even elements of optimizing. To realize desired changes, the support of (top) management is an absolute requirement. Situations may occur where it does not make sense to go against the existing organizational culture. The best that can be done is to support the marketing problem-solving mode actually employed—even if, from an outsider's perspective, a different mode would be more beneficial to the company.

(2) How does the use of marketing management support systems affect the marketing problem-solving mode?

So far we have mainly followed a one-way analysis, where the decision characteristics determine the marketing problem-solving mode, which in turn leads to the most suitable marketing management support system(s) (Figures 7.2 and 7.3). However, there is also a process in the other direction. The availability and use of an MMSS may very well change the decision situation. For example, the use of a particular MKIS or MDSS may increase the amount of data about a marketing problem. It may also contribute to the level of knowledge about a problem and thereby help the decision maker to acquire better insight into the structure of the problem. In this way a problem might migrate from a reasoning problem to an optimizing problem. It is also well known that the availability and use of a decision aid significantly affects the way decision makers solve problems (Todd and Benbasat 1991; Glazer, Steckel and Winer 1992). The use of a particular MMSS may even have an affect on the culture within a company. For example, the introduction of an MKIS or MDSS may stimulate a more analytical attitude. Therefore, in studying the effect of a marketing management support system, we need to perform a dynamic analysis. Such an analysis takes into account the feedback of the MMSS on the decision situation. In Figure 7.4 there is a dominant arrow from MPSM to MMSS: the marketing problem-solving mode determines the type of marketing management support system that is needed. However, over a longer time period, there is also an effect in the opposite direction: an MMSS can change the MPSM. And this opposite effect should be taken into account when, after a certain period of time, the marketing management support system gets updated or replaced. The next generation of MMSS in a company might have different requirements than the generation of systems it replaces. Of course, the effect of the marketing management support system(s) on the marketing problem-solving mode is closely related to issue (1), described above. As we argued earlier, a particular type of decision support system may deliberately be used to change the prevailing MPSM.

(3) Should a marketing management support system reinforce the strengths of a decision maker, or should it compensate for his limitations?

On the one hand, matching marketing management support systems with the demand (user) side implies that decision makers get MMSS that are consistent with their competencies. This implies that, for example, analytically oriented decision makers get sophisticated marketing models. On the other hand, it also seems natural to use MMSS to compensate for the limitations of decision makers. For example, Van Bruggen, Smidts, and Wierenga (1998) found that low-analytical decision makers benefit most from using an analytical MMSS. Trying to compensate for limitations in human cognitive capabilities is a common approach to decision support. Suppose that an MMSS has to support the reasoning mode. In the case of reasoning, the decision maker has a mental model that may consist of cause-and-effect relationships. In principle this model allows the decision maker to make what-if simulations. However, because of human decision makers' cognitive limitations (e.g., Simon 1979; Hogarth and Makridakis 1981) a decision maker will only be able to consider a limited number of alternative solutions. A computer system offering what-if capabilities can extend the decision maker's mental capacity in the reasoning mode, and we therefore expect such a system to improve the decision maker's performance. In this way, a system that compensates for the weaknesses of a human decision maker may be effective.

Sometimes decision makers seem to be aware of their own limitations. In a study done by De Waele (1978), individuals appeared to prefer the decision aid that complemented their weakest style instead of the one that supported their strongest. For example, low-analytical decision makers preferred analytical aids. In other studies, however, decision makers were found to be less enlightened. Designers of decision support systems have paid little attention to the psychology of the decision maker (Hoch and Schkade 1996). Figure 7.7 shows the importance of taking the personality of the decision maker into account when designing and/or choosing marketing management support systems. Perhaps the issue of reinforcing existing strengths versus compensating for weaknesses is not an either/or question. Marketing management support systems can fulfill both roles. Such systems should be designed not only to take advantage of the distinctive competencies of decision makers, but also to compensate for their inherent weaknesses (Hoch and Schkade 1996).

7.4   Understanding the Evolution of Marketing Management Support Systems

So far, we have used the framework developed in this chapter for determining the required decision support given the characteristics of the decision situation. Our integrating framework is also helpful in understanding the evolution of marketing management support systems and their use over time. In Chapter 3 we discussed the four components of MMSS: information technology, analytical capabilities, marketing data, and marketing knowledge. These components are also depicted in the right-hand side of Figure 7.4. The evolution of MMSS so far has clearly been directed by these factors, which is to say that the evolution of such systems has clearly been supply- and technology-driven. Developments in the components of MMSS were dominant. In the 1960s and 1970s the major driving forces behind developments in MMSS were developments in the analytical capabilities component (e.g., progress in optimization and estimation techniques). During the 1980s the driving forces were advances in the marketing data component (i.e., the scanning revolution). Nowadays, developments in the marketing knowledge and information technology components are dominant, and marketing management support systems are being equipped with knowledge and intelligence.

However, the evolution of *the use of* marketing management support systems did not automatically follow their supply. When marketing models (the first type of MMSS) were introduced in the 1960s, it was expected that this scientific approach to marketing management problems would soon have a major impact on marketing practice. However, it turned out that (marketing) managers were not so eager to adopt these models (Little 1970; Eliashberg and Lilien 1993). According to Simon (1994) "the practical significance of marketing science has remained very limited." However, this does not imply that marketing model builders have not been trying very hard to develop better systems to really help managers. Nor have they been oblivious to the importance of managerial judgment for marketing decision making. As early as 1970 Little introduced "decision calculus," a procedure in which managerial judgment is used for the parameterization of response functions.

Several reasons have been proposed to explain the reluctance of marketing managers to use marketing models. These reasons relate to the models as such (they are not robust enough, not simple enough, or too difficult to understand [Little 1970]), to the lack of selling capabilities on the part of the model builder (Lilien 1994), and to the lack of relevant data (Simon 1994). Although such factors may be important, our analysis suggests that there needs to be a match between the marketing problem-solving mode and the marketing management support system used. Marketing models are an appropriate type of MMSS in the case of the optimizing mode. Given our discussion of the factors conducive to the optimizing mode (a highly structured problem, high degree of knowledge, ample time frame, stable market, and so on), it is unlikely that this mode will occur frequently. Although developing better models and selling models more effectively will help promote their use, these steps alone will not turn the situation around. We believe that managers will only be inclined to use marketing management support systems if these match with the marketing problem-solving mode they use.

The framework also explains positive developments (Little 1991). For example, the success of marketing models on practitioners in the domain of sales management (Vandenbosch and Weinberg 1993; Lodish et al. 1988) is probably due to factors like a highly structured problem, the presence of analytical decision makers with quantitative skills, an ample time frame, and a stable market situation. In addition, the fact that marketing information systems are implemented in companies more often than marketing models may be because the reasoning mode is more common than the optimizing mode. Of course, the ongoing research in marketing (science) will further increase our knowledge of marketing phenomena, which helps to structure marketing problems, thus making them more amenable to optimizing. Many unharvested fields are still out there, waiting to be reaped by the analytical power of marketing science. The limited use of marketing models does not imply that marketing science is on the wrong track, as Simon (1994) seemed to conclude, nor that we need a "paradigm shift." What can be learned from several decades of research in marketing, though, is that progress will be slow. New knowledge tends to have relatively little impact on improving marketing management practice (Silk 1993). On this count alone, it will take a long time before the majority of marketing problems are solved in the optimizing mode (if this ever happens). For the time being, efforts should be made to develop marketing management support systems that can support marketing decisions made in the reasoning, analogizing, and creating modes.

Key Points

- *Three different objects of support can be distinguished for marketing management support systems: the decision outcome, the decision process, and learning.*

- *Marketing management support systems can offer decision support by means of three different modes of support: automating, informating, and stimulating.*

- *To support the optimizing mode, marketing models and marketing expert systems are the most appropriate marketing management support systems.*

- *To support the reasoning mode, marketing information systems, marketing decision support systems, marketing neural networks, and marketing knowledge-based systems are the most appropriate systems.*

- *To support the analogizing mode, marketing case-based reasoning systems and marketing neural networks are the most appropriate systems.*

- *To support the creating mode, marketing creativity support systems are the most appropriate type of marketing management support system.*

- *The complete mapping of decision situation characteristics and marketing management support systems can be presented in an integrating framework linking the demand and supply sides of marketing management support systems.*

- *One application of this integrated framework is the marketing management support recommender, which uses characteristics of the decision situation as input and provides (heuristic) recommendations about the most appropriate type of marketing management support system as output.*

- *Marketing scientists should focus on developing marketing management support systems for each of the four marketing problem-solving modes. So far, a lot of effort has been put into support of the optimizing mode, whereas less effort has been put into support of the reasoning, analogizing, and creating modes.*

Chapter 8

BRANDFRAME: A Marketing Management Support System for the Brand Manager

Berend Wierenga, Arco Dalebout[1], and Soumitra Dutta[2]

Learning Objectives

- *To understand how the characteristics of a specific marketing function— that of a brand manager—can be translated into the requirements for a marketing management support system.*

- *To learn how the different functionalities of data-driven and knowledge-driven marketing management support systems can be used in designing an integrated system.*

- *To evaluate the effectiveness of a demand-side approach to designing marketing management support systems.*

8.1   Introduction

In this chapter we will apply the ideas about matching the marketing management support system with the decision situation of the marketer by developing an MMSS that is tailor-made to a specific marketing function, that of a brand manager in fast-moving consumer goods (FMCG). The brand management or product management system originated at Procter and Gamble in the 1920s and has become the dominant way of organizing the marketing function in FMCG companies (Buell 1975; Arnold 1992). The principal difference between the brand management system and the so-called

[1] Arco Dalebout was a PhD student in marketing at the Rotterdam School of Management. To our deep regret, he passed away on 8 April 1999.
[2] Soumitra Dutta is Professor of Information Systems at INSEAD, Fontainebleau, France.

functional organization of marketing is that in the former the different marketing functions for a product (i.e., product definition, pricing, advertising, sales promotion and distribution, and market research) are the responsibility of one and the same person: the brand manager, also called the product manager (Kotler 1997). Although no two products or markets are identical, all product managers use a common set of concepts, indicators, and ways of reasoning in carrying out their jobs. This makes it worthwhile to develop a system that can support everyone who fulfills the function of brand manager in FMCG markets.

This chapter will continue with a discussion of the tasks of a brand manager, the problems he or she must solve, the data that he or she has available, and the resulting need for decision support. We will then describe BRANDFRAME[3], a system specially designed for supporting brand managers. We will also pay attention to the first results of implementing BRANDFRAME in actual brand managers' decision situations. Finally, we will reflect on further developments and perspectives for systems such as BRANDFRAME.

8.2   The Tasks of the Brand Manager and the Implications for Decision Support

The work of a brand or product manager can be appropriately described using the concept of the *management control cycle* (Ackoff 1978; Courtney, Paradice, and Mohammed 1987). The management control cycle of a brand manager is depicted (in a condensed form) in Figure 8.1.

First of all, a brand manager is constantly *monitoring* the brand. If the brand manager observes something worrisome (e.g., a drop in market share) or discovers opportunities for improving the position of the brand, he or she starts *diagnosing* the situation. After having obtained better insight into what is going on in the market, the brand manager starts *planning* specific activities aimed at putting the brand in a better position, which may include *designing* specific marketing programs (e.g., advertising or sales promotions). These programs then have to be *implemented*, after which *monitoring* must begin again to see if the actions have the desired results.

---

[3] BRANDFRAME is a registered trademark.

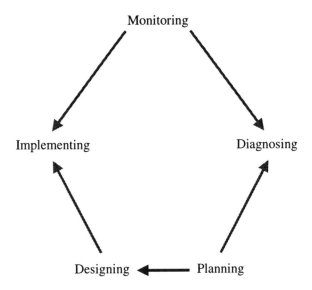

Figure 8.1   The Management Control Cycle of a Brand Manager

How does a brand manager perform his or her job in practice? To answer this question, Dalebout (1993) investigated the contents of "yesterday's diary" for ten product managers at a major FMCG company in the Netherlands (see Figure 8.2). It turned out that the attention of a product manager is dispersed over a large number of activities. Each day there were, on average, 5.7 planned agenda items in a product manager's diary; in addition, though, there were also many unplanned phone calls and other interruptions.

Activity in Product Manager's Diary	No. Who Listed It
• Ad hoc activities: reading mail, phoning, paying bills	10
• Preparation of introductions/relaunches	8
• Preparation of promotion activities	7
• Working on annual plan	5
• Market research–related activities	5
• Consultations with other departments: subjects not mentioned	5
• Advertising-related activities	3
• Social activities: drinks, visitors	3
• Packaging-related activities	2
• Organizational/personal affairs	2
• Writing reports: subjects not mentioned	2
• Education	1
• Presentations	1
• Lunch	1
• Other	2
Total	57

Average per product manager per day: 5.7 items

Figure 8.2   Activities of a Product Manager

Dalebout (1993) also conducted more in-depth interviews with four of these product managers, asking them to estimate the percentage of time they typically spent on several (categories of) activities. The results are presented in Figure 8.3.

Categories of Activities	Current %	Ideal %
Strategic planning: working on the long-term strategy and preparing the annual marketing and action plans for their products	18	28
Gathering/analyzing data concerning the current position of their products in the market	17	23
Preparing/implementing activities in the areas of advertising, promotion, distribution, price, and product improvements/introductions	51	41
Other (some of the activities mentioned were talking to the sales department, delegating, steering other departments, talking/meeting for planning, and taking courses)	15	8

Figure 8.3   Time Spent by Product Managers on Categories of Activities

These results show that more than half of the time of a product manager is spent on concrete, ad hoc activities related to the various marketing instruments, that is, product improvements/introductions, (sales) promotions, advertising, distribution, and price. Other activities, each taking somewhat less than 20 percent of a product manager's time, are strategic planning (including the annual marketing plan) and marketing research–related activities (gathering and analyzing data). The general picture pretty well illustrates Mintzberg's (1973) observation about managerial work in general. He found that brevity, fragmentation, and variation characterize the activities of a manager. Interestingly, Figure 8.3 shows that product managers themselves would like to spend more time on long-term planning and gathering and analyzing data than they currently do. With regard to the question of how product managers make decisions, Figure 8.4 shows that, according to the brand managers themselves, experience, insight, and intuition are much more important than testing or models. In order to be effective, a decision support system for a brand manager should support this basic modus operandi.

Manner of Evaluating Alternatives	Average*
Experiment (e.g., in a test market or through market research)	3.6
Use of models (e.g., mathematical models or models for simulation)	2.0
Experience, insight, and intuition	6.0
Other	5.3

*Scale: 1 = never; 7 = always

Figure 8.4   How Product Managers Evaluate Alternative Actions

Brand managers in FMCG typically operate in an information-rich environment. The amount and variety of data and knowledge that product managers can use for making decisions is enormous. The "hard" data usually consists of a combination of scanner data, household panel data, ex-factory sales data, and marketing research figures and reports. The "soft" data or knowledge can consist of information on competitive introductions, (re)launches, promotional campaigns, economic indicators, and so on. This vital knowledge reaches the product manager through various sources: the press, conversations with colleagues, observations in shops, consumer complaints, and so on.

A product manager combines the incoming information with his or her own experience, insight, and intuition to make a decision. Goldstein (1993) studied how product managers use and learn from scanner data. After interviewing six product managers from an American grocery manufacturer, he concluded that managers' analyses of scanner data are guided by a prior understanding of the market environment. When studying scanner data, managers modify their views in light of new findings. This seems to imply that the mental models (containing a priori knowledge) of brand managers play an important role in how the managers reason about the phenomena observed in their market. In addition, brand managers tend to retain the information about specific events in the form of coherent "chunks" of information. In the terminology of Chapter 5, these chunks are called *cases*. These insights are in agreement with our conclusion in the last chapter that for a product manager in FMCG the dominant marketing problem-solving modes are *reasoning* and *analogizing* (see Figure 7.8). The recommended types of marketing management support systems that follow from these modes are marketing information systems, marketing decision support systems, marketing knowledge-based systems, marketing neural networks, and marketing case-based reasoning systems. These recommendations are summarized and explained in Table 8.1.

Table 8.1   Matching the Product Manager's MPSM with Appropriate MMSS

MPSM	**Mode of Support**	**Appropriate MMSS**	**Purpose**
Reasoning	Informating	Marketing information system	Provides data for monitoring
		Marketing decision support system	Simulates marketing actions
		Marketing knowledge-based system	Represents marketing knowledge
		Marketing neural network	Discovers patterns in data; updates mental models
Analogizing	Stimulating	Marketing case-based reasoning system	Stores and retrieves past events
		Marketing neural network	Learns from experiences

The purpose of an MMSS for a brand manager should be to increase both the efficiency and the effectiveness of decision making. The system should produce answers quickly, given the large number of activities a brand manager is engaged in and the usual time pressure. The MMSS should not only respond to questions, but should also play an active role by drawing the manager's attention to significant events it has discovered in the data heaps and suggesting courses of action. Since reasoning and not optimizing is the dominant marketing problem-solving mode of a product manager in FMCG, an MMSS should not so much come up with final decisions (automating), but should rather support the brand manager's decision process (informating and stimulating). After all, the manager will continue to use his or her own mental model of the situation. The system should fulfill the role of sparring partner for the product manager, including providing evidence for updating mental models, if needed. A more elaborate discussion of the management support requirements of a brand manager can be found in Dutta, Wierenga, and Dalebout (1997a).

8.3   The BRANDFRAME System

This section gives an overview of the BRANDFRAME system and describes a BRANDFRAME consultation.

8.3.1   Overview

BRANDFRAME offers a structure for representing the marketing knowledge relevant for a particular brand. It offers facilities for the storage and retrieval of data and supports the brand manager in monitoring his or her market and diagnosing particular events. Finally, BRANDFRAME can make recommendations for particular marketing programs. The BRANDFRAME system consists of five modules, as depicted in the system's main screen (Figure 8.5). These five modules also serve as menu items for the user.

The five BRANDFRAME modules and their functionalities are as follows:

1. *Define/change brand situation.* In this module the product manager can define his or her market in terms of naming and characterizing the product class, the subproduct classes, brands within the different subproduct classes, retailers, and market segments.

2. *Set targets and budgets.* This module contains the targets for each period for volume, sales, and market share. The budgets for advertising and other marketing activities are also entered in this module.

3. *Report market data.* This module is a marketing information system that provides information about the focal brand and its competitors with respect to a series of key indicators: sales volume, sales value, volume share, value share, price, distribution channel, and so on.

4. *Analysis of a specific period.* This module makes an in-depth analysis of the position of the focal brand in a specific period. It also provides an

extensive diagnosis and makes suggestions for the marketing instruments that can be used to steer the course of the brand in a desired direction.

5. *Design a marketing program.* This module helps the product manager to develop a marketing program for the instrument that he or she thinks needs attention.

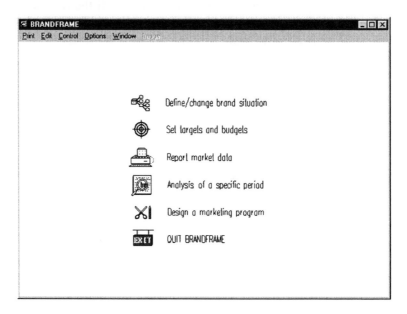

Figure 8.5   Main Screen of the BRANDFRAME System

The different modules are accessed with different frequency. *Define/change brand situation* has to be initialized once. After that, the product manager only needs to access that module if he or she wants to add, modify, or delete subproduct classes, brands, market segments, and/or retail chains. The information in *Set targets and budgets* is typically changed only once or a few times per year. The remaining modules are designed to support the product manager in his or her day-to-day activities with respect to the brand. BRANDFRAME is especially aimed at supporting the monitoring, diagnosing, planning, and design stages of the management control cycle. For this purpose the system is continuously fed with ex-factory sales data, retail panel data, household panel data, and possibly in the future Internet purchase data.

8.3.2 A BRANDFRAME Consultation

We will now work through the modules of BRANDFRAME in the same way a product manager would do. The implementation of BRANDFRAME described in this chapter uses real-life data. For confidentiality reasons we altered the names of the market and the players. The example product class is called *fopro* (an abbreviation for *fo*od *pro*duct), and the names of the moons of Saturn and Uranus have been substituted for the brand names in this product class. First we will review the overall picture of the market as it is represented in the module *Define/change brand situation*.

Figure 8.6 (a screen dump from this module) shows what the market looks like for the product class fopro. The tree that is depicted in this figure is the *market view*. The structure of the market as depicted here reflects the product manager's personal vision of his or her market. For example, the "view" of the fopro market in Figure 8.6 is the perspective of the product manager of Atlas, one of the fopro brands. The product manager's view of the market (mental model) is an important starting point for any monitoring, diagnosis, or design decision he or she makes. Thus BRANDFRAME can accommodate the specific view of an individual product manager.

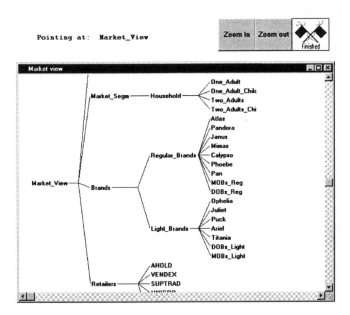

Figure 8.6   The Fopro Market

Within the fopro product class, this product manager distinguishes two subproduct classes, regular fopro and light fopro. Each subproduct class consists of a set of brands. In a specific implementation of BRANDFRAME, there is one particular brand that is the focal brand: the brand the product manager is responsible for. All the other brands are considered as competitors, though some of them might be from the same company as the focal brand. The module *Define/change brand situation* is fed with many pieces of knowledge about the focal brand, the competing brands, and the (sub)product class that are relevant for making marketing decisions for the brand. This knowledge can be quantitative (e.g., brand awareness) or qualitative (e.g., stage in the product life cycle). For a more extended discussion of this knowledge, see section 8.4.

The module *Set targets and budgets* represents the goals and constraints of the product manager. Typically, in the fall of a given year a product manager makes a marketing plan for his or her brand for the coming year, including goals and required marketing resources, such as advertising and sales promotion. Once he or she has obtained approval from his or her superiors (e.g., the vice president of marketing), this marketing plan becomes the input for the module *Set targets and budgets* for the following year.

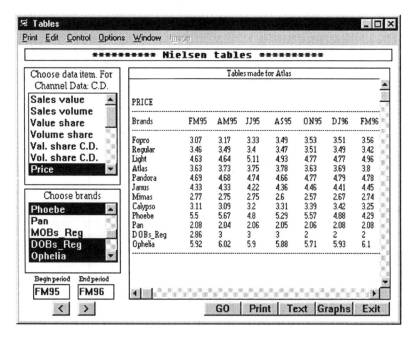

Figure 8.7   BRANDFRAME's Market Data Report

The module *Report market data* contains a lot of quantitative information (sales, market shares, prices, etc.) about the focal brand and competing brands, in both numeric and graphic form. Figure 8.7 shows an example of the output of this module: the prices of a number of Atlas's competitors. For this example we used Nielsen data collected in the bimonthly data collection era.

Apart from providing numbers and graphs, the module *Report market data* also verbally highlights the most striking changes between the current time period and an earlier one (to be specified by the user), both at the level of the market and at the level of specific retail chains (see Figure 8.8).

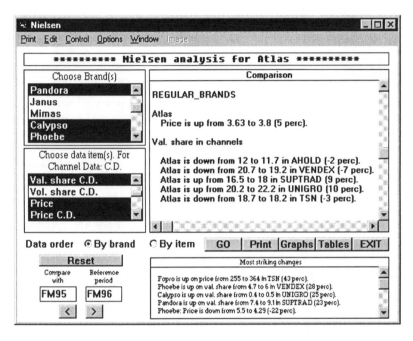

Figure 8.8   BRANDFRAME's Market Analysis

Whereas the previous module supports the overall monitoring task of the product manager, the module *Analysis of a specific period* makes an in-depth analysis of the position of the focal brand. It starts with a numeric and graphic summary of the current market situation and advises the product manager whether or not further analysis is needed (see Figure 8.9). In the example of Figure 8.9 BRANDFRAME recommends to continue further analysis because the volume sold in the most recent period was below target and the market share was also lower than it had been in the previous period.

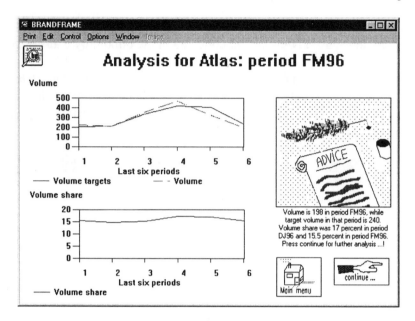

Figure 8.9   BRANDFRAME's Analysis of a Specific Period

If the product manager continues with the analysis (a BRANDFRAME user can always overrule a recommendation from the system), he or she will see a screen with meters similar to those in an airplane cockpit. These meters correspond with the marketing instruments "Sales promotion," "Advertising," "Retailing," "Price," and "Product" (see Figure 8.10). Each of these meters has a pointer, which starts at a value of zero. After the analysis of a period is completed, each meter will show a value between 0 and 100, expressing the urgency of using the corresponding marketing instrument.

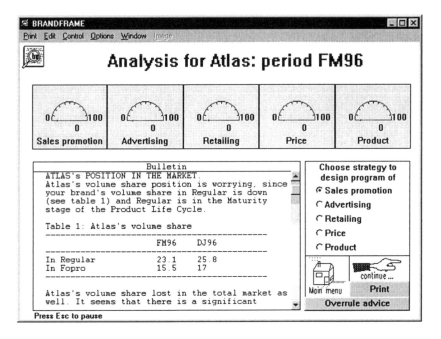

Figure 8.10   BRANDFRAME's Analysis Meters

BRANDFRAME begins its analysis of a specific period by considering the position (market share) of the focal brand in the product class, in the subproduct class, and in the several retail channels. Next, the system considers significant mutations (as compared to "normal" market volatility) that occurred during the last period. The system pays special attention to competitors to whom the focal brand lost market share. BRANDFRAME also considers the importance and current values of brand awareness and assesses whether brand awareness needs to be increased. During the BRANDFRAME consultation, the system presents its conclusions verbally and also provides tables to demonstrate the changes with numbers (see Figure 8.11).

BRANDFRAME is supposed to stimulate the product manager's thinking process. It was the intention of the developers of BRANDFRAME to provide the manager with a sparring partner that has a similar "mental landscape" to that of the manager. In order to make the relationship between the manager and the system as lively as possible, BRANDFRAME uses randomly selected alternative formulations of verbal statements at different moments. Simple parts of sentences have several alternatives. The manager's own brand is sometimes called "your own brand," sometimes "Atlas" (in the case of the example we use), and sometimes "the focal brand." "Is down" can be replaced by "decreased," and so on. The manager can therefore run the same analysis or parts of the same analysis without getting bored or starting to think about problems too mechanically.

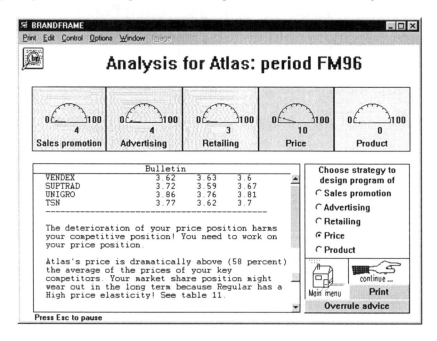

Figure 8.11   BRANDFRAME's Conclusions

The situation with respect to distribution is also analyzed. BRANDFRAME determines whether the situation of the brand, relative to competing brands, can be improved. The system examines display share and draws the manager's attention to possible discrepancies between market share and display share (e.g., if display share is above market share in a specific retail channel, this might be a reason for this retailer to decrease the number of facings for our brand). Next, BRANDFRAME examines whether or not the (relative) price position has deteriorated over the last period(s) and, if so, in which channel(s). During the consultation BRANDFRAME makes connections between the situation of the focal brand and the different marketing instruments. If, for example, brand awareness is low, increased advertising might be considered. Alternatively, to increase brand awareness a sales-promotion campaign might be carried out. Low distribution levels and/or low display shares imply a need for investments in the relationship with the retailer. A price that is too high might call for a price decrease or a price promotion. During the consultation, the system's findings are translated into movements of the pointers of the several marketing instrument meters. Additionally, the color of a meter box changes if it becomes more urgent to use that marketing instrument (red means very urgent). After a complete analysis, the BRANDFRAME screen looks something like Figure 8.12.

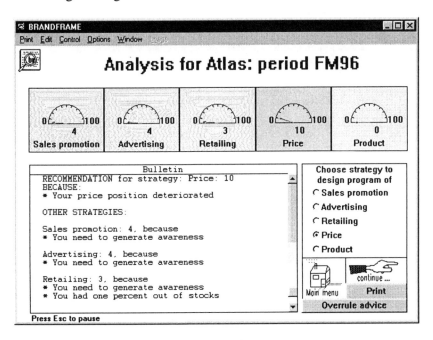

Figure 8.12 BRANDFRAME's Recommendations

In this case the deterioration of the price position of Atlas is judged to be the most serious problem, and BRANDFRAME suggests considering the *Price* strategy component. Second, awareness needs to be increased, which might be done through advertising, sales promotions, or paying attention to retailing. BRANDFRAME produces verbal recommendations with respect to the strategy. It suggests which marketing instrument should be given first priority, which should be given second priority, and so on. Besides making recommendations, the system summarizes the reasons why certain recommendations are made the way they are made. In essence, the module *Analysis of a specific period* diagnoses the events that have led to the current situation of the brand. Furthermore, it also suggests how the marketing instruments can be used to change the position of the focal brand in a desired direction. Again, the user can overrule BRANDFRAME and give priority to a different marketing instrument than the one the system recommends.

The fifth and last BRANDFRAME module is *Design a marketing program.* As an example, Figure 8.13 shows a screen from the *Sales-promotion designer* portion of this module.

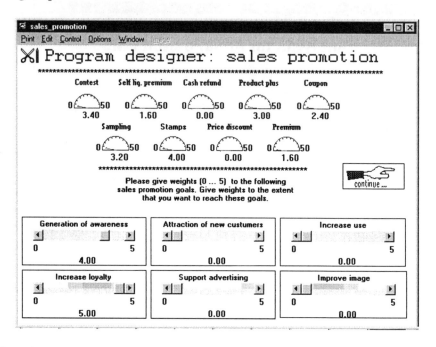

Figure 8.13   BRANDFRAME's Sales-Promotion Designer

When using the *Sales-promotion designer,* the brand manager has to provide the system with the desired goal(s) of the sales promotion (e.g., generate awareness, attract new customers, increase use, increase loyalty, etc.). BRANDFRAME will recommend a sales-promotion device (in this case, stamps) and will also provide a short description of that type of sales promotion. Figure 8.14 depicts an example of these recommendations.

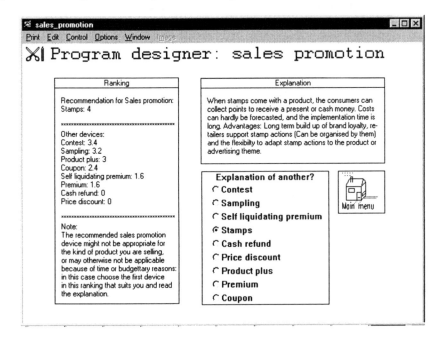

Figure 8.14   BRANDFRAME's Sales-Promotion Recommendation

In the *Advertising designer* portion of the *Design a marketing program* module, BRANDFRAME first analyzes whether or not increasing brand awareness is advisable (see Figure 8.15).

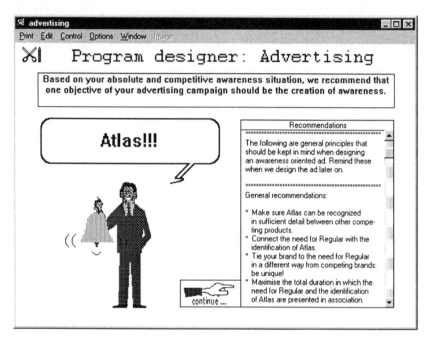

Figure 8.15   BRANDFRAME's Analysis of the Brand Awareness Situation

Subsequently, BRANDFRAME recommends which attribute should be emphasized most in an advertisement. Furthermore, it advises the user on how the advertisement should be executed (see Figure 8.16).

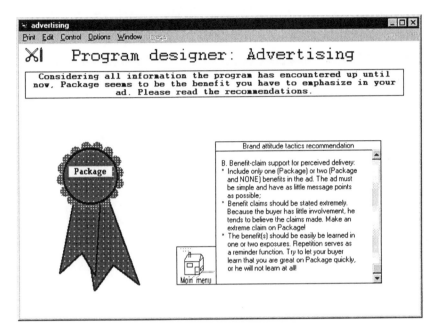

Figure 8.16   BRANDFRAME's Advertisement Recommendations

A final example from the *Design a marketing program* module is a feature that supports advertising budgeting decisions. For this purpose BRAND-RAME uses the decision-calculus method that we discussed in section 4.2.2.

In this procedure the product manager has to provide the system with four different input values (see Figure 8.17): the maintenance rate of advertising, sales at maintenance rate + 50%, the market share if advertising were cut to zero (min), and the market share that could be reached with unlimited advertising (max).

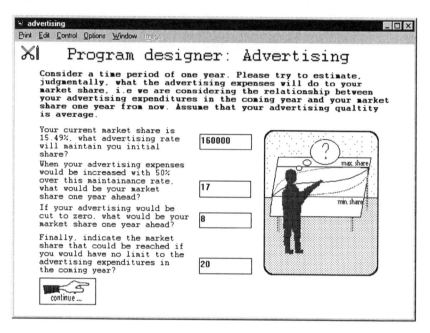

Figure 8.17   Input Requests in the Advertising Budget Routine

Using these four inputs, the system estimates the parameters of the ADBUDG response function. This response function is then used by BRANDFRAME to carry out what-if analyses for the user.

The parameterized decision-calculus model, estimated by using the four input values of the manager of Atlas, is shown in Figure 8.18.

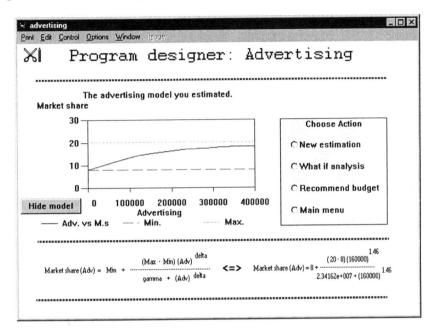

Figure 8.18   The ADBUDG Response Function

If the product manager is not interested in the mathematical details of the model, he or she has the option of hiding them. The product manager can play around with the assumptions, that is, perform sensitivity analyses.

Furthermore, the decision-calculus model can also be used to find the advertising budget that is optimal, given the assumptions (see Figure 8.19).

| advertising | □ □ × |

Print Edit Control Options Window Image

Program designer: Advertising

Advertising expenditures	Deviation from maintainance level	Marginal market share (Percentage)	Marginal gross profit
80000	−50%		
96000	−40%	0.77	74051
112000	−30%	0.67	62356
128000	−20%	0.58	51830
144000	−10%	0.51	43644
160000	****	0.44	35458
176000	+10%	0.38	28441
192000	+20%	0.34	23763
208000	+30%	0.3	19085
224000	+40%	0.26	14407
240000	+50%	0.23	10898

Recommendation

New estimation

We find the highest return per advertising dollar at an expenditure level of 80000. This is the level at which your expenses reach the highest efficiency.

There seems to be no limit, within the given range, to your advertising expenses being profitable. You can raise your adver-tising expenses over 240000, because at

Main menu

Figure 8.19   The Optimal Level of the Advertising Budget

We have now described how BRANDFRAME supports a product manager in monitoring tasks, diagnosing the situation of a brand, making suggestions for the use of particular marketing instruments, and designing marketing programs. In the next section we describe the different types of knowledge that BRANDFRAME contains to carry out these functions.

8.4   The Knowledge in BRANDFRAME

How does BRANDFRAME arrive at its suggestions and recommendations? What knowledge does the system contain, and where does this knowledge come from? The very concept of BRANDFRAME comprises a lot of knowledge: how a brand manager operates, the key indicators of how a brand performs, the variables driving these indicators, and so on. In addition, BRANDFRAME is continuously fed with data: retail panel data, household panel data, internal data, data from market research projects, and so on. This data also forms a constant source of knowledge. More specifically, we distinguish four different types of knowledge in BRANDFRAME, which we will describe in the following subsections.

8.4.1 General Marketing Knowledge

BRANDFRAME is driven by general marketing knowledge that can be found in marketing textbooks and in the minds of experienced product managers. In BRANDFRAME this general marketing knowledge is codified in three different ways: in decision tables, in association tables, and in theory-driven procedures. A *decision table* produces an output for a particular variable based on the values of a number of specified other variables. Variables can be qualitative (e.g., the position of the brand is "alarming") or quantitative (e.g., the urgency of using the marketing instrument sales promotion is 85 on a scale running from 0 to 100). There is, for example, a decision table that determines the position of a brand ("alarming," "worrying," "satisfactory," or "excellent"). This is done by considering whether its market share is down, its stage in the product life cycle (a drop in market share is more serious in a growth market than in a declining market), the number of dangerous competitors, and the overall perceptual score of the brand. *Association tables* are used to connect the situation in the market to the urgency of acting with particular marketing instruments. Association tables can be constructed from marketing theory, but they can also be obtained from real-life managers. To illustrate this, twelve product managers were asked to distribute ten points over five different marketing instruments. The points had to be divided according to the urgency of using each of these five instruments in reaction to a specific indicator in the market (Dalebout 1993). The average values are presented in Figure 8.20.

The results in Figure 8.20 show, for example, that when the degree of distribution of a particular brand declines, managers are most inclined to work on their relationships with retailers (54%), followed by carrying out sales promotions (25%) and increasing advertising (11%), to rectify this situation.

The third way that BRANDRAME exhibits general marketing knowledge is in its use of *theory-driven procedures*. An example would be the advertising theory developed by Rossiter and Percy (1987) for the development of a rule base, which BRANDFRAME uses in the *Advertising designer* portion of the *Design a marketing plan* module.

Changed Indicator	Adver-tising	Promotion	Retailing	Price	Product
Distribution is down	11	25	54	07	03
Out-of-stocks increased	01	20	54	14	12
Relative price increased	12	22	06	45	15
Awareness is down	67	28	03	00	02
Share of purchase by distributors is down	06	35	41	12	06
Share of stocks at distributors is down	02	20	63	09	06
Display share is down	09	42	37	10	02
Share in advertising expenditures is down	75	14	02	05	04
Share in promotion expenditures is down	12	74	02	06	06
Quality image worsened	49	12	00	04	35

Figure 8.20   An Illustration of an Association Table

8.4.2   Knowledge About the Brand Manager's World

In the module *Define/change brand situation* a lot of information is entered about the focal brand, competing brands, and the total environment (e.g., the retail situation). We have observed that when a product manager starts using BRANDFRAME, that person must put his or her "world" into the system. The product manager defines the structure of the market and provides the characteristics of the product class and the different brands. Figure 8.21 shows the first part of the fill-in form for the fopro product class. Part of the input is objective information that should be readily available (e.g., last year's sales); however, another part is more subjective (e.g., whether a product is expressive or instrumental).

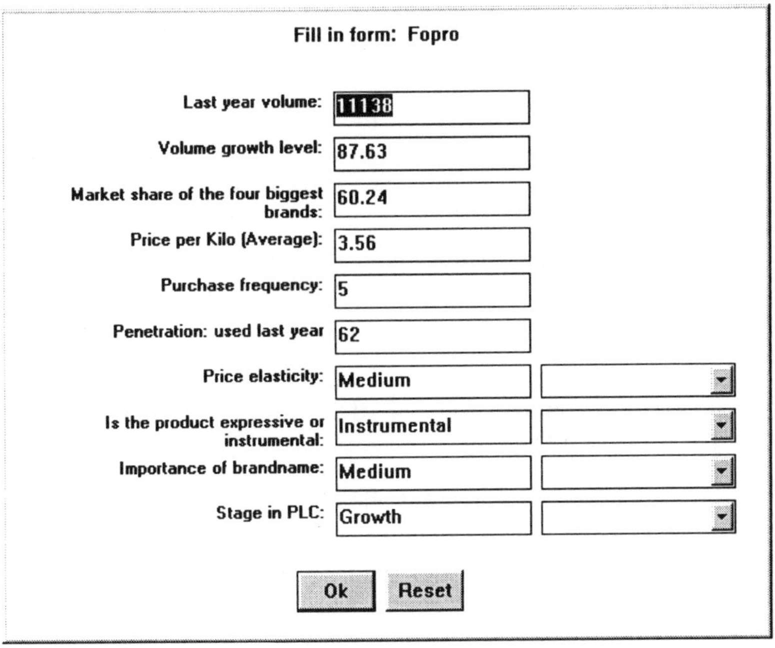

Figure 8.21   Part of the Fill-In Form for the Fopro Product Class

After the user enters knowledge about the product class, BRANDFRAME
needs information on the subproduct classes, the segments, and the brands in
the product class. BRANDFRAME acquires this information by means of
additional fill-in forms, similar to the one shown in Figure 8.21.
BRANDFRAME requests the following information about a brand:

- Market share.
- Price.
- Distribution.
- Advertising expenditures last year.
- Awareness.
- Penetration.
- Brand loyalty.
- Brand added value (brand equity).
- (Heuristic) ratings on perceptual attributes.

8.4.3   Continuous Data About the Position of the Focal Brand and Its Competitors

Continuous data about the position of the focal brand and its competitors is the type of data that is made available by syndicated services practically all over the world. This data typically comes from retail panels and household or consumer panels. The data items we referred to earlier, such as volume sales, dollar sales, market shares, prices, distribution shares, and out-of-stocks per outlet type, serve as a continuous input to BRANDFRAME. They drive the modules *Report market data* and *Analysis of a specific period.*

8.4.4   Specific Inputs Asked of the Product Manager During a BRANDFRAME Consultation

During a consultation, BRANDFRAME can ask the product manager for specific inputs—for example, whether he or she agrees with a specific recommendation. The philosophy behind BRANDFRAME is that although the system comes up with suggestions and recommendations, the product manager can overrule these at any time. BRANDFRAME will then continue in the direction suggested by the product manager.

8.5   Functionality of BRANDFRAME as a Marketing Management Support System

In earlier chapters we discussed several types of marketing management support systems, both data-driven and knowledge-driven. How should BRANDFRAME be characterized in the terminology we have introduced? BRANDFRAME is primarily a knowledge-based system (an MKBS). However, as a comprehensive tool it also has features of other systems. Although the BRANDFRAME "engine" basically uses qualitative reasoning, the system is continuously fed with quantitative data. Furthermore, BRANDFRAME also contains quantitative modules, for example, the component on advertising budgeting. In this sense BRANDFRAME is an *integrated system.* A general tendency of knowledge-based approaches seems to be that, rather than functioning as stand-alone systems, they are combined with quantitative models. The combination of (quantitative) model building and (qualitative) knowledge processing can be very powerful.

For the development of the *knowledge-oriented* part of BRANDFRAME, several different knowledge representation and knowledge-processing methods are applied. The prototype version shown here was developed in KAPPA-PC. KAPPA-PC is a 4GL tool that supports different methods for representing knowledge and dealing with it. The KAPPA-PC development environment is comparable to environments like Art*enterprise, CLIPS, Level 5 Object, and LPA Flex (see Chapter 5). KAPPA-PC is an object-oriented environment, where systems are modeled as sets of cooperating objects (see Chapter 3). According to the principles of object orientation, the system contains slots, methods, and inheritance. Examples of slots in BRANDFRAME are given in Figure 8.22. In the AI literature the list of slots that characterize an object is called a *frame*. In BRANDFRAME the brand is the central element and the brand frames are the most elaborated frames. This was the reason for naming the system *BRANDFRAME*.

The inheritance principle implies that when a new brand is created, it automatically inherits all the slots of its parent. Thus the user only has to specify values for those slots for which the new brand differs from the other brands in the product (sub)class.

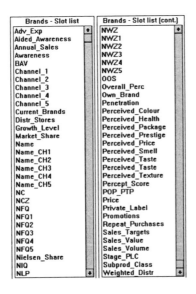

Figure 8.22   List of Slots for Brand Objects in BRANDFRAME

In an object-oriented system the behavior of objects is modeled by so-called *methods*. Figure 8.23 shows an example of a method in BRANDFRAME— in this case, for the computation of the overall perceptual score of a brand. Whenever the overall perceptual score of a brand is needed, a message is sent to the object in question, to execute this perceptual-score method and return the result.

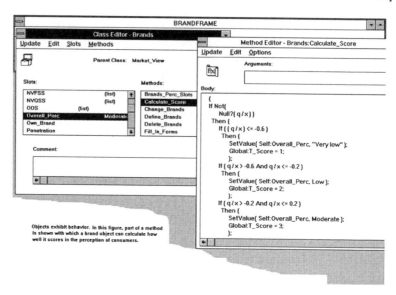

Figure 8.23   A Method for Computing the Perceptual Score of a Brand

Although KAPPA-PC is object-oriented, knowledge processing can also occur through the use of *rules*. For example, the translation of the decision tables into knowledge-processing methods is done by means of rules. Figure 8.24 shows an example of a rule that determines whether or not the situation of a brand is "alarming."

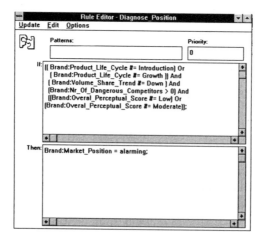

Figure 8.24   An Example of a Rule in BRANDFRAME

BRANDFRAME also has a case-based reasoning functionality. After each consultation, the system stores the particular brand situation, together with the system's recommendation and the decision actually made by the product manager. Later, the results of this decision can also be added to this information. All the information about a particular event constitutes a case. The cases of the same brand that emerge over time are put in a case base. Cases of other brands from the same company, from the same or different product categories or countries, might also be added to this case base. The case base can be used to support finding solutions for new problems (see Chapter 6). The use of cases is in accordance with the habit of brand managers to store marketing events in their memories in the form of chunks (Goldstein 1993).

In terms of knowledge-processing methods, BRANDFRAME constitutes a "hybrid environment." It makes use of several of the knowledge representation and knowledge-processing methods that we discussed in Chapters 5 and 6. These include frame-based representation, rule-based reasoning, and case-based reasoning. Notwithstanding these advanced knowledge technologies, we should remember Feigenbaum's "knowledge principle," which states that the power of an AI program to perform at high levels of competence depends on the amount and quality of the knowledge that program contains about the problem domain. The reasoning method, while necessary, plays a secondary role (Feigenbaum, McCorduck, and Nii 1988, p. 7). So it is of crucial importance that a system like BRANDFRAME be equipped with adequate brand management knowledge. Furthermore, such a system should contain efficient procedures for continuously updating this knowledge using feedback from the marketplace.

8.6   Evaluation and Perspective

The prototype version of BRANDFRAME was implemented at Holland Fast Moving Company (HFMC)[4]. Two product managers (in different product categories) worked with BRANDFRAME for an extended period of time. They used BRANDFRAME each time new Nielsen data arrived and also for ad hoc purposes, such as the analysis of specific problems, discussions with the sales department, and brainstorming about promotions. After four months their experiences with respect to using BRANDFRAME were evaluated.

The product managers found BRANDFRAME to be useful, complete, important, and timesaving. The latter is relevant, given the very busy schedules of brand managers. The product managers especially valued

---

[4] This is a pseudonym for an actual Dutch company.

BRANDFRAME's customizability ("It lets the product manager define his own mental model of the world") and the fact that all the information is brought together around the focal brand. They felt that the product manager using the system remained in charge ("I find it easy to let BRANDFRAME do what I want"). In this respect BRANDFRAME was evaluated favorably compared to the existing systems. The two product managers also found their interactions with the system to be stimulating. During these interactions they were forced to make their ideas and assumptions explicit. The product managers were convinced that BRANDFRAME made better use of Nielsen and comparable data than the existing systems did. They observed that BRANDFRAME is also a good learning device because it represents a realistic marketing environment.

Managers do not always engage in active search to perform the monitoring tasks for their brands. Therefore, the monitoring function of BRANDFRAME was very welcome. The same was true for the diagnosing task. Product managers spend a lot of time evaluating alternative marketing actions and designing marketing programs. However, they showed less interest in using computer support for this task than for the monitoring and diagnosing tasks. This might be due to limitations of the current BRANDFRAME version with respect to designing marketing programs, but there may also be an implicit view that designing marketing programs is the core business of a brand manager and should therefore not be relinquished to a computer.

In addition to the experiences of the two product managers who worked with BRANDFRAME for several months, the Holland Fast Moving Company also had a group of eight product managers work with the system during a two-day session. BRANDFRAME was implemented for each product manager's own brands. The results of a after-use survey are presented in Figure 8.25. What the product managers appreciated most about BRANDFRAME was its capacity to stimulate thoughts and support their decision-making process. However, they did not have the impression that BRANDFRAME was automating their jobs.

Based on these results, we conclude that the BRANDFRAME concept is successful in that it has a good fit with the requirements of the specific decision situation of a brand manager in fast-moving consumer goods. BRANDFRAME recognizes the expertise and judgment of the decision maker (brand managers in FMCG tend to be highly educated professionals) and acts as their sparring partner. A lesson we may learn from the experience with BRANDFRAME is that a demand-oriented development might very well be the secret for the success of future marketing management support systems. An MMSS should be built "around" the decision maker. This can start with a quite basic system, which incrementally becomes more sophisticated. The BRANDFRAME version discussed here, although it has many interesting features already, is still a prototype and must be developed further.

The BRANDFRAME system	Average score
Imposes serious restrictions when I look at my market	4.1 *
Is very useful in pointing at good analysis and results	4.6
Is sufficiently adaptable to the wishes of the user	4.5
Automates the job of the product manager	3.0
Provides information on my market	5.4
Stimulates the thinking of the product manager	5.4
Provides information on my market	4.1
Aims to support the process by which the product manager decides	5.3
Aims to let the product manager learn while practicing his job	5.1
Is userfriendly	5.3
Is fast	3.9
Is fun to work with	4.9
Is accessible	5.3
Is easy to learn working with	5.5
Is very flexible	4.0
Matches the way of thinking of a product manager	4.4

Sevenpoint scale: 1 = does not apply at all; 7 = applies very much

Figure 8.25   Results from an After-Use Survey or BRANDFRAME among an international group of brand managers (n=8)

So far we have discussed the advantages offered by BRANDFRAME to individual product managers. There are also advantages at the company or corporate level. A system like BRANDFRAME can help to conserve company-specific knowledge about brands and markets. This is no luxury, given the quick turnover of brand managers. For a new brand manager, learning the situation about the brand becomes much easier if BRANDFRAME has already been implemented for that brand. Furthermore, by storing consultations, BRANDFRAME can be used to develop a "corporate brand memory" containing information about past events with brands, the actions that were taken, and the outcomes of these actions. Such a corporate brand memory facilitates learning and the accumulation of valuable brand management knowledge in the company.

Key Points

• *A marketing management support system for a brand manager should support the different stages of the management control cycle: monitoring, diagnosing, planning marketing actions, and designing marketing programs.*

• *A marketing management support system for a brand manager should play an active role and, combining incoming data with knowledge about the brand, informate and stimulate the brand manager in supervising the brand. The system should also give quick responses to questions.*

• *BRANDFRAME is an integrated system (using elements of data-driven and knowledge-driven MMSS) that acts as a sparring partner for a brand manager. It contains both general marketing knowledge and specific knowledge about the particular brand manager's world, and it is fed with a continuous stream of market data.*

• *Brand managers who have used BRANDFRAME judged it to have fulfilled its requirements and considered it useful, complete, important, and timesaving.*

• *The BRANDFRAME approach demonstrates the success of an MMSS designed for a specific type of decision maker.*

PART IV

*Perspectives on Marketing Management
Support Systems*

Chapter 9

Factors That Determine the Success of Marketing Management Support Systems

Learning Objectives

- *To acquire a comprehensive view of the different factors that influence the success of marketing management support systems.*

- *To become familiar with the most important empirical studies on the effectiveness of marketing management support systems.*

- *To learn how the design characteristics of marketing management support systems influence their success.*

- *To learn how the implementation characteristics of marketing management support systems influence their success*

9.1 Introduction

The fourth and last part of this book focuses on how to increase the success of marketing management support systems in companies, in terms of both their adoption and implementation and their contribution to more effective and efficient decision making. In the present chapter we develop a framework of the factors that determine the success of MMSS. In the next chapter we discuss the developments in marketing and in the environment of marketing that are relevant for MMSS in the future.

Compared to the work put into the *development* of marketing management support systems, the effort spent investigating their impact on the quality of real-life marketing management decisions (i.e., their *success*) has been modest. This is remarkable considering the large investments that companies often make in developing and implementing MMSS. Of course, many studies on the development of MMSS have paid attention to the implementation of a specific system in one or more companies and have sometimes commented on the success of these systems. However, research with the primary purpose of obtaining systematic, generalizable insight into the factors that determine the success of marketing management support systems is scarce. At this stage there is no comprehensive theory regarding the effectiveness of MMSS. In this chapter we attempt to develop such a theory by combining conceptual ideas with the empirical evidence available today.

We start by describing the most important studies on the effectiveness of marketing management support systems available to date. Next we present a conceptual model (one could also call it an *integrating framework*) of the factors that determine the success of MMSS. Given the discussion of the previous chapters, it should come as no surprise that the *match* between the demand and supply sides of marketing management support systems is the central construct in this framework. However, as we shall see, *design* and *implementation* characteristics are also important for getting MMSS successfully implemented and used in companies. The framework is not only based on the work on *marketing* management support systems, but also makes use of insights developed in the field of (general) management support systems, also referred to as decision support systems (DSS) or information systems (IS). Furthermore, the framework is not only useful for structuring our current knowledge about the effectiveness of MMSS, but also shows the gaps in this knowledge and thereby suggests a list of issues that should be high on the research agenda for MMSS. These insights will be used in the next (and last) chapter, which focuses on how to develop marketing management support systems that are fit for the future.

9.2   Empirical Research on the Effectiveness of Marketing Management Support Systems

In this section we briefly discuss the most important empirical studies on the effectiveness of marketing management support systems. One of the first systematic studies on the impact of MMSS was conducted by Fudge and Lodish (1977). Sales managers of United Airlines used the CALLPLAN model (Lodish 1971) for determining optimal sales-call frequency schedules for their clients. In a controlled experiment, these researchers found that the sales reps who used CALLPLAN realized significantly higher sales (+8.1% on average) than sales reps using the habitual planning methods. A more recent study confirmed the success of a CALLPLAN-type approach to sales planning in an application in the pharmaceutical company Syntex (Lodish,

Curtis, Ness, and Simpson 1988). This study won the Franz Edelman Award for Achievements in Operations Research and the Management Sciences.

Another study, which also won the Franz Edelman Award, described the successful implementation of a marketing management support system at ABB Electric (Gensch, Aversa, and Moore 1990). The particular MMSS used a multi-attribute choice-modeling approach to describe the preferences for transformers among different (segments of) customers of ABB Electric. Comparison of sales results in the geographical districts where the MMSS was implemented with those in districts where traditional marketing methods were used showed that the use of the MMSS had a significant impact on sales. Sales were up 10–18% in the districts using the MMSS and down 10% in those not using it. The subsequent companywide implementation of the MMSS led to an enduring increase in the market share of ABB Electric. According to the authors, one of the key factors for the success at ABB Electric was the direct involvement of the CEO of the company in the development and implementation of the MMSS. In the Syntex case, although the actual implementation was very successful (an increase in annual revenues of $25 million), management did not carry out all the major reallocations of resources over products and markets that the model recommended (Lodish et al. 1988).

Wierenga and Oude Ophuis (1997) report on a cross-sectional study about actual marketing management support systems in companies, covering a broad range of marketing decision situations and different MMSS. A survey was held among 525 companies, of which 194 had adopted an MMSS. These researchers found that the adoption of an MMSS was positively related to top management support, the stage of development of marketing in the organization (marketing orientation), and communication (as measured by the number of information sources about MMSS and knowledge of successful MMSS in other companies). They also found that use of the system by its adopters was higher when users had access to the system through direct interaction instead of through an intermediary and when there was a champion for the system within the company. In addition, satisfaction with the system was higher if it was accessible through direct interaction, if it was more adaptable, and when there was a higher level of perceived participation on the part of the user in the implementation process (user involvement).

The studies just referred to deal with the use of marketing management support systems for real-life decision making in companies. However, most of the empirical studies on the effects of MMSS were conducted by means of laboratory experiments. Chakravarti, Mitchell, and Staelin (1979) carried out an experiment in which they measured the effect of using the ADBUDG model (Little 1970) for supporting advertising decisions. They found that using this system led to poorer decisions in terms of operating profit and the accuracy of predicted market share. McIntyre (1982) carried out a similar experiment, using the same type of MMSS, but he found a positive relationship between the use of the MMSS and profits.

Zinkhan, Joachimsthaler, and Kinnear (1987) studied the effects of several decision maker characteristics on the success of marketing management support systems, measured by use and satisfaction. They found that cognitive differentiation (a cognitive style variable) and prior involvement with DSS (an experience variable) were positively correlated with the use of an MMSS. Van Bruggen, Smidts, and Wierenga (1998) carried out an experiment in the MARKSTRAT (Larréché and Gatignon 1990) environment. They found positive relationships between using this MMSS and market share and profit. However, subjects using the MMSS did not have more decision confidence than those not using the system. McIntyre (1982) found the same result, that is, no relationship between the objective effect(s) of using an MMSS and the subjective evaluation of the user/decision maker.

Also in an experimental setting, Hoch and Schkade (1996) studied the effect of the decision environment on the impact of marketing management support systems. In their study subjects had to predict the future credit ratings of applicants given four financial characteristics. In a predictable environment, historical cases and a pattern-matching strategy offered adequate support to decision makers. However, in less predictable (more dynamic) environments, linear models were more effective decision aids. This finding demonstrates that the extent to which a decision support tool is effective may depend on the decision environment.

We can draw several conclusions from the studies that have been conducted so far. First, the success of marketing management support systems in terms of their positive effects on profit and other company results has been demonstrated several times. However, MMSS have *not always* been found to be successful. Apparently, the performance of an MMSS depends on the specific characteristics of the situation in which the system is used and the specific success measure(s) one is looking at. This observation generates at least two issues for further research. First, it is important to gain better insight into the conditions under which an MMSS is successful. From the studies reviewed above, several antecedents of MMSS success emerge: support from top management, organizational culture (marketing orientation, internal communication), the design characteristics of the particular MMSS (accessibility, sophistication), characteristics of the implementation process (user involvement), and decision maker characteristics such as experience and cognitive style. The IS literature describes even more variables that can affect the success of a (marketing) management support system.

Second, there are many *different measures* for the success of a marketing management support system. Examples encountered in the studies to date include the extent to which the MMSS was actually used by decision makers, acceptance of the system's recommendations by management, and the effect of such a system on market share, profit, forecast accuracy, and decision confidence. As an issue for further research, it is important to distinguish between different success measures, to examine their mutual relationships, and to be clear about which dependent variable(s) to include in empirical studies on the effects of using an MMSS.

In the next section we present a comprehensive framework of the factors that determine the success of marketing management support systems.

9.3   A Framework for Explaining the Success of Marketing Management Support Systems

We distinguish five main factors that determine the success of a marketing management support system. These are (1) the *demand* for decision support, (2) the *supply* of decision support (the decision support offered by the MMSS), (3) the *match* between demand and supply, (4) the *design characteristics* of the particular system, and (5) the *characteristics of the implementation* of the particular system. Together with (6) the dependent variable "*success* of the MMSS," these five factors constitute the main building blocks of the framework presented in Figure 9.1.

We suppose that the primary determinant of the success of a marketing management support system is the match between the demand side (the decision processes to be supported) and the supply side (the functionality of the management support systems employed). Here we distinguish between the *potential* success of an MMSS and its *actual* success. We think that the match between demand and supply determines the *potential* success of an MMSS. To what extent this success will be realized depends on the *design characteristics* of the MMSS and the *characteristics of its implementation* (Davis 1989; Alavi and Joachimsthaler 1992).

The first three factors in the framework correspond directly with the three preceding parts of this book. The *demand side of decision support* is the subject of Chapter 2. The *supply side of decision support*—that is, the different types of MMSS and their functionalities—is the subject of Chapters 3 through 6. The *match between demand and supply* is the topic of Chapters 7 and 8. Finally, *design* and *implementation* aspects (blocks 4 and 5 in Figure 9.1), although important, are not specific to *marketing* management support systems and have therefore not been covered by separate chapters in this book. More information about the effect of these factors can be found in the general DSS literature (see below).

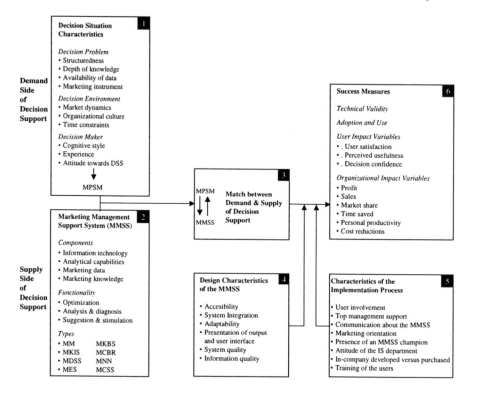

Figure 9.1   An Integrating Framework of Factors That Determine the Success of Marketing
Management Support Systems (*Source:* adapted from Wierenga, Van Bruggen, and
Staelin 1999)

9.3.1   The Demand Side of Decision Support

Management support systems have to play their role in the context of
problem-solving activities of (marketing) decision makers. Therefore, it is
important to start our analysis with the *demand* side of decision support, that
is, the decision situation (block 1 in Figure 9.1). The early writings in the
DSS/IS literature (Mason and Mitroff 1973; Mock 1973; Chervany,
Dickson, and Kozar 1972; Lucas 1973) mentioned three basic factors that
characterize the decision situation: (1) the *problem* to be solved, (2) the
environment in which it must be solved, and (3) the *decision maker* who has
to solve it.

In Chapter 2 the different demand-side factors were discussed as
antecedents of the marketing problem-solving modes (MPSM). We will only
highlight a few elements here. The problem characteristic *structuredness*
refers to Simon's (1977) notion of "programmability" of a problem.
Marketing problems vary enormously in their level of structuredness. Sales-
force allocation and media planning are examples of relatively structured

problems; marketing communication and marketing strategy are examples of less structured problems. The decision environment characteristic *market dynamics* suggests that there is a big difference between operating in a stable market versus operating in a turbulent one (Simon 1994). In stable markets it is relatively easy to build mathematical models and perform some form of optimization. However, in turbulent markets decision makers will be hard-pressed to understand and interpret what is going on (Bucklin, Lehman, and Little 1998). An important decision maker characteristic is *cognitive style,* which refers to the process by which (marketing) decision makers perceive and process information. Most common is the classification of decision makers into analytical and nonanalytical or heuristic types. It seems that an analytical cognitive style facilitates the *use of* marketing management support systems (Larréché 1979; Zinkhan et al. 1987; Van Bruggen et al. 1998). However, Benbasat and Dexter (1982, 1985) found that low-analytical decision makers have the most to gain from decision support aids if they actually use them. Van Bruggen et al. (1998) also observed that an MMSS can reduce the difference between high- and low-analytical decision makers.

9.3.2 The Supply Side of Decision Support

The counterpart of the demand side is the *supply* side, which refers to the decision support offered by the marketing management support systems (block 2 in Figure 9.1). As we have seen in Chapter 3, an MMSS is a combination of four *components:* information technology, analytical capabilities, marketing data, and marketing knowledge. Depending on the relative prominence of the different components, different types of MMSS offer different decision support *functionalities.* For example, an MMSS can help to carry out optimizations, it can support the analysis and diagnosis of a specific situation, or it can come up with suggestions for users that stimulate the generation of (new) solutions. These different functionalities have led to different *types of* marketing management support systems (see section 3.6). The development of MMSS started with data-driven systems, such as marketing models, marketing information systems, and marketing decision support systems. However, more recently a new class of managerial support systems has emerged: knowledge-driven systems. Benbasat and Nault (1990) were among the first to distinguish expert systems as a separate class of managerial support systems. Since then several other types of knowledge-driven management support systems have appeared. In marketing, marketing expert systems, marketing knowledge-based systems, marketing case-based reasoning systems, marketing neural networks, and marketing creativity support systems have become available. These different kinds of MMSS and their specific strengths and weaknesses were discussed in Chapters 4, 5, and 6.

9.3.3   The Match Between Demand and Supply

Which marketing management support system is most suitable depends on the decision situation. As early as 1967, Cox and Good mentioned the "system-manager balance" as an important element of marketing information systems. Therefore, the *match* between the demand and supply sides of decision support (block 3 in Figure 9.1) is the central element in our framework of the factors that drive the success of MMSS. Chapter 7 discussed in detail how to achieve a match between the demand and supply sides of marketing management support systems. Here we do this only in a summary form. The decision situation characteristics lead to a specific marketing problem-solving mode. Factors that favor the *optimizing* mode are an analytical cognitive style for the decision maker, a highly structured problem, stable market conditions, and an ample time frame. If the problem is less structured, the market is changing quickly, and the time frame is more constrained, the *reasoning* mode is more likely to be employed. A nonanalytical or heuristic decision maker who is dealing with an ill-structured market under severe time constraints will use his or her experiences with similar cases to solve a current problem. This means that the *analogizing* mode is being used. If there is no precise problem formulation and no time pressure, and if the purpose is to come up with novel ideas and solutions, the *creating* mode will prevail. In order for an MMSS to be successful, there must be a match between the marketing problem-solving mode and the actual system used.

In order to effect such a match, a structured approach should be followed (see Chapter 7). For example, under the *optimizing* mode the primary task of a marketing management support system is to find the best solution within a given problem space. In the case of a quantitatively formulated problem, this means using marketing models. If the problem is formulated in qualitative terms, using marketing expert systems would be most appropriate. In the *reasoning* mode there will be a need for analysis and diagnosis, functionalities that are offered by marketing information systems, marketing decision support systems, and marketing knowledge-based systems. In the *analogizing* and *creating* modes support systems should have the functionalities of making suggestions and stimulating the decision maker, features that are offered by marketing case-based reasoning systems and marketing creativity support systems.

9.3.4 Design Characteristics of Marketing Management Support Systems

The match between the demand and supply sides of decision support determines the *potential* success of a marketing management support system. However, whether or not this potential materializes will depend on two sets of factors, *design* characteristics and *implementation* characteristics. For example, two different systems for media planning may both take an optimization approach, but one system may require the input of a lot of technical parameters, whereas the other system may receive its input through a user-friendly dialogue. In such a case the chance of success of the more user-friendly design is much higher. The effects of design and implementation characteristics on the success of a system have been studied extensively in the *general* DSS/IS field. There is much literature on these topics, summarized in several review papers and meta-analyses, such as those by Zmud (1979), Kwon and Zmud (1987), DeLone and McLean (1992), Alavi and Joachimsthaler (1992), and Gelderman (1997). Papers that have studied the effects of design and implementation characteristics for *marketing* management support systems (e.g., Zinkhan, Joachimsthaler, and Kinnear 1987; Wierenga and Oude Ophuis 1997) tend to find effects that are similar to those found in the general DSS/IS field. In the remainder of this subsection we present a contemporaneous account of the insights (gained through research) into the most important design characteristics of marketing management support systems. These characteristics are listed in Figure 9.2.

- Accessibility
- System integration
- Adaptability
- Presentation of output and user interface
- System quality
- Information quality

Figure 9.2   The Most Important Design Characteristics of Marketing Management Support Systems

Accessibility refers to the way the user has access to the system. In the mainframe era managers did not have direct access to the computer; specialized intermediaries (sometimes referred to as "marketing science intermediaries") were needed for interaction with the system (Little 1979, p. 23). Now managers often interact directly with the marketing management support system from their desktop or laptop PC, but there are still many instances where the MMSS can only be accessed from dedicated computers elsewhere in the company. Greater accessibility has been found to have a positive effect on the success of MMSS (Paisley 1968; Igbaria and Nachman 1990; Mawhinney and Lederer 1990). Furthermore, the research of Glazer, Steckel, and Winer (1992) makes clear that information that is more easily accessible will be given more attention. This may even lead to biased decision processes if more value is attached to this information than it deserves.

System integration is the extent to which marketing management support systems are integrated with other systems. There is a tendency toward companywide information systems—so-called *enterprise resource planning* (or ERP) systems—with modules for the different functional areas (i.e., marketing, logistics, finance, etc.). System integration implies that marketing cannot unilaterally determine the specifications of MMSS any longer. At the same time, system integration makes marketing information accessible to a wider range of managers, including nonmarketing managers. This may well be a critical success factor for MMSS.

Adaptability, also called *flexibility,* is the extent to which the system can be made usable for new purposes without major technical intervention. Little (1970) observed that marketing models should be "adaptive." Moreover, the flexibility of (marketing) decision support systems has been found to be highly correlated with success (Barki and Huff 1990; Udo and Davis 1992; Wierenga and Oude Ophuis 1997).

Presentation of output and *user interface:* Several studies have investigated the effects of graphic and tabular presentations or other aspects of output presentation (Lusk and Kersnick 1979; Benbasat and Dexter 1985; Cleveland and McGill 1987; Wainer 1984). The most effective output form turns out to depend on many factors, including the cognitive style of the user. Day and Glazer (1994) make a plea for "analog representation" of information. With an analog device—for example, a clock—information is processed very quickly, which is critical when real-time performance is required (compare the ratio of analog to digital instruments in the cockpit of an airplane). The BRANDFRAME system (see Chapter 8) makes use of such clocks. Using modern multimedia technology, systems are now capable of combined presentation modes: figures, tables, graphics, audio, and video.

System quality is defined as the extent to which the system fits with the needs of the user (DeLone and McLean 1992). Examples of variables that are typically dealt with in this context are ease of use, perceived usefulness, ease of learning, and ease of understanding (Davis 1989; DeLone and McLean 1992). Other system quality elements are response time, accuracy, and reliability (DeLone and McLean 1992). Ease of use of an information system and perceived usefulness have been found to influence the extent to which decision makers use a system and thus its effectiveness (Davis 1989; Davis, Bagozzi, and Warshaw 1989; Adams, Nelson, and Todd 1992).

Information quality refers to the quality of the system output, including such aspects as the accuracy of information, reliability, precision, currency, and timeliness (DeLone and McLean 1992).

9.3.5 Characteristics of the Implementation Process

Characteristics of the implementation process have been a long-standing concern for both decision support systems (Schultz and Slevin 1975) and marketing models (Naert and Leeflang 1978). There have been a lot of studies on the implementation of DSS. In the remainder of this subsection we summarize the state of knowledge with respect to the most important implementation characteristics. These characteristics are listed in Figure 9.3.

User involvement is the extent to which users—that is, marketing decision makers—participate in the design and maintenance of marketing management support systems. User involvement is the most studied implementation variable in the DSS/IS field. Two recent meta-analyses found relatively large positive effects of user involvement on system use and satisfaction with the system (Alavi and Joachimsthaler 1992; Gelderman 1997). For *marketing* management support systems the importance of user participation and involvement of marketing in the purchase/development of an MMSS was demonstrated in the study by Wierenga and Oude Ophuis (1997).

- User involvement

- Top management support

- Communication about the MMSS

- Marketing orientation

- Presence of an MMSS champion

- Attitude of the IS department

- In-company developed versus purchased

- Training of the users

Figure 9.3   The Most Important Implementation Characteristics of Marketing Management Support Systems

Top management support refers to the extent to which the superiors of the users support the development and use of marketing management support systems. There is an overwhelming agreement in the (M)DSS literature that top management support is an important success factor for decision support systems (Zmud 1979; Kwon and Zmud 1987; Lilien, Kotler, and Moorthy 1992; Lee and Kim 1992; Gelderman 1997; Wierenga and Oude Ophuis 1997).

Communication about the marketing management support system to (future) users: For a marketing audience the importance of this factor will be clear, but in the DSS/IS literature communication has not received much attention. In general, the number of information sources through which a company becomes aware of a new technology has been found to be an important factor leading to its adoption (Zaltman, Duncan, and Holbek 1973; Gatignon and Robertson 1989). Imitative behavior also plays a role. Apparent success that other innovators have with a new technology is a motivation to adopt the innovation oneself (Swanson 1994). Wierenga and Oude Ophuis (1997) found that the number of different information sources and knowledge about successful MMSS applications in other companies were significantly related to MMSS adoption.

Marketing orientation: The successful implementation of a marketing management support system requires a certain level of marketing development in the company: the presence of marketing expertise and the existence of some form of marketing organization (a marketing department, use of an annual marketing plan, resources for marketing, etc.). This development of marketing in an organization reflects the company's state of market orientation. The presence of a marketing organization is significantly related to MMSS success (Wierenga and Oude Ophuis 1997).

Presence of a marketing management support system champion, a person who is seized by the idea of an MMSS and pushes for it throughout the company: It has been found that the presence of a (marketing) management support system "champion" can have a very positive effect on its success (Sviokla 1989; Wierenga and Oude Ophuis 1997).

Attitude of the IS department: The IS department of a company is almost always involved in the implementation of a marketing management support system. This can be as the developer of the system or as a major adviser to (top) management if the system is purchased from outside. A cooperative attitude of the IS staff was found to be an important factor for (marketing) management support system success (Joshi 1992; De Jong, Huizingh, Oude Ophuis, and Wierenga 1994).

In-company developed versus purchased: The trade-off between these two ways of realizing a marketing management support system is faster implementation and lower costs (for a commercially purchased package) versus more flexibility and a better fit with the specific situation (for a tailor-made customer-developed system) (Lucas, Walton, and Ginzberg 1988). The consideration of fit might lead one to expect a relative disadvantage for a commercially purchased package; however, the study by Wierenga and Oude Ophuis (1997) found no difference in success between the in-company developed MMSS and the purchased systems.

Training of the users: Training appeared to have a significant positive effect on marketing management support system performance in several studies (Sanders and Courtney 1985; Barki and Huff 1990; Alavi and Joachimsthaler 1992; Udo and Davis 1992). The quality of *user documenta-tion* is also positively related to the effectiveness of MMSS use (Torkzadeh and Doll 1993).

9.3.6 Success Measures for Marketing Management Support Systems

As we have seen before there are different ways to *measure* the success of a marketing management support system. From the start of DSS/IS research, the question of what the dependent variable should be has occupied an important place in the literature (Zmud 1979; Keen 1980; Ives and Olson 1984; DeLone and McLean 1992). So far, this debate has not led to the adoption of *one* IS success measure. DeLone and McLean (1992), who examined dependent variables in 100 empirical DSS/IS studies, concluded that "there are nearly as many measures as there are studies" (p. 61). In the remainder of this subsection we review the most important success measures for MMSS. These are listed in Figure 9.4.

- Technical validity

- Adoption and use

- User impact variables

- Organizational impact variables

Figure 9.4   The Most Important Success Measures for Marketing Management Support Systems

Technical validity—that is, the extent to which the marketing management support system is a valid representation of the marketing processes and makes (statistically) accurate predictions—is a necessary condition for the success of an MMSS. However, it is not a sufficient condition, since even the most technically advanced systems may not be accepted by the decision maker. Therefore, the next success measure is *adoption and use,* which are also (obviously) necessary for the success of an MMSS. If a system is not both adopted and used, it cannot possibly be successful.

Regarding the impact of a marketing management support system, we follow DeLone and McLean (1992) in distinguishing between user impact variables and organizational impact variables.

User impact variables refer to how well the marketing management support system performs in the perception of the user. By far the most frequently measured dependent variable in DSS/IS research is *user satisfaction.* Of 39 studies considered in a meta-analysis, 27 (69%) had user (information) satisfaction as a dependent variable (Gelderman 1997). Sometimes slightly different concepts are used to express the user's psychological assessment of a system, like *perceived usefulness* of a system (Davis 1989; Adams, Nelson, and Todd 1992). Besides studying the evaluation of a system as such, one can also study the effects the MMSS has on the evaluation of behavior. A variable measuring behavior evaluation is *decision confidence* (Aldag and Power 1986; Goslar, Green, and Hughes 1986).

Organizational impact variables such as profit, sales, and market share have a more objective character. Ultimately, the costs of a marketing management support system should be outweighed by the extra *profit* it generates. Prior to that evaluation, one could examine the effects of an MMSS on *sales* and *market share.* It may be difficult to assess the profit contribution directly attributable to an MMSS. Sometimes when it is not possible to determine the MMSS's contribution to overall company performance, more limited performance measures have been used in the DSS/IS literature. Examples of such measures are *time saved,* increased *personal productivity,* and *cost reductions* achieved by using the system, for example, in production scheduling and ordering costs (DeLone and McLean 1992). The impact of an MMSS on the user does not necessarily coincide with its impact on the organization. Goal congruence between the two does not always exist. Individual employees may use computer systems just for fun (Davis, Bagozzi, and Warshaw 1989), for providing (erroneous) information as a means of justifying poor decisions (Ives, Olson, and Baroudi 1983), to increase the power of oneself or of the department (Markus 1983), or just to impress others. In such cases computer systems may serve the personal goals of employees, which can contradict or undermine the goals of the organization.

We have now discussed the different elements of the success framework of Figure 9.1. The framework can be used to explain the success (or lack thereof) of marketing management support systems by highlighting which success factors are favorable or unfavorable in a particular implementation of an MMSS. The framework also helps to formulate the most important research questions regarding MMSS. Such questions should be positioned in the context of the future conditions under which marketing management support systems will be operating. This is the subject of the next and final chapter of this book.

Key Points

- *The success of marketing management support systems is determined by five main factors: the demand for decision support, the supply of decision support, the match between demand and supply, the design characteristics, and the characteristics of the implementation process.*

- *The most important design variables for MMSS are accessibility, system integration, adaptability, presentation of output and user interface, system quality, and information quality.*

- *The most important characteristics of the implementation process are user involvement, top management support, communication about the MMSS, marketing orientation, presence of an MMSS champion, attitude of the IS department, whether the MMSS was developed in-company or purchased, and training of the users.*

- *We can distinguish four main types of success measures for MMSS: technical validity, adoption and use, user impact variables, and organizational impact variables. Within each of these categories several different measures are available.*

- *The success framework developed in this chapter can be used to explain the success (and failure) of MMSS in particular company environments and to formulate the most important research questions about MMSS.*

Chapter 10

The Future of Marketing Management Support Systems

Learning Objectives

- *To learn about recent developments in the marketing decision-making environment and how these changes affect the need for marketing management support systems.*

- *To learn about developments on the supply side and how these will enhance opportunities to develop more powerful marketing management support systems.*

- *To become aware of the most important research issues with respect to marketing management support systems.*

- *To develop a vision of the future role of marketing science with respect to marketing management support systems.*

10.1   Introduction

So far in this book we have described the state of the art of marketing management decision making, marketing management support systems, and their constituent components. We have argued that the demand side, that is, the decision situation, determines the requirements for marketing management support, and we have discussed the various types of data-driven and knowledge-driven MMSS that represent the current supply of decision aids. The fields of marketing management and marketing management support systems are not static, however. Both the decision situation of the marketer and the marketing environment itself are rapidly changing. One can be sure that ten years from now the state of the art of marketing science will be very different from what it is today. This implies that the requirements for MMSS will also change. At the same time, developments on the supply side are constantly offering new possibilities for MMSS. In this final chapter we reflect on these developments and their implications for marketing management support systems in the future. We also develop an agenda for further research into MMSS.

10.2   Developments on the Demand Side

The main demand-side factors of marketing management support are the decision problem characteristics, decision environment characteristics, and decision maker characteristics (Figure 9.1). We expect that the most pronounced changes will occur in the decision problem and the decision environment. Without a doubt, the most prevalent change with respect to the decision problem is the ever increasing amount of data that is available for solving marketing problems. The role that marketing management support can play in extracting the maximum of actionable knowledge from this data is the first issue we will address.

10.2.1   Ever Increasing Amounts of Marketing Data

The enormous quantities of data offer opportunities for a systematic analysis and for the support of marketing policies. Prior to the availability of all of this data, marketing was usually considered an art where the creativity of the marketer was an especially important asset (Ing and Mitchell 1994). Although creativity remains a key asset of marketers, decision makers now can and should benefit from the availability of more and better data by incorporating the information derived from this data into their decision-making processes (Blattberg and Hoch 1990).

In processing information, however, decision makers show cognitive limitations. These limitations may lead to biased decision-making processes in decision environments that have become complex because of data and information abundance. Biased decision-making processes will lead to nonoptimal decisions, and marketers will thus not fully benefit from the opportunities that the marketing information revolution offers. Marketing management support systems should help to circumvent these biases in human decision making.

Marketing management support systems can be effective both by reinforcing the strengths of marketers (e.g., creativity, domain knowledge, flexibility, and so on) and by compensating for their weaknesses. We distinguish two mechanisms by which MMSS can be effective: (1) by means of organizing data, which reduces the amount of perceived complexity, and by transforming marketing data into marketing information, insights, and knowledge, and (2) by means of reducing the biasing effects of a decision environment that has become (too) complex because of data abundance. The different types of MMSS that we described in Chapters 4, 5, and 6 each have specific characteristics that make them useful for performing one of the functions through which MMSS can be effective.

Organizing Data and Generating Insights and Knowledge

Blattberg, Glazer, and Little (1994) introduced the concept of the *information value chain*. This chain contains five successive stages (or elements): (1) data collection and transmission, (2) data management, (3) data interpretation, (4) models, and (5) decision support systems. Each of these five elements adds value to the collected data, leading to a higher information value and more potential market insight. After the data has become available and is organized in a marketing information system, systems like a (diagnosing) marketing knowledge-based system and a marketing expert system are useful for data interpretation and thus the conversion of marketing data into actionable knowledge. Conditions that call for action will be identified, relationships between variables can be investigated, and diagnoses will be performed. Next, marketing decision support systems can capture relationships between marketing variables. Models can be used to summarize the information from massive databases and can identify empirical regularities not observable to the human eye (Blattberg and Hoch 1990; Hoch 1994). Marketing neural networks can also be helpful for this purpose. Finally, the results of data interpretation and modeling can be the input for marketing decision support systems and (predictive) marketing knowledge-based systems, which can subsequently be used for generating alternative courses of marketing action and selecting the proper choice from among these alternatives.

Removing Bias from Decision-Making Processes

While the sheer volume of available data has grown exponentially, the human brain has not advanced in any comparable way to process and interpret this data (Simon 1997). The marketing manager of today, living in the time of the "marketing data revolution," is equipped with the same cognitive abilities as his or her colleagues from the "prehistoric" marketing era before the computer. Marketing management support systems should come to the rescue. An important function of MMSS is their ability to remove bias from decision-making processes. Several studies have demonstrated these effects. Hoch and Schkade (1996) found that in forecasting tasks decision makers often use their experience from earlier situations. This strategy performs reasonably well in highly predictable environments but shows biases when the environment is less predictable. Their experiment (which we discussed in the previous chapter) showed that a marketing decision support system in the form of a simple linear model can prevent or overcome these biases. In a laboratory experiment using the MARKSTRAT simulation, Van Bruggen, Smidts, and Wierenga (1998) found that in a complex decision environment the use of an MDSS makes decision makers less susceptible to applying the anchoring and adjustment heuristic for making marketing-mix decisions.

Unlike human experts, models are strong in that they are not subject to decision biases of perception and evaluation; experts often suffer from overconfidence and may be influenced by politics, whereas models take base rates into account and are immune to social pressures for consensus; experts can get tired, bored, and emotional, whereas models do not; and experts do not consistently integrate evidence from one occasion to another, whereas models weight this evidence optimally (Blattberg and Hoch 1990; Hoch 1994). The strengths of models also extend to the use of marketing expert systems, marketing knowledge-based systems, marketing neural networks, and marketing decision support systems. All of these systems are computer-based, derive information from data, and develop suggestions for decisions based on a *systematic analysis* of data. Such a systematic analysis will not be affected by decision biases, overconfidence, fatigue, or inconsistencies.

The ever growing quantity of available data is a fact of life. In the future competitive advantage will derive not so much from having lots of data, but from having the right marketing management support systems in place to get the most out of it.

10.2.2   Changes in the Marketing Decision Environment

There will be continuing demand for MMSS in the "traditional" areas, such as FMCG, but the demand will also grow in other domains, due to the emphasis on efficient supply chains, the advances in electronic commerce and organizational changes of companies.

Continuing Need for Marketing Support in Mass-Marketing Environments

Mass marketing has traditionally been the dominant approach in most consumer-goods industries, including fast-moving consumer goods and consumer electronics. Over the years the fast-moving consumer goods sector has been the most sophisticated marketing domain in terms of measurement, analysis, knowledge about customer and competitor behavior, and the way this knowledge is used in developing and implementing marketing strategies. Based on information collected through marketing research, marketers in various industries have been developing sophisticated marketing policies, very precisely targeted at specific markets or segments. Especially through further advances in the exploitation of scanner data (collection, storage, and transmission), the FMCG industry will continue to be at the forefront of the use of marketing management support systems.

Global competition and the increasing power of resellers makes it mandatory for manufacturers, especially those in FMCG industries, to keep investing in marketing management information systems. Increased reseller power—for example, of internationally expanding and concentrating supermarket chains—can negatively affect the results of manufacturers (e.g., by lowering margins). By using marketing management support systems, manufacturers will be able to generate valuable information and knowledge about the market, which will improve their position in terms of information and/or expert power relative to that of resellers. Thus the use of MMSS can create countervailing power. Retailers themselves are also starting to use the data collected in their stores for the support of marketing decisions. So far, they have used scanning data predominantly to support logistical operations. Retailers should also strive to develop an understanding of the way they can use MMSS to support their marketing activities. Since manufacturers have more experience and expertise in this field than retailers do, some form of cooperation might be beneficial for both parties.

In short, we can expect mass-marketed consumer-goods industries to remain a major target for the further development and implementation of marketing management support systems.

Increasing Cooperation Within Supply Chains

In several industries we see that organizations operating in different stages of the supply chain have started to cooperate and sometimes have developed partnerships. The efficient management of logistical operations has been a major driver of this development. There are several noteworthy examples of the successful sharing of *logistical information* in marketing channels. One of the best known is between Wal-Mart and Procter & Gamble (Buzzell and Ortmeyer 1994). By extensively sharing logistical information (using electronic data interchange), the two companies were able to improve the efficiency of their product flow. P&G's on-time deliveries to Wal-Mart improved significantly, while inventory turnover also increased dramatically. The success of logistical information sharing is also reflected in the emergence of Efficient Consumer Response (ECR) as an industry-wide initiative in the grocery industry. To guarantee a smooth, continuous product flow matched to consumption, the grocery industry requires a timely and accurate information flow. Besides logistical information, this information flow should also contain *marketing information.* Logistical information (e.g., ordering information) facilitates supply-chain management and can be characterized as cost-saving operational information that improves the efficiency and profitability of the relationship in which the information is exchanged. Marketing information (e.g., information about assortment management or new product development) is focused on enhancing revenues and has a more strategic character. Although the exchange of marketing information can be seen as a logical extension of supplier-reseller partnerships, which were originally designed to improve the efficiency of order-handling and shipping processes, so far organizations have been reluctant to share marketing information. Results obtained when manufacturers and supermarket chains cooperate suggest that both sides could increase sales results by working together to customize offerings at different stores and for different customers (Kumar 1996). This type of cooperation will benefit from the application of marketing management support systems that will not only increase the value of the information that is exchanged but will also facilitate the exchange process as such. It is important to realize that new technologies can help to respond to this demand for closer cooperation. At the same time, however, we also see that computer networks like the Internet and the recent proliferation of on-line auctions have given both companies and consumers more options for which companies to do business with.

Growing Importance of Electronic Marketing and Customization

Given the nature of mass-marketed products such as consumer food products (i.e., low price, small orders, voluminous choices, and so on) it is questionable (Bucklin 1966) whether a substantial share of the purchase transactions for these products will soon be processed through direct or on-line marketing (electronic commerce). Mass marketing is expected to remain an important branch of marketing in the future. However, in other markets the role of electronic commerce and customization will quickly gain importance (e.g., business-to-business marketing, services, and consumer durables). In the computer industry Dell has been very successful in introducing a strategy of customization. Customers can design a computer from available components so that it fits exactly with their demands and order it directly from Dell. The success of this strategy has completely changed the way computers are distributed.

Direct electronic links between suppliers and customers make it possible to engage in interactive or one-to-one marketing. In companies that apply such an approach, the customer database becomes the "engine" of marketing activities and all other processes derive from that. The Internet will increasingly be used to communicate with customers, to effectuate transactions, and, for specific products such as software and other information products (e.g., entertainment, news, consulting, and so on) even to deliver the products to the customers. Since each contact with a customer can be registered electronically, increasing use of the Internet will generate enormous amounts of data. This new data will have an acceleration effect on the use of more advanced approaches in areas such as business-to-business and services, which until recently trailed behind FMCG in terms of the analytical level of their marketing. Customization will generate a specific demand for marketing support. Transaction data will have to be analyzed to measure the effectiveness of specific marketing actions, and algorithms will be needed to develop optimal marketing propositions for individual customers. Organizations such as the virtual bookstore Amazon (www. amazon.com) and virtual CD shop CDNow (www.cdnow.com) are among the first to apply such approaches. Based on their analysis of individual customer's interests and buying histories, these companies develop personal recommendations for individual customers. CDNow even creates a personalized shopping outlet and personalized products for its visitors. In these types of channels, the supplier and the customer are building intimate relationships in which they cooperate in the development of products and services that fit customer's particular needs.

We can expect that the rapidly growing number of companies and households that have access to the Internet will increase the importance of customization strategies. To be able to respond quickly, accurately, and effectively to customers' behavior, sophisticated marketing management support systems are necessary. These systems will be able to process large quantities of data and respond with effective marketing programs, which can target at the level of individual customers.

New Institutions in the Marketing Channel

The advance of the Internet does not only change the relationship between suppliers and customers; it also changes the roles of traditional channel intermediaries. Since it will become more easy to establish direct contact between suppliers and customers, "traditional" resellers have to figure out a way to survive in the channel. To be able to do so, resellers must find a way to deliver added value—for example, by performing logistical operations or after-sales services in a superior way.

In contrast to the changing and sometimes reduced role of resellers, we also note the emergence of new organizations in industries such as the financial industry and the travel industry. These new organizations have specialized in collecting, analyzing, and using information and have therefore been called *infomediaries*. The core business of infomediaries is to match the needs and wants of customers with the products and services of suppliers. They can do this either in a specific industry (e.g., Travelocity in the travel industry) or across several industries (e.g., a portal like Yahoo). Since the analysis and manipulation of information is the primary activity of infomediaries, marketing management support systems will be indispensable tools for these types of organizations. The increasing prominence of infomediaries will thus also increase the demand for MMSS.

Changing Organizational Environments

Not only is the larger environment in which organizations operate changing, but the day-to-day organizational environment of the marketing decision maker is also changing. Organizations have flattened (Lilien and Rangaswamy 1998), and marketing staff support analysts have gone (Peacock 1998). As a consequence marketers have to deal with data and information themselves. Marketing management support systems will help them to do that. In another development, intra-organizational cooperation— that is, cooperation between the departments within a company—is increasing. Cooperation between R&D and marketing improves the chances of successful new product development (Leenders 1998; Van den Bulte and Moenaert 1998). Cooperation between marketing and production will increase the assurance of supply (Daerden, Lilien, and Yoon 1999). Similarly, the cooperation between marketing and other departments (e.g., finance) will be beneficial. Organization-wide information systems will facilitate interdepartmental cooperation, and marketing management support systems can be an important component of these systems.

10.3   Developments on the Supply Side

In addition to demand-side developments we also observe developments on the supply side of marketing management support systems that will enhance their sophistication and importance. Developments are occurring in all four of the comonents of marketing management support systems.

10.3.1   Information Technology

With respect to the hardware component of information technology, there is no reason to doubt that the exponential growth in storage capacity and computer speed (which we discussed in Chapter 3) will continue in the near future. Because of advances in telecommunication (e.g., wireless communi- cation), computer networks (i.e., the Internet, intranets, and extranets) will become increasingly powerful. This will make it possible to transfer sales data from different subsidiaries to central data warehouses in almost real time. Bringing together detailed data from multiple sources enhances the opportunities for valuable information. Multimedia possibilities will also grow and improve. In the near future marketing management support systems will make it possible, for example, for a marketer pondering the causes of a sudden drop in sales in a particular region to view the TV commercial(s) of local competitors on-line while studying sales data. The work on human-computer interfaces will make computers user-friendlier and in this way remove one of the barriers to the use of MMSS. Advances in the development of speech recognition software will make it possible for marketers to communicate with their MMSS as they do with colleagues and assistants nowadays. The increasing diffusion of handheld computers and personal digital assistants (PDAs) will also make support systems more accessible. Using these devices together with wireless communication technology, marketers can store and retrieve information from almost every location.

Software designers will increasingly use the object-orientation paradigm. As we saw in Chapter 3, this will produce reusable pieces of software—for example, software for the analysis of market share dynamics or the design of sales promotions—which will enhance the quick development and diffusion of marketing management support system tools. The work in AI will continue to produce knowledge-processing methods that can be used for MMSS. The ongoing work on expert systems, case-based reasoning systems, neural networks, genetic algorithms, and knowledge discovery methods is relevant in this regard. The same comment applies to the ongoing work on techniques such as qualitative reasoning and machine learning.

Also important are the advances in the development of group support systems (Dennis 1996). Decisions are often made by *groups* of decision makers rather than by individuals. These groups can consist of multiple marketers but also of decision makers from different departments and sometimes even from multiple organizations. Group support software enhances information sharing, stimulates discussions, and improves the quality of group decisions.

An emerging AI technology that has great promise for marketing management support systems in the near future is *autonomous agent* technology, also referred to as *intelligent agent* technology. An agent is a computer software system whose main characteristics are situatedness, autonomy, adaptivity, and sociability (Sycara 1998). The agent receives some form of input from its environment (situatedness), can act without direct intervention by humans (autonomy), can learn from its own experience (adaptivity), and is capable of interacting with other agents or humans (sociability). These autonomous agents can be active on the World Wide Web as so-called *softbots* (Etzioni 1997). In marketing these softbots are encountered as agents who look for special offers on the Web on behalf of consumers. An example is Andersen Consulting's BargainFinder, which searches for interesting audio CD offers on the Web, within the specifications given by its principal (the consumer). Another interesting example is the interactive buyers guide CompareNet (http://compare.net), which performs a search function in multiple product categories. Autonomous agents can also play a role in marketing management support systems. Agents may, for example, be authorized to make tailor-made offers to specific customers, based on their characteristics and buying history (situatedness). Such agents may learn from the customers' reactions to the offers and adapt their behavior accordingly. A marketer might also authorize an autonomous agent to develop, for example, sales promotions based on successful sales promotions in similar situations in the past (using the principles of case-based reasoning), by executing the appropriate adaptations.

10.3.2   Analytical Capabilities

Marketing management support systems have benefited tremendously from the developments in such fields as econometrics, statistics, and operations research, and will continue to do so. The more data we have in marketing, the more we need sophisticated techniques, for example, to estimate the parameters of complex brand choice or market share models or to carry out advanced clustering procedures. In addition, progress is being made in the simultaneous optimization of marketing, production, and logistics over the several components of a marketing channel. These analytical capabilities will allow marketers to extract more information and knowledge out of the enormous quantities of marketing data that have become available.

10.3.3   Marketing Data

The first wave of the "marketing information revolution," which resulted from the development of scanner technology, is likely to be followed by a second wave. This second wave will result from the growth of database marketing and electronic commerce. Not only will there be abundant data on customer transactions, but data about customers' movements on the Web (their behavior while at specific sites, their information-search behavior, and so on) will also be collected in abundance. The collection of this so-called *clickstream data* will lead to enormous databases. Furthermore, the Internet can also be used as a source for obtaining all kinds of secondary information, for example, on the development of new products and services by competitors (Graef 1997). Direct contact with customers has also created opportunities to obtain more qualitative responses from them about their experiences with products, their ideas about adapting existing products and services, and also their ideas for new products and services. Finally, databases with secondary data, made available by syndicated services such as A.C. Nielsen, IRI, GfK, Reuters, Dunn & Bradstreet, and others, will increasingly be available on-line.

10.3.4   Marketing Knowledge

Marketing knowledge in the sense of generalizable insights into marketing phenomena will continue to grow. However, as we argued in Chapter 3, the number of hard relationships in marketing science is still modest. We expect that the growth of insights at this stage will be roughly linearly related to the number of active marketing scientists, which will probably not increase in any spectacular way. This observation implies that, in the foreseeable future, for many relationships between marketing variables there will continue to be no hard knowledge that can be used as a basis for decisions. In this respect a marketing decision maker will remain in a less desirable position than an engineer, who can build on hard relationships determined in the physical sciences. By using advanced econometric techniques, a marketer will sometimes be able to determine "locally hard relationships"—like, for example, the price elasticity for a particular brand. Such local marketing knowledge can then be used as a basis for decisions. Alternatively, the marketer can use (subjective) mental models and expertise to support marketing decisions. In Chapters 5 and 6 we described how the field of AI has developed tools for representing knowledge in systems and how these tools can be used for reasoning and decision making in marketing.

10.4   Implications for Marketing Management Support Systems

From the developments we have observed on both the demand and the supply sides of marketing management support systems, we can derive a number of conclusions with respect to the future of these systems.

First, the developments on the demand side of marketing management support systems indicate a further *growing need* for such systems. The explosive growth of data and information will motivate a strong demand for systems that can help marketing managers transform this information into actionable marketing decisions. As we have seen, this demand will come not only from those who are traditionally interested in MMSS, that is, manufacturers of FMCG. But because of the rapid growth in database marketing and electronic commerce, companies in a much larger set of industries will develop a need for marketing management support systems, most notably in the business-to-business sector and in service industries. Besides increased demand we also expect increased impact from MMSS, because several of the developments on the supply side match very well with those on the demand side. The availability of sophisticated data analysis techniques will make mass-marketing activities in data-rich environments more effective. The increased availability of user-friendlier software will facilitate the use of MMSS by marketers themselves rather than by support staff. The availability of autonomous agents as part of MMSS will be especially effective in environments where customized marketing activities are being applied. Furthermore, the emergence of group support software and organization-wide systems will facilitate the coordination of activities across departments, while the availability of supply-chain management procedures will facilitate interorganizational coordination.

Second, there will be a strong *differentiation* in the types of marketing management support systems needed by different companies and within companies in different decision situations. It makes a big difference whether a company is active in a more or less stable FMCG market or in a very turbulent market in the IT or telecommunications industry. As we have seen earlier, stable markets can benefit from modeling and optimization, whereas more turbulent markets need MMSS that support reasoning, analogizing, and creating. Also, customization and interactive marketing pose their own requirements for MMSS. Following classical marketing principles, we might divide the market for MMSS into *segments* with relatively homogeneous needs for such systems within each segment. A more tailor-made approach to the design of marketing management support systems will definitely foster their success.

Third, the tendency toward *integrated systems* will continue. We distinguish two types of integration here. The first is the integration of different data-processing and knowledge-processing technologies in one and the same system. Optimization models and expert systems used to be very different from each other as technologies but are now coming together in the same marketing management support system. A marketing decision maker is not interested in technologies as such, but in what systems offer in terms of functionality. (The BRANDFRAME system, which we described in Chapter 8, is an example of a system that integrates a large number of different data and knowledge technologies.) The second type of integration is integration over functional areas of management. We have seen already that companies increasingly strive for intra-organizational cooperation and approach their activities from a *business process* point of view. Such a view emphasizes the integration of such different areas as marketing, production, logistics, finance, and so on. This process orientation is stimulated when the customer database is taken as the starting point for all the sales and consecutive transactions and delivery activities of a company. In such a situation there is a need for integrated information systems, systems that cover all the relevant functional areas. These integrated systems are often referred to as *enterprise resource planning* (or ERP) systems. In recent years organizations like SAP, Baan, PeopleSoft, and Oracle have implemented thousands of these systems. Increasingly, these ERP systems also contain so-called front-office components, which support the commercial activities of companies. The emergence of ERP systems implies that marketing management support systems should be accessible and useful to a wider set of decision makers, including nonmarketing ones. Similarly, MMSS should be able to tap information from the systems of other departments.

Fourth, there is still a *significant gap* between the potential benefits of marketing management support systems and what is actually realized in companies. The data- and knowledge-processing methods currently available make much more possible than what is realized today. Although the expenditures on MMSS are definitely increasing, companies do not seem to be keen enough on creating a *competitive edge* with marketing intelligence. It seems as if many companies consider marketing management support systems as a qualifier, and are satisfied when they have the same information as their competitors, rather than wanting to "out-informate" them. For example, in the Netherlands practically all companies in fast-moving consumer goods subscribe to one of the retailing panels (A.C. Nielsen or GfK/IRI) and use their standard marketing report systems. However, very few companies go beyond that. One of the reasons might be that higher management finds it notoriously difficult to judge whether or not IT expenses are justified. This is especially the case if it is not possible to measure the effects of these systems directly, as is typical in marketing. This limitation is important since top management is a critical factor for the success of MMSS. It is often claimed that the actual benefits of IT spending are disappointing at best and that IT spending has failed to yield significant productivity gains. The evidence is fragmented and somewhat mitigated (Pinsonneault and Rivard 1998). Marketing decision makers themselves have also had difficulties determining the value of MMSS. There have been several studies in which marketing management support systems led to objectively better marketing decisions, but where this was not reflected in the subjective perceptions of managers (McIntyre 1982; Van Bruggen, Smidts, and Wierenga 1998). This negative perception is an important impediment for progress in the development and use of marketing management support systems. Marketers should thus realize that using the same tool that one's competitors use does not lead to a competitive advantage. However, finding a new, more advanced tool that is *not* used by the competition might create an advantage comparable to the advantage that is gained by introducing a new product to the market or developing an advertising campaign that is very different from those of competitors. Clearly, more research is needed to bridge the gap between the potential and the actually realized benefits of marketing management support systems.

10.5   Research Issues for Marketing Management Support Systems

Marketing decision situations have many unique characteristics associated with the marketing problems being studied, the decision makers interacting with the marketing management support systems, and the environments in which decisions are made. Having reviewed the changes we expect with respect to the development, use, and impact of marketing management support systems, we will now discuss the most relevant and interesting issues for future research.[1]

10.5.1   Need for Studies in Real-World Company Environments

As we described before, marketers often have difficulty judging the value of a marketing management support system. To stimulate the implementation and use of these systems, it will be important to present evidence to marketers that these systems work. Laboratory studies have generated important knowledge about the success of MMSS and the variables that affect that success. However, the external validity of these laboratory experiments remains an issue and may limit the credibility of the reported effects in the eyes of marketers. The results of real-life studies will have more credibility than the results of laboratory studies. We noted earlier that the number of studies on the effectiveness of MMSS that have used real-life marketing management situations is scarce. We would like to see more such studies that use controlled experimentation within real-world field settings.

10.5.2   Need for More Insight into Managerial Decision Processes

Although the decision maker and his or her decision process constitute the core element of the demand side of marketing management support systems, our knowledge of this element is still fairly limited. The marketing management literature abounds in recommendations about how marketing managers *should* make decisions. However, it is surprising that in a field that knows so much about consumer decision making, we know so little about how marketing managers actually make decisions and how MMSS affect their decision-making processes. In this book we have presented a conceptualization of the way marketers solve problems. It will be interesting

---

[1]   Several of these issues were discussed in Wierenga, Van Bruggen, and Staelin (1999).

and necessary to test the validity of this conceptualization by investigating the decision processes of real-world marketers. We acknowledge that it is harder to "study" managers than consumers, but the payoffs from such studies could be great. Often business students are used as proxies. However, now that many academics are involved in executive instruction, it should be possible to use the participants in such courses, real-life marketing decision makers, as research subjects.

The list of possible topics to explore in studying the managerial decision-making process is extensive. Besides marketing problem-solving modes, several other relevant topics exist. As reported earlier, much of the work to date has centered on *cognitive style*. Another relevant variable is *experience* (i.e., professional experience as a marketing decision maker). Recently, Spence and Brucks (1997) found that novices especially benefited from using a decision aid. In fact, these researchers questioned the usefulness of marketing management support systems for experts. Experience has also been found to influence the use of information by marketing managers (Perkins and Rao 1990).

Another recent line of research on managerial decision making is the work of Boulding, Staelin, and their coauthors. These researchers initially studied managers involved in the launch of a new product offering and the subsequent decision of whether or not to terminate the launch. They noted that many managers tended to stick with a losing course of action (Boulding, Morgan, Staelin 1997). They then proposed and tested the veracity of a number of decision aids that were designed to help managers overcome this bias (often referred to as an *escalation* bias). In a follow-up study, Boulding, Biyalogorsky, and Staelin (1998) found that managers exhibit a tendency to overweight their prior beliefs when they obtain and evaluate new information. Thus, if they start out with a positive belief about a project, they tend to see new (negative) information more positively than a neutral observer would. Moreover, they weight their prior opinions more than predicted by a normative Bayesian updating model. All this leads to an overly optimistic viewpoint and thus the tendency not to disengage from a losing course of action. Studies of this type provide the designers of MMSS with deeper insights into how managers decide how to decide. Such knowledge should help construct new, more effective decision aids. Furthermore, it should also improve implementation procedures.

10.5.3   The Role of Time Pressure

Time windows for marketing decisions tend to be very small, and time constraints often preclude the execution of elaborate solution procedures. Time pressure has been recognized as an important variable in information systems design, but empirical studies on this variable have been sparse

(Hwang 1994). Time pressure causes selective and reduced information search and superficial processing (Hogarth and Makridakis 1991). Furthermore, time pressure leads to a tendency toward "locking in on a strategy" (Edland and Svenson 1993) and to simplifying strategies and conservative behavior (Hwang 1994). Van Bruggen et al. (1998) reported that decision makers benefited most from a marketing management support system when they were under little time pressure. On the one hand, an MMSS can help decision makers to refrain from suboptimal behavior; on the other hand, using an MMSS takes time. Further research should provide better insight into the trade-off between these two factors. Furthermore, research should try to find a way of making marketing management support systems that are clearly effective in terms of improving the quality of decisions also efficient. This means that these systems help marketers not only in responding effectively but also in responding in time.

10.5.4   From Relatively Structured to More Complex Problems

There is a continuum of marketing problems for which marketing management support systems can be developed, ranging from very structured problems in scientifically well-charted areas with substantial data, to ill-structured problems in scarcely explored areas about which little is known. Many of the MMSS developed to date address relatively structured problems with easily obtained data, such as sales planning, media planning, and shelf-space allocation. However, it is encouraging to see that problems in other industries are also being addressed. For example, systems are being developed for decision makers in the movie industry, an industry with a very complex decision-making environment and one in which managers tend to be very skeptical about analytical approaches (Swami, Eliashberg, and Weinberg 1999). Other areas for which marketing management support systems are being developed are the auto supply industry (Montoya-Weiss and Calantone 1999), the digital TV industry (Gupta, Jain, and Sawhney 1999), and the advertising industry (Goldenberg, Mazursky, and Solomon 1999). All these settings are very different from the well-known packaged-goods situation: problems are more complex and relatively ill structured. Moreover, managers in these industries tend to make their decisions using a mix of traditional decision rules or heuristics, intuition, experience, and hope. As we have argued before, in such a situation marketing management support systems can be especially effective.

10.5.5 From Data-Driven to Knowledge-Based Marketing Management Support Systems

Most marketing management support systems developed to date have been of the mathematical-modeling and optimization type, with a strong *data-driven* orientation. How can efforts be directed toward decision support for more complex or even ill-structured problems? One possibility is to cut the larger, complex problem into smaller "pieces," which can then be structured and made amenable to quantitative analysis. After all, many problems of the world that are presented as ill-structured problems become well-structured in the hands of the problem solver (Simon 1973). In this approach, which can be characterized as a "divide-and-conquer" approach, smaller problems are isolated out of larger ones and solved using an optimizing type of MMSS. Another way of addressing complex problems is by developing different types of decision aids. An important characteristic of ill-structured problems is that they are formulated in qualitative rather than quantitative terms. In such a situation *knowledge-driven* marketing management support systems can be used. These systems are based on knowledge representation and knowledge-processing methods developed in the fields of artificial intelligence and cognitive science. As we have seen in Chapters 5 and 6, a rich supply of expert systems, case-based reasoning systems, neural networks, and creativity support systems is emerging, and these systems can be applied in the marketing domain. For decisions in areas such as innovation, communication, and marketing strategy, case-based reasoning systems (making use of analogies) and creativity support systems can be very useful. Such MMSS typically do not provide recommendations for the "best decision." Instead, these knowledge-driven aids weed out poor decisions, make suggestions, and stimulate the thinking processes of the decision maker.

The effects of knowledge-based marketing management support systems have not yet been systematically studied. Since the kind of decision processes that are supported by these systems (e.g., being creative, searching for analogous situations) appear quite frequently in the daily activities of marketers, more insight is needed into the contributions of these systems and the conditions in which these contributions can occur.

10.5.6 The Optimal Combination of Managerial Judgment and Marketing Management Support Systems

Marketing decisions are rarely left completely to marketing management support systems. Although different points of view have been expressed on this issue (Bucklin, Lehman, and Little 1998), we do not think that a substantive part of marketing decisions can be automated. Marketing problems are difficult, often ill-structured, and the state of (generalized) marketing knowledge is inadequate for making decisions without the judgment of the human decision maker. It is not just coincidence that highly educated and skilled personnel tend to be recruited for marketing management jobs, even for uncomplicated products such as margarine or beer. Unlike the relatively more structured jobs in accounting or control, marketing tasks cannot easily be taken over by a computer. Instead of replacing the marketing manager, the role of a marketing management support system should be that of the ideal sparring partner, which enhances the manager's effectiveness as a decision maker. What is (or can be) especially successful is the *combination of* manager and system (Blattberg and Hoch 1990). In this combination managers need to be aware of the risk of allowing the MMSS to guide their activities, instead of the demands of the decision situation at hand (Glazer, Steckel, and Winer 1992; Pinsonneault and Rivard 1998). Marketing management support systems should not replace managerial cognition but rather extend the human cognitive capacity. More insight is needed into how to accomplish a match that gets the most out of the combination of marketing management support systems and managerial judgment.

As the designers of marketing management support systems become more involved in complex, unstructured problems, they will need more information on how managers now go about making these complex strategic decisions. The already discussed work of Boulding, Staelin, and their coauthors is one such effort. Other examples are the work of Moore (1992), Moore and Urbany (1994), and Glazer, Steckel, and Winer (1992). We want to encourage others to study the managerial decision-making process and to provide new insights into how to blend managerial knowledge with decision aid output to arrive at better decisions.

The requirement of a good fit between the decision maker and the marketing management support system raises the question of *reinforcement* versus *compensation*. Should the decision maker be provided with a system that reinforces his or her strengths, or should the system compensate for the decision maker's weaknesses? In the former case, analytically oriented decision makers would be provided with sophisticated marketing models. The latter strategy, however, would suggest providing less analytical (i.e., more heuristically oriented) decision makers with marketing models. Although this latter group probably has more to gain from using such a system, getting such people to work with systems that do not fit with their cognitive style requires more effort and may not even be feasible. A trade-off needs to be made, and the question as to whether it is more effective to give a marketing management support system a reinforcing or a compensatory role needs attention in future research.

10.5.7 From Technical Validation to Organizational Validation

As we discussed in Chapter 9, there are several potential measures of success for marketing management support systems. Technical validity is an a priori condition for the positive impact of marketing management support systems on company results. However, technical validity is still far removed from the ultimate measure of success, that is, a positive impact on company results. We already discussed the need to move MMSS from the academic arena into the corporate world. Only then will it be possible to determine the impact on organizational performance. Also, based on prior results (Van Bruggen et al. 1996; McIntyre 1982; Chervany and Dickson 1974; Schewe 1976) that show a weak correlation between self-assessment measures (e.g., satisfaction, perceived accuracy, etc.) and objective measures of performance, we suggest moving away from self-assessment measures as proxies for better performance. The lack of a relationship between objective and subjective variables also leads us to believe that this discrepancy may be a barrier to the increased adoption and use of MMSS since decision makers do not seem to be able to independently judge the (positive) impact of an MMSS on company performance. This lack of a relationship between objective and subjective variables also highlights the need to establish some baseline of performance that would have occurred if the MMSS had not been implemented. It might be interesting if the company were to use an independent third party to formulate and determine a metric for the performance of an MMSS prior to its implementation. Suppliers of ready-to-use marketing management support systems could then provide performance measures relative to these predetermined standards.

10.5.8 Dynamics

When considering the match between the demand and the supply sides of marketing management support, one should be aware of the dynamics of the situation. The availability and use of marketing management support systems may very well change the demand side of support. For example, a particular decision aid may increase the knowledge about a problem and make the problem situation more structured. This changes the characteristics of the decision situation and may make it possible to apply optimization where it was not possible to do so before. It has been documented that the availability and use of decision aids affects the way(s) decision makers solve problems (Benbasat and Todd 1996; Pinsonneault and Rivard 1998). Organizations may also learn from the use of marketing management support systems. Changes in the characteristics of the decision situation may lead to a different marketing problem-solving mode, which may, in turn, require a different marketing management support system. These dynamics in the demand for MMSS pose an interesting research topic. Companies may go through successive generations of marketing management support systems, where for each subsequent system the requirements differ from those of its predecessor.

10.6   Marketing Management Support Systems and Marketing Science

Marketing science has contributed a great deal to marketing management support systems. We distinguish three main areas where these contributions have been made.

First, methodological research in marketing has been an important supplier of components of marketing management support systems and an important driver for the growing sophistication of these systems. Over the last thirty years a rich collection of measurement, estimation, modeling, optimization, and simulation techniques have been developed (Lilien, Kotler, and Moorthy 1992; Eliashberg and Lilien 1993). These methodological contributions, which have their disciplinary roots in econometrics, statistics, and operations research, have been of invaluable importance for marketing management support systems.

Second, the extensive research efforts in marketing have resulted in an impressive body of knowledge (i.e., generalized knowledge) of marketing phenomena (see, for example, the 1995 Special Issues of *Marketing Science*), which can be employed in MMSS.

Third, research in marketing science has produced knowledge about the antecedents of the effectiveness of marketing management support systems. With respect to this issue several interesting insights have been obtained already, but this is an area that needs more research.

These three areas of marketing science will (hopefully) continue to produce results that are relevant for marketing management support systems. However, considering the gap between the potential of MMSS and what is actually achieved, the contributions from these three areas are not enough. Marketing management support systems are products or tools for which (just as with other new products) R&D efforts must be undertaken. The research in marketing science typically is the "R part" of this process. New methodologies and new generalized marketing knowledge make or constitute important contributions to the "components" of marketing management support systems. However, components as such do not represent full-fledged systems. These components are of the same order as the insights from operations research, computer science, and artificial intelligence, which are also indispensable ingredients of the R part of MMSS. The problem is that the "D part" in the R&D on marketing management support system seems to be missing. Sometimes management scientists develop a new methodology into an actual MMSS (successful examples are ASSESSOR and SCANPRO), but more often they leave this development to other parties. Sometimes data suppliers, such as A.C. Nielsen, GfK, and IRI carry out these activities, but it is not their core business. Furthermore, consulting and software companies sometimes develop and supply marketing management support systems, but they often seem to lack the expertise to deliver state-of-the-art systems.

What is needed in the field of marketing management support systems is a *design tradition*. In such a tradition the major question would be how to design MMSS for specified purposes. This new field should use the methodologies and insights accumulated in the R part of new marketing management support systems (information technology, analytical capabilities, marketing data, and marketing knowledge) and combine them for the development (the D part of the R&D process) of state-of-the-art MMSS. This design activity perhaps has more similarity with engineering (Lilien and Rangaswamy 1998) than with the traditional theory and testing-oriented approach of marketing science. Fields such as mechanical engineering and construction—and also information systems—have a strong design tradition. In marketing, with its roots in economics and the behavioral sciences, this design tradition has been lacking so far but is necessary for further progress in marketing management support. The principles of designing new objects (artifacts such as buildings, bridges, and tools, but also systems) clearly belong to the academic realm, as the technical universities have demonstrated in their long tradition. Therefore, we make a plea for defining *the design and engineering of marketing management support systems* as a new domain in marketing science. Of course, this field is interdisciplinary in nature, and marketing scientists will therefore have to apply insights from multiple fields. Input is needed from information systems, computer science, and artificial intelligence for the actual development of marketing management support systems. Input from cognitive psychology and organizational science is needed for insights into individual and organizational decision-making processes. A concerted effort in this respect will greatly enhance the successful implementation and use of advanced marketing management support systems in companies. It will also contribute significantly to the reputation of marketing science as a supplier of relevant and implementable knowledge that has a substantial impact on real-life marketing decision making.

The need for marketing management support systems is growing rapidly. Insights regarding which type of decision support to provide in which marketing decision situation are increasingly becoming available. The resources needed for the development of marketing management support systems are there. A rich collection of such systems are available already, and new technologies are continuously being developed. Taken together, all of these considerations make marketing management support systems a booming area of marketing science and a fascinating field to contribute to.

Key Points

- *The need for marketing management support systems is growing quickly. The most important drivers of this growth are the ever increasing volume of available data (in both mass marketing and one-to-one marketing environments), the value that can be realized by transforming this data into knowledge, increasing cooperation within supply channels, the emergence of new institutions, and the restructuring of organizations.*

- *Developments in all four of the components of marketing management support systems (information technology, analytical capabilities, marketing data, and marketing knowledge) enhance the potential impact of these systems.*

- *There are several research issues regarding marketing management support systems that need to be investigated. Studies on MMSS need to be performed in real-world environments, more insight into managerial decision-making processes is needed, systems need to shift their attention from well-defined and highly structured problems to complex and ill-structured ones and adopt a knowledge-based approach instead of the data-based approach they normally tend to take. Furthermore, the interplay between human decision makers and systems needs more attention, as does the (organizational) validation of marketing management support systems.*

- *Marketing science has contributed significantly to the development of marketing management support systems. More research is needed on the factors that determine the effectiveness of MMSS, and the design and engineering of marketing management support systems needs to be recognized as a new domain of marketing science.*

References

Aaker, D.A. 1975. "ADMOD: An Advertising Decision Model." *Journal of Marketing Research,* vol. 12, February, 37–45.

Aamodt, A., and E. Plaza. 1994. "Case-Based Reasoning: Foundational Issues, Methodological Variations, and Systems Approaches." *AICOM,* vol. 7, no. 1, 39–59.

Abraham, M.M., and L.M. Lodish. 1987. "Promoter: An Automated Promotion Evaluation System." *Marketing Science,* vol. 6, spring, 101–123.

Abraham, T., and L.W. Boone. 1994. "Computer-Based Systems and Organizational Decision Making: An Architecture to Support Organizational Innovation." Creativity Research Journal, April/May, 111–123.

Ackoff, R.L. 1967. "Management Misinformation Systems." *Management Science,* vol. 14, December, 147–156.

Ackoff, R.L. 1978. *The Art of Problem Solving.* New York: Wiley.

Ackoff, R.L., and E. Vergara. 1981. "Creativity in Problem Solving and Planning: A Review." *European Journal of Operational Research,* vol. 7, no. 1, 1–13.

Adams, D. A., R.R. Nelson, and P.A. Todd. 1992. "Perceived Usefulness: Ease of Use and Usage of Information Technology. A Replication." *Management Information Systems Quarterly,* vol. 16, no. 2, 227–247.

Adriaans, P., and D. Zantinge. 1996. *Data Mining.* Harlow, U.K.: Addison-Wesley.

Alavi, M., and E.A. Joachimsthaler. 1992. "Revisiting DSS Implementation Research: A Meta-Analysis of the Literature and Suggestions for Researchers." *Management Information Systems Quarterly,* vol. 16, March, 95–113.

Aldag, R.J., and D.J. Power. 1986. "An Empirical Assessment of Computer-Assisted Decision Analysis." *Decision Sciences,* vol. 17, no. 4, 572–588.

Alpar, P. 1991. "Knowledge-Based Modeling of Marketing Managers' Problem-Solving Behavior." *International Journal of Research in Marketing,* vol. 8, no. 1, 5–16.

Alter, A. 1996. *Information Systems: A Management Perspective.* 2d ed. Menlo Park, CA: Benjamin/Cummings.

Althoff, K.D., E. Auriol, R. Barletta, and M. Manago. 1995. *A Review of Industrial Case-Based Reasoning Tools.* Oxford: AI Intelligence.

Amstutz, A.E. 1969. "Market-Oriented Management Systems: The Current Status." *Journal of Marketing Research,* vol. 6, November, 481–496.

Anderson, J.R. 1983. *The Architecture of Cognition.* Cambridge, MA: Harvard University Press.

Andrews, J., and D.C. Smith. 1996. "In Search of the Marketing Imagination: Factors Affecting the Creativity of Marketing Programs for Mature Products." *Journal of Marketing Research,* vol. 33, May, 174–187.

Anthony, R.N. 1965. *Planning and Control Systems: A Framework for Analysis.* Cambridge, MA: Harvard University Graduate School of Business.

Arnold, D. 1992. *The Handbook of Brand Management.* London: The Economist Books, Ltd.

Assmus, G. 1975. "NEWPROD: The Design and Implementation of a New Product Model." *Journal of Marketing,* vol. 39, January, 16–23.

Assmus, G., J.U. Farley, and D.R. Lehman 1984. "How Advertising Affects Sales: Meta-Analysis of Econometric Results." *Journal of Marketing Research,* vol. 21, February, 65–71.

Axelrod, R., ed. 1976. *Structure of Decision: The Cognitive Maps of Political Elites.* Princeton, NJ: Princeton University Press.

Ayel, M., and Laurent, J., eds. 1991. *Validation, Verification and Test of Knowledge-Based Systems.* Chichester, U.K.: Wiley.

Bagozzi, R.P. 1996. *Principles of Marketing Research.* Cambridge, MA: Blackwell Publishers.

Bagozzi, R.P. 1997. *Advanced Methods of Marketing Research.* Cambridge, MA: Blackwell Publishers.

Bailey, D., and D. Thompson. 1990. "How to Develop Neural Network Applications." *AI-Expert,* June, 38–45.

Barabba, V.P., and G. Zaltman. 1991. *Hearing the Voice of the Market: Competitive Advantage Through Creative Use of Market Information.* Boston: Harvard Business School Press.

Bariff, M.L., and E.J. Lusk. 1977. "Cognitive and Personality Tests for the Design of Management Information Systems." *Management Science,* vol. 23, April, 820–829.

Barker, V., and D. O'Connor. 1989. "Expert Systems for Configuration at Digital, XCON and Beyond." *Communications of the ACM,* vol. 32, no. 3, 298–318.

Barki, H., and S.L. Huff. 1990. "Implementing Decision Support Systems: Correlates of User Satisfaction and System Usage." *INFOR* (Canada), vol. 28, no. 2, 89–101.

Bass, F.M. 1993. "The Future of Research in Marketing: Marketing Science." *Journal of Marketing Research,* vol. 30, February, 1–6.

Bass, F.M., R.D. Buzzell, M.R. Greene, et al., eds. 1961. *Mathematical Models and Methods in Marketing.* Homewood, IL: Irwin.

Bass, F.M., and J. Wind. 1995. "Introduction to the Special Issue: Empirical Generalizations in Marketing." *Marketing Science,* vol. 14, no. 3, G1–G5.

Bayer, J., and R. Harter. 1991. "'Miner,' 'Manager' and 'Researcher': Three Modes of Analysis of Scanner Data." *International Journal of Research in Marketing,* vol. 8, no. 1, 17–27.

Bazerman, M. 1998. *Judgment in Managerial Decision Making.* New York: Wiley.

Bellman, R. 1957. *Dynamic Programming.* Princeton, NJ: Princeton University Press.

Benbasat, I., and A.S. Dexter. 1982. "Individual Differences in the Use of Decision Support Aids." *Journal of Accounting Research,* vol. 20, no. 1, 1–11.

Benbasat, I., and A.S. Dexter. 1985. "An Empirical Evaluation of Graphical and Color-Enhanced Information Presentation." *Management Science,* vol. 31, November, 1348–1364.

Benbasat, I., and R. Nault. 1990. "An Evaluation of Empirical Research in Managerial Support Systems." *Decision Support Systems*, vol. 6, 203-226.

Benbasat, I., and P. Todd. 1996. "The Effects of Decision Support and Task Contingencies on Model Formulation: A Cognitive Perspective." *Decision Support Systems*, vol. 17, 241-252.

Berenson, C. 1969. "Marketing Information Systems." *Journal of Marketing,* vol. 33, October, 16-23.

Blattberg, R.C., R. Glazer, and J.D.C. Little, eds. 1994. *The Marketing Information Revolution.* Boston: Harvard Business School Press.

Blattberg, R.C., and J. Golanty. 1978. "Tracker: An Early Test Market Forecasting and Diagnostic Model for New Product Planning." *Journal of Marketing Research,* vol. 15, May, 192–202.

Blattberg, R.C., and S.J. Hoch. 1990. "Database Models and Managerial Intuition: 50% Model and 50% Manager." *Management Science,* vol. 36, 8, 887–899.

Bloom, D., and M.J. Stewart. 1977. "An Integrated Marketing Planning System." *ESOMAR Seminar no. 42*, 168–186.

Bockenholt, I., M. Both, and W. Gaul. 1989. "A Knowledge-Based System for Supporting Data Analysis Problems." *Decision Support Systems,* vol. 5, no. 4, 345-354.

Boden, M.A. 1991. *The Creative Mind: Myths and Mechanisms.* New York: Basic Books/Harper Collins.

Boden, M.A. 1994. "What Is Creativity?" In *Dimensions of Creativity.* Edited by M.A. Boden. Cambridge, MA: Bradford Book/MIT Press, 75–117.

Boulding, W., R. Morgan, and R. Staelin. 1997. "Pulling the Plug to Stop the New Product Drain." *Journal of Marketing Research*, vol. 34, 164-176.

Boulding, W., E. Biayalogorsky, and R. Staelin. 1998. "Stuck in the Past: Managers Persist with New Product Failures." *Working Paper MSI.*

Brehmer, B. 1980. "In One Word: Not From Experience." *Acta Psychologica,* vol. 45, 223–241.

Brien, R.H., and J.E. Stafford. 1968. "Marketing Information Systems: A New Dimension for Marketing Research." *Journal of Marketing*, vol. 32, July.

Bruner, J.S. 1962. "The Conditions of Creativity." In *Contemporary Approaches to Creative Thinking.* Edited by H.E. Gruber, G. Terrell, and M. Wertheimer. New York: Prentice Hall.

Buchanan, B.G., and E.A. Feigenbaum. 1978. "Dendral and Meta-Dendral: Their Application Dimension." *Artificial Intelligence,* vol. 11, 5–24.

Bucklin, L.P. 1966. *A Theory of Distribution Channel Structure.* Berkeley: Institute of Business and Economic Research, University of California.

Bucklin, R.E., D.R. Lehman, and J.D.C. Little. 1998. "From Decision Support to Decision Automation: A 20/20 Vision." *Marketing Letters,* vol. 9, no. 3, 235–246.

Buell, V.P. 1975. "The Changing Role of the Product Manager in Consumer Goods Companies." *Journal of Marketing,* vol. 39, July, 3–11.

Bultez, A., and P. Naert. 1988. "SH.A.R.P.: Shelf Allocation for Retailers' Profit." *Marketing Science,* vol. 7, no. 3, 211–231.

Burke, R.R. 1991. "Reasoning with Empirical Marketing Knowledge." *International Journal of Research in Marketing,* vol. 8, no. 1, 75–90.

Burke, R.R., A. Rangaswamy, J. Wind, and J. Eliashberg. 1990. "A Knowledge-Based System for Advertising Design." *Marketing Science,* vol. 9, no. 3, 212–229.

Buzzell, R.D. 1964. *Mathematical Models and Marketing Management.* Boston: Harvard University, Division of Research.

Buzzell, R.D., and G. Ortmeyer. 1994. *Channel Partnerships: A New Approach to Streamlining Distribution.* Report No. 94-104, Marketing Science Institute, Cambridge MA.

Camerer, C.F., and E.J. Johnson. 1991. "The Process-Performance Paradox in Expert Judgment: How Can Experts Know So Much and Predict So Badly?" In *Toward a General Theory of Expertise: Prospects and Limits.* Edited by K.A. Ericsson and J. Smith. New York: Cambridge University Press, 195–217.

Chakravarti, D., A. Mitchell, and R. Staelin. 1979. "Judgment-Based Marketing Decision Models: An Experimental Investigation of the Decision Calculus Approach." *Management Science,* vol. 25, no. 3, 251–263.

Chervany, N.L., and G.W. Dickson. 1974. "An Experimental Evaluation of Information Overload in a Production Environment." *Management Science,* vol. 20, no. 10, 1335–1344.

Chervany, N.L., G.W. Dickson, and K.A. Kozar. 1972. "An Experimental Gaming Framework for Investigating the Influence of Management Information Systems on Decision Effectiveness." Working paper 71-12, Management Information Systems Research Center, Minneapolis, MN.

Choffray, J.M., and B. Charpin. 1986. "Les Systemes Experts: Outils de Mise en Valeur de la Competence Marketing." Working paper, no. 86003, ESSEC, CERESSEC.

Chung, C.H. 1987. "Modelling Creativity for Management Support via Artificial Intelligence Approaches." In *Expert Systems for Business.* Edited by B.G. Silverman. Reading, MA: Addison-Wesley.

Churchill, G.A. 1999. *Marketing Research, Methodological Foundations.* 7th ed. Fort Worth, TX: Dryden Press.

Cleveland, W.S., and R. McGill. 1987. "Graphical Perception: The Visual Decoding of Quantitative Information on Graphical Displays of Data." *Journal of the Royal Statistical Society A,* vol. 150, no. 3, 192–229.

Cognitive Systems. 1992. *ReMind Developer's Reference Manual.* Boston: Cognitive Systems.

Collins, A.M., and M.R. Quillian. 1969. "Retrieval Time from Semantic Memory." *The Journal of Verbal Learning and Verbal Behavior,* vol. 8, 240–247.

Collopy, F., and J.S. Armstrong. 1992. "Rule-Based Forecasting: Development and Validation of an Expert System Approach Combining Time Series Extrapolations." *Management Science,* vol. 38, no. 10, 1394–1414.

Courtney, J.F., D.B. Paradice, and N. H. Ata Mohammed. 1987. "A Knowledge-Based DSS for Managerial Problem Diagnosis." *Decision Sciences,* vol. 18, no. 3, 373–399.

Cox, D.F., and R.E. Good. 1967. "How to Build a Marketing Information System." *Harvard Business Review,* May/June, vol. 45, no. 3, 145–154.

Craik, K. 1943. *The Nature of Explanation.* Cambridge: Cambridge University Press.

Crawford, C.M. 1997. *New Products Management.* 5th ed. Chicago: Irwin.

Dearden, J.A., G.L. Lilien, and E. Yoon. 1999. "Marketing and Production Capacity Strategy for Non-Differentiated Products: Winning and Losing at the Capacity Cycle Game." *International Journal of Research in Marketing,* vol. 16, no. 1, 57-74.

Daft, R.L., and K.E. Weick. 1984. "Toward a Model of Organizations as Interpretation Systems." *Academy of Management Review,* vol. 9, no. 2, 284–295.

Dalebout, A. 1993. *Management Support for the Product Manager.* Master's thesis. Rotterdam School of Management, Erasmus University Rotterdam.

Davis, F.D. 1989. "Perceived Usefulness, Perceived Ease of Use and User Acceptance of Information Technology." *Management Information Systems Quarterly,* vol. 13, September, 319–340.

Davis, F.D., R.P. Bagozzi, and P.R. Warshaw. 1989. "User Acceptance of Computer Technology: A Comparison of Two Theoretical Models." *Management Science,* vol. 35, no. 8, 982–1003.

Day, G., and P. Nedungadi. 1994. "Managerial Representations of Competitive Advantage." *Journal of Marketing,* vol. 58, April, 31–44.

Day, G.S., and R. Glazer. 1994. "Harnessing the Marketing Information Revolution: Toward the Market-Driven Learning Organization." In *The Marketing Information Revolution.* Edited by R.C. Blattberg, R. Glazer, and J.D.C. Little. Boston: Harvard Business School Press, 270–288.

Dearborn, DeWitt C., and H.A. Simon. 1959. "Selective Perception: A Note on the Departmental Identification of Executives." *Sociometry* vol. 21, 140–144.

De Geus, A.P. 1988. "Planning as Learning." *Harvard Business Review,* vol. 66, March/April, 70–74.

De Jong, C.M., K.R.E. Huizingh, P.A.M. Oude Ophuis, and B. Wierenga. 1994. *Kritische succesfactoren voor marketing decision support systemen.* Delft: Eburon.

DeLone, W.H., and E.R. McLean. 1992. "Information Systems Success: The Quest for the Dependent Variable." *Information Systems Research,* vol. 3, no. 1, 60–95.

Dennis, A.R. 1996. "Information Exchange and Use in Group Decision Making: You Can Lead a Group to Information, but You can't Make It Think." *MIS Quarterly,* December, 433-457.

Den Uyl, M.J., and E. Langendoen. 1997. "De inzet van adaptieve analyse-technieken in direct marketing." *Jaarboek Nederlandse Vereniging van Markt-onderzoekers,* 107–121.

DeSarbo, W.S., A.K. Manrai, and L.A. Manrai. 1997. "Latent Class Multi-dimensional Scaling: A Review of Recent Developments in the Marketing and Psychometric Literature." In *Advanced Methods of Marketing Research.* Edited by R.P. Bagozzi. Malden Ma: Blackwell Publishers Inc., 190–222.

De Waele, M. 1978. "Managerial Style and the Design of Decision Aids." *OMEGA,* vol. 6, no. 1, 5–13.

Dewey, J. 1910. *How We Think.* New York: D. C. Heath.

Dorfman, R., and P.O. Steiner. 1954. "Optimal Advertising and Optimal Quality." *The American Economic Review,* vol. 44, 826–836.

Dreyfus, H.L., and S.E. Dreyfus. 1986. "*Mind over Machine.*" New York: Free Press.

Drucker, P.F. 1993. *Post-Capitalist Society.* Oxford: Butterworth-Heinemann.

Dutta, S. 1993. *Knowledge Processing & Applied Artificial Intelligence.* Oxford: Butterworth-Heinemann.

Dutta, S., B. Wierenga, and A. Dalebout. 1997a. "Designing Management Support Systems Using an Integrative Perspective." *Communications of the ACM,* vol. 40, no. 6, 70–79.

Dutta, S., B. Wierenga, and A. Dalebout. 1997b. "Case-Based Reasoning Systems: From Automation to Decision-Aiding and Stimulation." *IEEE Transactions on Knowledge and Data Engineering,* vol. 9, no. 6, 911–922.

Edland, A., and O. Svenson. 1993. "Judgment and Decision Making Under Time Pressure: Studies and Findings." In *Time Pressure and Stress in Human Judgment and Decision Making.* Edited by O. Svenson and A.J. Maula. New York: Plenum Press.

Elam, J.J., and M. Mead. 1990. "Can Software Influence Creativity?" *Information Systems Research,* vol. 1, no. 1, 1–22.

Eliashberg, J., S. Gauvin, G.L. Lilien, and A. Rangaswamy. 1992. "An Experimental Study of Alternative Preparation Aids for International Negotiations." *Group Decisions and Negotiations,* vol. 1, 243–267.

Eliashberg, J., and G.L. Lilien. 1993. *Handbooks in Operations Research and Management Science, Volume 5: Marketing.* Amsterdam: Elsevier Science Publishers.

Engel, J.F., R.D. Blackwell, and P. W. Miniard. 1995. *Consumer Behavior.* 8th ed. Fort Worth, TX: Dryden Press.

Eppen, G.D., F.J. Gould, and C.P. Schmidt. 1993. *Introductory Management Science.* 4th ed. Englewood Cliffs, NJ: Prentice-Hall.

Esch, F.R., and W. Kroeber-Riel. 1994. *Expertensysteme fur die Werbung/Computer Aided Advertising System.* Munchen: Verlag Franz Vahlen.

Esch, F.R., and T. Muffler. 1989. "Expertensystemen in Marketing." *Marketing: Zeitschrift fur Forschung und Praxis,* vol. 3, no. 3, 145–151.

Eskin, G. 1993. "POS Scanner Data: The State of the Art in Europe and the World." ESOMAR/EMAC/AFM Symposium: *Information-Based Decision Making in Marketing.* Paris, November 17–19.

Etzioni, O. 1997. "Moving Up the Information Food Chain: Deploying Softbots on the World Wide Web." *AI Magazine,* vol. 18, no. 2, 9–18.

Eysenck, H.J. 1994. "The Measurement of Creativity." In *Dimensions of Creativity.* Edited by M.A. Boden. Cambridge, MA: MIT Press, 199–242.

Fayyad, U.M., G. Piatetsky-Shapiro, P. Smyth, and R. Uthurusamy, eds. 1996. *Advances in Knowledge Discovery and Data Mining.* Cambridge, MA: MIT Press.

Feigenbaum, E.A., P. McCorduck, and H.P. Nii. 1989. *"The Rise of the Expert Company."* New York: Vintage Books.

Forbus, K. 1988. "Qualitative Physics: Past, Present and Future." In *Exploring Artificial Intelligence.* Edited by H. Shrobe. San Mateo, CA: Morgan Kaufman.

Frank, N.D., and J. Ganly. 1983. *Data Sources for Business and Market Analysis.* Metuchen, NJ: Scarecrow Press.

Frank, R.E., A.A. Kuehn, and W.F. Massy, eds. 1962. *Quantitative Techniques in Marketing Analyses.* Homewood, IL: Irwin.

Fudge, W.K., and L.M. Lodish. 1977. "Evaluation of the Effectiveness of a Model-Based Salesman's Planning System by Field Experimentation." Part 2. *Interfaces,* vol. 8, no. 1, 97–106.

Gatignon, H. 1993. "Marketing-Mix Models." In *Handbooks in Operations Research and Management Science, Volume 5: Marketing.* Edited by J. Eliashberg and G.L. Lilien. Amsterdam: North-Holland, 697–732.

Gatignon, H., and T.S. Robertson. 1989. "Technology Diffusion: An Empirical Test of Competitive Effects." *Journal of Marketing,* vol. 53, 35–49.

Gaul, W., and M. Schader, eds. 1988. *Data, Expert Knowledge and Decisions.* Berlin: Springer Verlag.

Gaul, W., and A. Schaer. 1988. "A Prolog-Based PC Implementation for New Product Introduction." In *Data, Expert Knowledge and Decisions.* Edited by W. Gaul and M. Schader. Berlin: Springer Verlag.

Gelderman, M. 1997. *Success of Management Support Systems: A Literature Review and an Empirical Investigation.* Amsterdam: Thesis Publishers Amsterdam.

Gensch, D.H., N. Aversa, and S.P. Moore. 1990. "A Choice-Modeling Market Information System That Enabled ABB Electric to Expand Its Market Share." *Interfaces,* vol. 20, no. 1, 6–25.

Gentner, D., and A.B. Markman. 1997. "Structure Mapping in Analogy and Similarity." *American Psychologist,* vol. 52, no. 1, 45–56.

Gentner, D., and A.L. Stevens, eds. 1983. *Mental Models.* Hillsdale, NJ: Lawrence Erlbaum Associates.

Girod, G., P. Orgeas, and P. Landry. 1989. "Times: An Expert System for Media Planning." In *Innovative Applications of Artificial Intelligence.* Edited by H. Schorr and A. Rappaport. Menlo Park, CA: AAAI Press.

Glazer, R., J.H. Steckel, and R. S. Winer. 1992. "Locally Rational Decision Making: The Distracting Effect of Information on Managerial Performance." *Management Science,* vol. 38, no. 2, 212–226.

Goldenberg, J., D. Mazursky, and S. Solomon. 1999. "The Fundamental Templates of Quality Ads." *Marketing Science,* forthcoming.

Goldstein, D.K. 1993. *Product Manager's Use of Scanner Data: A Story of Organizational Learning.* Report no. 93–109. Cambridge, MA: Marketing Science Institute.

Gorry, G.A., and M.S. Scott Morton. 1971. "A Framework for Management Information Systems." *Sloan Management Review,* vol. 13, fall, 55–70.

Goslar, M.D., G.I. Green, and T.H. Hugues. 1986. "Decision Support Systems: An Empirical Assessment for Decision Making." *Decision Sciences,* vol. 17, no. 1, 79–91.

Graef, J.L. 1997. "Using the Internet for Competitive Intelligence: A Survey Report." *Competitive Intelligence Review,* vol. 8, no. 4, 41–47.

Green, P.E., and A.M. Krieger. 1989. "Recent Contributions to Optimal Product Positioning and Buyer Segmentation." *European Journal of Operational Research,* vol. 41, 127–141.

Green, P.E., and V.R. Rao. 1971. "Conjoint Measurement for Quantifying Judgmental data." *Journal of Marketing Research,* vol. 8, August, 355–363.

Green, P.E., and Y. Wind. 1973. *Multiattribute Decisions in Marketing: A Measurement Approach.* Hinsdale, IL: Dryden Press.

Gupta, S. 1994. "Managerial Judgement and Forecast Combination: An Experimental Study." *Marketing Letters,* vol. 5, no. 1, 5–17.

Gupta S., D. Jain, and M. Sawhney. 1999. "Modeling the Evolution of Markets with Indirect Network Externalities: An Application to Digital Television." *Marketing Science,* forthcoming.

Haberlandt, K. 1994. *Cognitive Psychology.* Boston: Allyn and Bacon.

Hanssens, D.M., L.J. Parsons, and R.L. Schultz. 1990. *Market Response Models: Econometric and Time Series Analysis.* Boston: Kluwer Academic Publishers.

Harmon, P. 1995. "Object-Oriented AI: A Commercial Perspective." *Communications of the ACM,* vol. 38, no. 11, 80–86.

Hauser, J.R., and S.M. Shugan. 1983. "Defensive Marketing Strategies." *Marketing Science,* vol. 2, no. 4, 319–360.

Hayes, P. 1985. "Naïve Physics 1: Ontology for Liquids." In *Theories of the Commonsense World.* Edited by J. Hobbes and B. Moore. Norwood, NJ: Ablex.

Hennesey, B.A., and T.M. Amabile. 1988. "The Conditions of Creativity." In *The Nature of Creativity.* Edited by R.J. Sternberg. Cambridge, England: Cambridge University Press, 11–38.

Hess, S.W., and S.A. Samuels. 1971. "Experiences with a Sales Districting Model: Criteria and Implementation." Part II. *Management Science,* vol. 18, no. 4, 41–54.

Higby, M.A., and B.N. Farah. 1991. "The Status of Marketing Information Systems, Decision Support Systems and Expert Systems in the Marketing Function of U.S. Firms." *Information and Management,* vol. 20, 29–35.

Hill, T., M. O'Connor, and W. Remus. 1996. "Neural Network Models for Time Series Forecasts." *Management Science,* vol. 42, no. 7, 1082–1092.

Hoch, S.J. 1994. "Experts and Models in Combination." In *The Marketing Information Revolution.* Edited by R.C. Blattberg, R. Glaser, and J.D.C. Little. Boston: Harvard Business School Press, 253–269.

Hoch, S.J., and D.A. Schkade. 1996. "A Psychological Approach to Decision Support Systems." *Management Science,* vol. 42, no. 1, 51–64.

Hofstadter, D. 1995. *Fluid Concepts and Creative Analogies: Computer Models of the Fundamental Mechanisms of Thought.* New York: Basic Books/Harper Collins.

Hogarth, R.M., and S. Makridakis. 1981. "Forecasting and Planning: An Evaluation." *Management Science,* vol. 27, no. 2, 115–138.

Holyak, K.J., and P. Thagard. 1995. *Mental Leaps: Analogy in Creative Thought.* Cambridge, MA: Bradford Book/MIT Press.

Hruschka, H. 1991. "Einsatz kunstlicher neuraler Netzwerke zur Datenanalyse im Marketing." *Marketing Zeitschrift for Forschung und Praxis,* vol. 13, 4, 217-225.

Hruschka, H. 1993. "Determining Market Response Functions by Neural Network Modelling: A Comparison to Econometric Techniques." *European Journal of Operational Research,* 27–35.

Hulbert, J.M. 1981. "Descriptive Models of Marketing Decisions". In *Marketing Decision Models.* Edited by R.L. Schultz, and A.A. Zoltners. New York: Elsevier North Holland.

Huysmans, J. 1970. "The Effectiveness of the Cognitive Style Constraint in Implementing Operations Research Proposals." *Management Science,* vol. 17, September, 92–104.

Hwang, M.I. 1994. "Decision Making Under Time Pressure: A Model for Information Systems Research." *Information & Management,* vol. 27, 197–203.

Igbaria, M., and S.A. Nachman. 1990. "Correlates of User Satisfaction with End User Computing: An Exploratory Study." *Information and Management,* vol. 19, 73–82.

Ing, D., and A.A. Mitchell. 1994. "Point-of Sales Data in Consumer Goods Marketing: Transforming the Art of Marketing into the Science of Marketing." In *The Marketing Information Revolution.* Edited by R.C. Blattberg, R. Glazer, and J.D.C. Little. Boston: Harvard Business School Press, 30–57.

Ives, B., and M. Olson. 1984. "User Involvement and MIS Success: A Review of Research." *Management Science,* vol. 30, no. 5, 586–603.

Ives, B., M.H. Olson, and J.J. Bouroudi. 1983. "The Measurement of User Information Satisfaction." *Communications of the ACM,* vol. 26, no. 10, 785–793.

Johnson-Laird, P.N. 1988. *The Computer and the Mind: An Introduction to Cognitive Science.* Cambridge, MA: Harvard University Press.

Johnson-Laird, P.N. 1989. "Mental Models." In *Foundations of Cognitive Science.* Edited by M.I. Posner. Cambridge, MA: MIT Press, 470–499.

Joshi, K. 1992. "A Causal Path Model of Overall User Attitudes Towards the MIS Function: The Case of User Information Satisfaction." *Information and Management,* vol. 22, no. 2, 77–88.

Kabanoff, B., and J.R. Rossiter. 1994. "Recent Developments in Applied Creativity." In *International Review of Industrial and Organizational Psychology.* Vol. 9. Edited by C.L. Cooper and I.T. Robertson. New York: Wiley.

Kahneman, D., and A. Tversky. 1974. "Judgment Under Uncertainty: Heuristics and Biases." *Science,* vol. 185, 1124–1131.

Kant, I. 1787. *Kritik der reinen Vernunft.* Herausgabe von R. Schmidt, 1971. Hamburg: Felix Meiner Verlag.

Kao, J. 1996. *Jamming: The Art and Discipline of Business Creativity.* New York: Harper Collins.

Kaul, A., and D. R. Wittink. 1995. "Empirical Generalizations About the Impact of Advertising on Price Sensitivity and Price." *Marketing Science,* vol. 14. no. 3, G151–G160.

Keen, P.G.W. 1980. "Reference Disciplines and a Cumulative Tradition." *Proceedings of the First International Conference on Information Systems,* December, 9–18.

Keen, P.G.W., and M.S. Scott Morton. 1978. *Decision Support Systems: An Organizational Perspective.* Reading, MA: Addison-Wesley.

Klayman, J., and P.J.H. Schoemaker. 1993. "Thinking About the Future: A Cognitive Perspective." *Journal of Forecasting,* vol. 12, February, 161–186.

Kleinmuntz, B. 1990. "Why We Still Use Our Heads Instead of Formulas: Toward an Integrative Approach." *Psychological Bulletin,* vol. 107, no. 3, 296–310.

Kolodner, J. 1993. *Case-Based Reasoning.* San Mateo, CA: Morgan Kaufmann.

Kotler, P. 1966. "A Design for the Firm's Marketing Nerve Center." *Business Horizons,* vol. 9, fall, 63–74.

Kotler, P. 1971. "*Marketing Decision Making: A Model-Building Approach.*" New York: Holt, Rinehart & Winston.

Kotler, P. 1997. *Marketing Management: Analysis, Planning, Implementation and Control.* 9th ed. Englewood Cliffs, NJ: Prentice Hall.

Kroeber-Riel, W. 1993. "Computer-Aided Globalization of Advertising by Expert Systems." In *European Advances in Consumer Research.* Vol. 1. Edited by G.J. Bamossy and W.F. van Raaij. Amsterdam, Association of Consumer Research, 110–117.

Kroeber-Riel, W., T. Lorson, and B. Neibecker. 1992. "Expertensysteme in der Werbung." *Die Betriebswirtschaft,* vol. 52, heft 1, 91–108.

Kumar, A., V.R. Rao, and H. Soni. 1995. "An Empirical Comparison of Neural Network and Logistic Regression Models." *Marketing Letters,* vol. 6, no. 4, 251–263.

Kwon, T.H., and R.W. Zmud. 1987. "Unifying the Fragmented Models of Information Systems Implementation." In *Critical Issues in Information Systems Research.* Edited by R.J. Boland and R.A. Hirscheim. New York: Wiley.

Langerak, F., H. Commandeur, and T. Duhamel. 1998. "ICT-Mogelijkheden vaak onbenut, Onderzoek naar gebruik van ICT door marketingafdelingen in België." *Tijdschrift voor Marketing,* November, vol. 32, 18–21.

Langley, A., H. Mintzberg, P. Pitcher, E. Posada, and J. Saint-Macary. 1995. "Opening Up Decision Making: The View from the Black Stool." *Organizational Science,* vol. 6, May/June, 260–279.

Larréché, J.C. 1979. "Integrative Complexity and the Use of Marketing Models." *TIMS Studies in the Management Sciences,* vol. 13, 171–187.

Larréché, J.C., and H. Gatignon. 1990. *MARKSTRAT2.* Redwood City, CA: Scientific Press.

Larréché, J.C., and V. Srinivasan. 1981. "Stratport: A Decision Support System for Strategic Planning." *Journal of Marketing,* vol. 45, fall, 39–52.

Lavidge, R.J., and G.A. Steiner. 1961. "A Model for Predictive Measurements of Advertising Effectiveness." *Journal of Marketing,* vol. 25, October, 59–62.

Leake, D.B., ed. 1996. *Case-Based Reasoning: Experience, Lessons & Future Directions.* Menlo Park, CA: AAAI Press/MIT Press.

Lee, J., and S.H. Kim. 1992. "The Relationship Between Procedural Formalization in MIS Development and MIS Success: A Contingent Analysis. *Information and Management,* vol. 22, 89–111.

Leeflang, P.S.H., D.R. Wittink, M. Wedel, and P.A. Naert. 2000. *Building Models for Marketing Decisions.* Boston/ Dordrecht: Kluwer Academic Publishers.

Leenders, M.A.A.M. 1998. *The Marketing – R&D Interface and New Product Performance: A Study in the Pharmaceutical Industry.* Rotterdam: Erasmus University Rotterdam.

Lenat, D., and R. Guha. 1990. *Building Large Knowledge-Based Systems.* Reading, MA: Addison-Wesley.

Leverick, F., D. Littler, M. Bruce, and D. Wilson. 1997. "The Role of IT in the Reshaping of Marketing." *Journal of Marketing Practice: Applied Marketing Science,* vol. 3, no. 2, 87–106.

Levitt, T. 1983. *The Marketing Imagination.* London: Free Press.

Lilien, G.L. 1979. "Advisor 2: Modeling the Marketing Mix for Industrial Products." *Management Science,* vol. 25, no. 2, 191–204.

Lilien, G.L. 1994. "Marketing Models: Past, Present and Future." In *Research Traditions in Marketing.* Edited by G. Laurent, G.L. Lilien, and B. Pras. Boston: Kluwer Academic Publishers, 1–20.

Lilien, G.L., and P. Kotler. 1983. *Marketing Decision Making: A Model-Building Approach.* New York: Harper & Row.

Lilien, G.L., P. Kotler, and K.S. Moorthy. 1992. *Marketing Models.* Englewood Cliffs, NJ: Prentice-Hall.

Lilien, G.L., and A. Rangaswamy. 1998. *Marketing Engineering: Computer-Assisted Marketing Analysis and Planning.* Reading, MA: Addison-Wesley.

Lilien, G.L., and A.G. Rao. 1976. "A Model for Allocating Retail Outlet Building Resources Across Market Areas." *Operations Research,* vol. 24, no. 1, 1–14.

Lippman, R.A. 1987. "An Introduction to Computing with Neural Nets." *IEEE ASSP Magazine,* April, 4–21.

Little, J.D.C. 1970. "Models and Managers: The Concept of a Decision Calculus." *Management Science,* vol. 16, April, B466–B485.

Little, J.D.C. 1975a. "BRANDAID: A Marketing-Mix Model, Part 1: Structure." *Operations Research,* vol. 23, no. 4, 628–655.

Little, J.D.C. 1975b. "BRANDAID: A Marketing-Mix Model, Part 2: Implementation, Calibration, and Case Study." *Operations Research,* vol. 23, no. 4, 656–673.

Little, J.D.C. 1979. "Decision Support Systems for Marketing Managers." *Journal of Marketing,* vol. 43, summer, 9–26.

Little, J.D.C. 1991. "Operations Research in Industry: New Opportunities in a Changing World." *Operations Research,* vol. 39, July/August, 531–542.

Little, J.D.C., and L. M. Lodish. 1969. "A Media Planning Calculus." *Operations Research,* vol. 17, January/February, 1–35.

Lodish, L.M. 1971. "CALLPLAN: An Interactive Salesman's Call Planning System." Part 2. *Management Science,* vol. 18, no. 4, 25–40.

Lodish, L.M., E. Curtis, M. Ness, M. K. Simpson. 1988. "Sales Force Sizing and Deployment Using a Decision Calculus Model at Syntex Laboratories." *Interfaces,* vol. 18, no. 1, 5–20.

Lucas, H.C., Jr. 1973. "A Descriptive Model of Information Systems in the Context of the Organization." *Data Base,* vol. 5, 27–36.

Lucas, H.C., Jr., E. J. Walton, and M. J. Ginzberg. 1988. "Implementing Packaged Software." *Management Information Systems Quarterly,* vol. 12, no. 4, 537–549.

Luger, G.F., ed. 1995. *Computation and Intelligence, Collected Readings.* Menlo Park. CA: AAAI Press.

Luger, G.F., and W.A. Stubblefield. 1993. *Artificial Intelligence, Structures and Strategies for Complex Problem Solving.* 2d ed. Redwood City, CA: Benjamin/Cummings.

Lusk, E.J., and M. Kersnick. 1979. "The Effect of Cognitive Style and Report Format on Task Performance: The MIS Design Consequences." *Management Science,* vol. 25, no. 8, 787–798.

MacCrimmon, K.R., and C. Wagner. 1994. "Stimulating Ideas Through Creativity Software." *Management Science,* vol. 40, no. 11, 1514–1532.

Malhotra, N.K. 1999. *Marketing Research: An Applied Orientation.* 3d ed. Upper Saddle River, NJ: Prentice Hall International.

Marakas, K.R., and J.J. Elam. 1997. "Creativity Enhancement in Problem Solving: Through Software or Process?" *Management Science,* vol. 43, no. 8, 1136–1146.

Margherio, L., D. Henry, S. Cooke, S. Montes, and K. Hughes. 1998. *The Emerging Digital Economy.* Washington, DC: U.S. Department of Commerce.

Markus, M.L. 1983. "Power, Politics and MIS Implementation." *Communications of the ACM,* vol. 26, no. 6, 430–444.

Mason, R.O., and I.I. Mitroff. 1973. "A Program for Research on Management Information Systems." *Management Science,* vol. 19, no. 5, 475–487.

Massetti, B. 1996. "An Empirical Examination of the Value of Creativity Support Systems on Idea Generation." *Management Information Systems Quarterly,* vol. 20, March, 83–97.

Mawhinney, C.H., and A.R. Lederer. 1990. "A Study of Computer Utilization by Managers." *Information and Management,* vol. 18, 243–253.

McCann, J.M., and J.P. Gallagher. 1990. *Expert Systems for Scanner Data Environments.* Boston: Kluwer Academic Publishers.

McCann, J.M., J. Hill, and D. McCullough. 1991. "The Application of Marketing Experiences via Case-Based Reasoning." Working paper, Fuqua School of Business, Duke University.

McCann, J.M., W.G. Lathi, and J. Hill. 1991. "The Brand Manager's Assistant: A Knowledge-Based Systems Approach to Brand Management." *International Journal of Research in Marketing,* vol. 8, no. 1, 51–73.

McCann, J., A. Tadlaoui, and J.P. Gallagher. 1990. "Knowledge Systems in Merchandising: Advertsing Design." *Journal of Retailing,* vol. 66, no. 3, 257–277.

McClelland, J.L., D.E. Rumelhart, and the PDP Research Group. 1986. *Parallel Distributed Processing. Explorations in the Microstructure of Cognition. Psychological and Biological Models.* Vol. 2, Cambridge, MA: MTI Press.

McCulloch, W.S., and W. Pitts. 1943. "A Logical Calculus of the Ideas Immanent in Nervous Activity." *Bulletin of Mathematical Biophysics,* vol. 5, 115–133.

McIntyre, S.H. 1982. "An Experimental Study of the Impact of Judgment-Based Marketing Models." *Management Science,* vol. 28, no. 1, 17–33.

McIntyre, S. ., D.D. Achabal, and C.M. Miller. 1993. "Applying Case-Based Reasoning to Forecasting Retail Sales." *Journal of Retailing,* vol. 69, no. 4, 372–398.

Mehotra, K., C.K. Mohan, and S. Ranka. 1997. *Elements of Artificial Neural Networks.* Cambridge, MA: MIT Press.

Meseguer, P., and A. Preece. 1995. "Verification and Validation of Knowledge-Based Systems with Formal Specifications." *Knowledge Engineering Review,* vol. 10, no. 4, 331–343.

Minsky, M. 1981. "A Framework for Representing Knowledge." In *Mind Design.* Edited by J. Haugeland. Cambridge, MA: MIT Press.

Minsky, M. 1991. "Logical Versus Analogical or Symbolic Versus Connectionist or Neat Versus Scruffy." *AI Magazine,* vol. 12, no. 2, 52–69.

Minzberg, H. 1973. *The Nature of Managerial Work.* New York: Harper & Row.

Mitchell, A.A. 1988. "The Development of a Knowledge-Based Media Planning System." In *Data, Expert Knowledge and Decisions.* Edited by W. Gaul and M. Schader. Berlin: Springer Verlag, 67–79.

Mitchell, A.A., J.E. Russo, and D.R. Wittink. 1991. "Issues in the Development and Use of Expert Systems for Marketing Decisions." *International Journal of Research in Marketing,* vol. 8, no. 1, 41–50.

Mock, T.J. 1973. "A Longitudinal Study of Some Information Structure Alternatives." *Data Base,* vol. 5, 40–45.

Mockler, R.J. 1989. *Knowledge-Based Systems for Management Decisions.* Englewood Cliffs, NJ: Prentice Hall.

Montgomery, D.B., A.J. Silk, and C.E. Zaragoza. 1971. "A Multiple-Product Sales Force Allocation Model." Part II. *Management Science,* vol. 18, no. 4, 3–24.

Montgomery, D.B., and G.L. Urban. 1969. *Management Science in Marketing.* Englewood Cliffs, NJ: Prentice Hall.

Montgomery, D.B., and G.L. Urban. 1970. "Marketing Decision-Information Systems: An Emerging View." *Journal of Marketing Research,* vol. 7, May, 226–234.

Montoya-Weiss, M., and R.J. Calantone. 1999. "Development & Implementation of a Segment Selection Procedure for Industrial Products." *Marketing Science,* forthcoming.

Moore, M. 1992. "Signals and Choices in a Competitive Interaction: The Role of Moves and Messages." *Management Science,* vol. 38, no. 4, 483-500.

Moore, M., and J. Urbany. 1994, "Blinders, Fuzzy Lenses, and the Wrong Shoes: Pitfalls in Competitive Conjecture." *Marketing Letters,* vol. 5, no. 3, 247-258.

Moret, Ernst and Young. 1995. "Impact van de informatietechnologie; onderziek naar de invloed van de ontwikkeling in de informatie- en telecommunicatie-technologie op de bedrijfsvoering." Rotterdam: Report A 5090.

Mott, S. 1993. "Case-Based Reasoning: Market, Applications, and Fit with Other Technologies." *Expert Systems with Applications,* vol. 6, 97–104.

Mowen, J.C., and G.J. Gaeth. 1992. "The Evaluation Stage in Marketing Decision Making." *Journal of the Academy of Marketing Science,* vol. 20, no. 2, 177–187.

Naert, P.A., and P.S.H. Leeflang. 1978. *Building Implementable Marketing Models.* Leiden: Martinus Nijhoff.

Neibecker, B. 1990. *Werbewirkungsanalyse mit Expertensysteme.* Heidelberg: Physica Verlag.

Neibecker, B. 1996. "Validierung eines Werbewirkungsmodells fur Expertensysteme." *Marketing: Zeitschrift fur Forschung und Praxis,* vol. 18, no. 2, 95–104.

Nemhauser, G.L., and L.A. Wolsey. 1988. *Integer and Combinatorial Optimization.* New York: Wiley.

Newell, A., and H.A. Simon. 1972. *Human Problem Solving.* Englewood Cliffs, NJ: Prentice Hall.

Newquist, H.P. 1994. *The Brain Makers.* Indianapolis: Sams Publishing.

Nilsson, N.J. 1998. *Artificial Intelligence: A New Synthesis.* San Francisco: Morgan Kaufmann.

Nonaka, I. 1994. "A Dynamic Theory of Organizational Knowledge Creation." *Organizational Science,* vol. 5, February, 14–37.

Nonaka, I., and H. Takeuchi. 1995. *The Knowledge-Creating Company.* New York: Oxford University Press.

O'Connor, J., and E. Galvin. 1997. *Marketing & Information Technology.* London: Pitman.

Ogilvy, D. 1983. *Ogilvy on Advertising.* New York: Crown.

Orr, Ken. 1997. "Data Warehousing Technology." White paper, Kenn Orr Institute (http://www.kenorrinst.com).

Paisley, W.J. 1968. "Information Needs and Uses." *Annual Review of Information Science and Technology,* vol. 3, 1–30.

Pandeliaki, S., and A.N. Burgess. 1998. "The Potential of Neural Networks Evaluated Within a Taxonomy of Marketing Applications." In *Bio-Mimic Approaches in Management Science.* Edited by J.M. Aurifeille and C. Deissenberg. Boston: Kluwer Academic Publishers, 1–12.

Payne, J.W., J.R. Bettman, and E. Johnson. 1993. *The Adaptive Decision Maker.* New York: Cambridge University Press.

Peacock, P.R. 1998. "Data Mining in Marketing: Part 1." *Marketing Management,* Winter, 9-18.

Penrose, R. 1989. *The Emperor's New Mind.* Oxford: Oxford University Press.

Perkins, W.S., and R.C. Rao. 1990. "The Role of Experience in Information Use and Decision Making by Marketing Managers." *Journal of Marketing Research,* vol. 27, February, 1–10.

Pettigrew, A.M. 1979. "On Studying Organizational Cultures." *Administrative Science Quarterly,* vol. 24, 570–581.

Pinsonneault, A., and S. Rivard. 1998. "Information Technology and the Nature of Managerial Work: From the Productivity Paradox to the Icarus Paradox." *MIS Quarterly,* September, 287-311.

Polanyi, M. 1966. *The Tacit Dimension.* London: Routledge and Kegan Paul.

Pounds, W.F. 1969. "The Process of Problem Finding." *Industrial Management Review,* vol. 11, no. 1, 1–19.

Preece, A., and R. Shinghal. 1994. "Foundation and Application of Knowledge-Base Verification." *International Journal of Intelligent Systems,* vol. 9, no. 8, 683–702.

Pringle, L.G., R.D. Wilson, and E.I. Brody. 1982. "NEWS: A Decision-Oriented Model for New Product Analysis and Forecasting." *Marketing Science,* vol. 1, no. 1, 1–29.

Raiffa, H. 1968. *Decision Analysis: Introductory Lectures on Choices Under Uncertainty.* Reading, MA: Addison-Wesley.

Ram, S., and S. Ram. 1988. " Innovator, An Expert System for New Product Launch Decision." *Applied Artificial Intelligence,* vol. 2, 129–148.

Ram, S., and S. Ram. 1996. "Validation of Expert Systems for Innovation Management: Issues, Methodology and Empirical Assessment." *Journal of Product Innovation Management,* vol. 13, 53–68.

Rangaswamy, A. 1993. "Marketing Decision Models: From Linear Programs to Knowledge-Based Systems." In *Handbooks in Operations Research and Management Science, Volume: 5 Marketing.* Edited by J. Eliashberg and G.L. Lilien. Amsterdam: North Holland, 733–771.

Rangaswamy, A., R.R. Burke, J. Wind, and J. Eliashberg. 1986. "Expert Systems for Marketing." Working paper 86-036, Marketing Department, The Wharton School, University of Pennsylvania.

Rangaswamy, A., J. Eliashberg, R.R. Burke, and J. Wind. 1989. "Developing Marketing Expert Systems: An Application to International Negotiations." *Journal of Marketing,* vol. 53, October, 24–39.

Rangaswamy, A., B.A. Harlam, and L.M. Lodish. 1991. "INFER: An Expert System for Automatic Analysis of Scanner Data." *International Journal of Research in Marketing,* vol. 8, no. 1, 29–40.

Rao, A.G., and G.L. Lilien. 1972. "A System of Promotional Models." *Management Science,* vol. 19, no. 2, 152–160.

Rao, A.G., and P.B. Miller. 1975. "Advertising/Sales Response Functions." *Journal of Advertising Research,* vol. 15, no. 2, 7–15.

Reuters. 1996. "Dying for Information." Reuters Business Information.

Ries, A., and J. Trout. 1993. *The 22 Immutable Laws of Marketing.* London: HarperCollins.

Riesbeck, C.K., and R.C. Schank. 1989. *Inside Case-Based Reasoning.* Hillsdale, NJ: Lawrence Erlbaum.

Robbin, A. 1990. *Idea Fisher – An Introduction.* Irvin Ca: Fisher Idea Systems.

Rossiter, J.R., and L. Percy. 1987. *Advertising and Promotion Management.* New York: McGraw-Hill.

Rossiter, J.R., and L. Percy. 1997. *Advertising Communications and Promotion Management.* 2d ed. New York: McGraw-Hill.

Rumelhart, D., J.L. McClelland, and the PDP Research Group. 1986. *Parallel Distributed Processing, Explorations in the Microstructure of Cognition. Vol. 1: Foundations.* Cambridge, MA: MIT Press.

Russo, J.E., and P.J.H. Schoemaker. 1990. *Decision Traps: Ten Barriers to Brilliant Decision-Making and How to Overcome Them.* New York: Fireside.

Sakaguchi, T., and M.N. Frolick. 1998. "A Review of the Data Warehousing Literature." (http://www.people.memphis.edu/~tsakagch/dw-web.htr)

Sanders, G.L., and J.F. Courtney. 1985. "A Field Study of Organizational Factors Influencing DSS Success." *MIS Quarterly,* vol. 9, 1, 77–93.

Saunders, J. 1987. "The Specification of Aggregate Market Models." *European Journal of Marketing,* vol. 21, no. 2, 1–47.

Schank, R.C. 1982. *Dynamic Memory: A Theory of Learning in Computers and People.* Cambridge, England: Cambridge University Press.

Schank, R.C., A. Kass, and C.K. Riesbeck, eds. 1994. *Inside Case-Based Explanation.* Hillsdale, NJ: Lawrence Erlbaum.

Schewe, C.D. 1976. "The Management Information System User: An Exploratory Behavioral Analysis." *Academy of Management Journal,* vol. 19, no. 4, 577–590.

Schmitz, J.D. 1994. "Expert Systems for Scanner Data in Practice." In *The Marketing Information Revolution.* Edited by R.C. Blattberg, R. Glazer, and J.D.C. Little. Boston: Harvard Business School Press, 102–119.

Schmitz, J.D., G.D. Armstrong, and J.D.C. Little. 1990. "Coverstory: Automated News Finding in Marketing." *Interfaces,* vol. 20, 29–38.

Schultz, R.L., and D.P. Slevin. 1972. "Behavioral Considerations in the Implementation of Marketing Decision Models." In *Proceedings Spring and Fall Conference AMA,* 494–498.

Schumann, M., P.A. Congla, K.S. Lee, and J.G. Sakamoto. 1987. "Business Strategy Advisor: An Expert System Implementation." Los Angeles: IBM Scientific Center.

Scott Morton, M.S. 1971. *Management Decision Systems: Computer-Based Support for Decision Making,* Cambridge, MA: Division of Research, Harvard University.

SEI Center Reports. 1990. Workshop on the Impact of Artificial Intelligence on Management Decision Making and Organizational Design. February 10, The Wharton School, University of Pennsylvania, Philadelphia.

Senge, P.M. 1990. *The Fifth Discipline: The Art and Practice of the Learning Organization.* New York: Doubleday/Currency.

Senn, J.A. 1995. *Information Technology in Business, Principles, Practices, and Opportunities.* Englewood Cliffs, NJ: Prentice-Hall.

Shanteau, J. 1992. "How Much Information Does an Expert Use? Is It Relevant?" *Acta Psychologica,* vol. 81, 75–86.

Shaw, R. 1994. *How to Transform Marketing Through IT.* London: Business Intelligence.

Shortliffe, E.H. 1976. *Computer-Based Medical Consultations: MYCIN.* NewYork: American Elsevier.

Siegel, S., and N.J. Castellan. 1988. *Nonparametric Statistics for the Behavioral Sciences.* 2d ed. New York: McGraw-Hill.

Siekmann, P. 1994. *Expertsysteme fur die Werbeentwicklung und Beurteilung-Ein kritischer Vergeleich.* Master's thesis, University of Bielefeld.

Silk, A.J. 1993. "Marketing Science in a Changing Environment." *Journal of Marketing Research,* vol. 30, November, 401–404.

Silk, A.J., and G.L. Urban. 1978. "Pre-Test-Market Evaluation of New Packaged Goods: A Model and Measurement Methodology." *Journal of Marketing Research,* vol. 15, May, 171–191.

Silver, M.S. 1991. *Systems That Support Decision Makers: Description and Analysis.* New York: Wiley.

Simon, H. 1982. "PRICESTRAT: An Applied Strategic Pricing Model for Nondurables." In *Marketing Planning Models, TIMS Studies in the Management Sciences.* Vol. 18. Edited by A.A. Zoltners. 23–41.

Simon, H. 1994. "Marketing Science's Pilgrimage to the Ivory Tower." In *Research Traditions in Marketing.* Edited by G. Laurent, G.L. Lilien, and B. Pras. Boston: Kluwer Academic Press.

Simon, H.A. 1957. *Models of Man.* New York: Wiley.

Simon, H.A. 1960. *The New Science of Management Decision.* Englewood Cliffs, NJ: Prentice Hall.

Simon, H.A. 1973. "The Structure of Ill-Structured Problems." *Artificial Intelligence,* vol. 4, 181–201.

Simon, H.A. 1977. *The New Science of Management Decision.* Rev. ed. Englewood Cliffs, NJ: Prentice Hall.

Simon H.A. 1979. *Models of Thought.* New Haven, CT: Yale University Press.

Simon, H.A. 1995. "Machine as Mind." In *Android Epistemology*. Edited by C. Glymour, K. Ford, and P. Hayes. Menlo Park, CA: AAAI Press.

Simon, H.A. 1997. *Administrative Behavior: A Study of Decision-Making Processes in Administrative Organizations*. 4th ed. New York: Free Press.

Simon, H.A., and A. Newell. 1958. "Heuristic Problem Solving: The Next Advance in Operations Research." *Operations Research*, vol. 6, January/February, 1–10.

Sinkula, J.M. 1994. "Market Information Processing and Organizational Learning." *Journal of Marketing*, vol. 58, January, 35–45.

Sloman, S.A. 1996. "The Empirical Case for Two Systems of Reasoning." *Psychological Bulletin*, vol. 119, no. 1, 3–32.

Slovic, P., and S. Lichtenstein. 1971. "Comparison of Bayesian and Regression Approaches to the Study of Information Processing in Judgment." *Organizational Behavior and Human Performance*, vol. 6, no. 6, 694–744.

Smith, G.F. 1989. "Defining Managerial Problems: A Framework for Prescriptive Theorizing." *Management Science*, vol. 35, no. 8, 963–981.

Spence, M.T., and M. Brucks. 1997. "The Moderating Effects of Problem Characteristics on Experts' and Novices' Judgments." *Journal of Marketing Research*, vol. 34, May, 233–247.

Sprague, R.H., Jr. 1989. "A Framework for the Development of Decision Support Systems." In *Decision Support Systems: Putting Theory into Practice*. Edited by R.H. Sprague and H.J. Watson. Englewood Cliffs, NJ: Prentice-Hall, 9–35.

Sprague, R.H., Jr., and E.D. Carlson. 1982. *Building Effective Decision Support Systems*. Englewood Cliffs, NJ: Prentice-Hall.

Sternberg, R.J. 1977. *Intelligence, Information Processing and Analogical Reasoning: The Componential Analysis of Human Abilities*. Hillsdale, NJ: Lawrence Erlbaum Associates.

Störig, H.J. 1990. *Kleine Weltgeschichte der Philosophie*. ed. 21, Stuttgart: W. Kohlhammer Verlag.

Sviokla, J. 1989. "Business Implications of Knowledge-Based Systems." In *Decision Support Systems: Putting Theory into Practice*. Edited by R. H. Sprague and H.J. Watson. Englewood Cliffs, NJ: Prentice Hall, 125–151.

Swami, S., J. Eliashberg, and C. Weinberg. 1999. "SilverScreener: A Modeling Approach to Movie Screens Management." *Marketing Science*, forthcoming.

Swanson, E.B. 1994. "Information Systems Innovation Among Organizations." *Management Science*, vol. 40, September, 1069–1091.

Sycara, K.P. 1998. "The Many Faces of Agents." *AI Magazine*, vol. 19, no. 2, 11–12.

Tardif, T.Z., and R.J. Sternberg. 1988. "What Do We Know About Creativity?" In *The Nature of Creativity: Contemporary Psychological Perspectives*. Edited by R.J. Sternberg. Cambridge, England: Cambridge University Press, 429–440.

Tellis, G.J. 1988. "The Price Elasticity of Selective Demand: A Meta-Analysis of Econometric Models of Sales." *Journal of Marketing Research*, vol. 25, November, 331–341.

Todd, P., and I. Benbasat. 1991. "The Impact of Computer-Based Decision Aids on the Decision Making Process." *Information Systems Research*, vol. 2, 87–115.

Torkzadeh, G., and W.J. Doll. 1993. "The Place and Value of Documentation in End-User Computing." *Information and Management,* vol. 24, 147–158.

Torrance, E.P. 1988. "The Nature of Creativity as Manifest in Its Testing." In *The Nature of Creatvity.* Edited by R.J. Sternberg. Cambridge, England: Cambridge University Press.

Turban, E. 1995. *Decision Support Systems and Expert Systems.* 4th ed. Englewood Cliffs, NJ: Prentice-Hall.

Turban, E., and J.E. Aronson. 1998. *Decision Support Systems and Intelligent Systems.* Englewood Cliffs, NJ: Prentice Hall.

Turban, E., E. McLean, and J. Wetherbe. 1996. *Information Technology for Management: Improving Quality and Productivity.* New York: Wiley.

Turing, A. 1950. "Computer Machinery and Intelligence." *Mind,* vol. 59, October, 433–460.

Turner, A.M., and W.T. Greenhough. 1985. "Differential Rearing Effects on Rat Visual Cortex Synapses." *Brain Research,* vol. 329, 195–203.

Udo, G.J., and J.S. Davis. 1992. "Factors Affecting Decision Support Systems Benefits." *Information and Management,* vol. 23, 359–371.

Urban, G.L. 1970. "SPRINTER MOD III: A Model for the Analysis of New Frequently Purchased Consumer Products." *Operations Research,* vol. 18, 805–854.

Urban, G.L. 1975. "PERCEPTOR: A Model for Product Positioning." *Management Science,* vol. 21, no. 8, 858–871.

Urban, G.L., and G.M. Katz. 1983. "Pre-Test Market Models: Validation and Managerial Implications." *Journal of Marketing Research,* vol. 20, August, 221–234.

Van Bruggen, G.H., A. Smidts, and B. Wierenga. 1996. "The Impact of the Quality of a Marketing Decision Support System: An Experimental Study." *International Journal of Research in Marketing,* vol. 13, no. 4, 331–343.

Van Bruggen, G.H., A. Smidts, and B. Wierenga. 1998. "Improving Decision Making by Means of a Marketing Decision Support System." *Management Science,* vol. 44, May, 645–658.

Van Bruggen, G.H., A. Smidts, and B. Wierenga. 1999. "The Value of Experience-Based Expertise in Marketing Decision Making and the Role of Decision Support." Working paper, Erasmus University Rotterdam.

Van Campen, P., K. Huizingh, P. Oude Ophuis, and B. Wierenga. 1991. *Marketing decision support systemen bij Nederlandse bedrijven.* Delft: Eburon.

Vandenbosch, M.B., and C.B. Weinberg. 1993. "Salesforce Operations." In *Handbooks in Operations Research and Management Science, Volume 5: Marketing.* Edited by J. Eliashberg and G.L. Lilien. Amsterdam: North Holland, 653–694.

Van den Bulte, C., and R.K. Moenaert. 1998. "The Effects of R&D team Co-location on Communication Patterns Among R&D, Marketing and Manufacturing." *Management Science,* vol. 44, 11, 1–18.

Van Hilligersberg, J. 1997. *Metamodelling-Based Integration of Object-Oriented Systems Development.* Amsterdam: Thesis Publishers Amsterdam.

Wagenaar, A., M.J. den Uyl, and P. Van der Putten. 1997. *Data Mining in Marketing Databases*. Amsterdam: Nederlandse Associatie voor Direct Marketing, Distance Selling en Sales Promotion DMSA.

Wainer, H. 1984. "How to Display Data Badly." *The American Statistician,* vol. 38, no. 2, 137–147.

Watson, I. 1997. *Applying Case-Based Reasoning: Techniques for Enterprise Systems*. San Francisco: Morgan Kaufmann.

Wallas, G. 1926. *The Art of Thought.* New York: Harcourt Brace Jovanovich

Weber, E.U., and O. Coskunoglu. 1990. "Descriptive and Prescriptive Models of Decisionmaking: Implications for the Development of Decision Aids." *IEEE Transactions on Systems Management and Cybernetics,* vol. 20, no. 2, 310–317.

Wedel, M., and W.S. DeSarbo. 1997. "A Review of Recent Developments in Latent Class Regression Models. In *Advanced Methods of Marketing Research.* Edited by R.P. Bagozzi. Oxford: Blackwell, 352–388.

Wedel, M., and W.A. Kamakura. 1997. "Market Segmentation: Conceptual and Methodological Foundations." In *International Series in Quantitative Marketing.* Edited by J. Eliashberg. Boston: Kluwer Academic Publishers.

Weick, K.E. 1983. "Managerial Thought in the Context of Action." In *The Executive Mind: New Insights on Managerial Thought and Action.* Edited by S. Srivastava and Associates. San Francisco: Jossey-Bass, 221–242.

Weiss, C.H. 1980. "Knowledge Creep and Decision Accretion." *Knowledge,* vol. 1, no. 3, 381–404.

Wertheimer, M. 1959. *Productive Thinking.* New York: Harper and Row.

West, P.M., P.L. Brockett, and L. L. Golden. 1997. "A Comparative Analysis of Neural Networks and Statistical Methods for Predicting Consumer Choice." *Marketing Science,* vol. 16, no. 4, 370–391.

Wierenga, B. 1990. "The First Generation of Marketing Expert Systems." Working paper no. 90-009, Marketing Department, The Wharton School, University of Pennsylvania.

Wierenga, B. 1992. *Knowledge-Based Systems in Marketing: Purpose, Performance, Perceptions and Perspectives.* Management Report Series no. 112. Rotterdam: Rotterdam School of Management, Erasmus University Rotterdam.

Wierenga, B., and J. Kluytmans. 1996. *Prediction with Neural Nets in Marketing Time Series Data.* Management Report Series no. 258. Rotterdam: Rotterdam School of Management, Erasmus University Rotterdam.

Wierenga, B., and P.A.M. Oude Ophuis. 1997. "Marketing Decision Support Systems: Adoption, Use and Satisfaction." *International Journal of Research in Marketing,* vol. 14, no. 3, 275–290.

Wierenga, B., P.A.M. Oude Ophuis, K.R.E. Huizingh, P.A.F.M. van Campen. 1994. "Hierarchical Scaling of Marketing Decision Support Systems." *Decision Support Systems,* vol. 12, no. 3, 219.

Wierenga, B., and G.H. Van Bruggen. 1997a. "The Integration of Marketing Problem-Solving Modes and Marketing Management Support Systems." *Journal of Marketing,* vol. 61, July, 21–37.

Wierenga, B., and G.H. Van Bruggen. 1997b. *Matching Marketing Management Support Systems and Marketing Problem-Solving Modes as the Key to Effective Decision Support.* Management Report Series no. 37 (13). Rotterdam: Rotterdam School of Management, Erasmus University Rotterdam.

Wierenga, B., and G.H. van Bruggen. 1998. "The Dependent Variable in Research into the Effects of Creativity Support Systems." *MIS Quarterly,* vol. 22, 1, 81–87.

Wierenga, B., G.H. Van Bruggen, and R. Staelin. 1999. "The Success of Marketing Management Support Systems." *Marketing Science,* forthcoming.

Winer, B.J. 1971. *Statistical Principles in Experimental Design.* 2d ed. New York: McGraw-Hill.

Wiser, M., and S. Carey. 1983. "When Heat and Temperature Were One." In *Mental Models.* Edited by D. Gentner and A.L. Stevens. Hillsdale, NJ: Lawrence Erlbaum Associates, 267–298.

Wittink, D.R., M.J. Addona, William J. Hawkes , and John C. Porter. 1988. "SCAN*PRO: The Estimation, Validation, and Use of Promotional Effects Based on Scanner Data." Working paper, February.

Zaltman, G. 1997. Rethinking Market Research: Putting People Back In." *Journal of Marketing Research,* vol. 34, November, 424–437.

Zaltman, G., R. Duncan, and J. Holbek. 1973. *Innovations in Organizations.* New York: Wiley.

Zinkhan, G.M., E.A. Joachimsthaler, and T.C. Kinnear. 1987. "Individual Differences and Marketing Decision Support Systems Usage and Satisfaction." *Journal of Marketing Research,* vol. 24, May, 208–214.

Zmud, R.W. 1979. "Individual Differences and MIS Success: A Review of the Empirical Literature." *Management Science,* vol. 25, no. 10, 966–975.

Zoltners, A.A., and P. Sinha. 1983. "Sales Territory Alignment: A Review and Model." *Management Science,* vol. 29, no. 11, 1237–1256.

Zuboff, S. 1985. "Automate/Informate: The Two Faces of Intelligent Technology." *Organizational Dynamics,* Autumn, 5–18.

Subject index

A

ABB Electric, 267
Accessibility, 273
A.C. Nielsen, 65, 97, 100, 105, 112, 291, 293, 301
Adaptability, 274
Adaptation, 176
Adaptive techniques, 198
ADBUDG, 250
ADCAD, 144
ADDUCE, 162, 179
Adoption, 277
Advertising campaign(s), 23, 24, 27
Advertising designer, 248
Algemeen Dagblad (AD), 173
ALGOL, 52
Amabile, 36
Amazon, 66, 287
AMOS, 60
Ample time frame, 39
Amstel, 132
Analog representation, 274
Analogical reasoning, 26, 166
Analogizing (mode), 21, 27, 216, 272
Analysis of a specific period, 245

Analytical (style), 20, 37, 271
Analytical capabilities, 44, 57, 290
Anchoring and adjustment, 18, 19
Andersen Consulting's BargainFinder, 290
ANOVA, 58
Antecedents, 33
APACHE, 167
Application software, 51
Aristotle, 72
Artificial Intelligence, 121
Artificial neural network, 185
Aspiration levels, 26
Assembly languages, 51
ASSESSOR, 105, 301
Association tables, 253
Attitude, 276
Attributes, 54, 131
Automating, 213
Autonomous agent, 289
Availability heuristic, 18
Availability of data, 34

B

Baan, 293
BaanFrontOffice, 101

Back propagation, 190
Backward Chaining, 139
Ballpark solution, 176
Bar code scanners, 50
Bar code, 45
Baseline creativity, 202
BASIC, 52
Battle Planner, 178
Bayesian analyses, 86
Bayesian updating, 295
Biased decision-making, 282
Biological neural networks, 186
Bols, 128
Bounded rationality, 4, 18
Brand management, 231
Brand manager, 231
BRANDAID, 23
BRANDFRAME, 232
BRANDFRAME consultation, 243
Business process, 292

C

C, 52, 142
C++, 55
CAAS, 159, 203
CALLPLAN, 23, 62, 87, 90, 91, 114, 115, 266
Canary, 131
Case base, 259
Case histories, 37
Case retention, 177
Case revision, 177
Case-based reasoning, 27, 121, 166
Case-based reasoning cycle, 169
CDNow, 66, 287
CD-ROM, 50
Central processing unit (CPU), 49
Champion, 276
Channel intermediaries, 287
Chips, 46

Chi-square automatic interaction detection (CHAID), 60
Chunks, 236
City block, 175
Class, 54
Classes, 131
Classification tasks, 168, 178
Clickstream data, 290
Client-server computing, 57
CLIPS 6.04, 143
Clocks of mind, 21
Clouds of mind, 21
Cluster analysis, 59
COBOL, 52
Coca-Cola, 30, 129
Cockpit, 242, 274
Codified knowledge, 71
Cognitive differentiation, 268
Cognitive limitations, 282
Cognitive model, 22
Cognitive science, 21, 121
Cognitive style, 37, 271, 295
Combination of manager and system, 298
Common knowledge, 70
Common sense, 70
Communication, 276
Communication networks, 55
CompareNet, 290
Compensate (versus reinforce), 226, 298
Competitive advantage, 293
Compiler, 52
Completeness of knowledge, 34
Complex problems, 296
Components of MMSS, 44
Computer, 46, 47
Computer literacy/proficiency, 39
Conceptual spaces, 29
Condition-action pairs, 134
Confidence factor (CF), 140
Confirmatory factor analyses, 60
Conjoint analysis, 61
Connectionism, 187

Connectionist approach, 125
Consumer panels, 65
Controllable variables, 61
Convergent thinking, 29
Cooperation within supply chains, 285
Corporate brand memory, 261
Correlation analysis, 59
Cost reductions, 278
CoverStory, 155
Creating (mode), 21, 28, 272
Creating, 217
Creativity Support Systems (CSS), 165, 200, 201, 202, 203
Creativity, 19, 29
Croky Chips, 28
Cross-sectional analyses, 198
Customization, 286

D

DARPA, 124
Data Mining, 199
Data warehouses, 67, 199
Datadetective, 197
Data-driven marketing management support systems, 81-82
Data-driven systems, 271
Data-mining tools, 68
David Hume, 122
Decision bias, 17
Decision calculus, 85, 228
Decision confidence, 278
Decision environment characteristics, 35
Decision maker characteristics, 36, 221
Decision maker, 270
Decision situation characteristics, 219
Decision support functionalities, 271
Decision support models, 82

Decision support systems (DSS), 104
Decision table, 253
Decision-calculus, 249
Decision-making group, 289
Decision-making styles, 20
Deep Blue, 124
Deep knowledge, 34, 35, 70
Define/change brand situation, 240
Dell, 286
Delta rule, 190
Demand Side, 269, 270
Demand-side perspective, 10
DENDRAL, 123
Dendrites, 186
Depth of knowledge, 34
Derivational reuse, 176
Descriptive analyses, 58
Descriptive models, 62
Design a marketing program, 246
Design characteristics, 269
Design tradition, 301
Diagnosing, 232
Differentiation, 292
Digital Equipment Corporation, 142
Direct marketing, 196
Discriminant analysis, 59
Distribution, 30
Divergent thinking, 29
Divide-and-conquer, 297
Domain knowledge, 70, 123
Dominant matches, 213
Dominant mode, 32
Donor experts, 158
Dunn & Bradstreet, 66, 291
DVD, 50
Dynamic market, 36
Dynamic memory, 177
Dynamic programming, 62
Dynamics, 299

E

Ease of learning, 274
Ease of understanding, 274
Ease of use, 274
Edible-fats market, 25
Education, 37
Efficient Consumer Response
    (ECR), 285
Electronic data interchange (EDI),
    56
Electronic Marketing, 286
Elementary propositions, 136
Empirical generalizations, 72
Empirical research, 266
Empirical tradition, 74
Empiricism, 73
Empiricist school, 73
EMYCIN, 138
End-user software, 51
Engineering, 301
ENIAC, 47
Enlightenment, 69
Enterprise resource planning
    (ERP), 64, 274, 293
Estimation, 84
ESWA, 154, 158, 159
Euclidean distance, 175
Evolution (of MMSS), 227
Excitation, 186
Experience, 16, 37, 295
Expert Systems, 137
Expertise, 16, 75
Explicit knowledge, 71
Explorer, 56
EXPRESS, 52
EXSYS Professional, 143
External data, 64
External information, 94

F

Factor analysis, 59
Falsification, 72

Fast-moving consumer goods
    (FMCG), 231
Feed-forward network, 187
Fifth discipline, 69
Fifth Generation Project, 124
Fire, 134
Firing (of a neuron), 187
Flexibility, 274
Flippo, 28
Flow of ideas, 202
FMCG (fast-moving consumer
    goods), 131, 284
Fopro, 239
FORTRAN, 52
Forward chaining, 139
4GLs, 52
4Thought, 193
Frame(s), 130, 257
Frame-based, 130
Framework, 269
Franz Edelman Award, 267

G

Gains chart, 197
General knowledge, 72
General marketing knowledge,
    253
General problem solver (GPS),
    122
General problem-solving school,
    26
Generalized marketing
    knowledge, 75
Generations (of marketing
    management support systems),
    300
GENI system, 202
GfK, 291, 293, 301
Goal (of problem solving
    process), 134
GOLDWORKS III, 143
Grand mean, 76
Grolsch, 132

H

Hard relationships, 291
Hardware, 49
Heineken, 129, 132
Heuristic types, 271
Heuristic(s), 18, 37
Hidden layers, 187
Hierarchical structures, 131
Hierarchy of objects, 56
Holdout sample, 193
Human brain, 283
Human nervous system, 186
Hybrid environment(s), 161, 259
Hybrid systems, 133

I

If-then rules, 74
Implementation process, 268, 275
Implementation, 159
Implemented, 232
In-company developed, 276
Indexing, 170
Inductive retrieval, 176
INF*ACT, 97
Inference engine, 123, 137
Infomediaries, 287
Informate, 213
Information fatigue syndrome, 5
Information processing, 95
Information quality, 275
Information Resources Inc. (IRI),
    65
Information technology (IT), 44,
    45, 288
Information value chain, 283
Informational systems, 67
Inheritance, 54, 132
Inhibition, 186
Initial conditions, 134
INNOVATOR, 158
Input layer, 187
Inquiry center, 96
Instance(s), 26, 54, 131

Integrated circuits, 46
Integrated system(s), 256, 292
Integrating framework, 217
Intel, 47
Intelligence, 26
Intelligent agent, 289
Interdepartmental cooperation,
    288
Interdomain analogies, 167
Internal data, 64
Internal information, 95
Internet, 56, 286
Interpolative adaptation, 177
Intradomain analogies, 167
Intranets, 56
Intra-organizational cooperation,
    288
Intuition, 18, 75
Intuitive styles, 20
IRI, 291, 293, 301

J

Java, 55
Jenever, 128

K

KAPPA, 52, 133
KAPPA-PC, 256
Kasparov, 124
KDD, 199
Knowledge, 120, 252
Knowledge base, 137
Knowledge-creating company,
    200
Knowledge-creating organization,
    69
Knowledge discovery tools, 68
Knowledge discovery, 199
Knowledge manipulation, 125
Knowledge principle, 139
Knowledge processing, 125
Knowledge representation, 121
Knowledge-driven, 11, 121

Knowledge-driven systems, 271
Kuwait Petroleum, 29

L

Laboratory experiments, 267
Languages and Shells, 141
Latent class modeling, 60
Latent constructs, 60
Layers, 187
Learning in organizations, 6
Learning rate, 192
Learning, 69, 177, 212
LEVEL5, 142
LEVEL5 OBJECT, 143
Limited cognitive resources, 19
Linear programming, 22
LISP, 141
LISREL, 60
Local area networks (LAN), 56
Locally hard relationships, 75, 291
Locally rational decision making, 18
Locking in on a strategy, 296
Logic theorist, 122
Logistical information, 285
Logit analyses, 60
Long-term memory, 134
LPA Flex Expert System, 143

M

M1, 142, 146
Machine language, 51
Machine learning, 178
Magic Bean, 181
Mainframes, 47
Management control cycle, 232
Management information systems, 91
Mapping, 218
Market dynamics, 36, 271
Market research agencies, 65
Market view, 239

Marketer(s), 4, 16
Marketing automation, 6
Marketing case-based reasoning systems (MCBR), 8, 113
Marketing channel, 287
Marketing creativity support systems (MCSS), 8
Marketing data revolution, 283
Marketing data, 44, 63, 290
Marketing decision maker(s), 3, 4
Marketing decision making, 3, 16
Marketing decision support systems (MDSS), 7, 103, 114
Marketing expert systems (MES), 8, 115, 143
Marketing information and analysis center, 95
Marketing information revolution, 290
Marketing information systems (MKIS), 7, 91
Marketing information, 286
Marketing intelligence, 94
Marketing knowledge, 44, 68, 74, 291
Marketing knowledge-based system (MKBS), 8, 113, 143, 162
Marketing management support recommender, 219
Marketing management support system (MMSS), 7
Marketing manager, 4
Marketing models (MM), 7, 22, 82, 114
Marketing neural networks, 8
Marketing optimization, 22
Marketing orientation, 276
Marketing problem-solving modes, 16, 211
Marketing program, 62
Marketing programming problem, 22
Marketing science, 300

Marketing-mix instrument, 35
MARKSTRAT, 268
Mass marketing, 284
Match, 211, 269
Mathematical model, 22
Mead, 29, 202, 203
Media allocation schedule, 62
Media planner, 219
Media planning, 22, 34
MEDIAC, 23, 62
Megahertz (MHz), 49
Mental arithmetic, 21
Mental efforts, 19
Mental model(s), 24, 37, 69
Message passing, 55
Meta-analysis, 76
METAPHOR, 52
Methods, 54, 257
MIAC, 95
Microcomputers, 47
Microprocessors, 46
Microsoft, 51
Microsoft Windows, 51
Minicomputers, 47
Minkowski metric, 174
MIPS, 47
Mode of support, 212
Model parameterization, 83
Model specification, 83
Model validation, 86
Model world, 22
Model-based reasoning, 24
Model-building tradition, 22
Modus ponens, 127
Momentum parameter, 191
Monitoring, 232
Moore's law, 48
Moret, Ernst & Young, 5
Movie industry, 296
MS-DOS, 51
Multimedia technologies, 47
Multiple regression analysis, 59
MYCIN, 123, 137

N

Nearest-neighbor, 174
NEGOTEX, 159
Netscape Navigator, 56
Networked representation of
    knowledge, 126, 129
Neural networks, 126, 184
NeuralWorks, 193
Neuron, 186
Neurotransmitters, 186
New business manager, 219
New-product introductions, 27
Nielsen data, 241
Nodes (of a neural network), 187
Noncontrollable variables, 61
Nonoptimal decisions, 282
Nonprocedural languages, 52
Normative models, 62
Novel concepts, 28
Novices, 17

O

Object code, 52
Object of support, 212
Object orientation (OO), 53
Object, 133
Objective knowledge, 71
Object-orientation paradigm, 289
Object-oriented systems, 133
OLAP, 103
On-line analytical processing
    (OLAP), 68
On-line marketing (electronic
    commerce), 286
Operational systems, 67
Operations research, 62, 87
Opimizing (mode), 21
OPS5, 142
Optimal decision, 17
Optimization algorithm, 22
Optimization, 21
Optimizing (mode), 21, 214, 272
ORAC model, 16, 211

Oracle, 293
Organizational culture, 36
Organizational impact, 278
Organizational validation, 299
Organization-wide information
    systems, 288
Ossified cases, 28
Overfitting, 192

P

Packaged-goods industry, 45
Panels, 65
Parallel Distributed Processing,
    187
PASCAL, 52
Pattern-matching, 268
Pattern-recognition, 75, 185
PC, 47
PDP, 187
Pentium, 47
PeopleSoft, 293
Pepsi-Cola, 30
Perceived usefulness, 274, 278
PERSONAL CONSULTANT,
    142
Personal digital assistants
    (PDAs), 289
Personal productivity, 278
Personalized products, 287
Physical symbol hypothesis, 193
Planning, 232
Plato, 68
PLS, 60
Point-of-sale (POS), 50
POS data, 64
Post-it, 29
Potential success, 269
Power, 278
Predicate calculus, 127
Predictive models, 82
Prescriptive models, 83
Presentation of output, 274
Price changes, 27

Problem characteristics, 34
Problem finding, 29
Problem, 270
Procedural languages, 52
Procter & Gamble, 56, 285
Product manager, 219, 232
Production systems, 134
Programmability, 34, 270
Programming language, 51
PROKAPPA, 143
PROLOG, 141
Promotion planning system, 179
PROMOTOR, 159
Propositional symbol, 127
PUFF, 138
Purchased, 276

Q

Q8, 29
Quantitative skills, 39

R

R&D, 301
Random-access memory (RAM),
    49
Rational model, 17
Rationalism, 73
Rationality, 17
Reactions of competitors, 27
Read-only memory (ROM), 49
Reasoning (mode) 215
Reasoning from first principles,
    27, 71
Reasoning mode, 272
Reasoning, 21
Recognize-act cycle, 135
Recursivity, 142
Reframing, 29
Reinforce (versus compensate),
    226 298
ReMind, 179
Report market data, 240
Representation of cases, 170

Representativeness heuristic, 19
Research issues, 294
Reseller power, 285
Resource allocation, 62
Response function, 83
Response models, 61
Response reporting, 63
Retail store audits, 65
Retention, 177
Retrieval, 173
Reuters, 4, 291
Rule-based reasoning, 123
Rule-based representation of
    knowledge, 126, 127
Rules of thumb, 18
Rules, 27, 259

S

Sales management, 34
Sales promotions, 27
Sales-force decisions, 34
Sales-force, 23
SalesPartner, 155
Sales-promotion designer, 246
SAP, 293
SAS, 59
Satisfice (as a decision strategy),
    18
Scanning technology, 45
SCANPRO, 301
SCANTRACK, 65
Second-generation systems, 46
Self-assessment measures, 299
Semantic Networks, 129
Semantic similarities, 174
Set targets and budgets, 240
SH.A.R.P., 23
Shelf-space, 23
Similarity metrics, 174
Simplifying, 18
Simulation, 61
Skills, 39
SKUs, 64

Slots, 54, 131
Smalltalk, 55
Soft associations, 21
Soft knowledge, 75
Softbots, 289
Software, 49
Solution space, 29
Soni, 198
Source code, 52
Space Odyssey, 124
Sparring partner, 260
SPSS, 59
Stable markets, 36
Stanford certainty factor algebra,
    140
Status reporting, 58
Step function, 189
Stereotypes, 133
Stimulate, 213
Storage devices, 50
Stories, 166
Structural equation modeling, 59
Structuredness, 270
Structuredness, 34
Subclasses, 54
Subjective knowledge, 71
Suboptimal behavior, 296
Success measures, 277
Success, 265, 268
Sun microsystems, 55
Superclass, 54
Supercomputers, 47
Supply side, 44, 271
Supply, 269
Surface knowledge, 70
Survey, 114
Syllogism, 127
Symbolic approaches, 193
Symbolic representation(s), 24,
    125
Synaptic junctions, 190
Syntactical similarities, 174
Syntex (Laboratories), 23, 90, 266
Synthesis tasks, 168

System development software, 51
System integration, 274
System quality, 274
System software, 51
Systematic, 37
System-manager balance, 272

T

Tacit knowledge, 71
Technical validity, 277
Teknowledge Company, 146
Test set, 195
Thinking Man, 26
Third-generation computers, 46
3M, 29
Time constraints, 35
Time pressure, 296
Time saved, 278
Time-Series Analysis, 194
Top management support, 276
Topshots, 28
Trade-off judgments, 61
Training set, 195
Training the network, 190
Training, 277
Trait, 201
Transfer function, 188
Transformational reuse, 176
Transistors, 46
Travelocity, 288
T-tests, 58
Turbulent market(s), 36, 271
Turing test, 157

U

Uncertain premise, 140
Uncertainty, 141
United Airlines, 90, 266
United Biscuits, 28
Units, 186
UNIVAC I, 46
UNIX, 51
Use, 277

User documentation, 277
User impact, 278
User interface, 274
User involvement, 275
User satisfaction, 278

V

Validation sample, 196
Validation, 157, 299
Verification methods, 157
Visual Basic, 55
Visual C++, 55
Von Neumann, 49
VPEXPERT, 142

W

Wal-Mart, 56, 285
Weak-theory domains, 27
Weights, 188
What-If Questions, 60
What-Questions, 58
What-Should Questions, 62
Why-Questions, 59
Wide area networks (WAN), 56
Working memory, 134
World Wide Web, 55

X

XCON, 142

Y

Yahoo, 288

Author index

A

Aaker, 87, 114, 303
Aamodt, 170, 303
Abraham, 201, 303
Achabal, 182, 315
Ackoff, 29, 92, 232, 303
Adams, 275, 278, 303
Adriaans, 199, 303
Alavi, 269, 273, 275, 277, 303
Aldag, 278, 303
Alter, 46, 51, 304
Althoff, 167, 168, 174, 178, 179, 304
Amstutz, 93, 304
Anderson, 24, 304
Andrews, 203, 304
Armstrong, 216, 307, 318
Arnold, 231, 304
Aronson, 91, 321
Assmus, 76, 304
Auriol, 167, 304
Aversa, 267, 309
Axelrod, 24, 304
Ayel, 157, 304

B

Babbage, 122
Bagozzi, 58, 60, 275, 278, 304, 307, 308, 322
Bailey, 192, 193, 304
Barabba, 6, 96, 304
Bariff, 37, 304
Barker, 142, 304
Barki, 274, 277, 304
Barletta, 167, 304
Baroudi, 278
Bass, 72, 75, 76, 77, 82, 304, 305
Bazerman, 17, 18, 305
Bellman, 62, 305
Benbasat, 226, 271, 274, 299, 305, 320
Berenson, 92, 93, 305
Bettman, 19, 134, 317
Biyalogorsky, 295
Blackwell, 76, 308
Blattberg, 11, 105, 114, 282, 283, 284, 298, 305, 307, 311, 318
Boden, 29, 201, 305, 309
Boone, 201, 303
Boulding, 295, 298, 305
Brehmer, 17, 305
Brien, 91, 92, 305

Brittle, 161, 168
Brockett, 198, 322
Bruce, 6, 313
Brucks, 16, 295, 320
Bruner, 29, 306
Buchanan, 123, 306
Bucklin, 271, 286, 297, 306
Buell, 231, 306
Bultez, 23, 87, 114, 306
Burgess, 200, 317
Burke, 34, 143, 144, 153, 154,
    162, 179, 306, 317, 318
Buzzell, 56, 82, 285, 304, 306

C

Calantone, 296, 316
Camel, 173
Camerer, 17, 306
Carey, 25, 323
Carlson, 104, 320
Castellan, 58, 319
Chakravarti, 267, 306
Charpin, 143, 306
Chervany, 270, 299, 306
Choffray, 143, 306
Chung, 29, 306
Churchill, 58, 60, 306
Cleveland, 274, 307
Collins, 131, 307
Colmerauer, 141
Commandeur, 93, 313
Coskunoglu, 19, 322
Courtney, 24, 29, 232, 277, 307,
    318
Cox, 272, 307
Craik, 24, 307
Crawford, 200, 307
Crick, 166
Curtis, 23, 90, 267, 314

D

Daerden, 288
Daft, 36, 307

Dalebout, 212, 213, 217, 231,
    233, 234, 237, 253, 307, 308
Davis, 269, 274, 275, 277, 278,
    307, 321
Day, 7, 24, 274, 307
De Geus, 7, 307
De Jong, 276, 308
De Waele, 227, 308
Dearborn, 17, 307
DeLone, 273, 274, 275, 277, 278,
    308, 322
Den Uyl, 197, 198, 308
Dennis, 289, 308
DeSarbo, 63, 308, 322
Descartes, 73
Dexter, 271, 274, 305
Dickson, 270, 299, 306
Doll, 277, 321
Dorfman, 62, 308
Dreyfus, 124, 308
Drucker, 6, 69, 308
Duhamel, 93, 313
Duncan, 276, 323
Dutta, 124, 187, 212, 213, 217,
    231, 237, 308

E

Edland, 296, 308
Elam, 29, 202, 203, 308, 314
Eliashberg, 11, 22, 34, 60, 62, 82,
    87, 113, 143, 144, 153, 154,
    159, 228, 296, 300, 306, 308,
    309, 317, 318, 320, 321, 322
Engel, 76, 308
Epoch, 191
Eppen, 62, 309
Esch, 203, 309
Eskin, 77, 309
Etzioni, 289, 309
Eysenck, 201, 309

F

Farah, 6, 311

Farley, 76, 304
Fayad, 199
Feigenbaum, 123, 139, 259, 306, 309
Forbus, 24, 309
Frank, 63, 82, 309
Frolick, 68, 318
Fudge, 90, 158, 266, 309

G

Gaeth, 19, 316
Gallagher, 143, 152, 153, 154, 315
Galvin, 56, 67, 316
Ganly, 63, 309
Gatignon, 62, 268, 276, 309, 313
Gaul, 143, 153, 305, 309, 315
Gauvin, 159, 308
Gelderman, 273, 275, 276, 278, 309
Gensch, 267, 309
Gentner, 24, 166, 309, 310, 323
Ginzberg, 277, 314
Glazer, 7, 11, 18, 226, 274, 283, 298, 305, 307, 310, 311, 318
Golanty, 105, 114, 305
Golden, 198, 322
Goldenberg, 296, 310
Goldstein, 166, 235, 259, 310
Good, 272, 307
Goslar, 278, 310
Gould, 62, 309
Graef, 290, 310
Green, 61, 278, 310
Guha, 70, 313
Gupta, 296, 310

H

Haberland, 73, 124, 186, 187, 310
Hanssens, 59, 310
Harmon, 133, 310
Hayes, 24, 310, 320
Hennesey, 36, 310

Hess, 87, 114, 311
Higby, 6, 311
Hill, 154, 162, 179, 196, 311, 315
Hoch, 11, 18, 27, 184, 227, 268, 282, 283, 284, 298, 305, 311
Hofstadter, 26, 201, 311
Hogarth, 4, 17, 226, 296, 311
Holbek, 276, 323
Holyak, 26, 32, 311
Hruschka, 196, 311
Huff, 274, 277, 304
Hughes, 278, 311
Huizingh, 6, 58, 276, 308, 321, 322
Hulbert, 28, 311
Hume, 68, 73
Huysmans, 37, 311
Hwang, 296, 311

I

Igbaria, 274, 311
Ing, 64, 282, 311
Ives, 277, 278, 311

J

Jain, 296, 310
Joachimsthaler, 268, 269, 273, 275, 277, 303, 323
Johnson, 17, 19, 134, 306, 317
Johnson-Laird, 21, 24, 27, 124, 187, 312
Joshi, 276, 312

K

Kabanoff, 29, 312
Kahneman, 4, 18, 312
Kamakura, 63, 322
Kant, 68, 73, 312
Kao, 200, 201, 312
Kass, 167, 318
Katz, 112, 113, 321
Kaul, 76, 312

Keen, 34, 104, 277, 312
Kepler, 166
Kersnick, 274, 314
Kim, 276, 313
Kinnear, 268, 273, 323
Klayman, 24, 312
Kluytmans, 194, 322
Kolodner, 26, 27, 33, 166, 167,
    312
Kotler, 22, 60, 76, 82, 83, 84, 85,
    86, 87, 91, 92, 94, 95, 96, 113,
    125, 232, 276, 300, 312, 313
Kozar, 270, 306
Kroeber-Riel, 203, 204, 312
Kuehn, 82, 309
Kumar, 198, 286, 312
Kwon, 273, 276, 313

L

Lahti, 154, 162
Langendoen, 197, 198, 308
Langerak, 93, 313
Larréché, 87, 114, 268, 271, 313
Laurent, 157, 313, 319, 304
Lavidge, 144, 313
Leake, 167, 178, 313
Lederer, 274, 315
Lee, 276, 313, 319
Leeflang, 59, 60, 82, 83, 86, 103,
    104, 115, 275, 313, 316
Leenders, 288, 313
Lehman, 76, 271, 297, 304, 306
Lenat, 70, 313
Leverick, 6, 10, 313
Levitt, 200, 313
Lichtenstein, 19, 320
Lilien, 11, 23, 39, 60, 61, 62, 82,
    83, 84, 85, 86, 87, 113, 114,
    159, 228, 276, 288, 300, 301,
    307, 308, 309, 313, 314, 317,
    318, 319, 321
Lippmann, 187, 314

Little, 6, 11, 23, 37, 62, 63, 64,
    65, 72, 78, 85, 86, 87, 103,
    104, 114, 216, 228, 267, 271,
    273, 274, 283, 297, 305, 306,
    307, 311, 313, 314, 318
Littler, 6, 313
Lodish, 23, 62, 86, 87, 90, 114,
    115, 153, 154, 158, 228, 266,
    267, 303, 309, 314, 318
Lucas, 270, 277, 314
Luger, 124, 133, 134, 141, 162,
    314
Lusk, 37, 274, 304, 314

M

MacCrimmon, 29, 202, 203, 314
Makridakis, 4, 17, 226, 296, 311
Malhotra, 45, 60, 314
Manago, 167, 304
Manrai, 63, 308
Marakas, 202, 314
Margherio, 47, 48, 314
Markman, 166, 309
Markus, 278, 314
Mason, 270, 315
Massetti, 201, 202, 315
Massy, 82, 309
Mawhinney, 274, 315
Mazursky, 296, 310
McCann, 143, 152, 153, 154, 162,
    179, 182, 315
McClelland, 187, 315, 318
McCorduck, 139, 259, 309
McCulloch, 187, 315
McCullough, 179, 315
McGill, 274, 307
McIntyre, 182, 183, 184, 268,
    293, 299, 315
McLean, 51, 273, 274, 275, 277,
    278, 308, 321
Mehotra, 187, 197, 315
Meseguer, 157, 315
Miller, 182, 315, 318

Miniard, 76, 308
Minsky, 130, 193, 315
Mintzberg, 18, 35, 235, 313
Mitchell, 64, 154, 160, 161, 267, 282, 311, 315
Mitroff, 270, 315
Mock, 270, 316
Moenaert, 288, 321
Mohammed, 24, 29, 232, 307
Mohan, 187, 197, 315
Montgomery, 78, 87, 93, 114, 125, 316
Montoya-Weiss, 296, 316
Moore, 267, 298, 309, 310, 316
Moorthy, 22, 60, 82, 83, 84, 85, 86, 87, 113, 276, 300, 313
Morgan, 295, 305
Mowen, 19, 316

N

Nachman, 274, 311
Naert, 23, 59, 60, 82, 83, 86, 87, 88, 103, 104, 114, 115, 275, 306, 313, 316
Nault, 271, 305
Nedungadi, 24, 307
Neibecker, 153, 154, 158, 312, 316
Nelson, 275, 278, 303
Nemhauser, 62, 316
Ness, 22, 90, 267, 314
Newell, 122, 124, 125, 134, 137, 316, 320
Newquist, 124, 167, 316
Nielsen, 25
Nii, 139, 259, 309
Nilsson, 124, 316
Nonaka, 6, 69, 71, 200, 316

O

O'Connor, 56, 67, 142, 196, 304, 311, 316
Ogilvy, 144, 317

Olson, 277, 278, 311
Orr, 67, 317
Ortmeyer, 56, 285, 306
Oude Ophuis, 6, 58, 187, 267, 273, 274, 275, 276, 277, 308, 321, 322

P

Paisley, 274, 317
Pandelidaki, 200, 317
Paradice, 24, 29, 232, 307
Parsons, 59, 310
Payne, 19, 134, 317
Peacock, 288, 317
Percy, 76, 144, 253, 318
Perkins, 295, 317
Pettigrew, 36, 317
Piatetsky-Shapiro, 199, 309
Pinsonneault, 293, 298, 299, 317
Pitts, 187, 315
Plaza, 170, 303
Polanyi, 71, 317
Preece, 157, 315, 317

Q

Quillian, 131, 307

R

Ram, 154, 158, 317
Rangaswamy, 8, 34, 61, 82, 114, 143, 144, 153, 154, 159, 162, 288, 301, 306, 308, 313, 317, 318
Ranka, 187, 197, 315
Rao, 61, 198, 295, 310, 312, 314, 317, 318
Remus, 196, 311
Ries, 28, 318
Riesbeck, 26, 28, 166, 167, 318
Rivard, 293, 298, 299, 317
Robbin, 202, 318
Robertson, 276, 309, 312

Rossiter, 29, 76, 144, 253, 312.
   318
Rubicam, 144
Rumelhart, 187, 315, 318
Russo, 29, 30, 315, 318

S

Sakaguchi, 68,, 318
Samuels, 87, 114, 311
Sanders, 277, 318
Saunders, 83, 318
Sawhney, 296, 310
Schader, 143, 309, 315
Schank, 26, 28, 166, 167, 177,
   318
Schewe, 299, 318
Schkade, 11, 18, 27, 184, 227,
   268, 283, 311
Schmidt, 62, 309, 312
Schmitz, 153, 155, 216, 318
Schoemaker, 24, 29, 30, 312, 318
Schultz, 59, 275, 310, 311, 318
Scott Morton, 34, 104, 310, 312,
   319
Sculley, 30
Senge, 6, 69, 319
Senn, 46, 47, 49, 57, 319
Shanteau, 16, 319
Sharing, 285
Shaw, 6, 319
Shingal, 157
Shortliffe, 123, 137, 140, 319
Siegel, 58, 319
Siekmann, 203, 204, 319
Silk, 87, 105, 106, 114, 229, 316,
   319
Silver, 213, 319
Simon, H., 36, 228, 271, 319
Simon, H.A., 4, 17, 18, 20, 26, 34,
   122, 124, 125, 134, 137, 185,
   226, 270, 283, 297, 307, 316,
   319, 320
Simpson, 23, 90, 267, 314

Sinkula, 7, 320
Slevin, 275, 318
Slovic, 19, 320
Smidts, 17, 226, 268, 284, 293,
   321
Smith, D.C. 203, 304
Smith, G.F., 29, 320
Smyth, 199, 309
Solomon, 296, 310
Soma, 186
Spence, 16, 295, 320
Sprague, 34, 104, 320
Srinivasan, 87, 114, 313
Staelin, 267, 270, 294, 295, 298,
   305, 306, 323
Stafford, 91, 92, 305
Steckel, 18, 226, 274, 298, 310
Steiner, 62, 144, 308, 313
Sternberg, 27, 32, 36, 203, 310,
   320, 321
Stevens, 24, 310, 323
Stubblefield, 124, 133, 134, 141,
   162, 314
Svenson, 296, 308
Sviokla, 276, 320
Swami, 296, 320
Swanson, 276, 320
Sycara, 289, 320

T

Takeuchi, 6, 71, 200, 316
Tardif, 32, 36, 203, 320
Tellis, 76, 320
Thagard, 26, 32, 311
Thomson, 192, 193
Todd, 226, 275, 278, 299, 303,
   305, 320
Torkzadeh, 277, 321
Trout, 28, 318
Turban, 51, 53, 91, 321
Turing, 122, 157, 321
Tversky, 4, 18, 312

U

Udo, 274, 277, 321
Urban, 93, 105, 106, 112, 113,
   114, 78, 125, 316, 319, 321
Urbany, 298, 316
Uthurusamy, 199, 309

V

Van Bruggen, 17, 20, 21, 201,
   213, 226, 268, 270, 271, 284,
   293, 294, 296, 299, 321, 322,
   323
Van Campen, 6, 58, 321, 322
Van den Bulte, 288, 321
Van der Putten, 197, 322
Van Hillegersberg, 53, 55
Vandenbosch, 228, 321
Vergara, 29, 303

W

Wagenaar, 197, 198, 322
Wagner, 29, 202, 203, 314
Wainer, 274, 322
Walton, 277, 314
Warshaw, 275, 278, 307
Watson, 166, 167, 176, 178, 179,
   320, 322
Weber, 19, 322
Wedel, 63, 313, 322
Weick, 36, 307, 322
Weinberg, 228, 296, 320, 321
Wertheimer, 29, 306, 322
West, 198, 322
Wetherbe, 51, 321
Wierenga, 6, 17, 21, 58, 152, 160,
   162, 194, 201, 212, 213, 217,
   226, 231, 237, 267, 268, 270,
   273, 274, 275, 276, 277, 284,
   293, 294, 308, 321, 322, 323
Wilson, 6, 313, 317

Wind, 34, 61, 72, 76, 143, 144,
   153, 154, 305, 306, 310, 317,
   318
Winer, 18, 58, 226, 274, 298, 310,
   323
Wiser, 25, 323
Wittink, 76, 105, 114, 312, 313,
   315, 323
Wolsey, 62, 316

Y

Yoon, 288, 307
Young, 144, 316

Z

Zaltman, 6, 96, 276, 304, 323
Zantinge, 199, 303
Zaragoza, 87, 114, 316
Zinkhan, 268, 271, 273, 323
Zmud, 37, 273, 276, 277, 313,
   323
Zuboff, 213, 323